THE
MYTHIC
WEST IN
TWENTIETH-
CENTURY
AMERICA

THE MYTHIC WEST IN TWENTIETH-CENTURY AMERICA

ROBERT G. ATHEARN
Foreword by Elliott West

University Press of Kansas

Published by the University Press of Kansas
(Lawrence, Kansas 66045),
which was organized by the Kansas Board
of Regents and is operated and funded by
Emporia State University, Fort Hays State University,
Kansas State University, Pittsburg State University,
the University of Kansas, and Wichita State University

Library of Congress Cataloging-in-Publication Data

Athearn, Robert G.
  The mythic West in twentieth-century America.
  Bibliography: p.
  Includes index.
  1. West (U.S.)—Civilization—20th century.
2. West (U.S.) in literature. I. Title. II. Title:
Mythic West in the 20th century.
F595.A85   1986   978'.03   86-11106
ISBN 0-7006-0304-2

Printed in the United States of America
10   9   8   7   6   5   4   3   2   1

*To all my graduate students
and to the many others
who are following the
traditions of the
western historians who
have gone before us*

CONTENTS

FOREWORD

This, the last of eleven books written by Robert G. Athearn, is surely his most personal. Most of his works have shown the stamp of his feelings about the subject at hand, particularly those set in the "high country," the northern plains and Rocky Mountains where he spent most of his life. *The Mythic West in Twentieth-Century America,* however, is even more a blend of scholarship, personal observation, and opinion, and as such it is a fitting final statement from one of the West's most respected historians.

As he tells us in its opening sentence, Athearn began this book more than sixty years ago. His boyhood experience on his grandfather's Montana ranch sowed the seeds of questions he would pursue throughout his long career. Just what and where is the West? Why have so many been so obsessed with finding and saving that mythic time and place? What has the West meant to those who have lived there and to the millions more who have journeyed there only in their imaginations? And how have the answers to these questions changed with the years? The issues involved here—the place of the West and the frontier experience in our search for a national identity—have inspired a small library of important books during the last thirty years or so. Most of these writers have given their attention to those confident and aggressive years of the nineteenth century when the frontier was sweeping across the continent.

Athearn's contribution, in part, is to pursue the shifting perceptions of the West into the present century. There the story has taken new twists as Americans have confronted hard lessons about themselves and their land. Again and again the message of events has been much the same: We are running short of resources and of room to grow. The region that once seemed endlessly bountiful and forever wild has become a land of narrowing limits. With this realization, popular feelings about the West, "the most American part of America," have swung erratically between hope and disillusionment, affection and anger. Yet the myth has survived, however battered and bent into new shapes. Any political, economic, or social history of the modern West, Athearn is saying, must take that myth into account.

Historians at last are giving more attention to the West during the twentieth century. In particular they have begun to focus upon the enormous impact that the Great Depression, the New Deal, and

ix

World War II had on the region. Those years of catastrophe followed by spectacular growth did much to set the course of development since then. Athearn, too, finds that the period from 1930 to 1945 was of crucial importance, but his history is not of the sort done recently, for instance, by Richard Lowitt and Gerald D. Nash. Nor does Athearn analyze the western myth with the intensity and detail of such a writer as Richard Slotkin.[1]

The Mythic West in Twentieth-Century America is both less and more than these books. Admittedly impressionistic, it is by no means intended to be a full treatment of its subject. Instead, Athearn uses each chapter to consider, from a different angle, certain developments that have shaped the modern West and some of the ways in which these transformations have in turn molded what people have thought and dreamed about that land. As his raw materials he uses popular periodicals, films, novels, and the works of literary tourists, as well as more formal scholarly works. Shaping all this, however, are the astute insights of a native westerner who studied and wrote extensively about the country, who lived and taught there virtually all his professional life, and who apparently never considered leaving it. Athearn wrote of his subject with obvious affection but also with the critical squint of a scholar and veteran observer who knew his subject extraordinarily well.

Bob Athearn was close to completing this book at his untimely death in November 1983, shortly after the Western History Association had honored him with its first award for a distinguished body of writing on western history. At his request, I wrote one chapter on a subject that he thought should be included—the conservationist and preservationist movements. The result ("The Wilderness Evangelists") is based upon Athearn's own extensive notes, some research of my own, and a fragment of the chapter he had begun. Also at Athearn's request, I made a few minor additions and changes to his text, primarily as transitions between the various parts of the book. This was done with the generous help of staff members of the University Press of Kansas, as well as Bob's close friend Herb Luthin and Bob's son, Frederic J. Athearn. Maxine Benson, formerly the editor of Kansas History and a doctoral student of Bob's, diligently

---

1. Richard Lowitt, The New Deal and the West (Bloomington: Indiana University Press, 1984); Gerald D. Nash, The American West Transformed: The Impact of the Second World War (Bloomington: Indiana University Press, 1985); Richard S. Slotkin, Regeneration through Violence: The Mythology of the American Frontier, 1600–1860 (Middletown, Conn.: Wesleyan University Press, 1973) and The Fatal Environment: The Myth of the Frontier in the Age of Industrialization, 1800–1890 (New York: Atheneum, 1985).

searched out appropriate photographs to accompany Bob's text, and
Kathie Villard of Fayetteville, Arkansas, generously loaned samples from her collection of advertisements using western themes. Most ardent thanks of all, however, should go to Claire Raney Athearn, whose advice, perceptive suggestions, and encouragement were invaluable. Bob was fond of calling Claire Athearn his best and shrewdest critic, and all who have worked on this project now know why.

Whatever tinkering has been done by others, *The Mythic West in Twentieth-Century America* is still Robert Athearn's book alone. It is informed by his characteristic intelligence and graced by the humor and felicity of style that his readers have come to expect. As do his other works, it leaves us with a deeper, richer understanding of that elusive and complex place, the West, which he knew as well as anyone ever will.

Elliott West
University of Arkansas, Fayetteville

ROBERT ATHEARN'S WEST

Montana

North Dakota
MINOT
BISMARCK

Idaho

Wyoming

South Dakota
PIERRE
MISSOURI RIVER
SIOUX CITY

Nebraska
NORTH PLATTE
KEARNEY
OMAHA

Nevada

Utah

Colorado
HAYS
SMITH CENTER
KANSAS CITY

Kansas
WICHITA

Arizona

New Mexico

WOODWARD
VICI
OKLAHOMA CITY

Oklahoma

FORT WORTH

Texas
SAN ANTONIO
DEL RIO

N
W — E
S

Miles
0   250   500

Publisher's note: The boundaries of "Robert Athearn's West" reflect Athearn's mental map of the authentic West and the November 1985 sketch by Claire Athearn, who accompanied her husband on his travels throughout the region. (Map by Eva Williams)

PROLOGUE

This book really began in the summer of 1922. I have intended to write it ever since.

It was during this period of the early twenties that the faithful followers of what they imagined to be the "Old West" were lamenting the fading away of that treasured American heritage. Most of the mourners lived in the East. One aspect of this transition that they found most disturbing was the disappearance of cowboys, hitching racks, and livery stables in little western towns, which now were replacing these props on the western scene with paved streets, automobile dealerships, and Rotarians. To the faithful, this constituted a blight on the countryside of their minds—a form of municipal pollution, an environmental outrage.

I lived in one of these upstart violations of the Old West dream, a little burg of five or six thousand, located in north-central Montana. It was a town that had no cowboys, simply because it wasn't situated in cow country. It was a farming region, a place where Scandinavian farmers went to "the city" on Saturday mornings to sell their cream, poultry, and eggs, after which they bought supplies, perhaps went to a movie matinee, and went home.

This little town, built on the traditional unimaginative square with such inspired street names as First Street or Third Avenue, was representative of those bustling communities that the easterners now resented so much for their copycat ways. It had twice-a-day rail service on a transcontinental line, a telegraph office, a daily newspaper, telephones, and home mail delivery. It was not out of touch with the world.

For the convenience of residents, there were two multistory department stores that sold everything the modern American could want. One of them even had a tearoom. There were drugstores, a jewelry store, furniture stores, clothing stores, and hardware stores. The town even boasted of a modern steam laundry. A local photographer offered to take family portraits. There were a "dime store," a bakery, and a confectionary store, behind which was a dance hall that blared jazz on Saturday nights. There was no want of professional services: lawyers, doctors, dentists, and a good hospital. The town had two banks. There were several hotels—but no elevators.

In the way of public services the town was right up-to-date. We had a police force, a jail, a fire department, and city street crews that watered the boulevards and tidied up the few paved streets that the town boasted. We had daily mail delivery. There was a public library. Children had elementary schools, both public and parochial, and there was a high school, complete with a band and a football team. Private services delivered milk daily and picked up and delivered laundry and dry cleaning. An iceman kept the icebox supplied.

Social outlets were not wanting. Two movie theaters, several restaurants, the Elks Club, the Masonic Lodge, and a full supply of speak-easies—or "blind pigs" as they were known—gave couples an opportunity to get out now and then. Single men not only had the speak-easies to frequent; there were also several pool halls and card-rooms, not to mention a red-light district, which was not officially sanctioned but was condoned because it was discreetly located just outside the business district and was curtained off by a high board wall. The men also had service clubs, where they joined together at noon once a week to sing the praises of promised Harding prosperity and to share stories of their commercial progress.

Housewives had telephones with which they could order almost anything they needed. They enjoyed central heating, hot and cold running water, bathrooms, and indoor toilets, and some had electric kitchen stoves. Many had access to the family automobile. The men thought them quite pampered.

Then, one day, I was suddenly lifted out of this environment and thrust into an entirely different world, one that was only about one hundred and fifty miles away, but in terms of change and newness, it was like being dropped into the Land of Oz.

This was occasioned by our doctor's orders that my mother's health was frail and she needed a quiet rest in the mountains. My father had two young boys on his hands, one seven and one five years old; they had to be farmed out. The solution wasn't hard. My grandfather had a ranch along the Missouri River, down in the famous breaks of that waterway, a spread in which my father had an interest and which he visited occasionally anyway.

Of course I wasn't aware of it, but this was just the time when those who resented the "modernization" of the West and trumpeted that message through national magazines were arguing that the real article, the frontier West, lay not far removed from these nasty little commercial eyesores that were marring the western landscape, towns such as the one I lived in. This was quite true. The Missouri River ranch was a prime example; it would have more than pleased the most severe of the critics.

"My interest in the American West sprang from the soil. Perhaps that makes me a grass roots historian," Robert Athearn would write fifty-two years after he was photographed at age four on his grandfather's horse ranch in Montana, south of the Missouri River. (Courtesy, James L. Athearn)

Going there was like having the time machine slip a few cogs, thrusting one back almost a half-century. With a single exception, nothing on that ranch belonged to the twentieth century or even years earlier than that. The exception was an old Model T Ford touring car, but even that had a limited utility. The ascent out of the breaks was so steep that "Henry" couldn't negotiate the grade under its own power, and when a rare trip to the outside world was called for, it was necessary to hook a team of draft horses to it and drag that big modern mechanical magic slowly up the twin ruts that led to the flat country where the contraption could propel itself. Then the teamster had to make his way back down the decline; it was quite an operation, one that you didn't undertake every day.

The ranch. It had no well; we drank Missouri River mud that was slightly cleared up by throwing into the water barrel cactus leaves that had been sliced open, the theory being that whatever properties the cactus had would help to settle the silt. The main dwelling was made of cottonwood logs, topped with a dirt roof that sprouted cactus plants. The logs were chinked with triangular strips of wood and sealed with a mud plaster that was held together with some kind of binder. My little brother developed a fondness for the mud plaster and had to be broken of snacking on it. I think he had a mineral or vitamin deficiency of some kind. The main room of the house was a place where we ate, at a long picnic-type table, and after meals we took a siesta on kitchen chairs that were tipped upside down and used as back rests for those who were lying on the floor, much in the manner of the willow-woven Indian "lazy backs" that the Blackfeet Indians used and later made for sale to tourists. Behind that room were a bedroom on one side and a kitchen on the other.

The kitchen had an old, large iron range on which my grandfather, the self-appointed cook, turned out his prized sourdough flapjacks and sometimes corn bread that we called johnny cake and ate with butter and syrup. That particular summer, my aunt and uncle were at the ranch, so he was relieved of most of the cooking since there was now a woman in the house. The diners were relieved, too, because the cuisine picked up noticeably in quality.

Behind the kitchen was a root cellar, where stores were kept. Presiding over this dugout was an enormous black and yellow bullsnake named Jim, who was the official "mouser." The first time my grandfather ordered me into the root celler "to fetch a can of Carnation," I nearly failed to survive the shock of meeting Jim, not having been warned of his directorship of that domain. During the winter, Jim abandoned the cool of the place for a warmer spot. He curled up in the woodbox near the stove, and if you wanted a stick of wood, you had to disentangle the snake to get it. My aunt finally put an end to *that* form of nonsense and banished the beast. Believe me, Jim was quite a revelation to a city boy.

Beyond the main house lay the outbuildings. On one side was a cabin with extra sleeping space; on the other was a bunkhouse that accommodated the seasonal ranch hands. Near the latter quarters were a workshop, which always smelled of tar and turpentine; a chicken house; a barn, with an attached corral that was littered with manure; a hog pen; and an icehouse, where blocks of muddy ice were stored. A milk cow furnished not only daily milk but also cream and butter, the latter laboriously produced in a hand-driven churn that nobody volunteered to turn.

Our diet was varied. Fresh eggs were always available, and a large garden that lay next to the river kept the root cellar full. Fried chicken was plentiful and easy to prepare. Occasionally a calf was slaughtered, but beef was not always available. I have eaten horse-meat roast when stocks were low. The pork supply was steady; grandfather got out his 30-30 rifle when the time came to dispatch one of the hogs, after which it was thrown into a barrel of scalding water to remove the

bristles. The old man was a former butcher, so "dressing out" was
performed in a professional manner. Sometimes river catfish were nailed by the tail against one of the outbuildings and skinned with a pair of pliers.

This was not the traditional cattle ranch. My grandfather raised some alfalfa seed for sale because it was low in bulk, easily transportable, and brought a relatively high price. This helped to buy the "necessaries" for the larder, things such as sugar, coffee, salt, and flour. The manner in which these staples were acquired had not changed in a century. Each fall a boatman drifted down river, stopping at all the ranches along the way, selling these items in bulk— flour and sugar in large bags, coffee in five-pound tins. You bought a year's supply, much in the manner of the pioneers along the Cumberland or upper Ohio during the early 1800s.

Rather than run a herd of cattle, we dealt in horses. My father, who was a banker, also owned a horse company (not to mention a Buick car agency, to show that he had an eye to the future), and he financed an operation in which he and his brother bought horses from the Indians and later shipped them to the Midwest as saddle stock for farmers. While these animals were not candidates for a dog-meat factory, they were not very handsome horses. They were the ordinary wiry range ponies that had been around the West for a long time. Durable, sure-footed, reliable, and homely, they were quite serviceable. My father called them hammer-heads.

Because most of these horses were still a little on the untamed side, they had to be readied for their buyers—that is, halter broken and saddle broken. My first remembered employment was participating in the halter breaking. A long pole was mounted on two solid posts; then the horses, fitted with heavy halters, were tied to the railing, perhaps seven or eight at a time. It was the job of my brother and myself to stand in front of them and wave white flour-sack dishtowels in their faces. This frightened them and made them rear back against the tautness of their tethers. After they had done this until their necks and jaws were rubbed raw and sometimes bloody, you could easily lead them. This was utterly cruel but was commonly accepted at a place and time in which horseflesh was not highly prized. After this process, the horses were taken to the corral to be saddle broken by the resident ranch hand, who rode them and hazed them until they didn't have a buck left. Then they were pronounced fit for riding by Iowa farm boys, or perhaps by their mothers or sisters. We had hundreds of these range ponies; apparently the horse business still was profitable in 1922.

This was the Old West of that time. Primitive, simple to an extreme, and isolated. Now and then drifters passed our way, and they were warmly welcomed with a place in the bunkhouse and were given all the food they could eat—free. Perhaps they carried in an armload of stove wood now and then, as a courtesy, but no money ever changed hands. They were guests. This was part of the myth of western hospitality in that my grandfather and uncle kept these passers-by up late, grilling them on the latest news from the outside world and exchanging anecdotes and memories. The hosts weren't necessarily hospitable; they were lonely and starved for news, not having had any mail or newspapers for weeks on end. When everyone was "talked out," the stranger saddled up and moved on. Jaw-weary, the poor fellow had more than earned his keep.

There were other social aspects. This was the wilderness, a place that easterners mistakenly envied as an unsullied land that Rousseau would have praised, a land that was pure, where the invigorating climate and the clean moral atmosphere bred men, true Americans. Therefore, what better location in which to place a couple of small boys, a locale free of the sins of city life and the evil influences that could warp young minds.

How true. We had no company but each other. We had no toys. We played with washed and defanged tin cans; with a .45-caliber revolver, which was useful in practicing the quick draw that we had seen earlier at the movie's Saturday matinee; with a mangy mongrel dog, which we alternately petted and mauled; and with small barrel hoops, which could be rolled by guiding them with a small stick.

But that was all front—something for the elders to witness. Down at the river's edge was a small, quiet backwater which had a silted shore that was sandy enough to form roads, castle, and forts. We sailed boats made from the bark of huge cottonwood trees, little vessels carved out by my grandfather. This was sanctuary; it was Huck Finn country; it was escape from the world of discipline. And it was made especially attractive because I learned to roll cigarettes from Bull Durham tobacco stolen from the bunkhouse. By summer's end I could "build me a smoke" with fair accuracy, one that drooped properly from my lips in the manner I had seen cowboys use on the movie screen. Also, there we shared other treasures: sugar—especially brown, if available—stolen from the pantry to satisfy the hunger for nonexistent candy. While dragging on a fag, I explained life to my brother in language that was heavily interlarded with profanity that I had picked up from the men, especially as they watched some of the horses get out of the fenced area and head for the nearby breaks, where it would take a lot of effort to recover them. The hideout was a treasured place, one in which fantasies could be acted out in an uninhibited manner.

But when we were around the adults, there was discipline. This was a day before Dr. Spock had had a chance to blight an entire generation, one in which treasured old values of learning to toe the mark still were regarded as the only way to raise children. This sometimes came to us in unexpected ways and was somewhat more stringent than I thought necessary. For example, my brother was given to bed-wetting, which is not abnormal in a five year old. Grandfather, who thought my parents had done a singularly poor job in raising us, announced that there was only one cure for this senseless habit. "By God, you're just going to have to whale the hell out of the little whelp." It was a wet and very noisy summer, and I don't remember that Grandfather's therapy was entirely successful, but at least he got a lot of exercise, and it soothed his otherwise mean disposition.

A more cheerful example. Part of ranch life's dinner-table custom dictated that each member pick up his cutlery and his crockery and take it to the kitchen. That rule was ironclad, applied to all, and was rigorously enforced. That it was effective came home to me when my father picked us up that fall to take us home. At noon, en route, we stopped at one of those little towns that the Great Northern had sprinkled across northern Montana, to have lunch at one of the cafés. When the meal was over but before my father was aware of what was happening, my brother scooped up his plate, milk glass, and cutlery, marched to the rear of the establishment, kicked open the swinging door, and presented the startled cook with his burden. It caused much merriment among the customers and some embarrassment to my father.

So I had experienced the Old West. I had lived in its rarefied atmosphere, had breathed the air that made men, and had felt the uplifting influences of its moral climate.

By the time I got home, I had acquired a sneaky habit of petty pilfering in the pantry when hungry, had picked up the basics of draw poker by watching the men play their evening game, and had developed a vocabulary so shot through with profanity that it nearly got me kicked out of school a couple of times later; I also showed indications of having a mild smoker's cough. I shudder to think what might have happened had I missed this golden opportunity to experience the American Shangri-La and had been further exposed to the vices of the crowded city.

My reaction to the wilderness and its simplicity was negative. I was very glad to get out of the place, because it all seemed to be a reversal of life as it should be, or as I knew it. To me, the wilderness just couldn't hold a candle to indoor plumbing. Of course, I was just a kid, an unformed man whose regard for the freedom of the untouched country was yet nascent. I had not yet developed a sense of romance or the appreciation of idealized landscapes. I never before had felt suppressed or imprisoned. Not until I was locked into the Missouri River breaks and banished from the world, so to speak. It can be a very suffocating experience.

The principal intent of the foregoing is to try to show from firsthand experience something of what life actually was like in the last vestiges of the pioneer West. This isolated ranch, miles and miles from "civilization," was a holdover from that era, a frozen-in-time enclave that today would make a marvelous museum. But seeing it was one thing; living with it was another. Since I discuss the mythic West at some length in the following material, it seemed appropriate somehow to present a picture of the real thing.

While this prologue is not intended to be autobiographical, it certainly is reminiscent. As a matter of fact, so is much of the book itself, because I have drawn upon a lot of personal experiences and observations in making my statement. In addition to growing up in the region—I was twenty before I ever ventured as far east as the Mississippi—I have studied the frontier movement and the West in an academic sense. Much of the material that I use here is from periodical literature, from published reminiscences and monographic material, but very little of it came from statistical or purely documentary sources. It isn't that kind of a book. I gathered a lot of ideas over the thirty-five years I spent teaching at the university level, especially from numbers of graduate seminars in which I worked closely with students who were working at myriad projects dealing with the West.

I have written some books about the West myself, and these have been reasonably varied in subject matter. One gathers a lot of miscellaneous information while doing research for a book, much of which never gets into the finished product, but it sticks in the mind. It is like saving string; one day you have an enormous ball of it. Then I assembled a lot of this collected material, refined it, and dispensed it to thousands of respectful and sometimes interested undergraduates over the years.

For decades, all of this has been congealing in the back of my mind. It built up until I couldn't resist the urge to set it down on

paper as a kind of summation, an essay or series of essays, a collection
of impressions that were vivid to me. The story has no state boundaries, because they are artificial anyway; no important men; little or no political or economic history. So if you take this to be a history of the twentieth-century West, you'll find it as full of holes as Swiss cheese.

This is the way I intended it.

CHAPTER 1

THE
EPHEMERAL
WEST

As the nostalgically remembered gay nineties drew to a close, a tingle of anticipation coursed through the veins of Americans, some of whom had begun to count off the dwindling months and weeks of the nineteenth century. So preoccupied were they with their hopes for the future, so self-assured about bigger and better things to come, that one almost would have thought the upcoming great calendar change would occur only in the United States, the rest of the world presumably being so backward and nonprogressive that it had nothing in particular to realize from the days that lay ahead.

Yet, in the suppressed excitement over what surely would be the American century, misgivings lay submerged, scented with the sweet sting of nostalgia; and the good-bys that were being prepared had a sentimental cast that was almost unique in the nation's history. It was as if America was cutting itself loose from the past, surrendering a treasured family possession as one of the conditions for embarking upon some uncertain but necessary new course. Somehow, old values were to be traded for new ones, and Americans would have to explore the future without its old spiritual charts and compasses. They felt this only vaguely, many of them unable to identify the missing elements; and although the feeling was indefinable, there lingered a sense of impending loss. Philosophers and forecasters who pondered these things thought they could identify the missing item: it was the West.

But not just the West of geography. It was also the West of the mind, of the spirit, a concept that for generations had reassured Americans of a future, a place to go, even though most of them would not choose to move. Somewhere out there in the general direction of the Pacific Ocean lay a depository of unending resources, imperfectly described or understood, and a source of Lebensraum that often was one more of imagery than of substance, yet dreamers thought of it as being real. To some it constituted a personal legacy especially set aside for the individual; others saw it as a national heritage to be used, if ever, in a collective sense. For most it was something held in trust for one's children or perhaps for future generations, but nonetheless an inheritance that somehow would come in handy on that inevitable rainy day. And now, as the era of international involvement, of industrialization, and of urban sprawl loomed large, the mystical West appeared to be fading.

Sensitive men viewed the impending change with sorrow, even apprehension. As the novelist Owen Wister was finishing *The Virginian* in 1901, he saw the recent development of the country about which he wrote as constituting one of the final phases of American growth. He was not happy with the result.

Fifteen years earlier the Philadelphian had noted in his journal that those who lived along the Atlantic Coast were "all varnished with Europe," were no race at all; and he predicted that the ensuing years would erase them from the earth. In their places would emerge the real Americans, a people he would like to visit if he were permitted to return to earth in a couple of centuries. He then believed that time and the western environment would produce a new society, endowed with a moral superiority drawn from the pure atmosphere of an unsullied land.

But now, as Wister scratched away at the work that was to give him lasting fame, those earlier anticipations had faded. Sadly he concluded that the promise of the West had not fulfilled his expectations, nor would it, and that the unrealized dream was a part not only of the nation's past but also of his personal history. In a sense the book was doubly valedictory; it was to be his last novel about the West.

Even before Wister had begun to worry over the decline of eastern Americans, Edgar Wilson ("Bill") Nye, the Wyoming editor and humorist, had a lament of his own. Rather than place his hopes in the West, as Wister had, Nye felt that the true West of his mind was disappearing already, and he said so in a piece that he wrote in the mid eighties. In "No More Frontier" he argued that the practice of penetrating the wilderness with railroads, so that an area might develop, had taken all the joy out of pioneer life.

In Nye's view the coming of "civilization" had driven out the long-handled frying pans and flapjacks in favour of condensed milk and canned fruit; and old trails that hundreds of hopefuls had traversed, shovels over their shoulder, now were littered with empty beer bottles and peach cans. The change, he thought, had done little for the mining camps, many of which now looked half-civilized and grubby and were mere "sawed-off" towns. The Old West was so far gone, in his view, that a mere day's ride would get a man to where he could see daily papers and read them under electric lights.

Not all westerners were so sentimental. The little Colorado mining town of Ouray took the philosophical view that perhaps the frontier was gone but that in the last analysis, this was not to be regarded as necessarily a bad thing, for its disappearance seemed to denote progress. In support of that argument the *Solid Muldoon,* so famous in the West for its unusual journalism, reprinted Nye's article with the comment that mineral booms often served as a fertilizer for later commercial and civic growth, as a promise of better things to come. There were no lamentations in Ouray over the passing of primitive living conditions.

But these small western places, especially the mineral boom towns, had a hard time growing up in the family of communities. It was not only the so-called civilized East that wanted them to be fixed in time, as examples of the wild and unruly frontier, but even the larger western cities assumed the same paternalistic attitudes. What Ouray suffered in the eighties, so did Creede a decade later. When a Denver newspaper observed that the old frontier was fading, it suggested that one might yet sample the wild flavor by visiting that relatively new mining camp: "It is the only place of the true frontier type in Colorado and it is doing its best to keep up its end. A year from now it will have changed." So spoke Denver, as a proud relative of a two-fisted young western offspring that still was wild and woolly and full of fleas and seldom curried below the knees, to use an old cowboy description.

As miners and farmers continued to press into unoccupied pockets of the West, the notion that the great drama was about to come to an end magnified, grew stronger. By the turn of the century, as this physical frontier appeared to be fading, that belief began to have a real impact all across America.

When novelist Emerson Hough spoke at the requiem for the lately departed, it was only 1901. But even by then he could look back at yesterday and at a land that "begot character, grew mighty individuals." It was a place of special opportunity and a time of adventure, all of which had faded from view. This West, this frontier—the names were used interchangeably—was to him a priceless possession, a heritage he called "immortal," and now it seemed to be forever lost. He predicted that never again would there be another time in the nation's history so "vivid, adventurous, heroic." The day had passed when the true dreamer of the nation was a man who daily illustrated the realization of the American dream by showing the

Heavily loaded burros and quagmire streets testified that primitive frontier conditions still prevailed in such places as Ouray, Colorado, when William Henry Jackson toured and photographed the mountain West. (Courtesy, Colorado Historical Society)

world that with only a rifle and a saddle blanket, he could pit himself against a hostile environment and be sure of making a living.

The notion that the absence of high risk had altered the conditions, and therefore the excitement, of frontier life lingered in men's minds. Not long after Hough complained that the place was too tame, a western newspaper asserted that with the disappearance of hostile Indians and big game—as though both were objects of the chase—the West had lost its possibilities for adventure. The trouble was, said the writer, the area was becoming overrun by farmers who had taken the government's offer of free land too enthusiastically, and now, in some parts of the West, elbowroom was getting a bit scarce. As a result, the whole region had "settled down to a humdrum sort of existence."

Emerson Hough's explanation for this development was the coming of the railroad, the advent of which had been widely hailed by westerners as their savior. To him, this outrider of progress had stilled any voices that might call forth conquering heroes. Now, he said, it cost not so much in heroism to go west; rather, it was expensive in monetary terms—to go there, to live there. This meant that the West no longer was a place that was good for the poor man. "There is no land for the free," he concluded. "America is not American."

Others shared the feeling. In 1902 the well-known novelist Benjamin Franklin ("Frank") Norris wrote that "suddenly" his countrymen had felt the change. However, he said, the continuous movement westward had become "so much an integral part of our conception of things" that it would be a long time before the full impact of its loss would be realized. "We liked the Frontier," he wrote; "it was romance, the place of poetry of the Great March, the firing line where there was action and fighting, and where men held each other's lives in the crook of the forefinger." With that comment he pinpointed a reaction that future generations would share as they watched movies and television or read their pulp westerns.

Norris overstated the case when he suggested that the disappearance of the frontier had been sudden. Two historians, both of whom were to be American presidents, had watched its passing for a decade and a half. Theodore Roosevelt, who had been what old hands call a skim-milk cowboy out in the Dakota Bad Lands, prized his range-land experience, and since the eighties he had talked about the gradual disappearance of the Old West. By 1913 he concluded that "the West has gone now, 'gone with lost Atlantis,' gone to the isle of ghosts and of strange dead memories." For as long as he lived, Roosevelt felt he had been among those privileged to savor the charm, the vigor, and the unfettered freedom of the pioneer West, that land "of vast silent space, of lonely rivers, and of plains where the wild game stared at the passing horseman." He regretted that succeeding generations could not share, or perhaps even understand, what he called the pleasantest, the healthiest, and the most exciting chapter of American history.

Historian Woodrow Wilson, in saying his farewell to the frontier, took a commonly accepted view that the area had served as a depository for restless souls who could not adjust to the more settled ways of an older society, those for whom "mere steady industry" was not sufficiently fulfilling. On the assumption that there no longer was a place for these social mavericks to go, no release for their exuberance, Wilson thought new communities now would have to find some compensating way to make life sufficient without what he called an "easy escape." He based his conclusion on the mistaken supposition that the supply of free land was gone and therefore a principal outlet that had long been available to a growing nation was forever sealed.

These, then, were some of the valedictories offered by Americans, ranging from presidents-to-be to authors and working journalists, articulate men who acted as spokesmen for a large and generally

voiceless group whose members felt the loss of the western ideal in
their own way. The man on the street knew that something was
lacking, but he couldn't say where it last had been located; nor could
he even accurately identify it, a maddening situation when reporting
to the lost-and-found department.

Emerson Hough was one of the literati who confessed his inability
to locate that place which Denis W. Brogan was later to call the
American Zion, a land of milk and honey. Frustrated, he rationalized
that it must lie hidden somewhere "under the blue haze of the
years." In the manner of an empty-handed fisherman, he remarked
lamely that the object of his quest was "all the more alluring for its
lack of definition." But he need not have hung his head over this
apparent lapse on the part of his geography teacher. The problem, far
from being new, had stumped the Pennsylvania artist George Catlin,
who became so famous for his early-nineteenth-century paintings of
western Indians. Commenting that few people knew where the West
lay, he added: "Phantom-like it flies before us as we travel." From
Catlin to the Houghs and others, no progress appears to have been
made in the search. But now that the lost item was currently in
demand, a more earnest effort was instituted.

A problem as complex and abstruse as this called for help from the
experts. Fortunately, one was at hand. A young history professor
from the University of Wisconsin, named Frederick Jackson Turner,
had stirred his profession during the early nineties by suggesting that
the frontier had exerted a powerful force upon the nation's development. It was imagined that he knew where to find this elusive place
where an American species grew. But the answer to the question was
complex, and querying Turner was as unrewarding as trying to get
an unqualified response from the family lawyer. Always general in his
writing, he described the frontier variously as being a meeting point
between civilization and savagery, a process of change, or even a state
of mind, any of which identifications would make the frontier difficult
for a curious westward-bound traveler to find. While Turner took up
the chase with enthusiasm, he did little more than to cast a gossamer
net in the direction of the quarry.

Not that Turner gave up easily. He continued to study the western
landscape for more than three decades. Even in the mid 1920s, as he
neared the end of his career, he was unwilling to be more specific than
to define the West as lying generally somewhere beyond the Mississippi River. There were many Wests, he explained, various regions
within the American empire that had undergone, and perhaps still
were undergoing, a transformation from the primitive to the com-

plexities of modern civilization. After studying the frontier for a lifetime, he still handled that unpredictable creature with the utmost of care.

It had not been a very successful stalk, that lifelong search by Turner, but neither was it a very fruitful one for others. Despite such discouraging results, the chase continued during the first quarter of the twentieth century, the huntsmen apparently undiscouraged by their lack of success. That any clues to its probable location remained vague was suggested by an eastern magazine when it answered its own question "Where is the West?" by saying that it was a place where man presently was and that the East was where he or his father had come from. The West, explained the editor, was unlike the East or the South in that it had no geographical limits. It was more a mental image, an undefined generality.

There were those who argued that indeed the West did have a geographical definition, just as it had identifiable life styles, but, amoebalike, both these qualities shifted constantly, giving rise to the belief that this part of pioneer America had been and remained largely a state of mind. It was not hard to move from this premise to the notion that the Old West had never really existed, except in the public's imagination.

This notion of changing form and flowing boundaries was not uncommon among writers who watched the nineteenth century recede in the distance. When pressed for directions to the storied land, they frequently answered that unfortunately it was a vagabond, possessed of a name but not an address. As one of them remarked, in whimsical explanation, if a person faced north, the West was somewhere on his left, and one would know when he had arrived at his destination by the difference in the manners and the outlook of the people. This might occur in the Rocky Mountain region; then again, it might not, for the whole matter was relative. Given instructions as nebulous as these, it is not surprising that the intellectually curious turned to other mind teasers in the parlor game of historical hide-and-seek.

The caretakers of the western mystique were not trying to tantalize the uninformed. For years the concept of the West, as a physical frontier, had been poorly defined. It was thought of as an ever-shifting part of the back country, where manners and morals were thought to have a peculiarly western cast, but that was about as definite as average Americans could be as to its whereabouts. Their difficulty was that of an Englishman who took up the hunt shortly after World War I and, as had his predecessors, confessed that just when he thought he had reached the promised land, it slipped from his grasp and wriggled toward the Pacific Ocean. He was sure he had cornered his prey when he entered the Rocky Mountain West, but again he was disappointed, for the people in that part of the country would only say "maybe" when asked if they were westerners. Upon reaching California, he was dismayed to learn that Denver was "back East."

Those who searched for the West during the early years of the twentieth century shared an old disillusionment. Travelers long had found fascination in looking for what they conceived to be the West— a land of cowboys, gunslingers, and "red" Indians—only to be disappointed when they found black broadcloth suits, real-estate agents, tramways, and gaslit streets. With reluctance, their modern counterparts accepted the existence of automobiles, radios, and Rotary Clubs in this presumably unspoiled part of America; but still they clung to the dream that there must be a virgin country yet to conquer somewhere in the vast distance that stretched toward the Pacific. One latter-day explorer, who had spent some months in sparsely settled country well back from the railroads, believed that one still could find "the truest civilization" in more remote America. The quest for the missing heritage went on.

Meanwhile, the generality that the West lay somewhere beyond the Mississippi River seemed to satisfy less critical folks. But as time passed, it became more obvious that about the same kind of an economy and way of life were to be found on either bank of that waterway, and so the boundary had to be moved westward, this time to the Missouri River. However, that definition began to give trouble when residents of such places as Council Bluffs and Omaha developed a more and more midwestern outlook. As a result, it became increasingly popular, particularly among academics, to say that the West began somewhere in the vicinity of the ninety-eight to the hundredth meridian, where annual rainfall diminished to about twenty inches a year, a figure below which scientists and others defined the countryside as arid or at least semiarid. Because the lack of moisture determined the economy that could be pursued— stockraising, or such frontier crops as wheat—and because those who engaged in these followings looked and acted in the manner that easterners thought westerners should, it was concluded that such a place must be the West.

Katharine Gerould, who wrote some penetrating articles and a book about the West during the twenties, may have been speaking with tongue in cheek when she remarked that when the traveler

By 1949 the once-rowdy gold camp of Cripple Creek, Colorado, had automobiles and power lines along streets where bonanza kings had jostled among sourdoughs in gum boots. Could parking meters be far behind? (Courtesy, Colorado Historical Society)

reached North Platte, Nebraska, something happened to the landscape that smacked of the West, but anyone who has been there will understand her reference. At about that point, Nebraska towns change, and farming subtly gives way to cattle ranching, the countryside has a dryer scent, and the horizon takes on a Charley Russell pastel hue. The change is such that strangers do not always sense it, although some of them may notice more Levis than bib overalls on town streets. It is more likely that westerners, on their way home, will feel a strange prickling at the nape of the neck and a stirring that horses are said to experience when they imagine that the barn is not far ahead. Probably this is what Wallace Stegner sensed when he wrote, some fifty years after Gerould, that beyond the hundredth meridian, "something abides that is different, separate, uniquely itself."

The feeling persists. In 1982 a national news magazine reported that residents of the Nebraska panhandle were restive, and there was talk of secession from the "eastern" capital, Lincoln, where farm-oriented legislators tended to neglect the westerners. "The raw-boned ranching life in the panhandle, they argue, is kindred to the wild West of Wyoming," the state they were seeking to join.

The gradual blending of the Midwest into the West has generated
comment by the westward bound since the earliest days of mass movements over the various emigrant trails. Even before that, explorers, fur trappers, army men, and private travelers remarked about this blending, and each had a slightly different version of when the countryside began to change. This uncertainty was the basis for argument as to where the West itself began, a difference of opinion that was understandable enough unless one chose the eastern face of the Rockies as the marker; but equally open to question was the matter of where the West ended. The Pacific Ocean certainly ought to have supplied a definitive stopping point, but here again the West as a state of mind intervened. The Sierra Nevadas and the Cascades curtained off a West Coast people who had developed an economic and cultural empire of their own. They enjoyed greater rainfall, raised different crops than did those who farmed farther east, looked seaward in their thinking, and came to constitute a separate if somewhat provincial society that was more eastern than western, if one accepts the "frontier" as a way of life.

Journalists and academics shared the view that the Pacific slope could not be admitted to the western club. Its population was a modern, urban-oriented, rapidly growing body that had acquired far more quickly those eastern cultural and material characteristics so long envied and mimicked by the newer West. A widely read author, who published regularly in one of America's most popular weeklies during the twenties, called the coastal states the new East and remarked that places such as Portland or Seattle had little about them that was western. He noted that the Boston accent and a Scotch Presbyterian quality of mind, so commonly observed in cities such as these, marked them as belonging to another province.

Even Columbia University's colorful president, Nicholas Murray Butler, wanted to be heard on this subject, and he, too, excluded the trans-Sierra people from the West. Easterners harbored a strange possessiveness, even a jealousy, about that place or concept they regarded as constituting the West. In their minds, only real frontiersmen ought to live in it.

But it was not eastern academics, rendering such judgments, that set apart the littoral. From a very early day its residents had regarded the country lying immediately to the east as a hinterland, a place of trade and commercial exploitation for their merchants and financiers, a good example being the manner in which these businessmen supplied the mining frontier as it seeped eastward into Nevada, Idaho, and Montana. With the passage of time, those who lived along the Pacific Coast recognized that their moderate climate and their transoceanic commercial outlook bound them together as a region. The economist Morris Garnsey wrote in the 1950s: "People in the West recognize this distinction clearly. Both Californians and Coloradans are sure of the distinction between 'The Coast' and 'The West.'" Or in the words of Wallace Stegner, when one drives eastward from Oregon or Washington, "you . . . drive into the West."

Exclusion of the Pacific littoral made things easier for those who demanded a geographic definition of the West. It has been argued that the vast stretch of America extending from Canada to Mexico and from the high plains to the coast ranges constitutes an entity of a kind. While there are sharp differences of temperature, terrain, and local custom within it, there are some threads that draw these states together, the principal one being the lack of rainfall. As Ross Calvin put it, the sky determines.

Beyond aridity, it has been said that the area's economy is more directly influenced by environment than is that of any other American area. The shape of the land determines the location of agriculture, of irrigation possibilities, of timber resources, of mining locations, of transportation routes, of recreational feasibility and its commercialization. So, in turn, are the size, nature, and location of the labor force determined. And it is also argued that because of these dispositions, which tend to influence the economy, so are the manners, morals, and attitudes of those who live in the province sufficiently influenced to produce a recognizable and separate society. And perhaps the glue that finally binds them together is the myth of the Old West, so strongly endorsed by other parts of the nation, especially the East, and even now by Europeans. Add in the natural defensiveness of westerners, and the bond of unity is complete.

Not infrequently the region today is referred to as the Mountain West; often it is merely the West; in either case the purpose is to distinguish it from the Middle West, on the one side, and the Far West on the other. In any case, if one accepts the argument that Americans chose to think of it as their last West, in historic terms, it is at least possible to identify this fugitive phenomenon in an emotional, if not completely a geographic, sense. Not infrequently, one interpretation was associated with the other, and the emotional became the physical.

To settle upon the intermountain area and the western plains as being the West, as well as the last frontier, does not mean that other sections of the country were denied a share of the frontier experience.

Rather, it suggests that for them, it was a characteristic that passed so rapidly—mercifully so, some argue—that its legendary aspects did not have time to take root in history. Actually, the fading out of raw frontier qualities took place fairly rapidly in the land west of the magic meridian, but because it was the last to be settled and therefore was the closing scene of part one of the national drama, it quickly found a place in the hearts of nostalgic Americans. Helpful was the fact that this was the most colorful West of them all: its cast of characters included mountain men, goldminers, cavalrymen, cowboys, steamboat pilots, stagecoach drivers, railroad builders, and high-flying financiers. Of all the Wests, it was the most precocious, unruly, noisy, flamboyant, and well known. Europeans, as well as Americans, took this, the youngest and most thoroughly spoiled child in the national family, to their hearts.

Because this last frontier faded quickly, there was as much argument about the date of its demise as there had been over its probable boundaries and location. The time of disappearance always depended upon the age and the outlook of the respondent. For several decades after the turn of the century, its passing from the scene invariably occurred during some westerner's lifetime. During the twenties, old cow hands said that the last of the genuine articles had hung up their chaps in the 1880s, but middle-aged ranchers contended that it really had happened around 1900. Younger stockmen, who argued that the western landscape now was overrun by "Montgomery Ward Buckaroos," set the terminal date at about 1913. In 1933, Philip Ashton Rollins wrote a foreword to Lawrence Smith's *Dude Ranches and Ponies.* Referring to horses, Rollins wrote: "After all, the Old West has not wholly gone. The blow flies and the dust are still in evidence."

Other westerners, who had not punched cows for a living, saw their particular West as having faded out at some other time. Except for a few rich strikes yet to come in Nevada, for example, the heyday of the silver miners was over by the turn of the century; to those who recalled its glory, the decline of that occupation marked the passing of the Old West.

The process was continually transitory, something that always ended in one's own lifetime. Nor did the passage of time help to wipe out the "them was the days" notion, for each succeeding generation found something in its boyhood that had a ring of "pioneer" about it. Sam Peckinpah, the movie director, whose forbears had come west by wagon train in 1853, stated proudly, "My earliest memory is of being strapped into a saddle when I was two for a ride up into the high country [of California].'' He was convinced that his was the hinge generation. ''My brother Denny and I were in on the last of it,'' he said. ''Denny and I rode and fished and hunted all over the country. We thought we'd always be a part of it.''

The communicators, either by film or the printed word, seem to be particularly attracted to the notion of the Old West. As a well-known Coloradan said, the term had a special appeal for ''bookish people,'' folks who savored it because the connotations were pleasant and they felt better just by thinking about it. A good example is John Fischer, who was so successful as an editor and columnist for *Harper's Magazine.* When he wrote his memoirs in 1978 and recalled a west-Texas boyhood, he claimed to be a survivor of a ''generation that saw the last of the Old West slide around the corner of history.''

If, indeed, the West had a special meaning for people, bookish people included, and if each succeeding generation clung to the idea that it had watched that cherished American heritage ''slide around the corner of history,'' one asks what is was, in particular, that left such a void in the American heart.

John Steinbeck answered that in 1938 in *The Red Pony.* As Jody's grandfather explained to the youngster, it was not the goal that mattered but the pioneers' act of achieving it; and now that the objective had been reached, there was no further need for the game: ''It wasn't getting here that mattered, it was movement and westering. We carried life out here and set it down.'' And then it was over. ''No place to go, Jody. Every place is taken.'' But that was not the worst part of it, Grandfather said. The heart of the problem was that ''westering has died out of the people. Westering isn't a hunger any more. It's all done.''

That, perhaps, is what modern Americans felt as they grasped at what they thought was the last of a great adventure and prided themselves that at least they had tasted it, savored it, before the hunger had quite subsided.

Thus, in the final quarter of the twentieth century, the backward flight into time went on, with nuclear-age Americans claiming residual rights in that now almost mythical experience.

CHAPTER 2

HOW THE OLD WEST WAS LOST

Some of the old-timers, who while away their retirement in small western towns, now and then wipe away a figurative tear as the talk turns to generalities about a West that is no more. These are daydreams, re-created scenes of youth, that are sometimes a bit distorted in memory's mirror, nostalgic reruns that sound curiously like old John Wayne movies.

The yarn spinners sound vague. And they are, to the extent that what they see is a pleasant haze glowing in a distant past. But a closer look at the horizon of their recollections would bring their memories into focus. Chances are that their verbal etchings would include no covered wagons, shiny locomotives, or steamboats; no blue-legged cavalrymen, whiskered prospectors, or painted Indians; and certainly no sheepherders tending detested woollies. Nor would that idyllic scene depict a windmill, a sulky plow, a haystack, or a field of growing corn.

No, these ancients, who may have done nothing more "western" for a living than read meters for the local utility company, are likely to conjure up quite different images, ones that they have grown very fond of, even if they have gained them only from reading pulp magazines. Their mental pictures almost surely would include a vista of rolling grassland, with a hundred or so head of cattle sprinkled like cinnamon upon it; and riding easily among the grazing animals would be the central, inescapable figure of the modern Western myth—the cowboy.

The cowboy legend is the most enduring of western folklore. To many Americans and foreign observers of our country, this man on horseback, with his boots and Stetson, has come to epitomize the West, even America itself. "The feel for the cowboy is everywhere," historian Joe B. Frantz has written; "the symbol of the cowboy is just as pervasive." This notoriety is at least partly justified. The cattlemen of reality starred in one of the final acts of the frontier story, the finale of an American pageant that had lasted more than two

"This 'High Riding Cowboy' typifies the spirit of the West," the Denver
*and Rio Grande Western Railroad assured potential travelers in this
promotional photograph. Like most businessmen, these knew what their
customers wanted to see and hear. (Courtesy, Colorado Historical Society)*

centuries and had covered every westering experience from coonskin
caps to chaps. So great was the influence of the horsemen on that last
frontier—the seemingly endless empire of grass stretching northward
from Texas to the Canadian line—that this region became known
internationally as Cow Country. It followed that the passing of the
cowboy of the open range, and his replacement by less romantic
types, convinced many that the Old West at last was gone for good.

Wyoming cattle barons enjoyed fine art and vintage wines at the Cheyenne Club, opened in 1881. (Courtesy, Wyoming State Archives, Museums and Historical Department)

The cattlemen who dominated the plains country during the last years of the nineteenth century left a mark far deeper than their numbers suggested, and therefore, when newcomers arrived to take possession, the change seemed dramatic and even violent. These men—and it was largely a male society—were more than romantic figures wearing spurs that went jingle, jangle, jingle; they directed the social, economic, and political scene for about forty years and, in some areas—Wyoming, the "Cowboy State," for example—much longer than that. Theirs was a form of aristocracy, one in which the owners represented a titled element and the ordinary hands were at least knights, mounted and ready to serve their lords. In lieu of a heraldic system, cattle brands served as coats of arms. Some of these burned-on insignia became widely known and respected as sources of power and influence in the kingdom.

This sagebrush nobility, proud, arrogant, and cocksure, ruled the region through its ownership of governors and legislators, resorting to force of arms only when the peasantry became restless or stepped out of bounds. As viewed from horseback, the tillers of the soil were regarded as lesser beings because they boarded a saddle horse as if they were climbing a ladder, settled for small pieces of land, milked cows, pitched hay, and, worst of all, saved their money. Not only were they clods, they were invading, unwelcome clods, who had wandered off the agricultural reservation and were tearing up the turf. The "sodbusters," as they were contemptuously dismissed, were regarded as constituting as great a threat to the cattle kingdom as the coming of railroads and cowboys had posed to the original tenants, the Indians. And the society they brought along was just as unacceptable to the cowpuncher as his had been to the tribesmen. But in both cases the old gave place to the new, and at about the same time.

By 1900 the Indians were pretty well fenced in, and the cattle kings were fenced out. Other Americans might view the emergent twentieth century with optimism, but the horsemen of the plains, both red and white, foresaw little that looked hopeful. This was especially true of the cattlemen, who had outrun frontier conditions on the open range, had worn thin a giant pasture once regarded as inexhaustible, and were themselves now a fading species. *Outing Magazine* recognized this in 1906 when it talked about the disappearance of the cowboy in the Southwest, explaining that it was because the southern ranges, particularly those of New Mexico, had been hard hit by drought and because the region's herd owners were being forced to look northward for better grazing. There was an out migration of both cows and cowboys.

This shift put additional pressure on such areas as the Dakotas and eastern Montana, where some of the cattlemen, who had struggled for years to make ends meet, became discouraged and left the country or moved to town. Those who were determined to stay in business once more headed north, this time to Canada, where, as a contemporary historian put it, "the last West has been reached." Or they sought Indian reservation lands in the United States. In 1904, for example, the Matador Land and Cattle Company leased half a million acres on the Cheyenne River reservation in South Dakota, subletting part of it to the Turkey Track outfit of New Mexico.

Retreat to Indian lands or migration to Canada provided no more than a momentary sanctuary for the herders. Overstocking of the available ranges and an increased pressure by homesteaders meant an end to the famed outfits that once ruled great patches of the public domain.

As early as the turn of the century, westerners began to talk about the passing of the open range; one of them remarked that "modern youth" on a western ranch hardly knew how to go about roping a gatepost. "He simply stands guard over cattle whose character has changed with all things else in the West." So the ancient herder, for a brief moment romanticized as a cowboy, apparently was back to his custodial duties, and the "broad-horned, wild-eyed Texas steer of romance is no more."

*Barbed wire, developed in the early 1870s, solved a puzzle of the plains—
fencing without timber or stone. It was a boon to farmers and ranchers, but
many a cowboy resented becoming a Ph.D. (Post-hole Digger). (Courtesy,
Colorado Historical Society)*

Within another ten years it would be asserted that the remaining
large cattle ranches of the West could almost be counted on one's
fingers, and it was doubted that more than one in five westerners ever
had seen an honest-to-God cowboy. When a ranch foreman was asked
what had happened to this species, he responded: "Oh, cowboys are
like blackbirds; they don't stay anywhere. And the fifteen men that
we have got wouldn't be caught in a hay-field on their life."

While these hired hands disdained the pitchfork, changing times
had retired them as men handy with guns. So little need was there for
marksmanship that the pistol—so lovingly known to the western
history buffs as the six gun—already had been discarded as a relic of
the past. As a contemporary observed, a young man interested in
stock raising had a choice: he could become "a typical cowboy
nuisance, wear queer clothes, shoot off pistols and strange oaths to
frighten tenderfeet, or he may become a real ranchman." The
emphasis was on *real,* meaning one who recognized churches, schools,
broadcloth suits, and business methods as a more normal way of life.

Actually the young man had no choice at all. There was very little
market for the "typical cowboy nuisance," because the romance was
over; cold reality governed. The last of the freewheeling beef barons,
who had exploited the public domain with a minimum of control and
had ruled it with armed riders, had played out their hands in the great

range-land gamble. Unable to compete any longer with those who
wanted to use the land more intensively, they now were obliged to
join the common folk as stock raisers. Shorn of their titles, they had
no choice but to settle down on limited parcels of land to breed
animals for market and to make a living much in the manner of other
agriculturists.

Even before the new century had finished its first decade, *Collier's*
weekly began to reminisce, remarking that for forty years cattlemen
had served as outriders for the agrarian advance but that within the
very recent past, this skirmish line had disappeared somewhere to the
north. Only in a few sections of Arizona or in scattered other parts of
the West could one still see large herds on an open range. By 1915,
some of the elderly members of that equestrian society would found
the Old Time Trail Drivers' Association to commemorate a day that
already had become ancient history. It was in that same year, said a
former resident of eastern Colorado, that the pioneer era had closed
for his neighbors, because at that time the federal government had
asked for bids to carry mail by truck. Because there was not a single
automobile or truck in the community, the man who won the bid had
bought a Model T Ford in order to secure the contract. The horse
and the horseman now were out of date. This fact also struck that
renowned social arbiter Emily Post, who happened to be touring the
West that year in one of the new gas buggies. As she paused at the
fashionable spa Colorado Springs, she sensed the emergent cowboy
legend, remarking that Coloradans loved the very name *cowboy*
because they admired the attitudes of men who were fearless, direct
in their outlook, lived in the out of doors, and did not recognize
obstacles when they saw them.

Yet other men who lived out of doors, who recognized obstacles,
and who were equally ready to surmount them had already staked
their claims to the land. Readers who knew their western fiction had
met these strangers in B. M. Bower's novel *The Long Shadow* (1909),
the shadow referring to the approaching agrarian hordes. The
readers knew about Billy Boyle, who had tried to help a rancher
combat the invasion, only to go down in defeat. These scenes had a
feel of reality for those who had witnessed the transition from cows to
plows. A Dakota pioneer later recalled that by the early 1900s, ranch
cabins in the country west of the Missouri River had begun to be
interspersed with claim shacks, and a new breed of land seekers had
appeared. He wrote: "The wool-hat people with their kids and plows
had come. Some of the ranchers tried to hold onto the water holes and
the hay bottoms by hiring somebody to file on them. The going price

was $200 for building an eight-by-ten shack and putting a stove and cot in it.'' It was a last desperate effort to stop the flow of a big wound that had been gashed into the range country. But it was too late. By the time the writer had moved away in 1906, the homesteaders were ''pretty thick,'' and there was no sign that the influx would abate.

Teddy Roosevelt thought that this was a natural turn of events. As he said in his autobiography, it was right and proper that the open range should disappear, for this phase of American development, of necessity, had been transitory. Glamorous as it had been, said the one-time cattleman, this way of life had not represented the best of all possible uses of the land; it was the homesteader and his family, the permanent dweller, who was the most desirable tenant.

As the new rush of homesteaders flooded the high plains and beyond, their numbers grew until the limit of profitable farm land had not only been reached but surpassed. In the process, the cowboy frontier was diluted, then flushed away, and the countryside was claimed by the plowmen who peopled the limitless squares of land that were either parceled out by the government or sold by the railroads.

This was not accomplished without a certain amount of sentimentalizing by the fans of the horsemen. Viewing from their distant perch, they saw a nameless, faceless, colorless species of lesser beings taking over God's country, driving off his favored children, and despoiling the landscape. Another chapter in the western legend had been written.

What this invading army did was to dispossess the last of the West's colorful characters, one whose time had come anyway if one thinks in terms of the open range; and then the farmers set about making western communities that looked and acted much the same as those found in older areas of the nation. In truth, this was simply the most recent result of an agrarian expansion that had been a powerful force in American life from the start. At no time in the past, in fact, had the farming frontier changed the country more than during those same years when the cattlemen had moved onto the Great Plains. From the founding of Jamestown in 1607 until 1870, American farmers had occupied 407 million acres. Then, between 1870 and 1900, as the ranching industry was expanding from Texas northward through Colorado and Wyoming to the Dakotas and Montana, farmers occupied an additional 430 million acres. In just thirty years they had opened more land to the plow than their ancestors had during the previous two and one-half centuries.

This great expansion had taken the farmers to the fringes of Cow Country, the arid and semiarid grasslands and deserts. During the first generation of the twentieth century, they made their move onto this final land of challenge, and as they did so, they were effectively completing a westward trek that stretched back for three hundred years. But rather than seeing the coming of the farmer as the climax of an old tradition, romantics preferred to focus upon the passing of the open-range cattle business. This, they said, signified the disappearance of the Old West. The coming of the "plow chasers" to the high-plains country, they said, somehow was bringing a way of life that was not just new but, more important, less desirable.

To this the modern frontiersmen objected. As early as the eighties, in one of the successive agrarian rushes that swept toward the Rockies, the newly arrived hoe men had made it clear that their presence heralded the establishment of a new and better order. In Colorado, where the open range was closed out fairly soon, a small-town newspaper suggested doing away with the word *ranch* on the ground that the term had done more to "repel the home-loving farming people of the East and to deter them from settling among us, than any other thing." It called the usage a relic of frontier days, suggestive of more primitive times, and asked that it be replaced by "the good old English word 'farm' that we left in the states with our old names and our religion."

By the 1920s, said the crusty old cowboy artist Charley Russell, this terrible thing had happened. Viewing the decline and fall of the Old West through the eyes of Rawhide Rawlings he wrote:

> Most of the cow ranches I've seen lately was like a big farm. A bungalow with all modern improvements, a big red barn that holds white-faced bulls an' hornless milk cows. The corrals are full of fancy chickens, there's a big garage filled with all kinds of cars, and at the bunkhouse that sets back where the owner and his family can't see or hear them, are the hands. You might see a man with a big hat, boots and spurs—he's the fence rider—but most of them wear bib overalls. The boss wears puttees and a golf cap. The bungalow, that's got electric lights an' hot and cold water. There's a piana that you play with your feet, and a radio, a Mah Jong set and a phonograph.

How had this happened so quickly? The bib-overall pollution of the landscape that bothered Charley so much was the result of a land boom during the early years of the twentieth century. Our history had witnessed many such surges by farmers seeking fresh, cheap lands, but this was one of the greatest—and as things turned out, it was the last. The plowmen's occupation of hundreds of millions of acres during the years after the Civil War had slowed dramatically during the final years of the century. Drought had discouraged any forays onto the plains, while falling prices of farm products offered little incentive to ambitious farmers to try their luck in new areas.

Then, shortly after the opening of the new century, the tempo picked up again. Farmers who had a little money and a lot of dreams suddenly discovered reasons to believe they might survive on lands that they always had avoided before. Despite the market glut and depressed prices of the 1890s, there was a latent feeling that the nation's food supply could dwindle and even cause hardship if the day came when there were no more new lands to claim. The census taker had inferred as much when, in 1890, he had suggested that the era of American agricultural expansion might be coming to a close and, with this development, that the family dinner table could be affected. Such gloomy thoughts from learned men might be disturbing to consumers, but they also alerted midwestern farmers to the possibilities of what land was left on the western prairies. This sort of talk strengthened hunches and nudged at pervasive feelings that there was one last main chance westward for those with the courage to grasp it. These Americans did not believe that the West of opportunity was gone; but they did suspect that it was fast fading and might be history by tomorrow. The lateness of the hour seemed to suggest that the final opportunity to claim part of the public domain was at hand.

Those who chose to take advantage of fresh lands and higher prices were not necessarily foolhardy agrarians bent on going west just because it was the thing to do. True, the same old siren songs were being sung, and on the surface it appeared that the "garden of the world" tableau had not changed. For example, Hardy Webster Campbell, the high priest of dry farming, was turning out literature that told of fresh bonanzas hidden beneath that sterile-looking high-plains sod. But there was nothing insubstantial about the condition of farm prices. Between 1900 and 1910 they advanced by more than 50 percent. Even better, the upsurge was not just part of a general economic boom in which farmers paid higher prices for their necessities; rather, it was one in which they gained upon other segments of the economy.

The five years between 1909 and 1914 have been called the golden age of agriculture, a time so favorable to farmers that it later was used as the base period in determining parity prices for farm products. To make the age even more golden, it was one when there were fewer dry years than usual on the high plains. As a result, land prices soared. Both the Dakotas saw advances of over 300 percent. To fan the flames of excitement, credit was easy to find, money was available in large amounts, and interest rates were low. For many a midwestern farmer the temptation was just too much. Not a few of them sold out and headed west.

Thus the years that immediately followed the reported "closing" of the frontier saw a steady westward flow of settlers. It has been estimated that shortly after the turn of the century, some four hundred thousand newcomers entered the trans-Mississippi West each year, with various elements of this army penetrating the region as deeply as their purses would allow. Those who had funds, who perhaps had sold eastern lands for $100 an acre or had come from the city with a grubstake, often stopped early and paid as much as $40 an acre, while others moved to less desirable but cheaper farms. This was the traditional type of advance, one that westering people had engaged in since colonial times. Discounting the fact that there was much speculation in western lands during these later years, transactions in which there was no real intention of settling, the fact remains that for approximately the first two decades of the twentieth century, more lands were taken up under the Homestead Act than all that had been disposed of in the nineteenth century.

The last rush for free or cheap lands was encouraged by the federal government. It was influenced, perhaps, by the notion that the agricultural frontier had about run its westward course, thus necessitating the use of marginal lands to guarantee a future food supply, and by the traditional concept that the nation's landed heritage should go to the people who would cultivate it. Gifford Pinchot, the spokesman for so much of Teddy Roosevelt's conservation policy, was adamant on the latter subject.

For these reasons and because it was necessary for settling the remnants of the public domain, homestead legislation was further modified to facilitate the westward trek of the latter-day frontiersmen. The Enlarged Homestead Act of 1909, the Three Year Homestead Act of 1912, and the Stock-Raising Homestead Act of 1916—all were responses to the pressures that resulted from the post-1900 land boom in the West. This is somewhat surprising in view of the fact that for four decades after the passage of the original homestead legislation in 1862, settlers had responded to a series of legislative modifications by resorting to increasingly flagrant fraudulencies and evasions of the law. The abuse did not deter Congress from continuing its efforts to people the land with small, independent freeholders. As late as 1904, with the passage of the Kinkaid Act, which applied to the Sand Hills country of western Nebraska, the legislators tried to respond to the realities of aridity in the West and to allot sufficient acreages to support individual families.

With continuing incentives dangled before their eyes, latter-day pioneers followed the old "settle and sell" practice, disposing of their midwestern farms and pressing deeper into country that they had considered alien for so long. During the first decade of the new century, the population of western North Dakota quadrupled, and in some counties in western South Dakota the increase was as much as 200 percent. In twenty years, some 26 million acres were taken up by homesteaders in the Dakotas alone. The land rush was so great that for twenty years, eastern counties of Kansas and Nebraska declined in population. All over the West, in fact, Cow Country felt the pressure of the agrarian horde. In only three years early in the century, the Union Pacific Railroad sold all of its remaining land-grant holdings in western Kansas and eastern Colorado. The land entries in the mountain states during these two decades quintupled those of the preceding forty years. Between 1900 and 1910, the populations of Idaho and Nevada doubled, thanks mainly to irrigation. On the high plains and in the panhandle of Texas—which for years had been the exclusive riding and stomping grounds of Comanches and Kiowas and cattle barons such as Charles Goodnight and Christopher Columbus Slaughter—sodbusters at last were making their bid for the land, at least along the watercourses, where they had the best chances.

As these hopeful farmers moved beyond the once-forbidding hundredth meridian, exploring untapped pockets of an empire that until recently had been ruled by cattlemen or reserved to Indians, they were doing more than simply adding to the nation's land under cultivation. By closing in on that country, which many considered the homeland of the free-roaming symbols of the American spirit, they were also bringing their countrymen closer to a kind of psychological time of reckoning.

As the final waves of agrarians assaulted the bastions of the desert, an eastern establishment that once had clucked disapproval of such westering tendencies on the ground that they might drain off the flower of more civilized regions cheered on the venturesome plowmen. Noting the movement's renewed acceleration, a well-known national magazine followed the deepening thrust with interest, remarking that the nation was entering upon a marvelous period of internal development. Old seaboard sensitivities as to the fate of the Indians appeared to have waned; and the editor acknowledged that the promised prosperity was due in part to the opening of fresh tracts of fertile land, some of which had been held in trust for the tribes. A more specific view of this inferred concept of the "greatest good for the greatest number" was revealed in 1910, when almost a million and a half acres of land were made available in north-central Montana. The recent occupants, described by a local paper as "trifling, lazy, renegade Chippewa Indians," along with a few Crees, were shipped in boxcars to the agency at Browning, where they were received in an unfriendly manner by the Blackfeet Indians. But as members of the master race confessed, it was the only way, for if these indigents were not transported, they would become a burden upon the local folks, who were trying to civilize the country.

The aggressiveness of these civilizers was gratifying to businessmen who had staked a great deal on developing the tag ends of the Great American Desert. James J. Hill, for one, admitted that he and his associates of the Great Northern Railway Co. had based a good many of their earlier decisions more on hope than on sound judgment, and now the gamble appeared to be paying off. Yim, as his Scandinavian settler-friends called him, welcomed the boom that accompanied the new century, and in an almost euphoric mood, he pondered the new bonanza, wondering if the bottom of the golden bucket ever would be reached.

Western farmers, those inveterate gamblers, would ride their lucky streak for approximately two decades, and except for a few bad hands, they would play against heavy odds and win. For about ten years after 1900, land sales were brisk. In a period when available acreages in the United States increased by 5 percent, the number of farmers grew more than twice that fast, and the value of American farmland jumped by more than 100 percent. As in any boom, much of the land was bought, not for purposes of cultivation, but as an investment, and when the inevitable decline set in, there was much lamentation among the speculators.

In addition to the rising price of farm products and the reputed returns from "scientific" farming methods in the once-unconquerable West, the irrigation craze that developed about the turn of the century added another factor to the sharpened demand for western farm lands. Supported by congressional legislation and backed by federal funds, the section's potential for irrigation appealed to the more conservative as a better venture than the risks of dry-land farming, or "horse-leg irrigation," as that method of summer fallowing was called. Water conducted onto the land was visible and presumably provided a much more reliable method of acquiring moisture than did relying upon prayer. Irrigation, older than biblical days, carried an ancient implication of fructifying the desert.

"After all there is no desert," the popular journalist Ray Stannard Baker announced to American readers in 1902. He admitted that much of the West was so designated during the nineteenth century, a great patch of land that was the "dread-spot" of the continent, but now, he stated confidently, "you may seek it in vain." He chided earlier evaluators for being men of little imagination, doubters who lacked faith in humanity, but in the far-sighted, progressive twentieth century, even those remote spots of the West that still might be thought of as deserts were fast shrinking before the onslaughts of man's ingenuity. This, said the enthusiasts, was the real conquest of the West, one in which the government had taken up the task of providing moisture where nature had left off.

By 1910, reclamation officials were pointing to the miracles already wrought in the desert—to cities that had sprung from the sagebrush and to a new land of fortune and opportunity that had materialized in the desert at the wave of the magic wand of water. Such a community was St. Anthony, Idaho, called a "city of opportunity surrounded by a country of promise" by those who paraded it as a thriving community that water had rescued from the desert. As a result, one of the largest sugar-beet factories in the nation, a plant that was capable of processing nearly 100,000 tons of beets annually, had been built nearby. There were other examples. A few years later, men were talking about similar conquests in such places as New Mexico, where some of the valleys that had been barren wastes only a decade earlier now were producing millions of dollars worth of cotton each year. Thus, said the boosters, the worth of conducted water was becoming more and more apparent, proving, they argued, that there was no limit to the desert-killing capabilities of reclamation.

Even more than the dry farmers, those who built communities around irrigated land were changing the vast stretches of the wide-open West and the image of that country that was held by the world outside. The irrigation canal was more than a bearer of water; it served also as a link that drew people into a closely organized society, much in the manner of the early Mormon settlements that offered such amenities as mail service, telephones, electric lights, trolley lines, and even paved streets and cement sidewalks. While there has been much talk about the vaunted independence of the western

This same confident smile had graced the faces of tens of thousands of frontier farmers, but on the fertile plains, it depended on water, like that captured by this Kansan in 1939. (Courtesy, Denver Public Library, Western History Department; photo by B. C. McLean, Soil Conservation Service)

settler, it was his situation, not his desire, that made him live out in the great spaces where his neighbors might be miles away. Dry farmers rebelled against this situation as best they could, by, for instance, grouping their houses together on the corners of four quarter sections, so that they might have some company—a concept of cluster housing that twentieth-century architects would use in seeking, not avoiding, open space.

Residents of the little irrigation communities, those oases in a desertlike country, found that they could bring with them the social advantages that came with having neighbors nearby. The settlements they made did not seem to be so different from the thousands of farming villages in the green and well-watered East. Compared to the changes wrought by their dry-farming cousins, the transformations for the irrigators were particularly startling. The taming of a land portrayed in the past as a wild domain, unreachable by all but the hardiest, seemed to be well under way.

As the irrigators laid out their farms in selected places in the desert, the dry-landers made much larger sweeps, penetrating new and as yet agriculturally unexplored regions, ever confident that method had replaced madness and that arid America had been subdued. But there were reverses for the latter-day frontiersmen, the first of which occurred around 1910. Tight money, no stranger to western farmers,

was part of the cause. The Panic of 1907 had been just that, a
financial fluctuation of relatively short duration, but it was enough to add disruption to an increasingly unstable western economy. Then came drought. While some areas had passable crops, others saw a second successive year of almost total failure, and from the southern plains came a grim warning of sadder days ahead—incipient dust storms. Homesteaders, who had come as invading "nesters" to drive back the cattlemen, now began their own retreat. A western-Nebraska farmer, departing from his burned-out land, left these words on the abandoned claim shack: "Fifteen miles to the Post Office; Fifty miles to the Railroad; Two hundred and fifty feet to water and six inches to Hell; I'm going back to Missouri." Critics remarked that such epitaphs to unrealized hopes represented an admission that the dry-land-farming frontier had advanced too far and that, ironically, it had torn up the sod and wrecked the cattleman's domain before heading back east.

During this setback there were some "painful readjustments," to use a phrase employed by apologists of dry farming: the advancing battle line wavered, then slowly re-formed and made yet another stand in the desert. Although some had called it quits and never would return, others saw the price of wheat edge up, thanks to the demands of war-torn Europe, and they ventured westward to plow up more grassland in the hope of making enough from the first crop to pay for the land. For many of them the gamble paid off, and during the second decade of the twentieth century there occurred a false prosperity, born of wartime prices, that took up the slack caused by recent reverses. As a result, by 1920, land values had increased, the production of wheat, corn, oats, rye, and barley had risen sharply, and millions of new acres had been put into production.

Since 1910 a subtle change had taken place in the West, one that would be much more noticeable in the years to come. During this time the increase in the number of farmers had not been in proportion to the additional lands put to the plow, which suggested that not only was the average size of individual farms growing but that absentee ownership was on the increase and corporate ownership was becoming more common. Gifford Pinchot had forecast this development early in the new century, when he had complained that great chunks of the public domain were passing into the hands of large individual or corporate owners whose object was profit, not homemaking.

As the European war intensified the demands for farm produce, the move toward large-scale farming and agribusiness accelerated.

There were few complaints at the time, partly because such changes are not always obvious to the public until later and also because wartime prices were providing farmers with the satisfying combination of making money in wheat while fulfilling a patriotic duty. Since the notion of development and growth was basic to western thinking, little criticism from that part of the land was directed against the appearance of big farmers. A people accustomed to the existence of cattle "barons" had little difficulty in accepting wheat "kings" in the realm.

The appearance of financial royalty, whose members sought to exploit new western agricultural frontiers, was merely incidental to the movement. They just formed another part of an invading force that was seeking to penetrate the inner reaches of the desert, and they shared the blame, later laid at the farmers' door, for destroying the grassland, causing wind erosion, and precipitating ecological problems in general.

These tillers of the soil, large and small, have been hailed before the bar of history and charged with being wasteful, headstrong people who had no concern except profit, thoughtless Americans who operated in an economy of waste and took long gambles, only to beg for a new deal when the cards ran against them.

In looking at such accusations, there are several factors that ought to be considered. Despite the frauds connected with application of the Homestead Acts and despite the disastrous eighties and nineties on the plains, the government continued in its efforts to draw people onto western land through the further relaxation of land laws and by means of federally sponsored irrigation projects. Farm prices were attractive enough, especially after 1914, to lure settlers away from older areas. Some abnormally wet years at this time offered a further incentive.

It was, not the western farmer, but eastern congressmen and journalists who talked about increased production and about winning the war with food. In 1917 a writer for a respected national magazine argued that food conservation would not be necessary if more of the nation's vacant lands were put into production. He called farming "the greatest single industry in the United States," and he urged that millions of idle acres be planted.

Economists who watched the agricultural scene of that time talked about efficiency, as the industrialists presumably had perfected that quality; about getting more from the land; and about new equipment, commercial fertilizers, irrigation works, improved seeds, and advanced methods. As one of the experts wrote, the old, reckless

After hard times in the 1890s, dreamers could once again find Eden in the West early in the twentieth century. In fields like this one in Moffat County, Colorado, high prices, innovative techniques, and plenty of rain made the difference. (Courtesy, Denver Public Library, Western History Department; photo by L. C. McClure)

exploitation that had crested during the eighties was a fling that a new country could afford but once. Now that youthful improvidence had run its course, it was time for agricultural maturity and high-yield farming.

Yet the propagandists seemed to be calling out for one more roll of the dice on the arid plains, a final gamble with nature. "Minute men," those latter-day patriots who volunteered to spread the gospel of victory to every village and farm in this new crusade, crisscrossed the West, crying out "Plant more wheat!" and "Wheat will win the war!" as printing presses rolled off a deluge of pamphlets urging production at any price. Actually, the great expansion that has so often been attributed to the war had already taken place during the years 1909 to 1914, but now the government itself inferred the use of marginal lands when it asked for an increase of 7.5 million over the 45 million acres already planted in wheat.

The farmers responded to all these blandishments. They cropped more acres, often on borrowed money; expanded enthusiastically, even recklessly; enjoyed the inflation years; and faced the music when the fighting ceased. For them, too, the "big parade" was over, and the boom had busted. The main problem of the modern wheat-bonanza prospectors was that they were too lucky, too ingenious, too successful. High prices, a few wet years, and an innovative application of machinery to the land resulted in enormous crops. The wheat harvest of 1919, a record setter, was gathered at a time when the large gasoline tractor, the combine harvester, the truck, and related mechanical devices were coming into their own on the Great Plains. Within a decade and a half after that banner year the workhorse had become a victim of technological unemployment. For example, in Kansas during this period, the use of old dobbin sank from more than sixteen hours per acre to about twelve minutes.

During the nineties, farmers had complained that they were being advised to go out and plant more crops and to counter falling prices with increased production. Having done that, they were rewarded by bigger surpluses, falling prices, and more mortgage foreclosures. Then, in 1917 and 1918, they had been told to be patriotic, to apply machinery and American know-how to the land, to farm efficiently, and they would win both the war and personal prosperity. They had done this, and again they had outsmarted themselves. Once more they had been thanked for their effort with glutted markets and sagging price levels. By the early twenties, hard times were again haunting the plains farmers, especially those who had settled in marginal areas.

What had been a sea of unbroken sod two generations earlier and a homesteading frontier just a few years back now was being rapidly integrated into a complex national and international economic system. Some farmers, of course, still lived under conditions that were just as primitive as the ones faced by earlier settlers, those who had taken up farms far from the railroad, who had to haul water for miles and looked upon a monthly bath as a luxury. The appearance of the Model T Ford and perhaps the battery-powered radio updated the process slightly, but the main pattern was essentially a repetition of an ancient formula for westering. But behind this battle line in country that had recently been captured and subdued, some major changes were taking place. Already, agricultural writers had begun to complain that despite an apparent land rush, the rural population of the West was not increasing; in fact, some regions were undergoing a loss of population. The farmers were not retreating to the east, as they had during previous assaults upon the agricultural frontier; rather, they were heading for the towns. The comforts of central heating, indoor plumbing, and community social life were attractive to retired farmers. The problem lay in the fact that their children shared the feeling, many of whom had little inclination to stay on the farm, preferring to turn over its operation to a tenant or to return to the land only long enough to crop it and thus become members of a new class called suitcase farmers. Such developments, it was argued, lessened the standards of production, because tenants did not have the real interest of the land at heart, but only an immediate return from it.

Tenant farming was yet another incentive for cropping larger acreages, for an increased usage of machinery, and, in turn, for the emergence of a new dimension in western farming: a labor problem. Worker unrest on the plains appeared in 1914, when, under the impression that a large crop was in the making, states began to advertise for harvest hands. The response was a flood of workers, only about 20 percent of whom were hired, the remnants filling little western towns with idle, hungry, unsheltered men who frequently were deported by the civic fathers. The next spring the Industrial Workers of the World, the "Wobblies," chartered an agricultural section that was aimed, in part, at the problems of migrant laborers in the wheat fields. Wartime pressures stifled organizational efforts, but during 1919 and afterwards, the drive for membership was sharply increased. The resurgence coincided with a period of violent postwar reaction in America, and from it there developed some ugly scenes in western agricultural communities.

By adopting mass production methods and seeking to mine the land with modern, highly efficient methods, the "industrialized" farms approached a labor-management impasse that was unique in American farming. Organized workers, led by the IWW, demanded wage contracts but were willing to abide by them only as long as it was to their advantage. On the other hand, farmers tried to drive down wages, and they opposed organizations that sought to maintain higher levels. They complained that members of the IWW not only refused to work but also prevented others from taking jobs. During the 1920 harvest, some Dakota farmers offered as much as seven dollars a day, a figure considered to be high, and were turned down. Angry townsmen, who depended upon farm accounts, frequently sorted out those workers who would sign up and put the rest on the first freight train that passed through town. The townsmen also refused to allow "jungling," and they raided the transient hangouts, sending the bindle stiffs fleeing. Agrarian hostility to the migrants, as well as the greater availability of smaller and hence cheaper mechanized equipment that better fitted the family labor force, resulted in a diminished floating population in the wheat fields. By 1930 the size of the annual migration from Texas to Canada had been cut by more than one hundred thousand workers, leaving about that many who still made the trek in search of employment.

Contracts, strikes and unions, tenants and absentee owners, respectable villages, and irrigated fields—all seem to have almost wholly transformed the plains and deserts of the West in a short lifetime. Cowboys and cattlemen, the knights-errant of the mythic frontier, had surrendered their ground to the homesteader and his family; then, just as quickly, these pioneer farmers had given way to a kind of "industrial agriculture" that shared much more with eastern cities than with the western experience, which many believed had given Americans so much that was uniquely their own.

Even before the Roaring Twenties had ended, those who were sensitive to sociological trends had begun to ask if the farmer's total immersion at the baptismal fount of industrial efficiency had not washed away the highly prized characteristic known as individualism, a quality thought to be essential to the conquest of the West. The legendary yeoman might profit by adopting scientific methods and expert direction and by farming larger units of land. But some wondered, how was he to keep alive the traditional independence that had been so jealously guarded in the old days? Would not these operators of future factory-farms be mere wage earners, dependent on others for their very bread and subject to the whims of absentee land monopolists?

If that should come to pass, here might be further evidence that the Old West was finally gone.

CHAPTER 3

THE
NERVOUS
YEARS

During the first quarter of the twentieth century, as permanent tenants completed the occupation of western lands, a shakedown of the social and political structure occurred, an onset of community and personal maturity. It was accompanied by an economic stabilization. These changes suggested the arrival of "civilization" and the disappearance of a life style that was free-swinging, uninhibited, and somewhat primitive.

The transformation occasioned much emotional grinding of gears among sentimental Americans who cherished the notion of a more orderly society but agonized over the surrender of a condition that was, at least in theory, its antithesis. In other words, they expected progress because that ideal long had been viewed as the keystone of the American way. But if progress theatened to dull the shimmering mirage that reflected eastward from the sunset, there were second thoughts about supplanting this lovely aura with a more mundane atmosphere.

It was this period of transition from an older to a newer West that one Kansas journalist aptly called the "nervous years." He considered the nineties to have been an adolescent period, a time of offensive boasting by westerners, of paranoid attitudes toward the East, and of an undisguised inferiority complex. Nervous as the early years of the new century might be, the writer regarded them as a bridge between a relatively crude frontier society and the development of a more traditional life style, one that was influenced by a further industrialization of the nation. In other words, the West was growing up.

This was more than a rationalization by a sympathetic newspaperman. National magazines carried the same message. The West, once regarded as a somewhat wild and untamed relative, now was popularly viewed as a young, maturing member of the family. From older sections of the country came praise for those in the new society whose progressive ways were reflected, not so much in their politics, *43* as in their acceptance of the mores that were attributed to forward-looking leaders of the burgeoning business world.

An updated westerner was being processed and readied for the nation's approval. Needless to say, the pattern was cut and the product was assembled in the East, where everything else was manufactured. In this case, nothing original was created; rather, there was fashioned a recycled American, possessed of the virtues that had once been attributed to an early species of easterners and dressed to suit modern times.

The focus of the new western thrust was upon the townspeople. That flow was advertised as being heavily laced with small merchants, tradesmen, and even manufacturers, as well as lawyers, doctors, musicians, and teachers—all of whom migrated by train and entertained no fears of being scalped upon arrival. The newcomers mixed easily with westerners, who either were natives or had put in enough time to claim tenure as westerners. Many of the latter had drifted into nearby towns: some had given up farming through retirement; others, having temporarily achieved a county office, had simply hung on when the political stint ended. The new urban mixtures operated as agricultural service centers and existed only because of the farmers in their areas. Members of this instant city gentry slavishly mimicked the eastern establishment that was putting together the new western myth, taking seriously their roles as morally clean, progressive, civic-minded Americans of a higher order; and as a part of that role, they looked down upon the tillers of the soil who lived around them and supported them.

Readily, almost eagerly, the already-established townsmen accepted the notion, provided to them by molders of opinion, that they were indeed the genuine article, true descendants of those sterling characters who had carried westward the torch of civilization, had tamed the country, and had willed to later generations the rewards of this genetic refining process. The fact that a large number of these burghers were not western born—some were even relatively recent arrivals—did not disturb their thinking. It was a case of the wish being the father of the thought.

If the composition of the migration to western towns was changing, so was that of the movement to the agrarian West, especially during the first two decades of the century. Now a much larger proportion of those taking up fresh lands were coming from the cities, rather than from eastern farms. Contemporaries conceded that many of these people had once lived on farms or had been born there but that, having experienced big-city life, they now wanted to return to the healthy atmosphere of rural America. Part of this was attributed to disillusionment with the city, its moral climate, and its increasing economic strictures, but another reason advanced was the notion that modern farm life was a far cry from the drab loneliness that had driven these folks cityward in the first place. Many of the farmhouses now were said to have hot and cold running water, bathtubs, and indoor toilets, while much of the field labor was accomplished by machinery. This suggested that the rush to the big cities led by young people during the '80s and '90s may have been premature, and now, in modern America, the best place for starting over, while enjoying the latest conveniences, was in the West, where land was still cheap, farm life comfortable, and the air invigorating.

So it was that uneasy easterners, many of whom were said to have developed a distaste for the alleged social evils of increasingly decadent seaboard cities, were encouraged to think of making the westward passage in search of new economic opportunities as well as to experience a moral and spiritual cleansing process. Westerners encouraged the notion, by stressing, whenever they could, the safety and comfort of a new and orderly America that lay beyond the wide Missouri. The East might mourn the passing of the frontier, but at least for the time being, westerners welcomed its reported demise as offering the promise of a less hazardous and less tumultuous life, and they did all they could to advertise the tranquillity that had descended over General Custer's tracks.

It was assumed by critics, both eastern and western, that the character of this latest migration would result in different western institutions and, therefore, a different West. They were right.

Shortly after 1900, writers began to identify this latter-day westerner and to describe his characteristics. They made it clear that while he had "arrived" in terms of maturity and stability, he had done much more than merely to have drawn even with the East. To have achieved no more than parity would have admitted to a failure of the frontier process, not to mention degrading the American ideal of progress. If the nation had sowed the West, the harvest must accomplish more than merely getting back its seed.

Yet, those who sought to characterize the contemporary westerner reverted to phrases that also described the frontiersmen, as traditionally viewed. According to the *North American Review,* this son of the pioneer was "clear-headed, stout-hearted, frank-faced, . . . the product of years of trial, of experiment, of triumph."

Missing from the catalog of virtues was the emphasis earlier placed upon the desirability of rugged physical specimens. It was rationalized that since the westward advance now was being carried out by less primitive forms of transportation and into communities where such attributes were somewhat superfluous, there were fewer premiums on hairy chests. A contemporary scholar wrote that the economic and social conditions then obtaining in the West remained vigorous enough to perpetuate qualities such as those enumerated above without requiring more muscular evidences of manhood. Presumably, such conditions traded virility for polish, if those who unstintingly praised the embryonic young merchant prince are to be credited.

Even the Virginian, the cowboy protagonist of Owen Wister's novel of 1902 who epitomized the manly virtues of the Old West, showed some hints of the changes coming to the ideal sons of sunset land. After he had gunned down Trampas, this classic Western hero married Molly the schoolmarm, settled down as a ranch manager, and eventually, we learn in the last paragraph, became "an important man, with a strong grip on many various enterprises," and one who fit in comfortably during visits back East. The new Western hero was a man of the world who thought nothing of making quick business trips to Chicago or New York, where he was much more at home than would be, say, a visitor from Keokuk, Iowa. If he needed a million dollars for some new enterprise, "he takes a train for the most likely lending centre. He carries his dreams with him as security."

True, there were such beings. The description fits Colorado banker, mining magnate, and railroad entrepreneur David Moffat, on one of his periodic visits to New York in search of funds to build his dream railroad westward from Denver. That he failed, that he died bankrupt, alone in the big city of New York, need not mar the image or damage the myth.

This generalized worldly westerner, said *Harper's,* drew such enviable traits from his municipal roots, because the new western towns were possessed of a "larger metropolitan manner" than were eastern places of similar size. These young, fresh cities, described as being highly charged with vitality, hopes, and expectations, were expected to spawn individuals of the same mold. Such qualities once had been hailed as products of the frontier, but now they were interpreted to mean up-and-coming, commercially aggressive, modern. It was taken for granted that men of such origins surely would be found doing business in the humming financial districts of large eastern centers.

But even when cast in that role, these young businessmen, riding out of the West, were said to be different; theirs was a healthy, hitting-

Vital and energetic, Denver grew from a town of about 5,000 in 1870 to a metropolis of some 134,000 in 1900. Dominating this late-nineteenth-century panorama is the Arapahoe County Courthouse, completed in 1883. (Courtesy, Colorado Historical Society)

above-the-belt aggressiveness. In 1904 an educated Wyoming resident explained that when he went East, he was appalled by the mercenary, suspicious attitudes of the natives, a people who seemed to regard all others as cheats. Not so in the West, he said. Out there, folks simply were trying to make money, while in the East they were trying to get it away from each other. This said more about western resources than about business ethics, but even if that explanation is accepted, it revealed differences between the two regions, if not their people.

Admirers of this up-and-coming urban westerner did not shrink from praising his two-fisted business approach, for Babbittry had not yet become a naughty word; but for fear the public get the wrong idea and decide that the son of the pioneer had succumbed to materialism in favor of any other kind of progress, it was set forth that where money bloomed, culture could not be far behind. It had happened in the East, said the argument; rising fortunes there had meant money for higher education, for increased cultural facilities, and for literary outlets. In expressing his hope that in the West there would come about a recognition "of things not recorded in agricultural reports," a writer for the *Independent* may have anticipated Harvard historian Charles A. Beard's later comment that the only kind of culture the West had was agriculture.

There was, of course, a danger that in gaining so much material wealth, its owners would yield to the desire to acquire some of the cultural trappings of an advanced civilization. It was during this period that a midwesterner earnestly assured an inquiring journalist: "I'm taking the family abroad for culture and, by George we're going to get culture if we have to stay six months!" Westerners, who were then feeling an increasing sense of their own special regionalism, would have been horrified at the prospect of falling into the same class as the midwesterner, whom they looked down upon and denigrated at every opportunity.

Whatever the degree of cultural onset west of the big river, it was bound to alter the lives of the people. The emergence of schools, clubs, libraries, and publications promised enlightenment; but the same package contained the possibility of social changes. Compared to their cousins in more settled regions, those on the frontier traditionally had made less of a fuss about social distinctions, had asked fewer questions about one's origins, and had featured a one-dimensional society. Western men who were poor were willing to be thought poor, since that condition carried no stigma in the great democracy. On the other hand, those who were rich chose not to advertise it by dressing ostentatiously, because this was a land in which one could lose his fortune tomorrow; therefore, what a man knew or could do was regarded as being more important than worldly goods, for such qualities were his real and permanent assets. Easterners who were trying to cling to the fading frontier wanted to think that this was one of the characteristics still to be found in the West, but the natives said this wasn't so. By 1900, they confessed, that condition had pretty well passed. They hastened to say that though the clannish spirit was by no means dominant, class lines had by now been drawn and were visible, especially in the towns.

This was disappointing to those along the Atlantic seaboard who had watched the great western morality play unfold. They had hoped that the cast of characters—at least the male characters—would continue to appear in proper democratic garb, but if this time-honored test no longer was reliable, they contented themselves with the conviction that makers of ready-made clothing were obliged to allow just a little more material for these broad-shouldered, athletic outdoor men who lived in such a healthy, vigorous climate. Western women, on the other hand, never had stood for such nonsense and

had insisted upon the latest styles, even during frontier times. An
eastern woman, commenting on this subject in 1904, allowed that "in the matter of dress the women of Colorado are quite up to modern standards."

She suggested also that the practices and customs of western society were beginning to yield to modern influences. Usages that were quite liberal in frontier days "have become as conventional as the most strictly interpreted of social codes could demand." It was more the case in the larger cities, where the entertainment of one's guests was offered in the tradition of western hospitality, but now with many of the amenities found farther east. Her remark that newcomers who arrived in town willing to entertain and who exhibited "a reasonable degree of education and refinement" were received "joyously" suggested a measure of social stratification.

The problem faced by eastern sponsors of the new western hero was that while they did not want to discount his pioneer background, supposing he had one, or to minimize the positive traits that he was said to have inherited, they wanted to show that he had outgrown some of his less desirable characteristics. It was cheerfully admitted that bad men and women usually came early to new areas but that their heyday was transient, and more solid folks came hard on their heels to make up the permanent population. There were some exceptions to this rule, and they had to be rationalized away. There still lurked in the West that foot-loose individual, the "sagebrusher," who manifested the traditional western spirit of restlessness. Moving about constantly, with the conviction that more money was to be made more easily on the other side of the mountain, was his response to the natural seductiveness of the West, a place historically attractive to the dreamer and the idealist.

The belief that undeveloped country always offered opportunities had been a lodestone for carefree spirits in all parts of America, and although modern westerners and their eastern friends refused to admit that opportunity no longer stalked the setting sun, it was better to think that more conventional methods would realize them. Floaters, now generally thought to be peculiar to the West, no longer were regarded as restless frontiersmen, pursuing their destiny, but instead, as transients, homeless people who were unable to find the West of their choice, drifters who were unsure of themselves. Chambers of Commerce shunned them, for they that did not join the crowd were not apt to be taxpayers. Fortunately, said the city fathers, these wanderers were outnumbered by reliable, steady young businessmen who knew real gold when they found it and had settled in for the duration.

These solid members of the young western commercial fraternity, prosperous and confident, were praised as being men who did not have to take a back seat to anyone. They could visit old haunts in the East without entertaining any exaggerated views as to its prosperity, its progress, its refinements, for their secure place in the new country had shown them that the East had little to be envied and that happiness could be achieved quite as easily on the prairies as along the boulevards. There was less and less talk of "back East." Second- or third-generation westerners, as well as some newcomers, held "old timers" reunions to commemorate their long residence in the West. Local cemeteries were getting larger, and as more families added plots to them, these places became little parks, where trees and grass were forced along, shrines to yesterday, recent though it was, where local history could be viewed. For many a community the burying ground was the first permanent tie with the new country, and not infrequently it served as the town's only public monument.

The West was acquiring a past.

But here was a paradox. The new westerner was looking for a respectability that came from tradition and the stability of continuity. But as he searched his yesterdays, he was forced to recognize that one of the most obvious traits of his forebears was a rejection of roots. According to the myth, at least, the frontier was, above all, a Fresh Beginning. Its experience supposedly had conditioned its people to escape the bonds of precedent, to be more aware of present urgencies, and to solve such problems in an innovative manner while never surrendering an uncritical faith in a better tomorrow. The western past showed a rejection of the past; its most obvious tradition was a walking away from tradition. So the West, schizophrenic as always, wanted the respectability of conventional antecedents, but it could not shake the feeling that such a search in itself was part of a metamorphosis from wild and free-running days to a present that reeked of regularity. Thus it stood high centered on the dilemma of explaining how one could have it both ways. It required some fast talking to show how one could be a special western product, born of a unique past, and yet still boast of being as culturally advanced as easterners—creatures who were looked down upon as mere dudes and lesser beings precisely because they were too much shaped by tradition. No wonder that modern westerners, trying to sort all this out, became increasingly nervous.

In an effort to resolve the problem, a New York City magazine ventured the notion that the West was eastern but that the East was very far from being western. Only in that as-yet-unspoiled country

could one find a combination of the "culture and conservatism of the
East, the chivalry and fire-eating spirit of the South and the broad
unhampered gambler's view of life native to raw western soil. . . .
That combination . . . is the United States in essence, found only in
the West." This was to restate Lord Bryce, of a generation earlier,
who thought the West to be the most American part of America. The
updated version implied that only in the West did the true American
reside, the great white hope of the nation. Journalists and an
emerging breed of western "fans" were not alone in predicting great
things for this prototype of the new American and his part of the
country. A well-known historian predicted that "whatever the future
may be, it will find not only the West determining the destiny of the
Republic, but also standing wholeheartedly for that better life to
which we all look forward."

The next logical step in the argument that the West was a mature
member of the fraternity was to assert that as a result of such a
development, or at least coincidental to it, the area had achieved
economic independence. In 1903 the *Outlook* praised the West's
industrial advance, saying that a decade earlier it had been hopelessly
dependent upon the East but that with the advent of packing houses,
milling, and even some small industries, the situation was changing
rapidly. Another eastern periodical said that American business and
industrial methods were being revolutionized every decade and
added, "The westerner is never behind in his contribution to this
American overturning."

Such notions were based upon misinformation or wishful thinking.
The West was not economically independent, and it would not even
approach that status for more than a half-century. It might *act* and
sound independent, but this was only noise, the snarling of a tethered
colonial.

In an attempt to show that the West had reached a level of national
equality in its agricultural efforts, the argument was set forth that that
region had entered a new era in which agrarians knew exactly what
crops to raise, how to cultivate them, and how to receive steady,
permanent income from the land. It was admitted that booms had
occurred earlier on the plains and that when things went bad, there
were cries that the bubble had burst. But then, said the appraisers of
the new West, gradually it became apparent that no one was starving
in the hinterland, that the poorhouse was a curiosity, and that even
the most beleaguered of the farmers were making at least enough
money to survive. By around 1910 the new frontiersman's persistence was said to have paid off and to have reaffirmed the

possibilities of western farming to such a degree that a fresh land boom was under way. This cresting the wave of a new prosperity, of having survived the trough of despair and depression, was used as proof that the agricultural West was solid and was here to stay.

If claims that by this time the West was economically self-sustaining were without foundation, stronger is the argument that signs of a home-grown culture were surfacing. In his *End of American Innocence,* Henry F. May picked 1912 as the date that marked the end of the trans-Mississippi country's acute need for cultural aid from the East. By then, he said, the nation was tame and united, a condition that allowed emerging areas to strengthen their identities and to develop social structures. Contemporary West watchers earlier took this view, certain that as this young society matured, its people increasingly would become aware of the advantages to be drawn from settled conditions, among them the possibilities for social and cultural growth.

Already, said the famed New York journalist Jacob Riis, women's groups in western towns had made gains in keeping these places clean, in promoting children's playgrounds, in heading off slum development, in fighting against child labor, and in urging the creation of juvenile courts, while warring relentlessly upon a favorite western pastime, gambling. The Danish-born Riis, who wrote several books about social problems, was deeply interested in the treatment of community ills, wherever found; and to see an awareness of such matters among the residents of the Wild West of yesteryear not only was personally encouraging to him but it was also something that could be useful when making contrasts to slum-ridden eastern cities. The *Independent* also made note of these changes and praised the West for its success in "combining emotional exuberance and esthetic freedom with the requirements of social control."

Westerners were not displeased to hear such things said about themselves. They were anxious to repudiate allegations that they worshiped only things material and that they were eager to tinker with social, economic, and political innovations; yet they were careful not to venture out where the ice was thin. "In working out his vision," remarked a critic in 1917, "the Westerner experimented with legislation, producing weird effects at the time, but on the whole tending toward better things." This critic was amused at the outbreak of committees and boards that solemnly studied "everything from the length of hotel bed-sheets to the specific gravity of kerosene," and he noted that in one little prairie town, no less than six inspectors, all drawing state salaries, were hard at work checking every business within reach.

These were activities that gave the West a reputation for being
liberal, for being a place of advanced ideas and experimentation; but there were basic flaws in that assumption. In 1915, Coloradans earned a bad mark in progressives' eyes when the Republican legislature tried to torpedo the program of jurist Ben Lindsey, the "kids' judge," whose work with juveniles was drawing far more praise from the East than at home. Colorado was called economically brutal, socially unregenerate, and politically depraved by unhappy liberal easterners, who often idealized this new and untouched land where progress was supposed to march forward without encountering the same resistance it had faced in older parts of the nation.

These critics did not understand the degree to which the pioneers' cultural luggage had been laced with New England conservatism and a disposition to make haste slowly. Westerners were, as a writer for *Outlook* pointed out, not only religious; they were even somewhat narrow theologically. Morally they were unreservedly against tyrants, of either the domestic or the foreign variety, and so tenaciously did they guard their voting privileges that, with some exceptions, political machines found western ground hard to plow. This inability of politicians to discipline their followers was to remain a characteristic despite the heavy influx in later years of easterners who were used to following party lines. Despite being mavericks, westerners retained their pioneer attachment to equality and displayed a keen sense of social justice, one in which they were willing to employ collective control that limited the individual when it seemed necessary. Sterling qualities such as these could bring only approval from easterners who felt an erosion of them at home.

This was more than praise for a maturing country cousin. There were hints from the eastern intellectual establishment that the new and as yet unspoiled West might well be a final repository for the social and political achievements that those people regarded as the fruits of the American dream. It was thought of as a safe house for a way of life that appeared to be threatened by a dilution of the cultural bloodstream.

In the periodicals during these years, grumblings could be heard that America was declining. One of the most commonly offered explanations was that the nation was being resettled by Asians and central Europeans, who supposedly were polluting our Anglo-Saxon purity. *Americanism* and *individualism* long ago had become holy words to the country's chest-pounding patriots, but now these two terms were linked—equated, really—with the values of the old-stock Protestants who supposedly had brought out the country's best.

And the West, the argument continued, was the haven for these beleaguered virtues. This idea was not new. For years, those who thought of themselves as racial aristocrats had seen the country beyond the Missouri as the natural home for their kind, in part because it simply was so far from the insidious influences of the East Coast. When William Jackson Palmer, the builder of the Denver and Rio Grande Railroad Company, founded Colorado Springs, he envisioned a lovely and respectable community that would attract well-to-do home owners and vacationers. Soon, others would imitate this example, and a ''new and better civilization'' would grow up in the West, he predicted. The Atlantic Coast, alas, was a lost cause. ''We will surrender that briny border as a sort of extensive Castle Garden to receive and filter the foreign swarms and prepare them by a gradual process for coming to the inner temple of Americanism out in Colorado,'' he wrote to his wife-to-be. ''Isn't that a logical as well as a unique notion?''

The idea was not unique, and it was hardly logical, but thirty years later it had become increasingly popular. Some of the men who were most responsible for shaping the popular impressions of the West were themselves members of the eastern cultural establishment, sons of the old-stock families, appalled at the waves of new immigrants that were washing up on the Atlantic Coast. So when Harvard graduate Owen Wister created the Virginian, he made his cowboy hero a symbol of yesterday's America, a square-jawed and blue-eyed cultural sentinel who opposed the oncoming hordes of non-Nordic newcomers. And Frederic Remington, another Ivy Leaguer, who became the most famous illustrator of the disappearing West, was quite specific on his views of the situation. The Italians, Chinese, ''Huns,'' ''Injuns,'' and eastern European Jews were ''the rubbish of the earth . . . the rinsins, the scourins, the Devil's lavings,'' he wrote. ''I've got some Winchesters and when the massacring begins, I can get my share.''

Of the many ironies of the western myth, this was among the tastiest, for it can be argued that the West, not the East, was the country's great melting pot during these years. From the first gold strikes, the mining towns had been the most polyglot swarmings in our history, veritable Babels, in which Irish, Peruvians, Hawaiians, Portuguese, French, Italians, and Chinese were thrown together with English, Germans, and pilgrims from every part of this country. Between 1860 and 1890, Nevada, not New York or Massachusetts, could claim the highest percentage of persons born abroad, and the northern plains, with their thousands of farmers from Czechoslovakia, Germany, Scandinavia, and Russia, were close behind. In

"For my sake . . . for my sake," Molly begged the Virginian in this illustration from Owen Wister's classic tale published in 1902. The man, his woman, and the situation would reappear scores of times in copycat novels and movies. (Courtesy, Colorado Historical Society)

1900 the Census Bureau reported that nearly eight persons of every ten living in North Dakota were either immigrants or children of an immigrant. No other state or territory has ever matched that figure.

Still, the idea took root that in the West the "true Americans," the individualistic Anglo-Saxon elite, were making their stand. In praising the region's racial purity, one critic was pleased to report that it was not "peopled by a hodge podge of aliens." Perhaps he was not classing the Swedes, Norwegians, Germans, and other northern-European farmers, then taking up western lands in record numbers, as "hodge-podge people." It was as if the West were providing some kind of a cultural strainer, one that left eastern rural areas with "a substitution of Italian, Hungarian, Russian and Jewish farmers," and allowing the Nordics unrestricted westward passage. Left behind, also, were thousands of other southern Europeans, who preferred to settle in the cities and to seek industrial jobs. An eastern periodical complained that its area was getting three times as many of these people as was the West.

That the Scandinavians were a part of the purifying process was made clear in 1909 by Governor John A. Johnson of Minnesota. He laid his cards on the table when he announced that by a selective process the God of American destiny had drawn from the world's best races—presumably those of northern Europe—to supply the westward-moving army of Caucasians.

A Scandinavian governor of a state that was heavily populated by Norwegians and Swedes might have been forgiven his public praise of the Nordic strain, but so current was the notion of genetic priorities that a University of Wisconsin sociologist could use the term *selections* when writing about two centuries of the westward movement. The probable result of this process, he concluded, was a peculiar strength of will among Americans, a trait that appeared to show itself in those who had penetrated the more remote frontiers. This strength, this vigor, was what Americans feared was dissipating.

As those who treasured the utopian West of their minds worried about the possibility that it might become just like the rest of the nation, events were at work that would tend to blot out sectional differences for the moment. Hints that the West would be called upon to join modern America were seen during World War I years as the national urgency called for unified responses. It was the mushrooming of patriotism, extreme and often misguided, that offered the West its share of a widely held and popular sentiment. An Idaho farm wife later remembered the great crusade as being "a pleasure to us sagebrush folks" because it "injected into the monotony of our existence a romantic spirit which linked us with the outside world of action and emotion.''

In part she meant that the farming class, increasingly ignored if not denigrated by the rising industrial society, now was urged to partici-pate in the national effort by providing food for the Allies. Through this kind of call to arms, western agrarian communities found a place in world affairs, broadened their views, and thought of themselves as a factor in international business, as opposed to their traditional place as an annex to eastern states. True, it was a somewhat evanescent role, one that would make western farmers a part of the postwar ''lost generation'' as bad times returned, but for the moment it gave them a sense of belonging, and from this would emerge a feeling of permanency in the fraternity of American states.

One of the uglier manifestations of support for the war was the degree to which ultranationalism was carried. ''We were a mob of patriots out there in the brush,'' wrote the same farm wife. ''One Hundred Per Cent Americans, as intolerant and unloving as bigoted churchers.'' Historian Angie Debo recalled farm-country patriotism in her *Prairie City,* when she commented upon the distaste that members of the community showed for the culture of their German neighbors: ''In August, 1918 . . . the Evangelical Church discon-tinued its German service, and the telephone exchange forbade the use of the language over its wires.'' Beyond that there were book burnings and actual cases of physical violence in the West.

Ironically it was this period of high emotions that drew western folks momentarily closer. Farmers and townsmen found common ground in buying Liberty bonds, hunting subversives, and persecut-ing German-Americans. But as Coloradan Hal Borland later wrote, these were episodes, and over all, the war did not make nearly the impact in the West that it did farther east. As Borland said, the lasting memory was that the price of wheat went to record high levels.

Associating the West with patriotism was not a warborn response. Nationalism, flag-waving, and chauvinism long had been parts of the nation's belief in manifest destiny, the West frequently having been used as that program's cutting edge. As recently as the turn of the century, novelist Frank Norris had commented upon the link between the westward impulse and the development of what he termed ''true patriotism.'' Now, at a time when America was off on the great adventure in Europe, bent upon making the world safe for America's conception of democracy, the link between frontier values and patriotism became increasingly evident. Emerson Hough's volume *The Passing of the Frontier* appeared at the height of American participation in the conflict, and he made it clear to his readers, many of whom had sons "over there," that the doughboys in the trenches of France were carrying on a long tradition of bravery in the face of hardships. He savored the term *frontier* and asserted that to the *genuine* American it was "the dearest word in all the world." He was another of those who stressed the notion that authentic Americanism was largely a frontier product, albeit a characteristic that had been diluted, as Hough put it, "by far less worthy strains," but one, he hoped, that still showed some signs of strength in the West.

For those who eschewed the printed word, there was Theodore Roosevelt, a converted easterner who was afflicted by a terminal case of cowboyitis, who now railed at authorities for their refusal to let him charge up Teutonic San Juan hills and corral the kaiser. It was much more than Teddy's penchant for outdoor life and his image as a man of the West that captivated Americans of his day; they saw it as a connecting link between traditional frontier characteristics and red-blooded Americanism, then so much in vogue.

That much-admired latter quality, however, had not flowered in the West during the prewar years, any more than it had in the rest of the nation; and after America's entry into the war, the West merely responded to national reactions. In fact, during the neutrality period, there was criticism of westerners who profited from demands for food by hungry, wartorn Europe but who otherwise displayed little interest in the conflict. "They are so wrapped up in their own selfish affairs; the war doesn't touch them except to make money for them," complained one critic. This unexpected prosperity was welcomed by the plains farmers, commented another, but the beneficiaries of it showed little sympathy for the cause that brought them their riches. On the contrary, peace movements were said to have gained adherents here out of proportion to the rest of the nation.

Apologists for the West reacted to criticism by explaining that out on the ranges the cowboys and cattlemen were not concerned with the problems of faraway nations; they were self-sufficient individuals, men who long had disdained the military and generally were suspicious of politicians. However, beneath the surface lurked the sentiment that sooner or later the boys would have to saddle up and ride off to settle matters. Tim McCoy, who became famous as a movie cowboy, recalled an evening at Thermopolis, Wyoming, when the question of neutrality became the subject of taproom talk. Said one old hand: "Of course I'm neutral. I'm so damned neutral I don't care *who* kills the Kaiser."

To many outsiders, Theodore Roosevelt, here looking tanned and resolute during a visit to Colorado, personified the image of the West. To many westerners, however, he was a meddlesome dude. (Courtesy, Colorado Historical Society)

When war came, admirers of these individualists were pleased that westerners participated in the program of rounding up the kaiser as enthusiastically as did the dudes farther east. Montana people were inordinately proud of the way their young men responded to the call, boasting that the number of volunteers was the highest in per capita figures in the nation. One of them later wrote that this threat to America could be avenged only in the western tradition of direct action and that Montanans regarded the challenge as a personal thing. This may have been a slight overstatement in view of the fact that due to a gross error in the 1910 census, the state's draft allotment came to about twice the number it should have been.

Whatever moved western lads to rally around the flag, the results were pleasing to their fans in the East. In reporting that these hardies were flocking to recruiting stations in greater numbers proportionately than in the Atlantic states during the spring of 1917, the *Independent* hoped that such a patriotic response would "put an end to the nauseating nonsense" recently appearing in eastern dailies "about the effeminacy and cowardice of westerners." Just because those Americans had entertained doubts about entering a European war, lamented that journal, they had been subjected to scorn, abuse, ridicule, and contempt. Happily, the frontier tradition had been preserved, and indeed, this was still a place where men were men, despite any momentary doubt as to their virility.

After the brief adventure in Europe, Johnny and his friends came marching home, some to join the "lost generation" and all the disillusionment that the term implied, others to take up where they had left off in their workaday world of wages, houses, marriage, and families. The war hatred, so quickly and expertly generated by the propagandists, was as quickly put to use by fear mongers, who now used it as a weapon in the new anti-Red crusade that swept the nation during the early twenties. In the West, where things always are done in a bigger and better manner, the hunt for subversives was carried on with great enthusiasm, as the flag waving of yesterday became the Americanism of the day. A contributor to the *Saturday Evening Post* noticed it when he visited the West in 1922, remarking that "there was, practically everywhere, the talk and the activity of patriotism, still vibrant from the late Great War; but it was talk, a patriotism of the surface, of the present." In this respect, Bryce's comments about the West being "the most American part of America" held true. It was a region of 100 percent Americanism, not only of following the rest of the country, but of trying to go it one better.

Examples of misguided patriotism in those soiled years have been set forth elsewhere. Coloradans, for example, saw extremists in Klan garb take over the state government, threaten the university, and make life precarious for minorities. Coloradans read in the *Denver Post* that its management would pay the first month's dues for any qualified employee who wanted to join the American Legion, an organization that the paper endorsed as being 100 percent American. Violence accompanied the new crusade, as a Denver tramway strike

*Streetcars overturned during the 1920 Denver tramway strike were graphic
evidence that for some the West's sweet dream had turned sour. (Courtesy,
Colorado Historical Society)*

of 1920 produced overturned streetcars, rioting, and fatalities at the
hands of strikebreakers. The turmoil led to the sacking of the *Post*'s
offices, which that paper attributed to unions, the IWW, "the Soviet
and the revolutionists." Out on the plains, in the agricultural
communities, "Americanism" again surfaced as floating farm laborers tried to force higher wages through organization and found
themselves driven out by community leaders who would have no such
subversive nonsense.

This mixture of ultranationalism, isolationism, a postwar depression, and an unprecedented prosperity that followed it was colored by
efforts to enforce an unpopular prohibition amendment, generated,
in part, by presumed wartime shortages of grain, a product that was
by the twenties a glut on the market. The ensuing social unrest gave
the decade its name, the "Roaring Twenties," an era in which more
gunfire was heard on the streets of Chicago than Dodge City ever had
witnessed. Against this background of gang wars, submachine-gun
fire, bootlegging, gambling, dope peddling, and prostitution, academics and frontier aficionados continued to mourn the passing of the
Old West, where such lost American institutions as gunfighting,
lynching, range wars, gambling, drunken brawling, and bordellos
had flourished in the purity of the wilderness.

It was assumed that these practices had been all right in a newer
part of the land and that, rather than misconduct, they were passed
off as a youthful excess, long since forgotten in the light of other and
more acceptable attributes. Caught between the familiar ground of
traditional ways, now slipping from view, and a new, rough world

that called for American participation and leadership, this young and still-maturing nation suddenly longed for roots, something to cling to in the uncertain days that lay ahead. Ironically they grasped at a tumultuous past that they would have shunned as a future prospect.

This left westerners themselves in a puzzling, contradictory situation. Living in the most rapidly changing section of the country, they were starting to reach toward a respectability that many felt could grow only from some cultural refinements and more civilized behavior. At that point, some outsiders, whose acceptance westerners were ardently courting, began saying that the greatness of the West lay in its raw and vigorous past, including the bawdy and unvarnished side of life in those early days. In this, there were an energy and a toughness that were rapidly ebbing in modern life.

This paradox faced by westerners, together with the sweeping social change that fed the sense of unease among many easterners, produced the "nervousness" that so impressed that Kansas journalist. Especially, the members of the older generation in all regions were looking for some kind of emotional anchor as they dispiritedly watched what they felt was a moral unraveling during the immediate postwar years. As always, the young were a problem to their seniors. Now they seemed to be trying to destroy themselves with bootleg booze, abandoned social conduct, and a general revolt against all that was held dear by those who presided over society. Traditional values suddenly became more important than ever. But what—and where— were those values? There was a disposition, on the part of some, to think that the West, long known for its violence and turmoil, was somehow a final refuge for sterling American traits that had spread to the West but had not, as yet, been washed away in the general erosion that was threatening the nation. If anyone wanted to savor the moral toughness that had won a continent, the West was the place to look.

And yet, even then, there were cries that the Old West, that repository of virtue, was already gone, and without this life-support system, much of our heritage would soon wither and die. Hamlin Garland said it in 1919, commenting that "something fine and strong and free is passing from our national life, something which helped to make our fathers the unconquerable individualists they were." John Gould Fletcher took up the chant in this eulogy to an ideal that was "passing, departing, vanishing, not to be sung, not to be remembered, not to be known," concluding that "the last great stretch of sunlight, of loneliness, of silence, is forever gone."

Those who read lines such as these and who looked about the neighborhood as the twenties picked up the jazz-age momentum

must have found it easy to look over their shoulders and think of
better days. It is not hard to appreciate their suspicion that the
country was going soft. One of the field-and-stream school of writers
sounded the theme once more, warning that we were becoming a
physically weakened country, a people who now did their pioneering
vicariously, reading about the days of yore while lounging in an easy
chair or in a motion-picture theater watching the West being subdued
from the vantage point of a loge seat, a people unwilling to tramp
wilderness trails in search of the real item.

   If not somehow soothed, this kind of nervousness would soon grow
into panic and despair. In the face of it, writers time and time again
went back to the well, suggesting that it was in the West that the hope
of the nation's future lay, a land out beyond, where, as one author put
it, "its promise and greatness [would be] welded into a perpetual
West." This "perpetual West" would be a palliative for those
unnerved by the new "real West," the maturing West. In this never-
never land, where nothing would ever change and where the
nineteenth century would live on forever, war-weary and disillusioned Americans could place their hopes for the future.

CHAPTER 4

EDEN IS
JEOPARDIZED

Lamentations over the erosion of pioneer qualities, heard so frequently in the early postwar years, suggested that at least a segment of the eastern establishment had failed to go along with the updating, the paving, and the streetlighting of the West. The frequent pats on the back that westerners had received for about two decades, gestures of encouragement for their forward-thinking economic ways, faded from view. Or they were blotted out by the wash of nostalgia that was poured forth by sentimentalists for whom Chamber of Commerce talk had always been unappetizing.

This shift in eastern feelings was part of the nervousness of the generations of the '20s. With an uncertainty about the direction that the nation was taking came a tendency to question the march toward progress in that part of America closest to its pioneer past—the West. Possibly the East simply had changed its mind. It may have concluded that permission for the young West to wear long pants had been given prematurely. In any event, the change in emphasis, if not a substantial change in attitude, was evident in those restless, uncertain years that followed the great European adventure.

The political parents of the colonials need not have worried about sudden changes in the West at large. True, the little towns that had traditionally been thought of as capsulizations of western life styles were showing signs of being blighted by local efforts to go modern, and that, to some in the East, was discouraging. But beyond the city limits the land looked pretty much as it had since cowmen had reigned uncontested and cavalrymen had prowled the prairies in search of unruly tribesmen. To be sure, the open range now was squared off with barbed wire, and the sod had been torn up by grangers. Often these scraggly homesteads had a look of impermanence about them, however; and in much of the West, not a few of them had been abandoned to the elements. Rural westerners still could be regarded as the nation's somewhat rustic cousins, people who cautiously were coming to grips with the twentieth century and who were not inclined to absorb eastern ideas easily. These agrarians, who more closely represented the idealized residents of the last West, apparently were in no hurry either to recognize recent important calendar changes or to join the rest of the world.

This was perfectly acceptable to those in the East who were not anxious for the West to change. They were ready to talk about progress and the excitement of living in modern America, but a significant group of them had no intention of applying the term to that frozen-in-time land of breath-taking sunsets and living folklore. They wanted to set the West aside, so to speak, as a vast wilderness wherein quaintly garbed horsemen rode around doffing multigallon hats and drawling "Howdy, Ma'am" to womenfolks—virile men who spent a good deal of their time looking picturesque. Easterners viewed this vast and generally undeveloped region as having no need for a new century; indeed, its occupants really had had no place in it.

The emergent notion, at this particular time, of maintaining the West as an oversized museum for the curious or the historically minded is explainable. By the 1920s, Americans who had reached voting age included what was probably the first generation to have matured without a clearly recognized frontier somewhere "out West." Three centuries after Jamestown, there remained insufficient wild and lawless country to fit the generally accepted definition of the term. To those who sensed the change and thought it mattered, there was a realization that the growing industrialization and urbanization of the East made the necessity of having a traditional West, or some very real substitute for it, all the more apparent.

To set aside the trans-Missouri West as a kind of national green belt was a proposition not without its problems. There were signs that some of the natives, especially the businessmen, were getting restless, were showing signs of rebellion at the idea of posing as exhibits for visiting admirers. This reaction by the colonials annoyed easterners, many of whom only yesterday had praised the plainsmen for their up-and-coming attitudes. In reaction, the easterners began to float disturbing rumors to the effect that not only was some of the cultural decay, then said to be marring the old American scene, seeping westward but, worse, that the ungrateful residents of that nascent country to the west were beginning to imitate their betters, especially with regard to municipal development.

Sadly the easterners concluded that the one-time showcase was being corrupted. Colorful western settlements that once had featured gunslingers, swinging doors, slit-eyed gamblers, and honest, big-hearted prostitutes were being supplanted by unimaginative population centers loudly advertised as modern cities, places where Main

Street sprouted Rotary Clubs, radios, flivvers, Community Chests, and divorces. Cow hands who once had crabbed their way along dusty streets on cayuse-sprung legs were being replaced by flappers in skirts as short as those in the immoral East, girls with lips as painted as any seen in seaboard fleshpots, scrawny creatures who brazenly undulated down the avenues, underclad and unashamed, and all of this in broad daylight. The young men were said to be no better. In that legendary countryside where it had been imagined that men invariably were masculine, there now lived "college morons," who lounged about, smoking cigarettes, and idling, able-bodied western-ers who showed no interest in doing an honest day's work.

The agonized complaints coming from that group of easterners whose special claim to the West had not faded and has not, even today, suggested that the never-never land of their hearts, so long and jealously guarded, was rapidly surrendering to the forces of modern communications. Hal Borland believed that the process had begun in his little Colorado town about 1915, with the appearance of the motion-picture house. He said it was this medium—a later genera-tion would accuse television—that had served as a leading molder of uniformity, one that had "slowly dissolved so many of the local and regional patterns of time and personality."

Other forms of communication hastened these changes during that first hectic postwar decade. Travelers who crossed the once-feared desert and threaded the high mountain passes now rode in trains, buses, or automobiles; occasionally, they flew in airplanes. Speed cops cruised the country where rangers once had ridden; bootleggers haunted old cattle-rustling trails; and the lonely places where earlier prospectors had grazed their burros were overrun by tin-can tourists who burned off the forests with carelessly left campfires and littered picnic sites with discarded cans and whose fat wives, wearing knickers, ravaged wild flowers along mountain streams. The crown-ing blow, said critics of this change, was the awful truth that some of the westerners were beginning to look and to act just like these mindless outlanders.

The notion that the West was succumbing to both a material and cultural standardization during the twenties was noted with increas-ing frequency in eastern periodicals. These once-special frontier people were now wearing the same hats, shoes, dresses, and suits as were other Americans. Mail-order houses and chain stores made these things available, and the belief that these were the uniforms of modern times caused them to be purchased and worn. Westerners also drove the same cars, read the same magazines, and listened to the same radio programs as did more ordinary folks in the East.

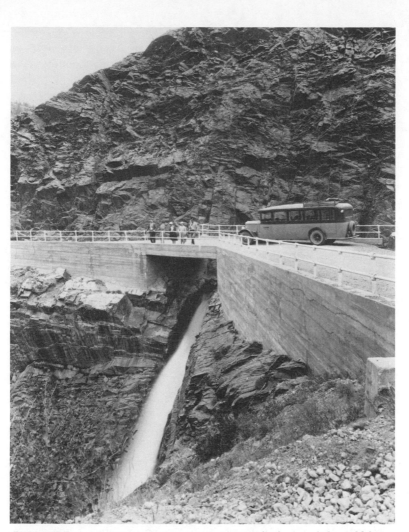

*By the 1920s and 1930s, Conestogas on pneumatic tires carried would-be
pioneers along paved roads to see sights such as Bear Creek Falls, near
Ouray, Colorado. (Courtesy, Colorado Historical Society)*

The famed Oswald Garrison Villard, publisher of the *New York
Evening Post* and the *Nation,* complained that coeds on western
campuses were "copycats of the worst kind," girls who went around
"dyed, marceled, painted, lip-sticked, 'nude'-stockinged." In general these people were not the rugged Americans whom he had
admired when he had ridden the first Northern Pacific train across
the continent some forty years earlier. On the contrary, they looked
just like householders in the East, a sure sign that the Old West had
disappeared, had surrendered to conformity.

Another of those who searched in vain for the "wild and woolliness that delighted my youthful dreams" confessed great disappointment at the tameness and conservativeness that he found, a condition he gloomily described as "civilized." Even those who grew up in these little western towns later chose to remember them as being a bit wild. Thurman Arnold's memory so recorded Laramie, but as Gene Gressley has pointed out, Sherwood Anderson would have had no trouble in identifying Winesburg in Laramie, so midwestern was the latter's appearance.

A good many easterners were upset that their "colony" was not conducting itself as they thought it should. Bernard De Voto ("Benny" to his friends), who shunned his Utah origins but made a living writing about the West for the rest of his days, poked fun at the surrender to conventionality beyond the wide Missouri. If the Chamber of Commerce proclaimed a "Smile-Damn-You!" week, he said, its enforcers would be on the streets to mandate bared teeth, and if almost any pioneer event was to be commemorated, beards were posted as official attire, with a commercial committee of public safety being on the alert to catch hairless malefactors.

While De Voto would not go so far as to say that such antics symbolized the decline of the West, he thought their existence represented a defect in American civilization. He was at his waspish best when lampooning boosterism, especially as it flourished in the service clubs in the once promised land. Elsewhere, he said, the Rotary badge might be set aside at bedtime, but the western partisan counted it as a "secret treason when he has slept without dreaming of giving Denver a million by 1930."

Another disillusioned easterner suggested that these civic and commercial tribal rites were part of a desperate attempt by little western towns to keep some sense of identity. Such a search was necessary because these places had surrendered their heritage of distinctiveness, thrown it all into the winds of progress. "They are all new, in the modern shape," he wrote of the places he saw; "all lighted and paved and policed in the same way; all clean, tidy and sinless." Some even had white lines down the middle of the streets and thirty-minute parking zones. What once had been the West now was no more than a geographic location, just a night's ride beyond Chicago.

Actually, those easterners who shook their heads and muttered that all the West was being taken over by flappers, lounge lizards, and glad-handing boosters were missing a distinction that was crucial to understanding the region. Life in many western towns had been different from outlying regions from the beginning. Urban inhabitants had been most concerned with cultural trappings, and because they had been the first to be connected by improved roads and, above all, the railroad, they were the most easily fed on refinements from the civilized world outside. For years, western urban dwellers had "puffed" their municipalities, primarily through local newspapers, and they had long anticipated the service-club injunction "Boost, Don't Knock" in their aggressive commercialism. In addition to serving their traditional roles as trade centers, county seats, or railroad stops, these enclaves were spiritually tied to the eastern business community.

Local farmers and ranchers, on the other hand, were usually much slower to accept the ballyhoo that villagers hawked as presaging the arrival of modern times. Through lassitude more than intent, those outside the towns pursued their old ways. It was almost as if the towns existed in one century and the surrounding countryside in another, the degree of difference depending on how far one lived from those urban centers.

In those towns the term *booster* was taken very seriously, and if one used it lightly or with a touch of irony, as was done by the likes of De Voto, westerners thought they were being made fun of and became angry. To them the expression implied local pride, economic success, as evidenced by growing civic grandeur, and community progress. One used it in a dignified manner; it was another "smile when you say that, mister," expression. The urban sons of the pioneers saw nothing out of place in forming booster clubs, of christening them with snappy, up-and-coming slogans, of wearing uniforms, or of sending delegates to state conventions to help boost boosting.

These young western business types saw nothing offensive in updating their towns, in paving, in policing, and in sanitizing. They were not slowed a bit by the complaints of Benny De Voto, who accused them of having "gone a-whoring after the false gods of Boosterdom" in their search for identity with what they conceived to be modern America. They offered heated denials when De Voto accused them of trying to drag the West down to the level of the vulgar Middle West, in order to make the West "democratically identical with portions of the country it has the good fortune not to resemble." Instead, when they looked outside of their town limits, these sharp young merchants, wearing straw sailor hats and bell-bottom trousers, sneered at the local agrarians in their straw field hats. The merchants called the agrarians "clodhoppers," and they could not agree with De Voto, who thought the nearby rural folk "altogether admirable," just because these rustics were presumed to be in touch with the soil, and therefore in contact with historical roots. To the merchants the honest plowman was a relic from a dead past they had abandoned in favor of a quest for the American holy grail of "bigger and better." When old-timers like the artist Charley Russell sneered back and referred to them as the "booster bunch" and "come-latelys," they shrugged him off as a nice old fellow bogged down in the nineteenth century.

In short, the West was, as usual, divided in its feelings about itself, its past, and its future. Particularly in the towns, westerners welcomed development and progress. Boosters there could not but watch with pride the prosperity that had been achieved in the preceding several decades, and thus no one was greatly surprised that these latter-day frontiersmen were inclined to enunciate their views on progress. Improved communications—a sharp growth of the information and news media—simply gave them a wider stage on which to perform than that afforded to their fathers.

Almost any time or any place seemed to provide a rostrum for economic evangelists who wanted to bless their respective communities. As Will Rogers remarked after visiting some of these small western towns, two men could not meet on the street without having one of them take a gavel from his pocket and call the other to order. Another guest at these community gatherings described the milieu in which the new faith was preached—the meetings in public halls, the service-club luncheon rooms—as places in which there were brotherhood and singing. After the singing and eating came the scraping of chairs and the lighting of cigars and cigarettes. He said the westerners took to cigarettes with the enthusiasm of college boys away from home for the first time. Then came the moment of truth, the delivery of the message of the day.

The readiness of western townsmen to organize, even to over-organize, was somewhat resented in the East, not just because it looked like mere mimicry—conduct that presumably belied the concept of the romantic West—but also because it smacked of acquiescence, not initiative; of conformity, not individuality. One easterner accused westerners of becoming humble minded and unassertive people who instinctively kowtowed to the East.

Suspicion that the germs of Babbittry were threatening the new country bothered such West watchers as novelist Joseph Hergesheimer, who traced the decline from the day of the individual—he thought trappers, cowboys, and miners were representative of this class—to the emergence of a breed that was far less independent, one that was being swallowed by the mass. This Quaker-educated writer reiterated the belief that the nation's moral fiber, as well as its vigor, strength, and reputation, was eroding; and in contrast to those who earlier had placed their last hopes in the West, he expressed his sorrow that the decay was spreading to the promised land. Even so, he caught brief glimpses of yesteryear, occasional suggestions of the region's linkage to the past, and he was grateful that he had been one of the privileged few to see such things. In another twenty years, he said, these dying examples of the Old West would be history.

Scholars agreed that the West was undergoing change. Frederick Jackson Turner, of frontier-thesis fame, looked at the area fifty years after the nation's centennial celebration and concluded that the spirit of adventure, which the westward movement earlier had carried with it, had been diminished by successive waves of settlement that had passed over the land beyond the Missouri. Individual competition, he said, was being replaced by "reliance on association," as evidenced by the growing subservience to such organizations as Chambers of Commerce and businessmen's service clubs, out of which had grown a steadily increased expectation of conformity to the dictates of community opinion. Admittedly, self-reliance still was stronger in this more recently settled region than in the East, but as time had passed, the margin of difference had narrowed. This metamorphosis was somewhat moderated by surface indications that remnants of the West's traditional initiative, optimism, and fondness for bigness still were around, thus coloring the change and seeming to give it a western flavor.

Observations such as these suggested that not all observers were ready to see the Old West finally and totally dead. In fact, a goodly number of writers in both the East and the West argued that survivals of the past were to be found, perhaps in modified forms, if one was willing to look hard enough. Even in western municipal societies there was some resistance to progress, a reluctance to give up yesterday's youth and to probe a new and uncertain future. The well-known magazine writer Will Irwin became conscious of this bridging process when he visited Leadville, Colorado, in 1923. There he saw the social flux as evidence of a cultural transformation then taking place in the West. "It was making its own kultur, clinging to some of its old, distinctive ideas on morals, on the comely customs of human life, even of costume," he wrote. But behind the outward change he saw these people as the inheritors of those who customarily had ridden a horse twenty miles and perhaps had taken a railroad train another fifty, just to attend a dance, distance being a western condition that time has merely modified.

Tried-and-true members of the Old West cult gloomily clung to the conviction that western towns had gone soft and were copying the East even more than before; yet, these people continued to clutch at straws, as Will Irwin had done when he talked about riding a county or so away to take in a dance, and they held that the West still was a big place, too big to become civilized all that fast. One of these last-ditchers, a nationally known newspaperman and author, soothed his readers with the concession that cities had indeed grown in the deserts and that highways and railroads now ran where rutty roads once wandered, but in so giant a land, these were only cosmetic changes. "There remain vast territories whence people emerge but seldom, and areas where men and women and children exist in a replica of the life which built America," he reassured them. Even now, in this modern day of fast autos and airplanes, he had seen homesteaders and even covered wagons, but far better, he sensed in such people a determination that made them by-pass an easier life for one that might even bring them face to face with death, so great was their desire to respond to the call of the land.

The persistence of the prairie schooner constantly attracted the attention of the autoists in their shiny brass and enameled toys. When one of them spotted a horse-drawn covered wagon in 1916, he commented that it still sheltered the "driver husband and tired wife and two or three small children and the household goods." He called these people intrepid Americans who were "pushing back the hand of the [Nevada] desert."

In that same year a popular West Coast magazine featured the life of a lady homesteader in southern Utah, who would prove up on her 320 acres in the fall. Aside from whatever pecuniary gain that might come from the land, the author of the story assured readers, "it is still a real inspiration to be part of a modern pioneer colony conquering the wilderness."

Reports of this unique breed that forsook civilization and threaded its way into the back country to wrest a living from nature fascinated travelers, some of whom sought out these latter-day pioneers as eagerly as if probing deepest Africa to study the primitives. An Englishman, who was raised in Paris and was enamored of the Old West, as only people of this background can be, grew absolutely lyrical when he visited the isolated mountain parks of Colorado in 1922. The more run-down and unprofitable a ranch looked, the greater was his fascination. Fences made out of sticks and tangled brushwood held together by wire, as well as yards choked with rubbish, told him that this was a normal condition, a necessary one "while the pioneer gets on with a more urgent job." When he saw log huts instead of bungalows, places "fit to breed a Lincoln," he grew excited. Livestock, grazing in what was and is still today normal cattle-raising mountain-park country, suggested that it was pastoral land simply because it was "at a stage earlier than cultivation." Proof of this came to him when he saw an occasional struggling cornfield and sometimes an orchard, all of which said eloquently that man was making only a tiny mark on the land. In search of the past, he found it in embryonic settlements, tucked away in remote areas where life was carried on in the same manner as it had been decades earlier and a thousand miles to the east. The Old West lived. He was charmed.

The belief that frontier America had not faded away but merely had headed for the hills was bandied about for at least two decades after World War I. It was argued that superficial indications might suggest its passing but that distinctively western types and the conditions that produced them were still around. It was agreed that anyone who visited Denver, Cheyenne, or Great Falls would have searched in vain for anything suggestive of the Wild West, but it took only a short trip from town to find working cow hands and bona-fide ranches. The absence of the old-time cow towns did not mean that the domain of the cattleman was extinct, as some later said it was, but rather that it had approached the limit of shrinkage and that henceforth it would operate under different and less glamorous conditions. The search for the purity of the wilderness, which reached back to the writings of early philosophers and beyond, would continue as the West steadily became more heavily settled. It is very much around today.

Those whose interest took them westward after World War I were drawn in that direction by the same set of beliefs that the eastern intellectual establishment continued to treasure, namely, that opportunities for individuals had been diluted by sheer numbers in older America and that only in the sparsely populated West could a man still stand apart from these crowds. In 1927, readers of a popular weekly learned that the westward movement of job seekers was then more pronounced than in pioneer days, when restless, migratory, and often discontented people sought changes in their lives. "There are men and women . . . who go to . . . western states merely to get a new deal, to be shaken up," said the magazine. Admittedly, there was more wealth and more actual opportunity in the East, "but the precious possession of their individuality is not so hard to keep in the West."

This notion that individualism historically had found the most fertile soil in a new and untamed country was believed and nurtured not only by academics such as Turner; it was so comfortable and attractive to the popular mind that its acceptance there also was easy. It stood as a symbol, as a pillar supporting the concept that a unique society had sprung up in the wilderness, the dominant strain of which had produced a new breed of man. It was one of the West's most potent myths; understandably, it was bound to die a lingering death.

Myths have the emotional pull of long-held family treasures, and lovers of the idyllic Old West clung to them tenaciously, grudgingly surrendering an item here and there as the real world closed in. If, as one writer has suggested, the only true individualist in the frontier era had been found at the end of a rope, the other end being manned collectively by civic-minded members of the community, known as vigilantes, then perhaps this highly regarded belief would have to be surrendered to the mediocrity of modern times. But surely, argued the romantics, if this alleged quality had been watered down, it must mean that society in the Promised Land was only slightly flawed, for its fabled attributes, so long cherished by tamer parts of the country, could not have disappeared overnight.

In short, the disciples of the western mystique were engaged in a stubborn retreat, willing to give only an inch or so at a time in the face of new forces that threatened to wipe out the last vestiges of the frontier heritage. These disciples clung to the belief that during the nineteenth century an original, vital, and even romantic social code had sprung from that special land and that it had been the core of a whole new civilization, one that its admirers wanted to believe was uniquely American. Not since colonial days, they insisted, had the nation possessed anything like it.

It was argued that the real westerner was aristocratic, as used in the favorable sense of being proud or distinguished, ''in just the way that most of the American colonists meant the country to be.'' The eastern critic who set forth this idea hastened to add that our forefathers never had objected to one man being better than another, but rather to the man who assumed this position without the requisite credentials. In other words, an accident of birth should not place one person above another. If, on the other hand, this distinction was earned, the idea was entirely acceptable, because democracy was ''the proper culture for a natural aristocracy.''

This quality of natural superiority, nurtured in the unpolluted atmosphere of a virgin land, was regarded by some observers as part of a distillation process that had produced the American spirit, which

their eyes saw as *true* Americanization. The crowded conditions of the
Atlantic seaboard—meaning the heavy injection of "lesser breeds"—
made this process difficult if not impossible in that area. Westward,
then, lay the best hope, because that part of the nation contained the
"last authentic haunts of the original American ideals, the distinctively American social philosophy." The concept smacked of
Bishop George Berkeley's prediction of another golden age westward
when he wrote the lines:

> Not such as Europe breeds in her decay;
> Such as she bred when fresh and young.

America, barely a teenager as nations go, suddenly experienced a
sharp pang of nostalgia.

Members of the Old West fan club badly needed to believe that this
process of rebirth was continuing somewhere, somehow, in the great
spaces westward. They hoped so, but reluctantly many admitted that
they had their doubts. Out toward the Rockies the picked breed of
men that legend had provided them with was fast disappearing.
Many worried that in place of the men who had wrested a wilderness
from the savages and had established a western Eden, there now
stood a run-of-the-mill people, stripped of individuality, devoid of the
pioneer spirit. Even the optimists agreed that mint copies of the
original heroic American no longer were in circulation, that such a
type had disappeared with the passage of time and now would "fade
and merge in the chaotic American Democracy." One part of
themselves reluctantly admitted the death of the old ways; another
part stubbornly refused to accept it.

In this mood, eastern visitors probed the plains and high country,
searching vainly for the remnants of yesteryear and reassessing the
region's presumably unique culture to determine its present characteristics and to measure the degree of decline that was reported to
have commenced. They watched for the traditional differences that
were believed to set westerners apart from others, for some evidence
that the moral decay that appeared to be undermining the East had
not yet infected God's country.

Their findings contained the seeds of hope. Out under that big sky
they sensed the presence of subtle qualities that suggested the
existence of old-time American values. The taxi driver who made
change as if he did not expect a tip, the friendliness of hotel clerks, the
dignified courtesy and absence of servility of those who served the
public—all were qualities noticed with pleasure. So were the use of

"lady" as a common form of address to a woman and the courtliness of men who were at ease with the world, who were independent without being surly.

In evidence also, especially in thinly populated areas, was the traditional informality of westerners, an easy interrelationship with one's neighbors, an openness to strangers, primarily because time had not yet closed distances or brought an equal degree of conventionality to those who lived outside the urban oases. As late as the twenties there remained vast stretches of western country where a man might ride for hours, even all day, without meeting another human being and where one still calculated distances in terms of the time consumed or between natural markers such as rivers or mountain ranges, as opposed to miles between points on the map.

Space, the West's great and lasting resource, gave man room to breathe, provided him with freedom of movement and fertile ground for the growth of personal dignity, which was so rapidly being lost in the crowded concrete jungles of big eastern cities. There, men had surrendered their identities, but out in this still-untamed land, such words as *stranger* or *pardner* had that special meaning, one denoting an unfenced society or the scarcity of humans, and it acted as a flavor or a scent whose fragrance hinted at older times when the West was new and wholesome.

This, at least, was the kind of information the scouts brought back to the East. What they did not say was that in a more objective sense the game was over, an era had come and gone and was no more. Scholars later would study this phase of American history and conclude that what the puzzled fans of the Old West had witnessed was the conclusion of a chapter of American history that has variously been described as the garden-of-the-world era, the agrarian myth, and the purity-of-the-wilderness concept.

As Richard Hofstadter and Henry Nash Smith suggested, the erosion of the agrarian symbol had been under way for some time. At first it was a possession of the intellectuals, but in time it became a generally popular notion. By the 1920s, commercial agriculture, recent land booms, and extensive—including "suitcase"—farming had pretty thoroughly eroded the vision of the honest plowman, except among the eastern intelligentsia, many of whose members had grasped at that tarnished myth and were hanging onto it with the determination of a grandmother clutching to her breast an old and worn family photo album.

Westerners were even worse off. At least eastern devotees of the legendary Old West had firm, unwavering beliefs, ephemeral as they might prove to be in the light of history. But those living in that country, still fresh from the frontier experience, faced another dilemma. On the one hand they wanted to believe in fairy tales as much as did anyone in Boston or Philadelphia. They, too, grasped at the idea that their own land, with its pioneer virtues, was host to the best in the national genius. Yet, on the other hand, they realized that life in a perpetual state of nature belied the American worship of progress, thus condemning them to be always social inferiors as well as cultural and economic colonials.

It was in this confused and contradictory frame of mind that the West, the youngest of the children of the historical frontier process, faced the real and ugly world of the "dirty thirties," which lay menacingly ahead. A lot of growing up would be called for. And in a hurry.

CHAPTER 5

"THE DREAMING IS FINISHED"

Until about 1920 the notion persisted and was broadcast to the East and Europe that the West was still a golden land. Its yet-hidden bounties would provide rich spiritual and, especially, material things for those who sought them. True, there was a nervousness growing among some who wondered whether the hard-baked individualism and the tough spirit of independence that had been associated with the earlier frontier era were dying out in the new century. But the West also had always stood for the chance to fashion a better life, to step up another rung or two on the economic ladder; and this feeling, at least, continued. In the West, there was still opportunity for all. The latest land boom, that of the war years, lent credence to the notion, for the euphoria of those bustling days still hung over the region.

As it was with the rest of the nation, the façade of false prosperity obscured basic economic and social ills; but in the West, if one looked more closely, there were indicators whose message ought to have seemed clear enough. The day was gone when successful immigrant pioneers sent sheaves of wheat back to the home country for the admiration and encouragement of relatives who still held back at the wharfs. The flow of "Atlantic letters," which Ray Billington talked about in his *Land of Savagery,* had dried up; indeed, the silence from the land of plenty was followed by an out-migration from the West, in some cases even back to Europe. Left behind were dried-up farms and unpaid mortgages.

Further obscuring the picture was the fact that in the West, during that decade and into the early thirties, there was a boom as false as the one going on in the East. The development of relatively inexpensive farm machinery, labor-saving equipment that allowed for extensive farming, drew speculators into the unplowed areas. Shopkeepers, bankers, doctors, and lawyers, who at the same time may have been "putting a little on the margin" in the stock market, also were buying undeveloped land and paying someone to work it. It was high-risk money, but profits were often made. In those years, over *78* five million acres of plains and grasslands were converted to wheat

*A Case tractor pulls a 21-foot disk harrow near Syracuse, Kansas. During
the 1920s and 1930s, machines with strong backs and long arms helped to
break millions of acres that had never known a plow. (Courtesy, Denver
Public Library, Western History Department; photo by J. I. Case Co.,
Racine, Wisconsin)*

land as the national agricultural sweepstakes picked up speed. In the
latter half of the twenties, grain acreages in thirteen southern-plains
counties increased from two to three million, and another raw patch
of land lay open to drought and blowing. Even in barren eastern
Wyoming, which was desolate enough to parch the passing eye, old
cow hands moved aside as breaker plows cruised into that once-
forbidden part of the West. By 1930, Laramie County alone had a
quarter of a million acres in crops. Marginal land had been stretched
to the limit; the stage was set for another agricultural defeat.

In retrospect, this rape of the countryside has generated considerable criticism; but at the time, westerners, in general, who had used
the land vigorously, sometimes recklessly since the opening of the
country, had no apologies. In their own day, miners, cattlemen, and
timber kings had extracted ruthlessly. Now the businessman-farmer,
either suitcase or sedentary, saw an opportunity to apply the results of
industry and technology to the land, and there seemed to be a chance
to succeed where others had not. Farms that had been left behind by
those who earlier had failed or had lost heart now sold for next to
nothing. Low property values and minimal taxes, especially on

acreages without buildings, encouraged wheat prospectors to "take a flyer," to plant in the cheapest manner and then pray a little. With some rain and a bit of luck, there would be a payoff.

Despite the big "plow-up" and the apparent prosperous activity, farmers in the twenties were quietly packing up and moving out. Between 1918 and 1933 the population of Hill County, Montana, for example, experienced a steady decline, and property valuations fell as much as a million dollars in a single year. Montana and Idaho showed the largest out-migration of any of the western states during these years. As the big party of that roaring decade proceeded elsewhere, worried farmers in these states attended meetings at which they puzzled over their problems and sought solutions.

Many a young couple whose high hopes had been burned out by hot winds left with heavy hearts and a great sense of disappointment. A woman who spent a night in southeastern Colorado with a pair of newlyweds long remembered the pathos of the experience. "I have never forgotten the wistful, yet determined remark of the bride who lived in that dugout," she wrote. " 'If we can just hang on and make as nice a place out of it as the folks did of theirs, it will be worth being lonely and doing without things for a few years.' " Pensively the young woman added, " 'When we get the trees started, it will rain more don't you think?' " But for her the question remained unanswered. In a few dry years they were forced out, and no trees grew there to tease the heavens for water.

These young gamblers made their roll of the dice, and they lost, along with a lot of others who were convinced that they could buck the odds against the Great American Desert of old and somehow could win. They had their reasons. Wheat is a frontier crop, one of the best cash crops around when it comes to farming under chancy conditions, and more than one optimist had run the risk and had won. These were the few whose names appeared in print as evidence that in a good year a newcomer might pay for his land and machinery with a single crop. There was something irresistible about drawing a lottery ticket called a western homestead.

One of the farm women of the area commented upon the characteristic, remarking: "I suppose there is something of the gambler in all of us. We instinctively feel that the longer we travel on a straight road, the nearer we must be coming to a turn." Nor was there any likelihood that a streak of bad luck would make believers out of the losers. When a Kansas farmer told his friends that excessive risk taking would lead to a more cautious approach, one of them responded: "Don't fool yourself. Just wait until we get about two good wheat crops in a row, and at good prices. Then see what happens. You can't make me believe we've learned our lesson so it will stick. It's just not in our blood to play a safe game.''

Because the plains farmers have engaged in high-risk agriculture, they have been criticized and charged with abuse of their fields. This is a bum rap. While they admit to gambling and sometimes playing long odds, they do not admit to carelessness with their land. They fully understand the dangers of blowing soil, of erosion, of aridity, and of any other destructive factors, if for no other reason than that these things reduce profits. In his *America's New Frontier,* the western economist Morris Garnsey defended the traditional farmers and blamed the suitcasers for tearing up the countryside. "By contrast," he wrote, "the settled farmers while joining the boom, tried to practice conservation in their expanded operations."

And he was right. Plains farmers were as experienced and intelligent as any in the world, according to a recent student of the calamity of the dust bowl. They did not deserve denigration at the hands of overnight journalists who gave up the city for a day or so to make penetrating analyses of the western problem. These agrarians were, however, the products of a revolutionary change in thinking that had begun two or three centuries earlier. From the time that men first scratched in the earth with sticks, most farmers had sought ways to adapt to overwhelming natural forces. Then, about the time when pioneers were pushing into and beyond the Appalachians, agrarians began to believe they could somehow rise above such forces, could "assert in every way possible the contriving hand of humanity," as Donald Worster has put it. American farmers were the most enthusiastic proponents of this new belief. They honed their skills, increased their mastery over land and weather, and pushed ever farther into the continent. They were remarkably successful. But this way of thinking could take them only so far. The grain growers who moved into new parts of the plains in the twenties were not wasteful, careless, or ignorant. Most of them were descended from a long line of farmers who had edged westward for generations, and they were joined by some of the best cultivators that Europe could offer. But they were now entering a place where a whole new set of rules was required and where Mother Nature suddenly lengthened the odds against them. These farmers were skilled professionals about to meet the limits of their philosophy.

Those who found themselves trapped in the dry and dusty thirties took a defensive attitude and sought to justify their presence on the plains in terms of a frontiering adventure that had gone wrong through no fault of their own. They argued that the government should share the blame, because it had encouraged the settlement of the area. They pointed the finger at avaricious land promoters, who had held out lures wrapped in golden promises, and at journalists, who earlier had praised the agrarian frontiersman for his daring, his hardiness, his utter courage. The hard-hit farmers even hinted at un-American activities, charging that it had been the big cattlemen, financed and encouraged by foreigners, who had led the way west and that the cultivators who followed were the victims, not the perpetrators. More recently, said the aggrieved, they had been enticed into expanding their operations by artificially high prices, born of a wartime necessity, when it had been regarded as an act of patriotism to produce crops.

Don't try to rationalize the nature of the failure, Caroline Henderson of Oklahoma advised them. Whether it was personal or providential mattered not; the question now was one of survival. She suggested that the less said about the problem, the better; Californians had learned to keep their mouths shut about earthquakes, and so the plainsmen who were in trouble ought not to advertise their woes by complaining. Be optimistic, she counseled her fellow sufferers, for in America's heartland that quality was the one durable basis for prosperity. She suggested that the farmers' best hope lay in their lifelong capacity for keeping at work, even in the face of failure, in their willingness to face hard facts, and in their inherent adaptability, a quality that had been honed fine over generations of frontiering experience.

Western farmers have been fortunate in that there has been no dearth of advice for them. It never dries up. At a national conference on land utilization, held at Chicago in 1931, the word came down from on high once more. Secretary of Agriculture Arthur M. Hyde reissued an old warning when he told his listeners that the boom days were over, that the bloom was off the rose. Even if the plains farmers had listened and had understood the precautionary message, there was not a great deal they could have done about it. They were growing a frontier crop on what was still thought of as an agrarian frontier, the underlying principle of which had been expansion and an extensive use of land, worked with a minimum of labor and expense. As the dry cycle of the thirties came into full play, they told themselves that it was just another of those periodic problems that would bottom out and then improve. As the saying went, it always rained at the end of a dry spell.

But it was not so easy to shrug off adversity this time. As early as the summer of 1933, some of the farmers in southwestern Kansas had to dig out their tractors, which had been buried in dust blizzards, before they could work their fields. That warning was reiterated during the summer of 1934, a season that was not only dry but was also searingly hot. What few spears of wheat managed to survive this onslaught grew into stunted immature stocks, whose shriveled heads were hardly worth the expense of harvesting. In terms of money it was estimated that the burnout of this disastrous season cost the nation approximately half of what it sank into World War I.

Heat and drought were bad enough, but there was more. As if the Maker wanted to be certain that the dry-land farmers fully understood the extent of their trouble, clouds of grasshoppers swarmed over that forlorn, bleached-out country, gleaning any stray spears of growth that may have survived the weather. Along graveled roads— blacktop was then a novelty in much of the West—darkened twin tracks, made by car tires running over grasshoppers, gave highways the appearance of having been oiled. So thick were the winged swarms that it was standard operating procedure for any service-station attendant to clean off the bug screen that protected the fins of car radiators. These screens were part of the normal accessories sold to drivers; without them, motors would quickly overheat. As early as the fall of 1933, representatives from seven western states and three Canadian provinces met at Fargo, North Dakota, to assess the grasshopper problem. The states turned to Congress and asked for help, which eventually came. Millions of dollars were spent to battle the 'hoppers with a poison bait made up of molasses, bran, arsenic, and water.

These were the early rounds in a major environmental war that was to rock the West with one savage blow after another. By 1936, about two million American farmers, a high percentage of whom lived in the old Louisiana Purchase country, would be drawing public assistance. As historian Walter P. Webb once remarked, the public domain itself had constituted the original relief fund for farmers, but they had lived with the notion that it was a birthright, not a grant to the poor. With the issuance of actual relief checks there came the humiliating realization that, at least for the moment, America had a new dependent class. Nature's bombardment during the mid thirties sent many a western farmer running for the nearest fiscal foxhole, desperately seeking aid from any and all sources.

What exacerbated the problem were the extended nature of the drought and the weakened condition of the farmers' financial re-

When the land picked up and left. "Dust blizzards," such as this one in Morton County, Kansas, smothered the hopes of many across the Great Plains in the 1930s. (Courtesy, Kansas State Historical Society, Topeka)

serves. Since 1934 was the fourth consecutive year of dryer-than-normal weather and of falling prices, they had not been able to build any reserve. Had the anticipated wet cycle appeared, they might have come out of the trough between financial waves, but 1935 and 1936 caused the fragile craft of high-plains farming to founder.

These years drew the attention of the federal government and of the national press. Even the Atlantic seaboard became aware of problems in the old American Desert. One embittered farmer put it thus: "Whenever Kansas breaks into the New York headlines it means one of two things has happened. Either we have suffered an act of God or else we have made fools of ourselves."

The people of the plains had experienced an act of God. In July of 1936 the temperature at Steele, North Dakota, hit 120°; and at Bismarck, farmers confined their ducks to coops because so many of them were passing out in the blazing Dakota sun. These people had experienced hot weather before and did not regard high temperatures alone as evidence that the heavens were against them. What really lowered their morale was excessive heat combined with continued aridity, which powdered the earth and made it subject to blowing. The entire plains country suffered from wind erosion, but it was the region of the Texas and Oklahoma panhandles, northeast New

Mexico, southeast Colorado, and southwest Kansas that earned the name "Dust Bowl."

When the wind blew, there was dust everywhere. To fight it the victims used nasal ointments, wore wet cloths over their mouths, and slept with the windows shut on stifling nights. Yet the dust filtered through, spoiling food, coating furniture and floors, irritating eyes, noses, and throats. In the hardest-hit areas, almost everyone sustained some kind of illness, dust pneumonia being the most severe and one from which fatalities were not uncommon. Those who fought the gray fog by buttoning their clothing to the chin went around bathed in sweaty mud. There was no escape.

Outside they found their cars' carburetors filled with "gasoline porridge," and the highways were blocked, as if by snowdrifts. Airplanes coughed their way through the same abrasive dust at amazingly high altitudes. Fliers joked about the pilot who took to his parachute when his plane's engine suffocated, and spent the next six hours shoveling his way to earth. With grim humor they solemnly recounted the story of the man who fainted when struck by a drop of water and required two buckets of sand to be hurled in his face to bring him around. Their tendency to make wry jokes was handed down to them by their forebears, who had developed a sardonic attitude toward the extremes of western weather. The region's climatic and geographic exaggerations historically have lent themselves to a tight-lipped kind of humor. In an effort to face the future with the same toughness that grandfather had been obliged to draw upon, these embattled plowmen recalled old rhymes, resolute lines intended to underscore a determination to hang on:

> Ashes to ashes and dust to dust
> The men folk raved and the wimmin cussed.
> Take it and like it; in God we Trust.

Despite outward efforts to pass over their difficulties, the plains farmers who watched the land blow away were as puzzled as they were discouraged. For generations their ancestors had disturbed the environment, even had fought against it as they spent lifetimes hacking down trees so that they could till the soil, and their efforts at turning the high plains "grass side down," as Charley Russell put it, merely were a part of the process of farming. When nature began to deal out punishment, they took it, hung on grimly, and told themselves that it was one of the implied risks that they had assumed. But by 1935 they had lost a lot of the faith that brought their forefathers west. Margaret Bourke-White, who made much of her early reputation photographing this flying farm land, said that in the spring of that year an atmosphere of utter hopelessness pervaded the plains country. A lot of folks concluded that it was time to pull up stakes and try agricultural prospecting somewhere else.

The ones who moved were the people who have been most written about. Those who stayed on commanded less attention. "Naturally you will wonder why we stay where conditions are so extremely disheartening," wrote one of them. The answer was that this was home. It was a place of friends, church, community, and roots. There was just too much to surrender. One of the wives put it thus: "I cannot act or feel or think as if the experience of our twenty-seven years of life together had never been. And they are all bound up with the little corner to which we have given our continued and united efforts. To leave voluntarily—to break all these closely knit ties for the sake of a possibly greater comfort elsewhere—seems like defaulting on our task." In her difficult position she clung to the notion that a move would not improve her lot, that it would rain again, as it had in 1926, 1929, and 1931, and then she would regret having surrendered her emotional investment in that little bit of the West.

A great many people from her part of the country did not feel a sense of place that strongly. As it had been with previous generations, they came, stuck it out as long as they could, and then left. The crudely lettered sign, tacked onto the earlier homesteader's shack, "Back to my wife's folks" had become legendary—and amusing. It suggested a double defeat. But this time the exodus was not eastward bound; rather, it was to the west, into the high country of the Rockies and beyond, even clear to the Pacific Coast.

Those who chose more attractive neighborhoods beyond the dust and the tumbleweeds sought out such areas as western Colorado. During a five-year period of that disheartening decade, over five hundred families settled in Mesa County, where they put tremendous pressure upon schools and other facilities of local communities, because only about one out of every five families had any money when it arrived. Coloradans found it difficult to complain about this particular roosting in their domain because a great many of the newcomers were from the dusted out part of their own state. As early as the summer of 1933, almost six hundred families in eastern Colorado's Baca County were on the relief rolls, and fifty were being added each month. Four years later a visitor in that general area said that people were living "in choking poverty," that there was not a doctor, a nurse, a hospital, or even an infirmary available in whole communities.

One would think that few people would want to migrate to such a place, but to Mexican-American beet workers it still held out the promise of jobs, and they moved in, many of them from New Mexico. Lest it be thought that the Old West lacked its prejudices, Governor "Big Ed" Johnson posted National Guardsmen at the state line and established what he called a "bum blockade" to keep out undesirables. The implied ethnic slur bothered few Coloradans because their leader's cordon sanitaire also was meant to be somewhat selective about the applicants' financial status, regardless of racial origins. These were troublous times, and one had to take care of one's own.

Those who circumvented such roadblocks headed for the West Coast. California took the brunt of it, as has been so well publicized. While no one knew for sure how many migrants had poured in during the thirties, those who lived there sniffed when the census taker said the state had grown by over a million during the period and allowed as how too many of them were unwanted "bowlers." However, historians have argued that the majority of the "Okies" actually came from poverty-stricken areas of Oklahoma, Arkansas, Missouri, and Texas that were not associated with the dust bowl. The Pacific Northwest felt less pressure, that region gaining some 460,000 migrants during the decade, about 40 percent of whom came from the northern plains country in the traditional straight-line movement from east to west. Members of this group escaped the Okie stigma and often were regarded as higher types who just had had luck at dry farming. When Oregonian Richard Neuberger interviewed a Scandinavian farmer with a family of five children, just in from South Dakota and with very little money, the journalist decided that the newcomer was a "typical American frontiersman" of that depressed period. Noboby had any such kind words for the Okies.

Novels were written and films were made that depicted this tattered agrarian army in retreat; grim-faced men, worn women, and hungry-looking children who stared dully at the overburdened stalled family car, its radiator pointed west. These dejected people differed from the earlier pioneers in that their attitudes did not reflect resolute optimism or hope for a better life farther west but, rather, one of desperate flight from disaster into a questionable but necessary tomorrow. So standard has the scene become, particularly because of the poignant photographs, featured by national picture magazines, made popular during the mid thirties, that it was easy to generalize about the problem.

If the latter-day pioneers were dusted out and the once-touted Garden in the Grasslands now showed a downturn in population figures, it seemed apparent that depression, low prices, and drought were driving people from their land and into other parts of America. Obviously, this was happening; statistics quickly confirmed movement. The question that remained was: How big was the exodus? During the difficult decade the plains, the mountains, and the Southwest lost between 5 and 10 percent of their population. All other states in the Union showed a gain. From the Dakotas to Oklahoma the result was a minus; New Mexico and Colorado squeaked into the plus column because of overflow from neighboring drought areas and because of shifting within these states from burned out areas to higher, greener ground.

While the size of the exodus from the region may have been exaggerated in the public mind, the flight of the farmers was greater even than the figures suggest. During the period, some of them simply gave up farming and moved to neighboring towns, with the result that the census figures indicated a statewide rural decline, whereas some of the urban areas actually grew. In North Dakota, for example, the urban increase was about 16 percent in a decade that saw the state's population drop by nearly 6 percent. The farms, of course, did not simply disappear. Usually they were bought or rented by neighbors who were determined to hang on. Between 1920 and 1940 the average size of farms in Montana jumped from 480 acres to 841 acres, the increase accentuating sharply during the depression years. A similar development took place in North Dakota and Wyoming. It was a trend that would continue, good crops or bad, for the ensuing decades, one signifying that the day of the small farmer in the plains West had passed.

Regardless of the size or the seriousness of the outflow from the area and despite the fact that it would be reversed, the heartland of the old, romantic West began to lose some of its earlier reputation in the eyes of Americans. Popular writers confessed that the streak of hard luck that westerners were having was setting some new records for adversity. Scientists argued that since the coming of the white man, the plains had experienced four dry years in every decade. But despite sympathy and technical explanations it seemed obvious to the man on the street that something was out of kilter if nine million acres had reverted to desert and another eighty million had been damaged.

And now that land of promise, of hope, of great expectation, had become merely another disaster area requiring public assistance. In recent years, especially since the end of World War I, the faithful had

Like a tombstone of the myth of Eden, a shriveled plant stands in a desolate field after a dust storm in Baca County, Colorado. (Courtesy, Denver Public Library, Western History Department)

stood fast in their belief about this treasured land. But as a large segment of America had shifted its admiration to the marvels being performed by business, industry, and technology, the West and, especially, the flat-land wheat-raising part of it had attracted less and less attention. As a matter of fact, the farming community beyond the wide Missouri never had excited the East very much. Ranchers excepted, the more recent rural residents of the plains were bib-overalled sodbusters about whom very few "westerns" were written. And when the dust began to envelop them, there was no general rush to help them or even to sympathize with them. The western farmer of the thirties was not a national folk hero.

By now the intelligentsia had concluded that the West was due a new image. Speaking of the frontier's passing, Lewis Mumford predicted that in the place of exploitation by "mere spread and plunder," a more stable and orderly society would be required to preside over the American agricultural hinterland. When Henry A. Wallace, then Roosevelt's secretary of agriculture, published his *New Frontiers* in 1934, he suggested much the same thing, but rather than foreclosing upon the old days and therefore the myth, he tried to bridge the gap between the romantic frontier West and the dusty disaster that was then in progress beyond the Missouri. Admitting that the days of agrarian expansion were over, he suggested that the most desirable transition would be one of preserving the good points of pioneer individualism while adapting to an environment that was devoid of opportunities for unlimited expansion and the further application of "free-booter democracy."

Wallace was confronted by the dilemma of a frontier psychology that was deeply rooted in the American emotional system, one that ran counter to the contemporary picture of an entire region's reverting to desertlike conditions. It is surprising that when Steinbeck's *The Grapes of Wrath* spoke that truth and laid bare the bankruptcy of an ancient American dream about going westward to the Promised Land, it was so widely accepted. The whole notion denied a long-established belief. It was like telling a child there was no Santa Claus.

The poet Archibald MacLeish wrote his farewell to the legendary West that decade in his *Land of the Free,* a poem in which he saw the dream being blown away by a west wind. "The land's going out from us," he wrote, "blown by a dry wind in the wheat." He asked himself if this spelled the end of a major phase of the nation's history.

> We wonder whether the great American dream
> Was the singing of the locusts out of the grass
>   to the West and the
> West is behind us now:
> The west wind's away from us.
> We wonder whether the dream of American liberty
> Was two hundred years of pine and hardwood
> And three generations of grass
> And the generations are up: the years are over.

That was the problem. To the dreamers the years were over, youth had passed, and there seemed to be no excitement on the horizon, no new worlds to conquer. And the West was to blame; that treasure house of spiritual as well as material things had passed a dividend, and the emotional investors were disappointed. Deeply embedded in the conscience of Americans was the notion not only that their nation was the land of the free and the home of the brave but also that in the West, at least in an economic sense, lay the very heart of this implied promise. Even westerners had convinced themselves of this, and they basked in the sunlight of this generally accepted notion, their

Chambers of Commerce playing that tune over and over again to willing ears. When the one-two punch of a world-wide depression, combined with an unusually lengthy period of drought, struck what had been touted as the breadbasket of the globe, it shattered some earlier convictions both in the East and in the West. As MacLeish said in one of his lines, "the dreaming is finished."

It was difficult for westerners to see it this way. Although the nonfarming westerners understood that farmers had experienced some difficulty during the 1920s, they shared the belief that the problem was cyclical. Despite the fact that in this presumably "roaring" decade, American farm income had dropped from 18 percent to 7 percent of the national income, real-estate values had fallen over 50 percent, and wheat prices had declined steadily, there seemed to be room for optimism. There had been ups and downs in crop yields, but there had been some rain, and the reverses were not severe enough to generate deep gloom. "Courage has returned," wrote Charles Moreau Harger in 1924. "The old cry that the farmer makes no profit and that prices rise only when he has nothing to sell has been forgotten." The *Literary Digest* called the West prosperous, an area that was thinly populated but one that spent more money per capita than did other sections of the country. For those who wanted to believe, the region continued to be recognized for its potential in resources; it was still regarded as the land of opportunity. As late as 1933, Courtney Ryley Cooper was selling this notion to readers of the *Saturday Evening Post*.

This suggests several things. Possibly Cooper was just another eastern journalist on a quick junket through the West who had no idea what was going on beneath the surface view; or westerners were reluctant to tell visiting reporters the truth, either because it might damage their image or out of sheer pride. There is something in this idea. Not a few of those who had made their move westward stubbornly defended their decision, and in the face of all adversity, they praised the place where they had chosen to settle. The descendants of earlier plains pioneers, those who had come to regard the West as their native place, told newcomers that rural folks historically had been slow to feel the effects of those eastern-bred financial panics. Money might be short for a while, but garden produce and barnyard fowls went a long way in staving off hunger. These people "forted up," resolved to combat adversity as they had in the past. There was not a great deal of advertisement of their plight, either by themselves or by outside observers.

Apparently, outward manifestations of the depression, at least in terms of popular unrest, were slow to surface in the West. When Mark Sullivan, a noted journalist, visited Idaho in the fall of 1932, he remarked that the state was "literally the last community in the United States to feel the depression." Perhaps the people there were just used to it; Idaho's agricultural depression had been going on for ten years. As a matter of fact, the average income of those people had declined by almost 50 percent between 1929 and 1932.

There were other small signs that the malady was slow to be noticeable, at least in the eyes of visitors. It was not until 1933 that a tourist, westbound out of Chicago, personally sensed any signs of trouble in Eden. As her train approached a western town, she heard a woman ask a whiskbroom-wielding porter if he had change for a quarter. "This was the first sign of a Western Depression," she wrote. When a passenger concluded a two-day trip with a dime tip, money indeed appeared to be tight.

But by that date, Pullman porters were not surprised at gratuities of this size. The problem for them was to find anyone on the trains. As Oswald Garrison Villard said, by then the star of empire was not taking its way west or anywhere else. He saw only ten passengers in all the sleepers of an eleven-car transcontinental train. Times were so bad, he said, that the sight of fifty-car freight trains caused excitement in the seedy little western towns through which they passed.

Granted that depending on what one did and where one lived in the West, there was a time lag before the depression hit with full force, its ultimate fury quickly showed westerners that they were not a favored people. Farmers might cushion the blow by growing a little food, but the townsmen, the salaried workers, and the nonagrarians found life decidedly hard. In the mountain states, copper, lead, and zinc went begging because eastern manufacturers were making fewer requests for such minerals. Thanks to the Roosevelt administration's response to pressure from western members of Congress, the silver-purchase act of 1934 resulted in the buying of around a billion dollars worth of the white metal during the next decade.

While this fiscal manipulation helped one extractive industry, it did little for the others. Fresh discoveries of oil in Texas and Oklahoma greatly increased the supply and sent the value of crude oil plunging to ten cents a barrel. By 1932, Montana's Kevin-Sunburst field hit its lowest production figure since its discovery. Except for the Cutbank field, where it was said to be impossible for wildcatters to hit a dry hole, Montana's oil business declined sharply. So did that of Wyoming and other oil-producing mountain states.

Another of the West's sources of income shrank during these years. Tourism—a business that dated back to the 1870s in some parts of the mountain West and one that promised to be of major importance as the "tin-can" tourist of automotive days discovered the national parks—wilted at just about the time when it had begun to flower. The optimism that resort owners had generated during the twenties faded as money grew tight, as visitors bearing that welcome item stayed home and watched the worrisome future. Hotels, motels, restaurants, and gas stations saw their returns fall off by 50 percent.

All across the West, men and women found themselves without jobs, and in that sparse country, there were few other places to look for them. A disheartened Montanan wrote, "When my last request for work brought me nothing but scorn normally accorded a horse-thief, I think I just quietly curled up and died."

Between 1929 and 1932, unemployment quadrupled in Colorado. Jobless transients created such a problem in Wyoming that by 1935 they were required to work for their board and room in camps set up for them in some of the towns. Old mining towns that still depended upon subsurface yields were hard hit. Squads of idle men sat around the streets of Butte, Montana, hoping for an upturn in copper prices. A 1934 survey of that city revealed a startling lack of even the most basic living facilities, especially such everyday expectations as toilets and showers. Idle mines set men adrift in other western areas, particularly Nevada and Arizona. In the latter state between 1932 and 1936, some fifty thousand people moved away, many of whom left because they could not find work in the mines.

Now and then the jobless grew militant, just as they did in the East. In Colorado, a state that had experienced such unrest in the past, there was anger and bitterness. When a group of unemployed people marched upon the state's capitol and pushed their way into the senate chamber, a national magazine screamed "Revolution!" But the locals were not all that upset about marching. Two years earlier, in 1932, they had watched the BEF (Bonus Expeditionary Force) depart their city to invade a foreign spot called Washington, D.C. So the folks in Denver did not show great alarm at the visitation paid the legislators; in fact, they were somewhat pleased when those who had been sent to the capital city to legislate got down to business and provided some matching funds to take advantage of money being offered by the federal government.

Not many people marched on the establishment demanding action. More often they took individual action, which ranged from leaving the West entirely, as had many before them, to moving in with relatives or doubling up with other families until the storm had passed. One example of "toughing it out" was a young couple named Henry and Helen Viets. When he lost his job in a western city, the pair headed for rural Nevada to join some friends who lived in a mud-and-log shack. The Viets fashioned an annex, made out of old railroad ties and boards that they took from an abandoned mine structure. They roofed it with tar paper and insulated the wall with rag chinking. She carried wood and water to her new home, emptied ashes from a hungry old stove, and doled out pennies from their entire fortune of twelve dollars to feed a flickering gas lantern. Henry occasionally found work in a nearby mine. This was back to rural living with a jolt. It was a negative kind of pioneering, a retreat and a reversion, but one that called for guts and resolution.

This was but one young couple who bit the bullet. Thousands of others chose to fight it out, to resist charity until the very end, to put their faith in the future and in the belief, bred into them through the generations, that things would take a turn for the better. Generally speaking, their faith was rewarded; but experiences such as that of the Viets left marks upon them that later years of prosperity never erased.

Aside from belt tightening and concern about possible unemployment, those who lived in the little western towns had other worries. One of these was the constant fear that the local bank, that ultimate financial barometer, would give them the dreaded news that it, too, had given up the ghost. Faith had built the West, and that was all that stood between depositors and bank management; there were no guarantees that the family finances would be protected. South Dakotans, among others, had a lot of experience with fiscal uncertainties. Between 1920 and 1934, over 70 percent of that commonwealth's state banks had failed, and the number of national banks that were still in business had dropped by more than half. Montanans knew the problem; during the early twenties, half of their banks had gone "belly up." For the townsmen, these happenings were unnerving; severed financial arteries quickly paralyzed business transactions, caused householders figuratively to bury their money in the backyard, and reduced the community to barter.

A scarcity of money and a loss of confidence in the economy's ability to recover prompted state and local officials to retrench. Among public employees, schoolteachers were a favorite target. Many school boards not only had to reduce salaries; they were also obliged to issue warrants in lieu of cash, pieces of paper that the merchants viewed with distaste and unhesitatingly discounted if they accepted them at all. In some areas, teachers "boarded around," as they had done during frontier days, glad to have a chance to eat and find shelter in return for bartered services. In South Dakota the governor pushed for a 10 percent salary reduction at institutions of higher education, thus recovering "a sizable sum" for the general fund. In 1933 Montana legislators considered closing down colleges at Havre and Billings but satisfied themselves with an across-the-board cut in the state's collegiate system.

The question at once arises as to whether westerners experienced problems that differed greatly from those that were besetting people all across America, whether they were any worse off than millions of their countrymen. The answer is a qualified yes. A decade of low agricultural prices, a shrinking world market, continuing indebtedness, high interest rates, and surpluses of products had placed an area that depended heavily upon farm prosperity in a very poor position to combat any extended period of financial adversity. It is true that agrarian communities all across the country could be said to have suffered from these things, but much of western agriculture was carried out under marginal conditions, and when all of the above negatives were present, the additional blows of drought and dust spelled the difference between a momentary defeat and absolute disaster. Caught in time between a timid Hoover administration, which was unwilling to take drastic relief measures, and an innovative Roosevelt program, which sputtered into action rather unevenly, a beleaguered region was caught in a cross fire of inaction at a time when it desperately needed help.

Except for the benefits received from a general New Deal agricultural-aid program, the West, especially the drought-stricken plains, did not receive special attention during Roosevelt's first two years in office. The president recognized that high-plains agriculture was different from that practiced farther east, and he agreed with Henry Wallace that a policy must be developed that would more effectively utilize the available sources of water. But until the dust storms assumed proportions that made national and even international headlines, he confined his efforts to dealing with depression problems that afflicted more populous parts of the nation.

If the New Deal was slow in initiating a program of massive aid to the high plains, it was not because Roosevelt was not aware of a mounting crisis in that region. His wife's friend Lorena Hickok, a journalist who investigated conditions for Harry Hopkins, wrote a devastating series of letters to Hopkins that are now available in book form.

In November 1933, from South Dakota, she reported a scene of mile after mile of "flat brown country," interspersed with snowdrifts and piles of Russian thistles, where houses were unpainted and the towns looked gaunt and grubby. What a country to stay out of, she commented. Here the people were reduced to eating Russian-thistle soup, the making of which Hickok described: "They cut the thistles green and stack them up. Inside the stacks the stuff is still green— although perhaps rotted a little. They haul that out, stew it up with a little flour and water, and eat it!" These people, she continued, lived in houses without fuel, without enough clothing or bedding, places "that a prosperous farmer wouldn't put his cattle in." In one of these houses she saw two small boys running around "without a stitch save some ragged overalls." They had no shoes or stockings, and their feet "were purple with cold." The parents weren't much better off. Referring to his tattered clothes, one farmer remarked: "They're all we've got now. We take turns wearing 'em."

Hickok referred to a comment made by one individual, who thought the country never should have been opened up. "I think he was right," she told Hopkins. But because it had been opened up, she had an idea about how it might better be used. She said that if Roosevelt ever became a dictator, she had a grand idea for him: "He can label this country here 'Siberia' and send all his exiles here. It is the 'Siberia' of the United States. A more hopeless place I never saw."

But people stayed on in "Siberia." One farmer said he hadn't had a really good crop since 1916, and when asked what prompted him to stick it out, he had a simple answer: "No place to go." So he stayed and worked his 320 acres with horses, while the tractor sat idle; there just wasn't any money with which to buy fuel. But even the farm animals were difficult to "fuel," and many a rib-studded, underfed horse tugged at creaking, rusted farm machinery as the farmer continued his hopeless fight against the desert. Obviously the agricultural economy of the Great Plains was possessed of a very narrow margin of reserve, and when that was expended, trouble was inevitable. Clearly the region was a disaster area, and immediate rescue measures were mandated.

Once the New Deal's programs picked up speed, especially with the granting of agricultural loans and benefit payments made under the Agricultural Adjustment Act of 1933, cash began to circulate in communities that had seen very little of it for years. Not only did the farmers benefit; bankers, merchants, and dealers in automobile and farm machinery responded in the manner of thirst-crazed men swallowing their first drink of water. As other programs touched these communities, commercial activity showed an even greater liveliness. More than mere pump priming, this amounted to opening a main irrigation valve.

In addition to aid being given to the plowmen, those who raised livestock in what was once the vast open range country also benefited. By 1932, cattle were selling for only half of what they had brought three years earlier, and ranchers all across the plains and mountain West, who had survived adversity in many forms, now began to go bankrupt. Proud and independent stockgrowers of a state such as Wyoming, faced by plunging prices and dried-up grasslands, reluctantly turned to the federal government for help. The Old West seemed light years away as they watched starving cattle and sheep being purchased by federal representatives and slaughtered on the spot because they were unfit for human consumption. The Federal government lent further assistance when it answered a long-standing range-land request for grazing on public lands. In 1934 Congressman Edward T. Taylor of Colorado sponsored an act, later described as a "major windfall," that opened some eighty million acres of land for use, in an orderly and controlled manner at reasonable rates. Even hardened old stockmen, who generally opposed the central government as a matter of principle, gave grudging approval to this legislation.

While farmers and stockgrowers, who constituted a major segment of the West's economy, received federal aid at a critical time, the New Deal pumped millions of dollars into outright relief, which provided money for hungry families in both town and country. By early 1935, one out of every five households in the plains drought area was receiving assistance of some kind. And they continued to need it. The year 1936 was a hard one for the western economy, and by the end of it, more than half the families in some counties were on relief. There would have been even more except for the fact that several federal agencies, such as the Agricultural Adjustment Administration (AAA), the Farm Credit Administration, and the Resettlement Administration sharply increased their activities in these hard-hit localities.

Some of the benefits that the central government bestowed were multiple and had far-reaching effects. For example, the Civilian Conservation Corps, popularly known as the CCC, took thousands of young men off the streets—a great many of them from the East— and put them to work building reservoir dams, mountain roads, and lookout stations and clearing forests. One writer called this agency

During the 1930s, thousands of young men built dams, carved out mountain roads, and cleared forests under the auspices of the Civilian Conservation Corps. (Courtesy, Colorado Historical Society)

Idaho's most popular New Deal agency and said the eighteen thousand boys, who worked in seventy camps, had a "definite and exciting impact" on the state. Neighboring western states had similar reactions.

This great conservation effort not only improved and protected millions of western acres; it also did a great deal for the health and outlook of some badly demoralized young men. Since much of the money that they earned was sent home, the benefits of the CCC program touched homes in every part of the country. The small amount of spending money that was left to the boys was welcomed by western merchants.

Viewed from a national standpoint or looked at in the light of subsequent inflation, the millions spent in the West may not loom large, but to that vast, lightly populated area the money that the federal government provided was a godsend. In a state such as Nevada, with a very high percentage of public and therefore nontaxable land, the fragile economy suffered heavily from the depression. Efforts to tease some money into the state by the legalization of gambling were not enough to offset the ravages of falling prices for minerals and livestock. Among the various states,

Nevada headed the list of per capita expenditures by the New Deal.
Even in neighboring Utah, where the Mormon Church was proud of
its ability to care for its own during difficult times, the situation
became so extreme that the Latter-day Saints had to ask for help.
Nevada and Utah received more money for relief, proportionately,
than did most of the other American states.

For a great many westerners the impact of this extensive aid
program was both dramatic and memorable. Older people in these
small communities still talk about those days of austerity, of hope,
and of change. A prosperous Denver doctor, who grew up in a small
northern-Montana town, was asked how he, who now drove an
expensive car, owned some valuable property, and belonged to a
politically conservative profession, could serve as an enthusiastic
precinct worker for the Democratic party.

"Do you remember those days when you and I were kids in that
busted little town?" he responded. "My Dad and I used to walk
along the railroad tracks looking for chunks of coal or bits of wood to
sell for what we could get. And the newspaper offered to trade
subscriptions for wheat because nobody had any money. The New
Deal changed all that, brought us the only cash we'd seen in ages. I
just never forgot it, that's all."

Some wanted to forget. The farmers often came from a long line of
agrarians, of native or foreign origin, people whose family traditions
featured independence and self-reliance. They found themselves in
an area of marginal rainfall, at a time when industrialized agriculture
was stripping them of their presumed economic freedom. What they
did not realize was the fact that they were failing as businessmen, as
opposed to tillers of the soil. Agriculture had changed. Still, to ask for
aid was a further strain upon an ingrained tradition of seeking favor
from no man, and when they put out their hands, they did it with
great reluctance. It was a confession of failure, both personally and
by a system that they believed in. That they wanted to ignore the days
of the dole is quite understandable.

A few resisted what they regarded as a great bureaucratic octopus,
reaching out for them from Foggy Bottom. They were led by
politicians who were anxious to show their individuality and their
perpetual enmity toward federal functionaries, who were thought to
hold the West in thralldom. These politically hairy-chested types
were epitomized by "Big Ed" Johnson, Colorado's maverick Democratic governor, who fought Roosevelt's administration tooth and
nail. When Edward Costigan ran for the Senate in 1930, his
enthusiasm for federal aid had given him a landslide victory, but by

1936, when Costigan's health broke down and he was forced out of politics, it was Big Ed whom the voters sent to Washington, where he could come to closer grips with the enemy, chiefly Harry Hopkins.

The people who sent Johnson off to the wars were those whose lachrymose complaints about Hoover's policies had seen them trooping into the Democratic camp in 1932, hopeful of receiving federal funds for dams, highways, and other public works, not to mention relief from the depression. During Roosevelt's first two terms in office, almost $400 million were pumped into Colorado for relief and recovery. Yet, by the early 1940s, visitors to that mountain redoubt were told over and over again about the evils of the New Deal. Thus, as the war in Europe turned things around for some of America's depressed economic sectors, Colorado's businessmen sufficiently recovered their nerve once again to trumpet an undying faith in the tradition of self-help and a perpetual opposition to high taxes and federal participation in the economy. Their vociferous opposition to an Arkansas Valley Authority suggested that they were ready to throw away their crutches and again walk unaided.

Colorado was by no means an isolated example of westerners' bucking the New Deal. Governor C. Ben Ross of Idaho opposed Roosevelt, as did Senator Pat McCarran of Nevada and, after 1937 especially, Senator Burton K. Wheeler of heavily Democratic Montana. In 1940 Senator Gerald P. Nye of North Dakota advised his constituents to vote for Wendell L. Willkie, and indeed, Willkie beat Roosevelt in North Dakota that year. In general, the West was inclined to bite the hand that fed it. Westerners rejected most of the New Deal labor reforms, failed to contribute their fair share of relief money, and fought guerrilla administrative engagements with federal officials who were trying to help them. This arose, in part, from weakness, for many of the western states did not have reform-minded governors or progressive state administrations. Very little reform in these years emanated from the states themselves. Basically what it amounted to was the unwillingness or inability of the states to reconcile what they conceived to be their rugged individualism, born of the frontier, with the planned society that was implied by the New Deal. The two concepts simply didn't mesh.

While westerners were flexing their biceps and making big talk about their presumed independence, eastern journalists were making fun of them for their fumbling of the scissors in an effort to cut parental apron strings. Those critics who scanned the colonial landscape from behind their Allegheny barricades gave a cold eye to that one-time land of individualism, daring, ruggedness, and romance. They saw another rescue taking place in that beloved wilderness, but it failed to excite them as in days of old, because this time it was the West itself. And they were disappointed. High noon was not Main Street and tied-down holsters; rather, it was a blazing sun that simply burned up the countryside. And the supermen who lived in never-never land now were yelling "uncle." It was too much.

By 1937 *Collier's* magazine complained that fifty federal agencies, not to mention those of individual states, had "puttered around" with the dust bowl for almost four years and had spent millions to bail out farmers who were scratching away at soil that wouldn't support lizards. Those once-fabled westerners, who had wrested the land from nature for God and country, now were transformed into plundering agrarian industralists, men who tore up nature's work in a fruitless effort to raise wheat that nobody wanted to buy and who, with their pulverizing machines, were bound to raise nothing but more dust.

Alarm over the upending of western sod marked a change in national attitudes. It signified a "back to grass" movement that would persist, and by another half-century the crusade for environmental preservation would reach national proportions. The problem of the thirties arose simply from a trial-and-error process that had seen the gradual edging westward of the "sodbusters," and until nature responded with weather that set new records for extremes, there had been no logical answer to the question of how far was too far west. And even then there was no convincing answer, as witness the renewal of speculative farming on marginal lands during the 1940s and 1950s. As recently as 1979 a dust-bowl historian averred that the New Deal drive to convert dust land to grassland was not an effort of far-sighted men to restore an area but rather was one made by men who were imbued with a missionary spirit as opposed to an understanding of a western problem or its solution.

The "missionary spirit" arose, in part, from the zeal of the idealists who surrounded Franklin Roosevelt. As it was with other Rooseveltian programs that were characterized as the New Deal, planners looked to both short-term and long-term solutions. Thus, in August 1936, when things were getting really serious in the dust bowl, the president appointed the Great Plains Drought Committee to recommend steps for early relief, but a month later he appointed another committee to recommend a long-term program for "the efficient utilization of the Great Plains area."

This Committee on the Future of the Great Plains concluded that the plains had not "responded favorably to a purely individualistic

*The New Deal pays for culture in what many still thought of as a
wilderness, here in the shape of a town library in Ault, Colorado. Libraries
appeared in hundreds of towns across the West. (Courtesy, Colorado
Historical Society)*

system of pioneering," and it suggested that farmers voluntarily
involve themselves in long-range planning that, while not surrendering local initiative or the treasured notion of self-reliance, would work
toward a more efficient system. This was necessary, it was pointed
out, because the steady progress that Americans had come to look for
in their frontier agricultural communities on their march westward
somehow had not only failed to work out on the plains but had,
indeed, reversed itself. Instead of becoming more productive, the
plains were becoming less so, and with that development, the
committee concluded, those tillers of the soil were becoming steadily
less secure on their western farms, and the quality of agricultural life
in the region was declining.

The so-called puttering around that the New Deal did both with
the dust bowl proper and with western agricultural lands in general,
as well as with water, time, and human beings, was so extensive that
it may well have left its footprints on that region more clearly and for
a longer time than was the case with any other part of the country.
That this relatively undeveloped region was hard hit is illustrated by
its national ranking in terms of aid received. A record of those states

that received the most federal funds of all types during that desperate decade places the first fourteen in the West. That region was awarded three times the national average for federal expenditures while it yielded only about one-third of that figure in locally generated revenues. This appeared to suggest that the West still was a colony but that it was no longer as productive to the parent as it once had been.

This posed some problems for the recipients of the largess. The more they received, the more their collective inferiority complex surfaced. That they understood their dilemma made the situation all the more irritating, yet they chose to go on, gnawing at the hand that fed them, while alternating between vituperation and lamentations over the sad role of the enslaved. Defenders of these politically schizophrenic people explained that such attitudes arose from defensiveness that was generated by the misfortunes of a normally hardworking, honest, independent people. In part, that was a rationalization of their disinclination to acknowledge any political debts to an administration that had bailed them out of deep trouble. An example is North Dakota, whose residents long had been known for their fondness for progressive programs, yet their support for the Democrats was ephemeral. These latter-day frontier farmers had hoped to free themselves from dependency when they had braved the new north country to make a living. Now they were uncomfortable in the role of takers.

Being on the take had some hidden costs as well. In a thinly settled country where the tax base was meager, the states were hard pressed to match federal grants that were being dangled under their noses. Fearful of letting some of this much-despised money escape, the legislators often laid on unpleasant levies such as sales taxes, or they increased the assessments on property. This produced an annoying drop in popularity among the locally elected. To compound the irritation the federal government posed conditions on how the allowance was to be spent, generated more agencies to carry out the proliferating rules, and produced spin-off state bureaucracies that grew like zucchini on a hot summer day.

All of which meant that the West, like a dope addict, came further under the control of the pusher. There grew what has been politely called a "new federalism" (not to be confused with the later Reagan version), one that so expanded the role of the central government that the man on the street tended to cast his eyes eastward, however reluctantly, to where a modern Great White Father dispensed trinkets, rather than to seek out the state capitol building. More precisely the occupant of the White House and his cohorts took a renewed grasp on the colonial West and wielded an influence that overshadowed that of Wall Street. By turning up the volume of programs that were aimed at promoting regionalism, the "feds" further diminished the power and local influence of the states.

When the magnitude of this evolution finally sank into western mentalities and into the thinking of that area's admirers in other parts of the nation, even the die-hards among Old West fans had to admit that, indeed, the land of their dreams was no more. The American dream had become an illusion as the myth of unlimited possibilities had run aground on the reality of drought, depression, and agricultural desolation.

In their preoccupation with the notion of the frontier, a good many Americans, scholars included, had ignored the problem of the West.

CHAPTER 6

COLONIALISM: THE ENDURING DILEMMA

At the start of the Great Depression, the legend of the Old West already was somewhat the worse for wear. Then, during the grim decade of the 1930s, the body blows dealt to the American economy gave the myth a further battering. Beleaguered easterners, fighting for their very existence, found little time for this kind of folklore. It was not that they did not enjoy the form of escapism it had provided, but their immediate problem was that the rugged individualism they had heard so much about in the immediate predepression years, a quality that seemed to ooze from the Old West, apparently had not saved the country from its present disaster. Westerns did not disappear, of course. Stars like Gene Autry and Roy Rogers warbled and strummed their way to popularity, but the vitality and unblushing optimism found in earlier movies and novels was missing. Those in search of vicarious adventure sought other means of escape, such as viewing the flood of war films that Hollywood was now offering as a substitute for horseback heroism in sagebrush country. Even the gangster films appeared to fill a need for armchair violence, excitement, and lawlessness, earlier thought to be western property.

In short, the West was out of fashion. The land was there, but the romance was gone, at least for the duration of the depression. It was like a passionate relationship gone stale, and the one-time object of affection now appeared to be quite plain and unprovocative. That favored region, once spoiled and pampered, was increasingly re-garded as a responsibility, one whose cost of maintenance was not worth the candle, a burden to the purse, a no-longer-needed emo-tional plaything. The master had begun to balk at supporting the mistress; the affair was over.

Word of its new status came to the West during that particularly trying year of 1932. It was delivered in the form of two public disavowals of the nation's orphan by a magazine not inappropriately named the *Atlantic*. From the seaboard of the same name, these complainants charged not only that the poor relatives across the wide Missouri were a drain upon the treasury but also that the mountain-plains region, in particular, had a disproportionate say in how federal receipts were spent, the result of which was undemocratic government. The idea that the tail was wagging the dog persisted; it surfaced again in the election of 1936.

Bernhard Knollenberg, whose finger-wagging article appeared in March 1932, reflected the impressions of a tour through what he termed some "sagebrush states" during the previous summer. As he drove through that sparse land, the visitor met with very few other motorists, a not surprising occurrence in a day when vacation money was hard to come by. But the loneliness of the road seemed to bother the vacationing lawyer, and instead of enjoying the majestic solitude, he fretted about the amount of money easterners had contributed through federal pipelines to provide for such travel. He concluded that such appropriations would have been better spent in the East, where its greater numbers could enjoy a more complete highway system. This inequitable allocation of funds, he wrote, was the result of having sagebrush senators secure pork-barrel legislation for their handful of constituents. The whole desolate region had a smaller population than had his home state, New York. As a group, these westerners paid less income tax than did the residents of the single state of Connecticut. He thought this unfair.

It wasn't that Knollenberg had anything against westerners, as people. He conceded that a refined and selected blood did indeed flow in their veins, an attribute that for some years had been touted by the West's eastern fan club, but this did not answer his complaint. "The rural, Nordic teetotaler . . . may be a more desirable type than the Celtic, Latin, Semitic, Anglo-Saxon potpourri that predominates the East," he admitted, "but the question is not whether an oligarchy selected from what·may be the soundest stock in the country is best fitted to govern." At issue was whether such minority rule was right and fair to the rest of the country. He thought the system of federal "aids" to the states heavily favored the lightly populated West.

The other critic, an aging rare-book collector from Philadelphia named Alfred Edward Newton, was less charitable when it came to issuing a grade to the westerners and to their respective states. His article, published in May of the same year, singled out Wyoming, Colorado, New Mexico, Arizona, Utah, and Nevada, which, along with several other "backward states," were urged either to relinquish their privilege of selecting senators or to get out of the Union. He was dismayed that the six "so-called states," with a population of only 2.7

million—"the least populated area in the whole civilized world"—
could speak with as much authority as the heavily peopled eastern
states. Idaho, he charged, was more a state of mind than a state, and
Nevada ranked even lower. The latter produced only driblets of silver
and copper, of which there was already too much, plus cactus,
rattlesnakes, and divorces, the last being a national scandal.

Newton's conclusion was simple and direct: "These miserable
Western States have nothing, and they are a drain upon the entire
country." To this particular piece of invective the magazine's editor
responded with a mild tut-tut; nevertheless he published it. He also
gave space in his June issue to a timid rejoinder from a Spokane
lawyer, who tried to show that on a per capita basis, westerners were
paying more than other Americans for their highways and were
receiving proportionately less federal aid.

The particular points that two dyspeptic easterners raised were not
entirely new, but the virulence of their attack was. Articles like theirs
heralded an important change in the way that eastern and western
states regarded one another. In the past, residents of each region had
complained about the pampered treatment being given to the other,
but even so, they had admitted that they had advantages and favors
of their own. Above all, the glorious hopes for the future cast a rosy
haze, obscuring all such distinctions. Only a few years before the
articles in the *Atlantic,* for instance, a national weekly suggested that
western states were getting back about 200 percent of what they were
paying in taxes, and their highways were being built largely with
eastern money. But, said the author, who called the West "the
youngest brother," the mountain states in particular had been
thoroughly drained of minerals by eastern investors, and if only a
small portion of that loot went into western highways, the expendi-
ture was more than justified.

Here, on the eve of the Great Depression, was an attitude that
expressed a warm, if paternalistic, relationship, an exchange of gifts.
But that was about to change. With the sickening slide of the national
fortunes, both the East and the West grew surly. Soon the first was
being portrayed as an exploitative, mustache-twirling master, while
the other appeared as a mooching, unwanted brother-in-law, who
lounged about the place when he should have been looking for work.
The lines of battle were drawn ever more clearly, and the debate over
"colonialism" threatened to drown out any voices of mutual good
will.

As with all modern changes in the Western image, this one had
roots in the previous century. The larger question of the West as a

national asset had existed for some time. During the region's formative years, doubters had been shouted down by the boundless enthusiasm of the land boomers, who were loud in their praise for the West's progress, its wealth, and the sterling characters it produced. Despite all that vocalizing, certain reservations had lingered on the part of more critical Americans as to the role of the nation's offspring and its proper place in the growing family. The notion that while the West might be a great place for exploitation, it also could be a drain upon the federal treasury dated well back into the nineteenth century. When Gen. William Tecumseh Sherman inspected New Mexico in 1866, he concluded that the acquisition of this territory had been a bad investment for the United States. Wryly he suggested that it be sold to Mexico, even if we had to loan that country the purchase money or, failing that, the United States should go to war with Mexico, defeat it, and make it take back much of the Southwest as a penalty for losing.

At that time, New Mexico, along with most of the mountain-plains West, was being ruled by Washington-appointed territorial governors, and it would remain as this type of a dependency for nearly half a century. While Americans long had boasted that they possessed no colonial system, that such exterior control was just a bad memory from which a free people had emerged, in truth the territorial structure was no more than the Republic's adaptation of an earlier British method. True, qualified territorial applicants eventually could gain full-fledged membership in the fraternity of states. But what easterners later complained about was that these colonials had achieved more than equality and that as nonsupporters they were threatening to bankrupt the family. Such arguments overlooked the fact that in many senses of the word equality, economic merely being the most obvious, the superior-subordinate relationship continued.

As late as 1897 William E. Smythe, who was well known for his studies on reclamation, viewed the trans-Missouri West as a great place to plant colonies. He remarked that it was common to think of colonialism as a thing of the dead past but that all growing nations tended to employ it as a means of economic expansion, the United States being no exception. The difference, he explained, was that this country had no need to go beyond its borders to find homesites for its growing population because the colonial movement "of today and of the future" would be directed toward the arid regions of the West. As the new century approached, there remained in American thinking the picture of a "desert" West that waited only to be "reclaimed"— that is, watered and colonized. Smythe was writing in a day of hope, of prospects for the further "developing" of American real estate out there someplace. A little over three decades later, in the depths of an unprecedented depression, such optimism no longer existed. Presumably the hinterland had been drained of anything worthwhile, and now taxpayers were being billed for a dead horse. Or so the Knollenbergs and the Newtons appeared to think.

For their part, westerners also were taking a fresh, hard look at their place in the economic scheme of things. It took some time, but they gradually came to see themselves as poor relatives, not legitimate offspring who had hereditary rights to the family fortune. Around the turn of the century they had been called "the children of the nation—and favored children," a status they had accepted with some reservations in the years that preceded American participation in World War I. It was in this phase that westerners had begun to display signs of an emerging resentment toward the spiritual domination of the East, and they even exhibited a certain political restlessness. But then came the troublous twenties, when agriculture, stock raising, and mining declined sharply. It was then that the pangs of a regional inferiority complex began to become obvious.

In this period of nationwide disillusionment and self-doubt, the West began to think of itself not only as a neglected colonial but also, more precisely, as a weaker element in an organization in which stronger factions were taking advantage of those who were less able to protect themselves. As the haze of optimism was burned away, westerners, their jaws clenched and their brows furrowed, were analyzing their situation and defining their grievances much more clearly than in the past. And they were feeling trapped. The conviction was growing that what was once thought of as development was, indeed, nothing more than exploitation by outsiders. The main burden of colonialism was, in their eyes, the economic tether by which they now were being constrained. It enforced a thralldom that went straight to the pocket nerve, overshadowing all other forms of subordination. In the eyes of easterners it threatened to create, for the first time in the nation's history, an American peasantry.

The traditional target of those who complained about outside control was, of course, the railroad industry. Discriminatory rates long had been a western grievance, one that dated back to the 1870s, climaxed about twenty years later, and remained a dormant dissatisfaction during the ensuing years. As was true in an earlier day, the outrage generated by the levying of inequitable freight rates ebbed and flowed with the price of grain and the general level of prosperity in the West. Not unexpectedly, the downturn in western economic conditions during the 1920s generated a search for a villain. An old and sure-fire one was waiting in the wings: rail rate schedules.

In 1926 an Idaho senator introduced a bill that was designed to better balance the differential between long-haul and short-haul rates. All mountain-state senators except those from Colorado voted for it. It goes without saying that the bill failed; even the Pacific Coast states voted against it. It was ironic that Colorado should have been among the negative votes, for its mineral and agricultural industries were no better off than were those of its sister states. Perhaps Colorado had not felt the bite sufficiently by 1926, but three years later there was evidence that times were changing. By then, Frederick Bonfils, publisher of the *Denver Post,* had come forth as a champion of those who wanted to control rail rates. He conceded that in an earlier day, when the West was thinly populated and railroads were fighting for their lives, they had to charge more, but now there was no justification for such conduct. He recommended the formation of a Rocky Mountain League of States, the combined power of which would force roads to moderate their charges. Bonfils argued that the region ought to be free from outside financial control, and in his demands for collective action he used such terms as *justice* and *square deal.*

In Colorado it was not only the little people, the small users, who had grievances against the financial giants who wielded power from afar. The sting of the lash had been felt by local corporations, the most recent of which had seen New York bankers and rival railroads stop David Moffat's efforts to build a line from Denver to Salt Lake City in the years before World War I. Before that, the Denver and Rio Grande Western Railroad had faced a similar situation, one that dogged it all during its early years; and one of the road's major goals while coming out of bankruptcy after World War II was to maintain control of its own financial destiny. That it succeeded was heralded by its directors as a landmark of progress for the line.

Although railroads were the traditional "enemy" and a favorite topic when westerners talked about financial peonage, the influence of the "foreign" money masters and large corporations had extended far beyond that by the twenties. "Even if you start a grocery store in a small town," said a western lawyer in 1927, "some chain may come along and beat you to it." He admitted that one could own a farm or practice a profession in the West, but any other avenue reached a dead end in the backyard of big business. And where were the big businesses? In the East, he said. As historian Walter Webb wrote of those years, the small-town merchants of the West were locked into a form of bondage that necessitated the payment of tribute to north-eastern financial centers.

Lamentations of this nature failed to move a great many residents in other parts of the country. Those who lived in the depression-ridden East already had expressed concern about supporting poor relatives out West, and now, at a time when belt tightening at home was called for, they were to have even greater complaints when New Dealers began to hand out money with a lavish hand to these sufferers of the sagebrush. Once again, said those from older sections of America, the country cousins were getting a larger proportionate slice of the federal pie.

Westerners did not object to generous helpings at the family table. Not yet. For the moment they were perfectly happy to see the New Deal bail them out. When criticized as deadbeats, they pointed out that they could hardly support themselves entirely, because much of their land was owned by the government and therefore was beyond their power to tax. Here was a refrain to be heard for generations to come. By the 1930s the government had given away or sold about all the land it ever would. A lot of the West was left under federal control, and it remains so today. In 1980 the federal government owned about 1 percent of New York and Ohio, 6 percent of North Carolina, and 9 percent of Michigan. Across the hundredth meridian, however, the numbers changed dramatically. Uncle Sam owned about 35 percent of Colorado and New Mexico, 50 percent of Wyoming, 65 percent of Utah and Idaho, and nearly 90 percent of Nevada. Particularly during the hard depression years, it seemed only fair that the Great White Father should pay his rent on the far side of the river.

Besides that, the western "colonists" during the 1930s still felt at ease accepting support from the national capital, though many of their children and grandchildren would feel differently. During the depression, westerners lived in the last of the "contiguous forty-eight" to be settled. They had waited as territories outside the union of equal states much longer than had their predecessors east of the Mississippi, and they were accustomed to thinking of Washington, D.C., not their own capital cities, as the controlling force. Federal agencies had been among them from the start and had parceled out the allotted money. Not infrequently these dispensers had constituted some of the better oases in the financial desert.

Thus, when the New Dealers arrived and renewed the greening of the West, the locals took their customary places in line—sometimes twice—and took all they could get. Then, as was the custom, when times got better, they attacked their benefactors and accused them of trying to prostitute the innocents with temptations from the big city.

Such behavior recalled earlier times, when westerners had damned the army for its bungling, for not killing off the red natives fast enough; but at the same time they eagerly had sought the establishment of posts to which they could sell horses and hay, beef, and booze. Now, in the thirties, government offices, often manned by outside political appointees, were doling out the largess. Local politicians, who did not have that kind of money, could not compete for votes on even terms, so they began to complain about remote control and to moan over the enslavement of a once-free people.

A foretaste of the militancy that was to emerge among western States' rights advocates made national news in 1943 with the outbreak of the comic-opera "Jackson Hole War" in Wyoming. That spring, when Franklin Roosevelt's executive order set aside 221,610 acres of land adjacent to Grand Teton National Park to establish Jackson Hole National Monument, local Paul Reveres saddled up and spread the cry that an invasion of outlanders was taking place. Those who felt that they had been set upon were further irritated by the realization that the withdrawn tract included 32,117 acres that had been acquired gradually by the Rockefellers, with the intention of giving it to the federal government for preservation purposes. As these westerners saw it, a second enemy, one representing financial royalty, had thrown in with the tyrants from Foggy Bottom to drive honest yeomen of the Rockies from the king's forest. Wyoming newspapers and politicians rallied around the folks of Teton County, who complained that they had been robbed of valuable taxable property, not to mention the loss of grazing, hunting, and fishing possibilities. The aggrieved struck back by calling for a moratorium on the buying of war bonds; Teton County quickly sank to the bottom of the state's list.

True westerners could do better than that. Talk was cheap, and passive resistance had no part in the pioneer tradition. Onto the scene now rode forty horsemen, armed to the teeth and accompanied by old-time movie actor Wallace Beery, who hit the saddle for some real-life drama. Well, almost hit the saddle; an ugly rumor had it that he was obliged to use a ladder to board his steed. Billed as a "rancher," Beery's sole claims to the title were a lease that he had on a half-acre of Forest Service land and his lone bovine, an old milk cow, which recently had expired.

The campaign fizzled as the light brigade drove a few startled cows across the newly forbidden land in a pallid show of defiance. The park superintendent, who had no taste for cattle wars, made no effort to deter the vigilantes in their quest for justice. Such acquiescence brought roars of protest from feisty Harold L. Ickes, secretary of the Interior, who called the horsemen "ghost-hunting cowboys" running around in "mail-order regalia" and engaged in mock heroics.

Nay, cried the head of the Wyoming Stockgrowers Association, no such thing. This was a mounted Boston Tea Party, carried out by patriots who were determined to preserve their God-given rights. "We will never rest until we are in fact, as well as in name, sovereign states," he informed his critics. Following along in the historical jet stream, Governor Lester Hunt struck a Lincolnesque pose and announced that his domain was "half free and half slave." Implications of revolution or a miniature civil war wafted eastward from Wyoming.

Washington listened. In December 1944, Congress passed a bill that abolished the Jackson Hole National Monument, and Roosevelt promptly gave it a pocket veto. But the complaints continued, and in 1950 another bill was passed that abolished the monument. As a trade-off, most of the contested land was added to Grand Teton National Park; the act had been performed, but under another cover.

By the end of World War II the western states were openly denouncing the degree to which federal control had fastened itself upon their part of the land. Early in 1945, governors and other western representatives, meeting at Reno, Nevada, spoke out against this encroachment by the central government and formally demanded the return of their "rights and functions lost to the federal government during the war." It was a public admission that the West simply had moved from one form of colonialism to another.

The war extended federal colonialism even in a negative way. During those years the region lost population to enlistments and to war industries outside the area. The vacuum thus created tended to drive out people who were not affected directly by either of these forces but whose businesses suffered; tourism serves as one example. There were, of course, isolated exceptions to the outflow. Cities such as Denver, Salt Lake City, and Las Vegas grew, but the fact remained that by V-J Day in 1945, the region's head count was smaller than it had been in 1940.

Lack of growth—which has traditionally been regarded as an American disgrace—generated cries of dismay and a sharpened antagonism from those who felt oppressed. Now it became popular to turn on the federal government and to accuse it of trying to stifle the West by smothering private enterprise. The Missouri Valley Author-

With its Texaco and Conoco service stations, Dillon, Colorado, was feeding on the West's growing tourism in 1949. Today it is submerged beneath Lake Dillon—part of a ski resort for modern vacationers. (Courtesy, Colorado Historical Society)

ity, for example, was loudly opposed by a group of westerners who listened to power-company lobbyists and came away convinced that their hereditary rights were being eroded.

These were merely signs that once more the natives were getting restless. Colorado poet Thomas Hornsby Ferril, a sensitive and perceptive man, watched the western emotional seismograph at the end of the war and noted some rumblings in the Rockies. In those early peacetime days he predicted: "The westerner is going to become more rampant, more articulate. He bristles and foams at hearing Thurman Arnold say that the western states are being treated as 'colonies of the mother country—the industrial East.'" The folks in Laramie, Arnold's home town, probably bristled and foamed a little more when, in 1937, he commented that anyone who had any sense would not settle in Wyoming, where he thought both money and intellectual contacts were in short supply. He was not mimicking De Voto, the expatriate who had heaped scorn upon Ogden, Utah; rather, he was trying to show that colonialism stunted development. "Economic disadvantage creates a backward country," he wrote. Like De Voto, however, Arnold felt that the West's lack of development was not simply a natural occurrence; it had been imposed. These critics were willing to compare the region to the American colonies before the Revolution in the mother country's denial of industry. Charges such as these brought nods of agreement from westerners and added to their already-well-developed sense of inferiority. As always, they welcomed a scapegoat when they were unable to pinpoint their own difficulties.

If all the charges of colonialism were true, then the West appeared to be held in thralldom by, not one, but two masters: Wall Street and Washington. In a series of articles, from his perch in the "Easy Chair" at *Harper's,* De Voto thundered his charges against the eastern establishment for half a decade after the war. Much of his writing simply reiterated or expanded upon his "Plundered Province" article of August 1934. Rail-rate inequities, usurious interest charges, absentee ownership, tariff protection for eastern manufacturers, the control of capital by casterners, the stifling of western industries by driving them to the wall with eastern monopolistic branches, and economic favoritism to the East in general—all were favorite launching pads for De Voto's multiple literary rockets. None of them was new, but there was a readership for these recycled ideas, and De Voto packaged them very attractively.

The surfacing of this postwar populism was not entirely surprising, if one considers the restlessness of the West during the preceding two decades, but it was not cast quite in the classic pattern. No William Jennings Bryan came forth; there was no "Sockless Jerry" Simpson, no Mary Elizabeth Lease, and no "Bloody Bridles" Waite to whip angry voters into a froth before sending them wild-eyed to the ballot boxes. There were writers, commentators, and university professors who held that the West still was a "company domain," and their warnings about the dire consequences of such a condition were gladly printed by eastern publishers, whose interest in the colonies was one of long standing.

This time, however, there was something hollow about the West's protest. Looking back, it was World War II that shifted and redefined the terms of the debate over colonialism, just as the global conflict changed so much else in the region. The war returned prosperity to the country at large and triggered a boom in the West that in many ways continues today. Though the East's complaints about the worthless hinterland continued in some quarters, businessmen began to look beyond the Missouri with a new interest after 1945. The view of the West as a wasteland and as an economic rathole no longer held the stage alone. In the West, business-oriented community leaders were working hard to wipe the dust off and to pound the dents from the old image of the country as a land of opportunity and sure profits. Under these circumstances, there was a need for a different villain. Western complaints about outside control still were heard, but now the oppressor was, not Eastern businessmen, but the national government, which had helped prop up the West during the depths of the depression.

So as Colorado economist Morris Garnsey noted, there was little outcry from the old Populist country about absentee ownership; instead, there was loud complaint about the government as landlord and as an enemy of States' rights. He was convinced that the traditional control that big business had exercised over the West's political apparatus had resulted in an ingrained notion that the federal government was out to stifle economic exploration and development. Garnsey strongly opposed the absentee ownership by the business world, but he also admitted that the federal government was the biggest absentee owner of all, a landlord in whose grasp most of the West lay. He added, however, that Washington had created more economic activity than it had suppressed and so was less harmful. Future western development, therefore, depended directly on the area's transportation, communications, and other major areas of economic activity.

In effect this is what the business-courting community leaders of the postwar West were complaining about. They wanted development at any cost, and they regarded the central government as the principal barrier to that expansion. They did not, to be sure, want Washington to release its western lands to them. Little of it would be profitable in private hands. Instead, they wanted to be able to use it with the fewest possible restraints. In the terms of the day, the debate raged over whether growth was to be "natural"—that is, unregulated and presumably "free"—or a controlled hothouse growth, supervised by planners from afar. The outriders and trumpeters of these latter-day business pioneers were the cattlemen, who still held a strong and somewhat disproportionate influence in various western legislatures and who were fond of making loud noises about the diminution of their legendary rights to grazing on the public domain. They were ready to ride once more, at the customary drop of a hat.

Meanwhile the argument grew hotter over just how tightly the West was being held in the coils of its ancient colonial subservience. Depending upon whom one read, the answer varied from no to yes, from somewhat to maybe. The freight-rates tether remained a popular part of the argument, with journalists and professors alike joining in the cry against these transportation companies, but in the decade and a half after the end of the war, there were those who contended that despite remoteness and discriminatory long-haul rates, the West had established a measure of economic independence.

Leonard J. Arrington, Utah's widely respected economic historian, supported this view in his study of the regional economy for the years 1940–60. He concluded that the West was moving in the general direction of economic maturity because of its declining reliance upon the exportation of its resources to sustain itself.

From the vantage point of 1940 the great "break through," which later was said to have resulted from the war and its immediate aftermath, did not appear to hold much promise. Scholars of that day still regarded the West as a "vast, new colonial empire," one that was potentially rich but was still poor because of its lack of development. The region continued to be viewed as a raw-material resource annex, one that was "destined to remain for many years to come a vast, unused storehouse of wealth, awaiting the needs of a future America."

However, said Arrington, the ensuing two decades belied that prediction. In citing four important changes in the Mountain West during those years, he summarized the observations of a great many people who had watched the unfolding panorama. Figures for tourism had soared, making climate and scenic attractions a major industry. There was far less dependence upon agriculture and mining than before. For the first time in history the Mountain West could boast of manufacturing on a significant scale, the steel complexes of Utah and Colorado being important examples. And lastly, the area was a beneficiary of enormous outlays for defense spending, a market that the West was now sharing with other portions of the country. While his tests applied especially to the mountain portion of the region and were true only in varying degrees to the plains country, there is enough application to the entire West that is being considered here to use the broader generalization when talking about colonialism.

As western financial leaders watched the peacetime economy emerge from the war years, they saw changes around them. They noticed that western bank assets, which had totaled a little over $7 billion in 1940, had tripled by 1948, giving rise to the feeling that local projects increasingly were able to rely upon "inside money" for assistance. Elroy Nelson, vice-president of Salt Lake City's First Security Corporation, expressed a hope that was shared by his colleagues when he said, "We're growing up industrially." The war, he thought, had accounted for a recent speed-up in that evolution. It was an episode that had "telescoped decades of development into a few years," and he thought it suggested the end of a century of colonialism.

Efforts to bring industry, and hence independence, to the West during these postwar years provided a new scenario, but even that was not without its problems. For about a quarter of a century after 1945, state and local community leaders made a concerted effort to attract new business to the western states. Each year, little groups of commercial missionaries were sent eastward to sing the praises of a new frontier and to woo capital. They offered climate, a cheap and docile labor force that could boast of little or no organization, favorable building sites, tax breaks, and other inducements. However, these solicitations in the big city were not indiscriminate. The scouting parties were on the lookout for small, clean "Swiss type" industries that would not pollute physical or civic atmospheres out there where the skies are not cloudy all day. It was hoped that through this selectivity the residents, both old and new, would have fewer complaints about the resultant growth; but as it turned out, these expectations were not realized.

As always, the eastern corporate establishment responded to the call, especially when the natives indicated a renewed urge to fondle a few trade beads. "Clean" industries began to plant outposts along the mountain front and throughout the Rockies. When *Esquire-Coronet*'s subscription department, Minneapolis-Honeywell Regulator, Hewlett-Packard, Beech Aircraft, Eastman Kodak, and IBM came to such a state as Colorado, they added to the tax base and hired the "right" kind of employees. Governmental installations, such as the Air Force Academy at Colorado Springs, the Central Radio Propagation Laboratory of the National Bureau of Standards (on donated land), the Atomic Energy Commission's cryogenics engineering laboratory, and the National Center for Atmospheric Research, all at Boulder, brought large payrolls and some highly trained personnel to the area. When Ball Brothers Research Corporation, a descendant of a well-known Indiana fruit-jar manufacturer, located at Boulder and began to process a number of federal contracts that were important to the space program, another nonpolluter had nestled against the Rockies.

The solicitation of these carefully selected industries offered yet another variation of the colonialism that had so annoyed westerners. As commercial implants, they were operated by remote control and were staffed, at least at the upper levels, by outsiders who at once sought to shape their new, if temporary, homes by demanding that these places retain their size, quaintness, and outlook. At the same time they lamented the fact that culturally the West was a desert. Those who followed the corporate flag westward were themselves

The National Center for Atmospheric Research, nestled against the foothills of the Rockies in Boulder, Colorado, one of scores of government-funded scientific agencies established after World War II. (Courtesy, National Center for Atmospheric Research/National Science Foundation)

colonists in a commercial sense. Frequently they thought of their jobs merely as assignments to one of their employer's outposts, and upon retirement, they would settle somewhere in a land of their particular dreams. They did not always hit it off well with the "old" colonists who, in the case of Colorado, responded by displaying bumper stickers that read "Native," a kind of family crest meant to put strangers in their places. The "strangers" posted "Who Cares?" bumper stickers on their cars.

During the years in which the search was on for noncontaminating industries, there were indications that some of the old reprobates, who had long been accused of befouling both the physical and the political climate of the West, were beginning to show signs of reform. One of these was the Anaconda Copper Mining Company, grimly referred to by Montanans as "old copper collar." As late as 1930, Oswald Garrison Villard was assuring his readers that Montana was a dual entity, one in which the influence of "the company" controlled the state by penetrating "every aspect of its business, social and political life."

By the early postwar years there were signs that the collar and the leash were less in evidence. True, the old reputation was hard to lose, and its echoes reached as far away as London, where Butte was called "an ugly and disgraceful monument to the search for corporate wealth" and where Anaconda Copper was said to control the press, radio stations, railroads, congressional representatives, state legislators, and even Montana's hotels. But closer to home the talk was softer. Joseph Kinsey Howard, who was often referred to as Montana's conscience, thought he detected a kindly look on Anaconda's countenance as it viewed the peons of its holdings. Before the astonished eyes of Butte, he wrote, the company had hit the sawdust trail and actually was assisting in community improvements, trying to make that declining, beat-up old mining camp a better family town. The company's subsequent relaxation of its long-time grip on the state's press was another indicator, but that one was more a palliative than a cure for colonialitis.

A generation later, Montana historian Michael P. Malone reexamined this issue and agreed that about the time Joe Howard made his assessment, the company indeed had begun to inch away from its nineteenth-century approach. It was his opinion that by the mid 1970s, Anaconda was no longer exercising much control over the state, and he even argued that while it once had been a big fish in a small pond, "it never had the place to itself." Perhaps. But there were other reasons for relaxing the leash. The company had suffered from some unhappy international experiences, had fallen on hard times because of depressed markets, and no longer had the stake in Montana that it once had coveted. Beyond that, it has been suggested that the state had commenced to grow up a little and was being less submissive to its former masters, of which Anaconda merely was one.

If, indeed, the corporate throat hold was slackening in Montana's case, there were complaints of a new threat from another part of the plains-mountains West. For years, Nevadans had thought of their state—the "rotten borough" as Gilman Ostrander called it—as a colony, not of the East, but of California. Over the years they had struggled for self-sufficiency, but as late as the 1950s, their personal income from mining was a mere 1.2 percent of the total and from ranching was only 2.5 percent. Comparatively, government employees accounted for 15.6 percent, while amusement and recreation stood at almost double that amount. The last two sets of figures indicated outside money and, with that, the suggestion of remote control.

But before outsiders become interested, one must show that the local gold mine is paying off. Offering a twin bill of easy divorce and legalized gambling, Nevadans gradually perfected a system that was open to even the poorest Americans, especially the masses from nearby California. Lures so numerous as to defy the imagination were concocted to entice folks across the Sierra. Weekend come-ons and freebies of all kinds sang siren songs to the wealthy, to the not-so-wealthy, and to pensioners, busloads of whom arrived as if in cattle trains. All of them were encouraged to divest themselves of their worldly goods. Lest any scraps be missed, Nevadans redesigned their tax structures to attract investors from the outside, especially Californians who once literally had pumped the Silver State dry. These hosts took particular satisfaction in plucking Golden State geese and settling some old scores.

Ironically, those who were making Las Vegas a gambling Mecca were creating from nothing a new gold rush, taking billions back from California and the world by appealing to the same sense of adventure and the grasping obsession that had brought the forty-niners flooding into the Golden State a century before. More than any other modern-day hucksters, they understood the possibilities of tapping the fantasy of the western bonanza, the hallowed belief that out in the wilds of the deserts or mountains, one could turn one's life around by panning the right gravel or turning the right card. And oh, how the money rolled in—for the owners, that is. By the 1960s, Nevada was one of the western leaders in per capita income, most of which came from what was tactfully called "trade and service industries." Gross revenues from gaming on the Las Vegas strip alone approached $270 million in 1969, and in most years the profits from the MGM Grand Hotel surpassed the total from all films made by the parent corporation. Success, however, had its price. In baiting

By 1948 a new gold rush was on, this time in Nevada, where Californians and other Americans were lured to cities such as Las Vegas by easy divorce and legalized gambling. (Courtesy, Nevada Historical Society)

the trap, a different set of visitors moved in, and now the cry was heard not only that was Nevada a long-time annex to California but, worse, that the place now was in danger of being taken over by outside financial masters, some of whom were said to have more than casual relationships with organized crime. Once more, western resources were being mined by strangers who were using the locals merely as the extractive labor force.

In the agonizing over its status, there were arguments that the West also remained a colonial region in a cultural sense. In 1973, *Newsweek* carried a complaint from a westerner to the effect not only that his area was shackled in an intellectual sense but also that the condition was getting worse. Once, he said, the West had had a score of vigorous regional magazines, but they no longer existed. Nor, he said, did a single national news program or political commentary originate in the West. Programming decisions, as well as media investment policies, had their sources in New York. "So gradually," he wrote, "I have grown to accept that I live in an intellectual, artistic and political suburb, a colony of the East."

There were other signs that in this sense the West remained a virgin land. Historian Gerald Nash suggested that the under-developed nature of the prewar West had left it open and available as a testing ground of all sorts, a place for experiments in education, science, architecture, cultural departures, and life styles. It also was a place where the original atomic bomb had been tested.

Use of a barren land as a testing laboratory speaks more of colonialism than it does of an emerging society. Even in residential land use, where suburban enclaves were developed in an irregular pattern within the conventional rectangular patterns, the effort was made to transplant an eastern trend rather than to originate. Despite arguments that the West was used as a hothouse for sprouting seeds of change, the results of which experiments sometimes were accepted elsewhere, the West that we are considering here remained mainstream and conservative in its outlook.

The political side of that conservatism emphasized increasingly the cry that it was not the business masters who posed the greatest threat from outside; rather, the bureaucratic overlords from the nation's capital were manipulating the sovereign's western satrapies. Part of this attitude derived from frontier days, when men were supposed to have moved west to get more breathing room and to find freedom from restraint. Settlers who came out, took up free land, demanded protection against the Indians, and complained when the rural-free-delivery carrier couldn't make it through the mud always reserved the right to be "agin the guvmint." It helped to preserve the fiction of their independence.

The hard liners among the conservatives were the cattlemen. The end of the open range had meant a considerable loss of political power; nevertheless, the one-time "Kings" were not without influence in the legislatures. In 1916, at a time when these lords of the open range were near the end of their heyday, a Nevada sociologist by the name of Romanzo Adams looked at the situation in his state and concluded that their fall from grace was more apparent than real. The 1910 census, he wrote, revealed that 82 percent of Nevada's so-called farmland was controlled by cattlemen. There were 344 "farms" that ranged in size from 1,000 to 175,000 acres, and although the amount of Nevada that was devoted to even this form of agriculture was relatively small, only 1 percent of it was "improved." For Nevada the Homestead Act had been a signal failure; the state's stockmen simply had moved from one kind of control to another. Adams suggested that the grazers should rent government land, subject to rules that would protect the grazing, and should pay nominal fees, only a portion of the full rental value of the range land. He anticipated the Taylor Grazing Act of 1934.

The Taylor Act was only part of the New Deal's efforts to alleviate the stockmen's difficulties and to provide a sensible, equitable plan for grazing. During the depression, problems on the range made many a rancher wonder if the days of raising cattle were about over;

severely depressed prices and drought had withered their future, just as it had that of the farmers. But the federal government came to the aid of these rugged individualists with substantial financial injections, and for many of them, it saved the day. Lorena Hickok wrote to Harry Hopkins from Cheyenne, in the fall of 1934, saying: "By and large, the cattlemen appear to be deeply appreciative of what the Government is doing to help them out. 'Many of us are desperate,' one of them told me. 'I think we'd just pack up and move out and leave our stock to starve if the Government hadn't stepped in. This gave us new hope, to try again.' "

But in the West, gratitude is a particularly fragile, evanescent quality, and memories of favors done by the government are spectacularly brief. War followed depression, and there was demand for agricultural products, especially beef. Within a very few years those agents who rode tall in the saddle or in the Ford pickup, who doffed their Stetsons to womenfolk, and who paid homage to no man had moved back into the nineteenth century, and cussing the feds again became a favorite indoor sport. The postwar years spawned a new generation of home-grown entrepreneurs, young business types who took up the cry that Washington controlled the purse strings; and here the cattlemen found new allies. Various interests that were desirous of utilizing the West's federal domain now joined in a propaganda campaign that would force this foreign power, which was located on the banks of the Potomac, to "give back" land to states that had never owned it in the first place.

It was entirely appropriate to western history that the cattlemen provided the outriders for the modern army of liberators. Theirs was the image of white hats riding to the rescue, of sacrifice and selfless contribution to the forces of right—the far Right in this case—and of justice in the land of the free. Actually they were motivated by no such high ideals; all they wanted was their own key to the range lands' executive washroom. They were not descendants of Owen Wister's hero; rather, they were men whose political views recalled the attitudes of their forefathers, who had once ruled the cow country; they were modern beef producers who had seen too many John Wayne movies.

What especially moved these latter-day beef barons to reach for their figurative shooting irons was the trumpeting of a fresh group of colonials, modern "nesters" who had fled the crowded regions of both coasts for the free air of the open and unsullied West. Many of these recent arrivals were attracted by the evangelism of a crusading element known to their detractors as "Ecofreaks," folks who appeared to be ready to fight against so much as the turning of a stone in a wilderness that they implied they had discovered and now claimed as their very own. Ironically the nature lovers tended to accept the garb of the cowmen and saw nothing inconsistent in wearing oversized Stetsons and in hobbling around in uncomfortable cowboy boots while admiring their recently claimed wilderness domain. The difference between the two groups lay in what was contained under the hats.

The average westerner fell between these two highly vocal groups as a faceless figure who appeared to have no opinion on the vital question of the day. This may have been due to the taciturnity attributed to his kind or because he was busy making a living and, as always, was chary of political noises in the background. He was not an alarmist, and therefore he came on as a mute and, even worse, an indifferent mute. Westerners, who long had complained about exploitation and tearing up the countryside, themselves were opposed to the destruction of the past, but they experienced some annoyance at the extremes to which some of the preservationists wanted to go.

What really generated the commotion over the use of western lands was the increased amount of economic activity in the postwar West, a transition that perhaps suggested the noisy birth pangs of the very independence that the area presumably was seeking. By the 1960s that growth was enough to excite westerners with its promise, while at the same time it alarmed a nationwide group of environmentalists, who began to push for wilderness areas. Lyndon B. Johnson's signature on the Wilderness Act of 3 September 1964 signified the extent of that group's strength, and it brought new cries from some westerners that the Old West was about to be turned into a preserve for bird watchers.

Earlier that year, Congressman Wayne Aspinall (D, Colo.) had identified the enemy when he had said, "If we let the East lock up these lands [for wildnerness] it will destroy the economy of the West." He argued, as did many of his constituents, that lands could be conserved while they were being utilized for limited and carefully controlled timbering, mining, grazing, and reclamation.

The threat of bureaucratic aggrandizement remained popular as one of the tools of the political trade. Fifteen years after Aspinall's warnings, presidential aspirant John Connally brought cheers from a group of Colorado Republicans when he declared: "I want to free the West of the bondage of bureaucracy in Washington." When he became president, he said, he would bring these colonials into the Union. Connally allowed as how he'd like to join the Sagebrush

Rebels. Later, Ronald Reagan expressed the same wish. Both men understood western Republican audiences.

During the tumultuous decade of the 1960s, when Americans were feeling a political irritation and a social nervousness, the complexities and contradictions in western attitudes toward the outside only deepened. For most of the region these were good years that promised to become even better. In such times, a leading news magazine noted, colonials were becoming leery of taking money from Washington on the ground that it merely would lead to tightened control over resources they wanted developed. The swelling conservation movement tended to stiffen the resolve of those who were trying to reduce the role of government regulation.

Even so, it was hard to break old habits. It was obvious that the new prosperity was due in part to the money that the federal government was shoveling across the hundredth meridian. During the '60s, New Mexico received more than $450 million from expenditures by the Atomic Energy Commission. Coloradans benefited from the payrolls of some thirty-seven thousand military personnel, not to mention some fourteen thousand civilian federal employees, and the spin-off from an additional $444 million in prime contracts. Neighboring Utah did only slightly less well at the national fiscal trough, while in Montana, government payrolls exceeded all others. In the "Treasure State" some forty-three thousand people worked for the state and local governments, and eleven thousand worked for the federal government, a figure that had doubled in twenty years. In 1969, Washington poured $644 million into Montana and got back $343 million in taxes. By 1981, Wyoming, Montana, and New Mexico were among the top five, per capita, in the amount of federal aid to state and local governments.

During these years this golden flow caused local politicians some problems. A good example of the dilemma facing those who stumped for reelection was the case of Republican Wallace Bennett of Utah in 1962. His published advertisements spoke out for better, not bigger, government and argued that federal aid should be sought only when state and local government could not afford to do the job. At the same time, Bennett reminded his constituents that he had worked hard for water projects, for aid to the Small Business Administration, and for research money to aid the local coal industry. In appreciation of this endorsement of independence, but one that included carefully drawn exceptions, the voters returned that solon to office. As one critic pointed out, the region argued that it could not live with the federal government, yet it gave every indication that it could not live without it. Its businessmen always endorsed cuts in federal spending while assuring the congressional delegation that their particular neighborhood had nothing it could sacrifice to the budgetary ax.

There were other evidences of the western political crunch. In 1963, when Senator Gale McGee (D, Wyo.) obtained for Park County, Wyoming, designation as an area of "persistent unemployment," in order to qualify it for emergency federal assistance, he was criticized by local residents. Yet his action was in response to a petition from the townsmen at Cody, the county seat, not a few of whom earlier had signed a "declaration of independence" from the federal government. Obviously these people had divided loyalties. Their city was the home of the state's first John Birch Society; and the Cody Club, a Chamber-of-Commerce-oriented organization, had originated the above-mentioned declaration. The fact that H. L. Hunt, one of the old-time economic gentry whom westerners had become used to saluting, had a summer place in the neighborhood added to the conservative ambience.

If westerners experienced a certain amount of bewilderment over the question of who were their masters, if indeed they had any masters, one of the explanations was to be found in the postwar changes being experienced by their part of America. At the beginning of that era one still heard numerous references to the sagebrush colonials, a sentiment that was most frequently evinced by liberals, both eastern and western, but as the years passed, there was more frequent talk of economic independence, one proof of which was said to be the region's increasing access to local capital. By the time the anticipated "Soaring Sixties" had come into view, the West was sharing a national expectation of prosperity, along with which came the cautious hope that the end of its own financial bondage was near. By then a national news weekly could say, "Today the West offers an industrial entity all its own," an entity that was said to be moving toward a long-cherished autonomy.

In many ways this was little more than a pat on the back from big brother. It cannot be denied that there was growth and development in the land of the Old West, but it was spotty and uneven. Colorado, with its historic economic connection with the East, worked hard to induce outside money and industry, while at the same time encouraging local enterprise, and the businesses that sprouted along this section of the Rocky Mountain front indicated a degree of success. Across the mountains, in Utah, there was similar development. These bits of evidence were encouraging to those who were promoting independence, and much was made of them in the press.

But others had second thoughts. In 1978 a writer for *American Heritage* looked again at De Voto's "plundered province" and concluded that while the Pacific Coast increasingly had found and developed its own resources, there was evidence to show that a replay was taking place in the part of the West that was traditioanlly accustomed to pillage. This time it included the strip mining of coal.

The picture was familiar. The energy-rich mountain region again was the scene of a boom, but it was one that appeared to pose more problems than it solved, and once more, the investment money had come largely from outside. Instead of being grateful for fresh income, the residents complained about overcrowded towns, a shortage of schools, an inability to cope with the imported crime wave, and, generally, of being brushed aside in the rush for riches by those who came to "git and git out."

As one visiting writer saw it, these industry-seeking communities had for so long been the poor stepchildren of the nation that when good fortune smiled, they "do not know how to react when the glass slipper finally fits." In other words, as De Voto once had suggested, it was again being inferred that the West did not really want to be liberated from the bondage that it so long had resented; rather, it wanted to "buy into it, cumulative preference stock if possible." There is, however, a difference between lying back supinely as the glass slipper is fitted and of owning part of the coach, the horses, and the coach-owners' kingdom. For a long time, westerners viewed the glass-slipper ceremony as one that suggested seduction, as opposed to a promise of wedlock and community property.

Thus, the notion of buying in was somewhat chimerical. A desire, a dream, but not a real prospect. At best the mineral-rich areas stood a chance to sell some of the subsurface holdings to outsiders. The mountain portions promised to remain largely as "diggin's" for the new prospectors, while out on the plains the modern coal miners were merely looking on the other side of the sod for a crop. As a well-known agricultural historian has remarked, the plains country would continue to be primarily a producer, surface or subsurface, and "its colonial status in relation to the rest of the nation will not change substantially." If anything, that status promised to become more pronounced because of a continuing decline in population among the agrarians. A diminished representation in Congress would reduce the already dwindling political influence of this group.

The prospect of a continued colonial role has not deeply concerned some elements of the western business community. The more aggressive commercial types have regarded the area, not as a cap-doffing dependent, but as one that had something to sell, as it always had something to sell; and from such transactions, westerners were supposed to make a living in the manner of their forebears. These latter-day traders, who still affected boots and broad-brimmed hats, liked to sit down with the monied folks from other parts and to join in economic games of chance—games called development—as opposed to acts of exploitation. They understood *independence* to be a word with positive connotations, but when dealing with land or resources, they held the short-run view that it mattered not if the money was local or imported. The long-run implications of financial control were not always a burning issue with those more interested in today than tomorrow and not at all interested in yesterday.

Therefore, those who regarded the central government's ownership and control of vast western regions as being a barrier to future development, not to mention a blot on the much-cherished notion of private enterprise, continued the arguments of yesteryear that the land was to be used, not hoarded. An opposing view held that a great body of westerners owed their living, not to mention their spiritual and physical well-being, to the fact that their government not only stood between them and the "developers" but also contributed to the West in a very positive way. They argued that even the cattlemen, who had spearheaded the "Sagebrush Rebellion," consistently had been helped, not hurt, by the officialdom that they appeared to hate so much. In addition to the vast amounts of land that stockmen earlier had controlled through an extremely liberal land policy, there were numerous instances of direct assistance from Washington. Mentioned were such things as help rendered in fighting foot-and-mouth disease, favorable legislation that offered protection against unfair packing practices, the subsidization of meat prices on occasion, and finally, numerous instances of direct, low-interest government loans.

As De Voto had suggested, the pervasiveness of the New Deal all across that thinly populated and yet undeveloped West later may have led to cries of a new servitude, but in truth, this penetration of the West rescued much of that region from the further ravages of economic colonialism by reversing the wasteful exploitation of resources with a program of rehabilitation, repair, and rebuilding. It offered alternative sources of credit, inexpensive electricity, which had never before been available to rural residents, badly needed water from expanded reclamation developments, and an impressive reforestation program by the Civilian Conservation Corps. It not only made life better for thousands of individual westerners, but in a field such as power development the government also helped to establish a base for the expansion of small industries, thereby initiating the first steps in the direction of economic independence.

And so it went. To some degree the relationship between the East and the West had always been one of parent and child, but the disastrous depression and the boom years that followed put new strains on the feelings between mom and her restless youngster. The West had stood for opportunities of various sorts—the chance to move and maneuver and wring fortunes from the land. But always westerners have required support from the outside, money from home to protect them and to get their various schemes off the ground. Behind this was the troublesome question of just how much profit and control the East could expect in return. The Great Depression threatened to destroy the mystique of a land of limitless possibilities. As eastern pundits advised cutting off the hinterland as a hopeless investment, westerners raged that all along, Wall Street had been milking them of their just rewards. Then, when businessmen of both regions again began to court one another after the war, the programs and controls of the government seemed to threaten both the image of opportunity and another sacred element of the mystique—independence.

The dilemma between support and control, investment and exploitation, has grown naturally from the economic realities of the West and the imagery of its myth. Consequently the debate over colonialism is probably with us for good. Often it has given the world a chance to see both sides at their worst. Eastern critics have sounded like a mother who has worked her children ragged on the family farm, then clutched a hankie to her bosom and sobbed how the brats have bled her dry. Westerners have taken advantage of eastern investment and, above all, government aid; but in the manner of ungrateful children, they have tried to bite the hand that fed them. True to their history, they have ignored the benefits and lashed out at their benefactors. As adolescents in the national family, they wanted the freedom to roam, but they still have turned up at mealtime and have always been around when the allowances were handed out. To them, Big Daddy in Washington remained the tight-fisted tyrant who unaccountably expected some kind of responsibility from the offspring.

CHAPTER 7

THE DUDES' WEST

The West's colonial relationship with the East has never been limited entirely to things economic. If investors have hoped to profit by long distance through the region's natural resources, millions of other Americans from Jersey City to Miami have been caught up in a similar enterprise during this century. Looking toward the sunset, these easterners also believe that the West can and should provide for some of their essential needs, but they are not concerned with coal, timber, copper, or wheat. Instead, they believe the West's most valuable commodities are wild, magnificent scenery, excitement, adventure, a bit of rusticity, and an occasional whiff of imagined danger. In other words, the chance to escape, briefly to be sure, the dailiness of their lives. As they pile into their station wagons and pull onto the interstate highways, they believe wholeheartedly that they are headed to see the "real" West, though much more often than not they will arrive somewhere else, in a place reconstructed by real westerners to fit the visions of these temporary pioneers with travelers checks.

These are some of the many constituents of the idealized West, and few of them are prouder of their claim to membership than those habitual visitors who technically may be called tourists but usually are referred to by the locals as "dudes."

As it is with many terms, the origins of the expression *dude* are not agreed upon. It is said to have come down from the Lowland Scots *duds,* or clothes. Canadian westerners used the term to describe certain immigrants and understood that it had derived from the German *Dudendop,* or lazy fellow. Webster's says it is an invented term that originated in 1883. Indeed, Bill Nye, the well-known Wyoming journalist-humorist, used the appellation that early. What it means is easier to explain. Purists used to describe such a person as being an easterner who was dressed in store clothes, as opposed to range-land garb. More broadly it has meant a stranger, a pilgrim, or a greenhorn—any of which has been used in a slightly deprecatory manner. Earlier it was associated with horseback-riding easterners, but in time it came to mean tourists in general.

More recently, young and irreverent westerners have taken to describing their guests as "turkeys"—behind their backs, but never

when standing behind the cash register. In kindness to those westerners, one might speculate that they refer to the tourist season as a time
of thanksgiving, in a financial sense. Conversely, the native-born are
called "savages." In any event, there are various grades of dudes,
and the ranking is broad enough to include those who head for
Wyoming or Montana to play cowboy for a couple of weeks and those
who stake out momentary homesteads with their Winnebagoes in a
KOA campground.

Whatever their descriptive title, these sightseers run the risk of
catching an old and virulent affliction that has struck down newcomers for well over a century. First-timers, who may show a proper
appreciation of the scenery, are not always deeply affected by the
atmosphere, social or climatic; but the jeans-and-Stetson disease
takes hold fairly rapidly. Second or third repeaters sometimes find
themselves drifting toward a possessiveness that surfaces early and is
identified by their announcement that the West is going to the dogs,
that too many tourists are cluttering up the place. They aspire to
membership in the club, and proof of their qualification is evinced by
a disdain for newcomers. If, after a respectable period of appren-
ticeship, one of the bronzed, bowlegged natives should by chance
infer in passing that there is a possibility for the pledge to become an
active, the result is a state of near euphoria. Should it happen, the
lucky recipient of the honor immediately sits tall in the saddle, even
without a horse. A summa cum laude, of course, would be the
initiation into one of the Indian tribes by somewhat bemused *genuine*
natives; but normally this is out of the question, because this is
usually accorded to presidents or to other members of the American
political royalty. The rank of honorary westerner is less difficult to
achieve, depending not so much upon rank or wealth as upon earnest
desire, unswerving faithfulness, and blind loyalty.

This is by no means a recent phenomenon. For at least two
centuries, travelers, of both foreign and domestic varieties, have
acquired special attitudes about the national hinterland. Their
accounts of a generously endowed land, exaggerations of its beauty,
distance, and climatic variations, not to mention the special breed of
people who seemed to grow out of this rare atmosphere, are replete
with such references. Not only has a great body of literature emerged
from these impressions; they have also made possible the firm rooting
of one of our principal national myths—the heroic frontiersman and
his stamping ground, the West. For many a young eastern boy it
became a lifelong ambition to see this fabled land and to breathe the
magic atmosphere. Now and then it took on near-religious propor-

Western tourism is new only in its scope. Resorts such as the Antlers, which opened in 1883 in Colorado Springs (nicknamed "Li'l Lunnon"), catered to well-to-do easterners and Europeans. (Courtesy, Denver Public Library, Western History Department; photo by H. S. Poley)

tions and produced a missionary zeal that called for a pilgrimage. A good example was the Bostonian Hall J. Kelley, one of the near fanatics of the nineteenth century, who became obsessed over Oregon.

The opening of western trails, over which pioneer families traveled, made the first inroads into the monopoly of masculinity that previously had characterized adventuring in these parts. Construction of the so-called transcontinental railroads went a step further, so altering the nature of western travel that outdoor-minded males were driven more deeply into the wilderness.

Now women and their children could see the West in comfort, and out of this grew resorts such as Marshall Sprague was talking about when he dubbed Colorado Springs "Newport in the Rockies." The late nineteenth century saw lawn tennis, genteel mountain climbing, cocktails, and high society at "Li'l Lunnon," as the new town was called. Those who were bored with summering at Saratoga, New York, could find their way west in comfort, and indeed, if they cherished the name, they could even try Saratoga, Wyoming.

Harvey Houses offered comfortable accommodations with a taste of local color for travelers on the Santa Fe line. The La Fonda Hotel, shown here around 1930, is still a popular Santa Fe, New Mexico, attraction. (Photo by T. Harmon Parkhurst; courtesy, Museum of New Mexico; neg. no. 10688)

Despite all the nostalgic drivel that has been written about cruising the wilderness by parlor car, the railroads never cared much for passengers, and almost from the beginning, the management of western lines complained that such traffic wasn't all that profitable. Not so very long ago, the president of one of these roads remarked, ''Freight doesn't complain.'' This, in pre-Amtrak days, was at a time when 95 percent of his company's income was from freight. But passengers were a necessary evil. Earlier the roads had put up with them because they did contribute something to the company coffers and, later, because the Interstate Commerce Commission held a whip over the railroads.

Tourism pleased the towns along the lines; places such as Denver counted heavily upon income from tour groups and conventions. Some of the early rail tourists had money, even enough to charter private cars, and the whole western business community, the railroads included, were anxious to offer these visitors opportunities to invest in a new and developing country. More than one wealthy tubercular brought his bank account west and bought in. James John Hagerman, who built the Colorado Midland Railroad, is one such example.

*Named for Buffalo Bill's youngest daughter, the Irma Hotel in Cody,
Wyoming, shown here in 1903, featured the latest in comfort and elegance.
(Courtesy, Wyoming State Archives, Museums and Historical Department)*

As the twentieth century got under way, there developed a growing
inclination on the part of the roads to give tourists more than a
routine plucking when they ventured westward. The Fred Harvey
system of Santa Fe Railroad fame is a case in point. Originally the
"Harvey girls" had minced about hungry travelers and railroad
employees, attending to their digestive systems; but other than that,
little effort had been made to attract customers. After 1900 the
Harvey Houses flossied up their surroundings and sought to induce
longer visits by adding a little luxury to their already excellent
accommodations and service. Few people who stop at Santa Fe today
miss a chance to see or possibly stay at La Fonda Hotel, one of the
town's leading tourist attractions. It is only one of the links in that
chain of Spanish-named hostelries.

Wyoming showed the traveling public that it could combine history
with comfort when, in 1902, the Irma Hotel—named for Buffalo
Bill's youngest daughter—was opened at Cody. This $80,000 luxury
spot featured "the celebrated Ostermoor mattresses and springs"; it
was heated by steam, lighted by gas, and had a telephone in every
room. For the gentlemen there were an elegant bar, a billiard hall,
and a barbershop. All milk, cream, and vegetables came from the
management's own farm. It also was ready for tourists, as distinguished from routine traveling customers. The livery stable was
equipped with "all kinds of rigs, saddle and driving horses, camp and

pack outfits, with experienced guides for hunting and fishing parties and tourists." Extending a hand to the eastern brethren, the owners announced, "Everything is modern and first-class." It sounded so good it almost killed any desire to see the Wild West.

But that was the job of the publicists. Their task was to transform the West into an attraction that had more to offer than endless horizons and fresh air. They denied that New Mexico was a land of "arid and sun-burned monotony," as some unkind soul had called it, and argued that it contained some sights worthy of the tourists' attention. Santa Fe was said to offer not only climate, history, and fine hotels but also a charming quaintness. This was to counter the contention that the West undeniably was grand but that it just wasn't picturesque.

That limitation had to be overcome, and westerners set about making improvements by quainting up the place at the risk of being ridiculous. Some of Colorado's modern ski resorts are an example of picturesque planning gone wild. The earlier, if ersatz, Swiss chalets of Glacier Park are somewhat more appropriate, being located in the "American Alps" and executed with moderation. The natives are not entirely to blame for the use of such lures. Highly paid eastern landscape architects and designers have produced what they imagine the dudes are looking for. This is just another price that the westerners have to pay to get their hands on some of that despicable eastern money.

Although tourism was undergoing a change at the turn of the century, this did not occur without resistance by those known as travelers, as opposed to the term *tourists,* people of means who for some years had been viewing the West as members of upper-crust society. One of the attractions of the western watering places was their remoteness from more populous areas and the likelihood that customers who paid well would not be trampled under foot by three-day trippers or, as a contemporary put it, by "hordes of hoodlums who desecrate the nearby beauty spots." That would come later. In a fiscal sense, expensive means exclusive, and those who had money for western vacations assumed that part of their prospective pleasure was to be found in such privacy. It was like going West in a Concorde—the airplane, that is, not the Concord stagecoach.

One of the refuges sought by those who disdained association with the common clay was the dude ranch. While it was nearly as old as the settled West itself—as early as the 1870s, Colorado ranches were taking paying guests—this institution reached the height of its popularity in the 1920s and 1930s.

During the 1880s, monied Britons had often stayed at ranches, using them as bases for hunting trips or just for enjoying the West. At about this time, Howard Eaton, a South Dakotan, began to charge for meals, which he had been giving away. The practice was regarded by neighboring ranchmen as being somewhat mercenary, but the degree of his success gave them pause for thought. In a few years, Eaton moved to the foot of the Big Horns in Wyoming for better hunting, fishing, and climate. Among members of the dude-ranching fraternity, he is generally accepted as the founding father, although there were other early dude ranchers, such as N. J. ("Dick") Randall of Gardiner, Montana.

As the popularity of these places grew, most of the clientele came, not from abroad, but from the more settled and citified parts of America. The men who ran the dude ranches soon learned that there was an important difference between the imported tourist and the home-grown variety. Daniel J. Boorstin, among others, has described the distinction. European travelers, particularly upper-class Englishmen who were taking "the tour" of the world's exotic places, traditionally were looking and hoping for the new, the unanticipated. They longed to be surprised. To them, travel broadened the traveler by exposing him to what he never dreamed could be. Americans, on the other hand, know full well what they want to find when they go a-touring. From the start, our people have traveled to find the expected, and if it is not there, we are outraged. Nowhere has this been more true than in the West. Americans demand yodeling Swiss in the Alps and bedouins on camels next to the pyramids; and in Colorado and Arizona they will have their breech-clouted Indians and cowboys in the saddle. This phenomenon has produced the false fronts and rough wood that are so characteristic of shops and stores in the region's tourist areas, not to mention places like Old Tucson, which sprang full blown from the popular imagination, with its staged gunfights, boot hills, and university coeds posing in saloons as saucy Miss Kittys. The dude ranchers were the first to face this peculiar American attitude, and they learned to play it beautifully.

During the initial phases of this new kind of western ranching, the visitors stood somewhat apart, much in the manner of Maine's summer crowd, their language, their attitudes, and, most of all, their clothing sharply distinguishing them from the locals, whose attitudes generally were those of amused toleration and, only rarely, of outright animosity. The tailored riding breeches, long-tailed coats, and occasional derby hats merely helped to identify the strangers as "dudes," but the eastern women's growing tendency to parade

For dude-ranch patrons, such as these who were paying to play cowboy in Wyoming's high country, horseback riding was an essential part of the experience. (Courtesy, Denver Public Library, Western History Department)

around in men's clothing raised the hackles of traditionally conservative westerners, whose own women were still wearing divided skirts and feminine jackets. As time passed and as the westerners got used to seeing these sartorial mavericks, the city cow hands attracted less attention. Working a herd of them was no different from hazing four-legged Shorthorns. It was just another, a newer, part of ranching, and the hired hands resigned themselves to it.

Working the dude herds remained hard for some of the older cow hands. But during the 1920s, cattle prices were low and jobs that called for herding honest-to-God cattle were hard to find; so some seasoned heel-squatters had to swallow their pride and to go to work as ''Show about Cowboys.'' One old-time Arizona cattleman wrote a poem called ''The Dude Wrangler,'' the last lines of which were:

> I shorely hated for to do it,
> For things that's done you cain't recall,
> But when a cowboy turns dude wrangler,
> He ain't no good no more at all.

Younger men, who were without these prejudices and who didn't mind being dubbed "Montgomery Ward Cowboys" by the old hands, accepted the change and entered the business with the knowledge that it was merely another part of the western economy.

Sometimes the shift to two-legged critters tried the patience even of the younger herdsmen. For years, one of the favorite stories around Glacier Park concerned a grim-looking old dudeen, as lady dudes were called, who informed the local wrangler that she would like to do a little trail riding. Courteously he asked her if she had any preference in saddles, and when she gave him a blank look, he explained that some folks preferred the eastern, or "postage stamp," saddle to the western style. Seeing that she still did not grasp his meaning, he said in a kindly way, "Ma'am, the western saddle has a horn." "Well," she responded in great alarm, "if the trails are going to be *that* busy today, I don't think I want to try it." And she fled back to her tourist group.

Those who piloted pilgrims around the western countryside often had a lot more to do than saddle the horses and act as guides. They were cooks and nursemaids, as well. One of them, who worked the Wyoming wilds, recalled preparing for an extended pack trip and being told by a doctor, who was to be a member of the group: "I want you to promise one thing. Oatmeal every morning for breakfast and hot applesauce twice a day." Since the customer is always right, the trail traveler got his wish, and the guide produced just what the doctor ordered.

While it was generally assumed that easterners who sought out the dude ranches were people who had means and who preferred the personal touch in their sightseeing, their motivation went beyond a desire to avoid sharing the Old West with the rabble who were beginning to cruise that country in their flivvers. It was indicative of a change in outlook on the part of those who were tired of summering at the eastern spas and whose interest in the West was not unlike that of other Americans who feared that the Old West was gone, or at least was slipping, and wanted to taste the flavor of that much romanticized place while time allowed. Since many of them were devotees of a conservation movement that swept the country in the early years of the twentieth century, it was entirely in keeping with their desire to savor the natural West, especially as guests of ranchers whose notions necessarily fitted this picture. Primitive beauty was a main stock in trade of the new herdsmen.

As it was with rail touring of an earlier day, where the cost was often more than the average man could pay just to wander the West for pleasure, so it was also with the handful of dude ranches that began what later was to become a big business by entertaining just a few ladies and gentlemen of means. But again to make the comparison with rail travel, summering in the West became more and more available to middle-class groups, and it became not so much a matter of cost as one of deciding upon what kind of vacation one wanted. For five dollars a day, schoolteachers, secretaries, and other "singles" who enjoyed group participation found that dude-ranch life offered the outdoors and a touch of the solitude that the wealthy once tended to monopolize. So many made this discovery that by 1937, Wyoming alone had 102 such establishments.

In reaching out for a larger clientele, dude-ranch owners were sensitive to the fact that the term itself was not an entirely complimentary one in the West, and more and more of these establishments, especially in the southern reaches of the West, tended to call themselves "guest ranches." With that, their activities broadened considerably, from just trail riding or helping out with the chores to a wide range of activities. Singouts, cookouts, dancing, and swimming gave the horses a welcome rest.

The opening of dude-ranch registers to the ordinary pocketbooks stripped some of their charm for the older patrons. As always happens, these vacation paradises are discovered by ordinary folks, and members of the elite have to look deeper into the travel folders. While the change did not take place overnight, it began fairly early. Chambers of Commerce, Boards of Trade, and various commercial clubs long had understood the virtues of volume and the profits that could be realized by enticing more visitors to the West. In January 1906 a See America First conference was held at Salt Lake City, a commercial missionary crusade of sorts, where participants thumped the tubs for the cause of home-grown scenery. Excursion rates, cheaper hotels, and attractive travel packages were advocated as means of snaring smaller wallets, those that would have been tossed back into the pond by earlier fishermen as being undersized.

In neighboring Colorado by that date, the drive to attract visitors already was well organized. In 1906 Denver attracted twenty-five conventions, involving seventy-five thousand conventioneers, many of whom took advantage of their brief stay to make side trips to Estes Park and other scenic mountain spots. Needless to say, the strangers were welcomed with open arms and treated to western hospitality; so they went home with light hearts and even lighter pockets. Coloradans were becoming increasingly aware of a subtle resource—scenery—that later would pay heavy dividends and cause tourism to be classified not only as an industry but as a leading industry.

Some cities cashed in especially well on the western mystique by drawing conventioneers who were looking for escape and a good time. These are some of the 75,000 Elks who visited Denver in 1906. (Courtesy, Denver Public Library, Western History Department)

By this time, tourists generally had discovered the ease with which one could reach the Rocky Mountains, and their numbers suggested that they were more than anxious to explore what was becoming everyman's West. It was estimated that the Rocky Mountain region was drawing as many as two hundred and fifty thousand people a year, a great many of whom were attracted to Colorado. As advertised, one could board an evening train at Chicago and be in Denver the next day before bedtime. The round trip fare was as low as $30.00, with sleeping-car fare extra. Eight different railroads were available to those with westering tendencies. One of them, the Northern Pacific, carried fourteen thousand passengers to Yellowstone Park in 1904.

The See America First movement presumably was an effort to entice tourists who might otherwise have gone to Europe—the Great

Like capillaries of a vast vein-and-artery system, smaller railroads, such as this one over Colorado's Poncha Pass, reached from the great lines into the western heartland. (Courtesy, Colorado Historical Society)

Northern made this phrase its motto—but in reality a majority of those who ventured out to the Rockies for the summer did not have the means or the intention of going to Europe. The westward pull was strengthened by promises of a comfortable and reasonably priced vacation. Already the western railroads were establishing a reputation for fast and even luxurious travel, generally not found on eastern lines, one that grew steadily and was widely known well into the 1930s and beyond. But these tourists were offered more. Better and less-expensive hotels were springing up; boardinghouse rates averaged nine dollars a week; summer cottages were less expensive; and the notoriously bad frontier cuisine was improving. Said one returnee, in wonderment: "I have been surprised to find out how fast the people out there are learning to live. I can order a better dinner in Spokane that I can in Pittsburgh." Indeed, the Old West was gone.

Roaming the West by train had developed quickly with the proliferation of major lines that followed the construction of the Pacific Railroad. Almost overnight, Colorado was reached by some of the principal roads, while at the same time it was being webbed with twisting little narrow-gauge routes that scaled impossible mountain heights and threaded through lovely river valleys and deep canyons.

It was ideal terrain for "exploring" by rail, whether in a private car or in an open observation car, which became highly popular with more ordinary visitors. The post-1900 period simply was one of expanding these facilities, of improving accommodations, and of lowering prices to increase the numbers. This, however, had a point of diminishing returns, partly because the curious always wanted to see more than the railroads could show them and because large families could not always afford even the excursion rates that the companies offered. What was wanted was a means of greater mobility and an even more economical way of taking the family on a vacation. Additionally, a growing desire for the outdoors and for camping suggested the need for individualized transportation. The automobile filled the bill nicely.

What was one day to be the day of the "tin can" tourist developed relatively slowly. The early automobiles were unreliable, expensive toys that found very few good roads to traverse. This was especially true in the West, and it would remain so for some time to come. By 1903, three automobile "trails" had been blazed across the continent, and that designation was accurate; they were little, if any, better than those used by covered wagons. It was almost another decade before any of the "name" highways would emerge.

Around 1909, some Colorado women proposed, to a state motorists' convention at Pueblo, that a coast-to-coast Lincoln Memorial Highway should be designated and lined with trees that were representative of the states through which it passed. In 1911, legislation was introduced into Congress that envisaged seven national highways, including a transcontinental one. In the following year the Yellowstone Trail (later U.S. 10 and then Interstate 90-94) was created, and a year later the Lincoln Highway (later U.S. 30 and then Interstate 80) came into being. These beginnings set in motion a development that saw the rapid spread of roadside facilities for the new auto traveler. Within a decade these and similar highways were reasonably well supplied with auto camps and cottages; by then the automobile was said to have revolutionized the average American's vacation.

It also moved that vacation westward.

But before it became common to load the family car with camp kits and kids and to set forth on a nomadic summer jaunt, a new breed of motorists had done the pathfinding. And pathfinding it was, for as a survey of 1904 showed, there were very few roads in the West that could be classified as "improved." That constantly violated term could mean anything; at best it conveyed the presence of shallow

Vacationers in search of the "real West" have rarely wanted to surrender entirely their favorite fast foods for local fare. Those stopping here, near Grand Lake, Colorado, could find popcorn, soft drinks, and hamburgers. (Courtesy, Denver Public Library, Western History Department)

ditches on each side of the pathway, intended as barrow pits, and enough scraping on the intervening space to call the road "graded." In the region under consideration—the plains and the mountain West—Utah led with 608 miles, the other leaders having around 200, but Montana and Nevada each had only about 65, Nebraska 23, and New Mexico a mere 2. Nationwide, some 7 percent of the roads were said to be improved; in the West the figure was slightly over 2.5 percent. The westward passage still provided its challenges.

That exploring the wilds in one of the new gas buggies was a venturesome undertaking came home to Milford R. McClelland in 1911, when he took his new Moline Dreadnaught—retail price, $1,850—across the plains from Iowa to Montana. He found the steppes of North Dakota to be so devoid of road signs that he had to fall back upon a crude sort of navigation, relying on railroad timetables and maps to estimate distance and on a "Blue Book" motorists' guide that offered only vague suggestions as to compass headings. This handy volume advised the motorist to start at some known point and then to proceed so many miles by the odometer, then take a fix on a red barn or on a white church, after which a right or a left turn was in order.

Taking into account stops for red barns and other identifiers, McClelland managed to make a hundred miles a day, occasionally pushing the Dreadnaught up to thirty or forty miles an hour when the terrain was not too choppy. He made a little over fifteen miles to a gallon of gasoline, which cost twelve cents, and paid thirty-five cents for dinner at North Dakota's better cafés. There were some hidden expenses that later tourists avoided; crossing the Missouri River at Bismarck necessitated paying the ferryboat operator twenty-five cents. Later, McClelland spanned the Little Missouri for nothing by using the Northern Pacific Railroad bridge and watching carefully for any oncoming unscheduled trains.

Despite navigational problems on the plains, Milford McClelland made a relatively easy passage. And a cheap one. This could have been misleading for others who aspired to adventuring in the modern manner. While McClelland was burning up the Dakota sod, others were not enjoying the West so much. A driver who made it deep into the Nevada desert wrote that some of those whom he met along the way swore that they must have found the last land on earth in this sea of sagebrush and that no power under heaven would ever induce them to endure such heat and dust again. Some of the explorers, dressed in khaki and wearing goggles, simply gave up and shipped their cars to Reno.

Despite such talk from the pessimists, those who boosted the new freedom of movement for travelers stressed, among other things, that automobile trips across yesterday's frontier were safe for women and children. When social arbiter Emily Post ventured out into the wilds in the spring of 1915, her readers learned that a whole new world awaited the so-called weaker sex. Of course, these presumably delicate creatures had to be prepared for some rather primitive going if they were going to take up modern trail travel. For example, the "highway" between Sterling, in northeastern Colorado, and Denver presented a picture of impassible mud, a landscape of innumerable autos glued to earth by gumbo, around which scene Mrs. Post circled and approached the mountain country by way of Cheyenne. It was advisable, she said, to select an American-made car for use in such country, because its ten-inch clearance minimized the chance of getting hung up on the high center between the ruts. She also mentioned the desirability of taking along ropes, shovels, spare parts, tire chains, and extra links for chain-driven cars. Extra gas, oil, and water, stored in the running-board rack, were a must.

There were rewards for the persistent motorist. After a hard trip, Mrs. Post luxuriated at Denver's Brown Palace Hotel and later at the

Antlers in Colorado Springs. These were well-known places, but anyone who had taken pleasure in thirty-five-cent Dakota meals was in for a shock. Lunch at the Brown could run to $3.50 or more. Double rooms cost $6.00, and coffee-and-toast room service was available at seventy cents. Breakfast cost ninety-five cents. As one descended on the map and stopped off at such ordinary places as Trinidad, Colorado, a room with bath at the Hotel Cardenas came to $4.50, with meals proportionately cheaper. But Trinidad was merely a place to stop and restore. Colorado Springs, or "Li'l Lunnon" as it had been called earlier, was more than that; it was a destination, a spa, a watering place, a resort that catered to folks disinclined to haggle over price. Emily Post found it charming, if a bit gay, and even a little racy.

Aside from the desire to play with the new gadget called the automobile and to go exploring where covered wagons once had rutted the sod, two events that had nothing to do with the lure of the mountain West's scenic attractions occurred about this time. One was the outbreak of war in Europe in August 1914; the other, a year later, was the opening of the Panama-Pacific Exposition at San Francisco and the Panama-California Exposition at San Diego. Both of these drew tourists westward, most of them by train, but a number of adventurous souls decided to make an outing of it and go by car.

As early as 1911 an advance party of automobilists was sent out to advertise the ease with which families might go to the West Coast in their family cars to attend the upcoming fairs. John G. Monihan, secretary of the Ocean to Ocean Motor Tourists, reported that because the expositions were bound to attract a flood of tourists, many of them by automobile, a convoy of twelve autos, driven by their owners, had completed the trip that year. The entire party, of wives, children, and friends, numbered forty; and Monihan stated proudly that the continent thus had been spanned, and without a single accident. Automotively speaking, the way west lay open.

Although the war in Europe probably diverted only a limited number of tourists westward, its influence was more useful as a device to advertise the West as an attractive alternative. Vacationers were advised that European spas were not then beneficial places for nervous health seekers or the curious. Instead, they were told, now was the appropriate (and patriotic) time to see America first. By venturing across the old American Desert and cresting mountains, which were so beautiful that they could be mistaken for the Alps, modern adventurers were promised pleasure in the Pacific's Mediterranean climate, as well as excitement and education at the fairs.

From the columned comfort and respectability of the Yellowstone Lake Hotel, guests could ride away in artifacts of the mythic West—and return to soft beds at night. (Courtesy, Colorado Historical Society)

The war and the acceleration of the See America First movement also coincided with the creation of the National Park Service. The parks were not new to the West; Yellowstone had existed since 1872, and by 1914, over four hundred miles of government road there were being used by tourists. This was one of the parks under the control of the War Department; the Interior Department ran such parks as Glacier, Rainier, and others. The National Park Service Act of 1916 drew the parks together under the Interior Department. Stephen T. Mather, who was appointed to direct the system, at once initiated a campaign to attract tourists. Coincidental to such advertising was the steadily increasing number of national parks being opened to motorists. During the first three decades of the twentieth century, seventeen of them were added to the existing one, national forests were expanded to around 160 million acres, and strong emphasis was placed upon outdoor family recreation.

The American public responded. During those years, national per capita travel increased sixfold, most of the gain being due to the wider use of the automobile. In this respect the West again was a frontier, a place that promised excitement, new experiences, and informative sightseeing. Best of all, the new frontiering was a family matter.

Much of the change took place within a decade. In 1924 the author of an article on auto camping talked of the transition since the opening of the Yellowstone Trail and the Lincoln Highway, a little over ten years earlier. The automobile, he said, had revolutionized the average American's vacation, sending out between five and ten million "motor gypsies" in the preceding year, and wherever they went—especially in the West—auto camps now beckoned them.

Denver is a good example of the oases that awaited the emerging "tin can" tourist. Calling Colorado one of the pioneers in tempting this fraternity to come its way, a *Saturday Evening Post* writer said that Denver's up-and-coming business leaders equated the importance of an auto camp with that of a railway station, hence the city's $250,000 Overland Motor Park. Support for such a statement came in a statistic: in the summer of 1923, over six hundred thousand campers were said to have used the park's facilities. This was twice the number of people who lived in Denver at that time.

Not only was the facility free to campers, but when it was opened in 1915, firewood, sawed and split, was thrown in. During the summer of 1917, when gasoline was supposed to be a war casualty, tourists arrived from thirty-eight different states. So great was the rush to see this part of America that the city fathers hastily set aside another plot of ground, sixty acres in size, and called it Genesee Park. But now tourists had to pay five cents for wood with which to cook a meal, because earlier guests at Overland had wasted so much of it. However, bricks were furnished free for those who wanted to set up small fireplaces. For those who were unacquainted with roughing it in the West or who did not want to build fires, there were electric cookers. Hydrants provided free water, city tankers sprinkled down the dusty park roads, and by night the encampment was illuminated by electricity. A nearby lake invited fishermen, whose kids meanwhile were amused at a nearby playground.

This was for the outdoor types. By the early twenties, Overland Park offered a three-story clubhouse that also contained a modern grocery and meat market, a grill and lunch counter with a steam table, a billiard room, a barbershop, comfort stations, and a laundry room. The second floor featured a large lounge with a dance floor, phonograph included, as well as a restaurant and a soda fountain. Above that there were women's toilets, showers, and lockers. An auto-repair shop and a movie were nearby. The complex had about a thousand small camp lots, or room enough for around five thousand tourists a night. Here the "motor nomads" found one of the West's new watering holes; here they rested, refurbished supplies, and

Denver's Overland Motor Park, shown here in the early 1920s, was a popular stopping place for the "tin-can tourists" descending on the West in droves. (Courtesy, Denver Public Library, Western History Department)

repaired their vehicles. Then off again, off to the wild, wild yonder, because somewhere out there lay another auto camp.

The West, in general, was quick to see the potential of this new source of income. The business of nursing along a few rich tourists had been rewarding in a limited way; now, with a mass market before them, westerners got downright hospitable and held out the latchstring to anyone who wanted to soak up some of that fabled western atmosphere. By the early twenties there was hardly a town that had not joined in the most recent gold rush. Sometimes the offering was no more than some open space, with running water, but it could be tent frames and even small cabins. Towns got into wars with each other in their all-out efforts to sidetrack some of the eastern money that passed by. They strove for one-upsmanship in offering fringe benefits to those who would stop and spend a dollar or so. For example, Boise, Idaho, furnished free hot and cold water as well as free electricity for cooking, washing, and ironing.

The theory was that the outstretched hand of western hospitality would come back filled with money that would be placed there by appreciative visitors. As one writer put it, to reap them, you had to get them; and to get them, you had to advertise. He said that enormous sums were spent to publicize the relative merits of these facilities, much of it appearing on highway signboards.

But the hopes of gold prospectors have been dashed before, and it happened again. To the great disappointment of the towns, some of their guests took the blandishments seriously and settled in, putting their children in the public schools and basking in the low-budget hospitality being dispensed by these traditionally friendly frontiersmen. The hosts responded by demanding money of their visitors, whom they now designated as "vagabonds." The newcomers then engaged in just enough work to pay for their new western abodes, amidst outcries from the citizenry about cheapskates, tightwads, and nonspenders. Ignoring the possibility that the western image might become a little tarnished by such mercenary attitudes, city fathers put their faith in private enterprise and turned these failing municipal hospitality houses over to private parties, who better understood the best methods of corraling two-legged mavericks. And thus was born a string of establishments that later became known as motels, the owners of which soon treated the advocates of public hosting to some illuminating lessons in monetary extraction. No wonder the campers began to grumble about the disappearance of the Old West.

One can't accuse western business types of not knowing a good thing when they saw it. It was estimated that, in 1924, two million "summer Bedouins" were roaming the Rocky Mountain West, carrying around money that other highwaymen might get from them. The idea that tourists were entering Yellowstone Park at the rate of one car a minute was enough to excite anyone who had ever seen a cash register. By calculating the cost of supplying food, housing, repairs, and fuel for that number of motor-driven nomads, even a westerner who could bulldog only a simple problem in arithmetic came up with mind-boggling totals. Montanans estimated that their share of the tourist take that year was $6 million, while Arizona guessed its haul to be $10 million. With numbers like that floating around, it was not necessary to yell "Tally ho" to signify that the prey was in sight.

Unhappily for westerners, the results were about as rewarding as that of the hunting dog who deposits the game at his master's feet: a pat on the head. Finders were not keepers. When it finally dawned upon outsiders that the West possessed yet another treasure that could be extracted, they moved in, and thus not a little of the gold that was rattled out of the tourists' pokes increasingly went to motel and restaurant chains, to corporate-owned gas stations, and to outside suppliers in general. As always, the masters of the purse let

the colonials hold the money for a brief moment, long enough to give
them a feel for it, but then they moved it out, for safekeeping. This is not surprising; what is surprising is that it took them a while to realize that the rustics had stumbled across another paying mine.

The emergence of the rubber-tired rovers did more than to motivate only those who wanted to set up deadfalls to trap unwary pilgrims who might wander their way. Westerners, in general, were so anxious to get things rolling that they were willing to pay dearly for more and better roads and to lobby more fiercely for additional federal aid from those tight-fisted folks in Washington who were always trying to enslave them. The natives were, so to speak, anxious to pave the way for this emergent group of contributors and, at the same time, to free their own bailiwicks from the seasonal gumbo fetters that isolated them during inclement weather. Nationally this phase of internal improvements was known as the Good Roads Movement, and it was one to which those who were becalmed on the western seas of grass enthusiastically subscribed.

Easterners were less enthusiastic about the movement, because they thought the West was getting more than its share of the funds. In 1912, Congressman Michael E. Driscoll of New York opposed a good-roads measure before the House, remarking that twenty-nine such bills had been introduced by the Democrats and ten by the Republicans, not one of which had been sponsored by members from the East and only a handful from the Mississippi Valley. The great majority had come from the West, including some from the South, but, in either case, from places where populations were small and distances between towns were great. Once more the East showed a reluctance to subsidize the "colonies."

The coming of the blacktop—or "oiled" roads, as westerners called them—was anticipated with nearly as much longing as had been the appearance of the railroads, both of which promised all-weather transportation. The West is big, very big, and its sparse population provides a small tax base with which to finance these expensive highways. They were slow in coming and painfully achieved.

The well-known author E. B. White noted in 1922: "Your popular conception of a national highway would be blasted were you to ride . . . into the capital of North Dakota on a road which had a grass center. . . . All the roads here are 'natural.' " Ten years later a fellow motorist noted that Montana, then the third-largest state in the Union, had but thirty-five miles of blacktop. At that time, New York had three hundred times as many miles of surfaced road as did Wyoming.

Although the streets were still dusty and unpaved, pristine sidewalks attested to the civic pride of Leadville, Colorado, shown here about 1910. (Courtesy, Denver Public Library, Western History Department; photo by George L. Beam)

The little towns of the plains and Rockies regarded it as a matter of civic pride to provide cement sidewalks and paved streets, these refinements being equated with the number of schools, churches, libraries, free tourist camps, and such amenities as they mentioned in their advertising. A passer-by remarked that Bozeman, Montana, in 1924 was much improved in this respect since he had seen it nearly two decades earlier. Now it boasted of fifteen miles of paved streets, which served the town's twenty thousand residents. Similarly, Phoenix, Arizona, now had paved streets; but rather than being praised for it, the eastern visitors, apparently wanting the Old West to stay muddy, said the place had lost its charm because the burghers no longer were interesting. They explained that these westerners were doing what other people wanted them to do, "rather than what they damn-please." It was very hard to satisfy the critics.

What the critics were saying was that the remote West, accessible to those with leisure time and money, should be preserved for them in a virgin state so that they could make occasional pilgrimages and commune with the ghosts of the New England naturalists. "To my mind the Good Roads Movement has become the Good Roads

Mania,'' complained a well-known conservationist. He conceded
that these roads gave ranchers access to nearby towns and permitted
the city people to enjoy recreation in the mountain forests, but the
momentum of the movement appeared to be punching holes in the
remaining patches of western wilderness. He called this sheer
stupidity, because ''by doing so we are cutting off, irrevocably and
forever, our national contact with Covered Wagon Days.''

Beyond describing succinctly the nostalgic yearning of the mid
twenties for a gone-but-not-forgotten frontier, it put very well some of
the secret feelings of the emerging wilderness enthusiasts, who were
seeking a form of clannish privacy in the forest primeval when they
argued for stretches of carbon-monoxide-free acres in the West. They
would have denied then, and they will do so even more vociferously
today, that this repudiated the concept of equal opportunity, either
financially or in terms of sex discrimination; but there existed then a
strong overtone of male desire to go deeper into the woods, where
outdoor ruggedness was monopolized by men. The financial aristocracy regarded the wilderness as their last recreational frontier.
Wealthy businessmen who charter flights into the Canadian wilderness today, for the ostensible purpose of finding better fishing, could
explain this quite easily—to anyone but their wives, that is.

By the 1930s, facilities for vacationers who wanted to drive around
the West began to improve. ''Tourist cabins'' became motels, and
the comforts that were offered to travelers approximated more what
earlier visitors had found in hotels. Except for the old resort hotels,
which were known for their cuisine, the food showed less improvement. As late as the post–World War II period, Bernard De Voto was
complaining that outside of Montana, he had not seen many good
restaurants. He advised visitors to seek out a dude ranch that served
meals, especially in Wyoming. But then, easterners always had
thought in terms of dining, rather than stoking up to avoid hunger. It
was a state of mind.

Despite depression and great financial difficulties during the dismal
thirties, there was a gradual improvement in roads as the hard-top
network began to spread across the West. The results often left
something to be desired, but blacktop of any kind was a great
improvement over gumbo or even gravel. In Montana, for example,
with money short and the need very great, the Highway Department
''stretched'' its available funds for blacktopping by making the
highways as narrow as possible. Since traffic wasn't heavy and since
Montanans were given to driving on either side of the road anyway,
the ''slim-Jim'' highways were no handicap to them.

Technology and tourism were transforming the West after World War II. Here power lines of the Colorado–Big Thompson project march across the land next to "tourist cabins" near the flatlanders' mecca of Estes Park. (Courtesy, Colorado Historical Society)

Understandably, tourists who were used to the paved roads in the East stuck to these smoother trails, despite the dangers imposed by the natives, who, even when sober, could be a little wild behind the wheel. The unwillingness to forsake the "straight and narrow" annoyed the westerners who had things to sell but who were off the main highways. One of the "beaters" of the tourist hunters complained that during 1935 there were almost three million visitors in his state of New Mexico, and half of them passed through the "Land of Enchantment" complaining that there just wasn't anything worth looking at. "They wouldn't get a yard off the highway," he complained. "We fooled 'em one place by building a highway right past White Sands, one of the natural marvels of the state, and they just had to look at it." Westerners were determined to make their scenery turn a profit if they had to rub the tourists' noses in it to get their attention.

Those whose tourist-oriented businesses were paying off belied the chronic complaint of low-paid westerners "you can't live on scenery." Thousands of them did, and still do so today. By the late twenties a newspaper photographer remarked, "Now every desert road is crawling with the flivvers of immigrants, and the flivvers are

crawling with babies, tin cans and folding phonographs.'' From
Montana to Arizona, all along the mountain ranges, the modern trappers set up their snares and awaited the annual opening of the hunting season. In Arizona, said one reporter, ''I find in all the trading posts great preparations to take care of the . . . tourist.'' This paid off. By 1939, Arizona, for example, claimed tourism as one of its thriving industries, one that added about $50 million a year to its income.

By ''taking care'' of the tourists—a term that could have some nuances—it was generally understood that this implied the furnishing of food, shelter, and perhaps some form of entertainment. Scenic beauty, of course, was one of the attractions. To it was added another time-tested appeal—the promise of better health and boosted morale. Earlier, this lure had brought railroad tourists to bask and soak at western spas, and now it was being offered to a newer and larger group, the motorists. During the thirties, tourist advertising increasingly emphasized the West's free and open life style, the purity of the air, the wholesomeness of the food, the freshness of the water, and the opportunities for restful quiet. Additionally, said one publicist, there was a hidden dividend, an important one, in ''the way the people take you, if you're the right sort.'' Even among the tin-can tourists, there were easterners for whom acceptance by the bronzed westerners was important.

Lamentably there were those among the new migrant masses who had no taste or sense of history, for whom even honorary membership in this elite meant nothing at all; but westerners shrugged this off as one of the gambles of the game. Playing upon the sentiments of those who were properly tuned in, the residents of the Stetson Shangri-La dug deep into their nostalgia bags and came up with memorabilia that could be converted into cash from more appreciative guests. Admittedly, said one magazine writer, the West had no monopoly on romance, but somehow visitors to that legendary place were emotionally receptive to it; as a matter of fact, to them it was part of the promised package. Westerns, in print and on celluloid, had done their work.

As always, the natives were ready to capitalize any resource, intangible as it might be, and they saw no reason to disappoint the dudes. That the western atmosphere was charged with some special kind of magic for easterners had long been recognized in the country beyond the wide Missouri. Teddy Roosevelt had shown them that a generation or more earlier. And for some time they had acknowledged what they regarded as a unique past with commemorative celebrations that recalled its color and excitement. Concurrently, they staged rodeos, usually for the sport of it, but in time this activity was merged with pioneer-day activities to include the heroes of the open range. Besides, chaps and cowboy hats, not to mention prancing cow ponies, spruced up any parade. Now, in the 1930s, the pioneer-day custom was put to a wider use, was publicized, dramatized, and, above all, commercialized. A mass market required mass production.

There now occurred a period in the region's history that will be known as the "wilding up of the West." Every place beyond the Big Muddy took part, the purpose being to give the visitors their money's worth. Even dull and desolate places that were closer to the river, those that had almost no "wild West" heritage, lent a hand, knowing full well that they had no mountains to sell but being well aware that those who were en route to the hills carried money and that any stops along the way would cause them to part with some of it. Dutifully the natives dressed up, wore hot and uncomfortable costumes on scorching August days, suffered beards and bonnets, and tried to look like carefree pioneers. Occasional profanity unintentionally lent an air of realism to the pageants.

Business districts were roped off, and the original Deadwood stagecoach—156 of which were identified—was put on display. Communities that missed out on this opportunity made up for it by parading an old Conestoga wagon, drawn by a couple of beasts that passed for oxen. Historical accuracy would have called for a representation of the ordinary farm wagon, accompanied by men wearing bib overalls and carrying pitchforks, but this would have been as unthinkable as the sight of two plow horses dragging a manure spreader down Main Street. Rather, these little wheat-growing communities preferred to think of their West in terms of horsemen, and so, mean-looking "cowboys" now lurked about town, occasionally staging fake gunfights, after which a frock-coated gent wearing a black plug hat measured the victims and had them boxed for shipment to a local Boot Hill that the place had never possessed.

There were, of course, some unexpected setbacks in the restoration of the Old West. Just when the program was hitting its full stride and the dudes were glassy-eyed with delight, some subversive soul would reveal that treacherous Shoshoni Indians on a Wyoming reservation were operating a canning factory. "Some relief director, with a warped outlook on life, had got them putting beets and carrots and spinach into cans," moaned one reporter. "Committees were at once named to get the miserable Shoshonis out of the kitchen and back to

From the friendly contests in practical skills such as riding and roping, the rodeo evolved into a major part of the modern entertainment industry. Crowds like this one at the Pendleton, Oregon, Roundup in 1923 got a whiff of an earlier working world. (Courtesy, Colorado Historical Society)

the ranges where a scalp or two might still be had, in a refined way.'' It was explained to the warriors that almost no money-bearing tourists carried can openers.

There were other embarrassing moments. For example, Cheyenne's chief of police displayed an appalling ignorance of the Old West's traditions when he went so far as to object when some of "the boys" took to shooting out the street lights. There was even worse to come. About this time a convention of beauticians met at Butte, and before anyone could muzzle him, the group's president horrified the natives by stating that hairdressing was one of the state's most promising young industries. Old hands slapped their chaps and exclaimed that the place was getting just too damned civilized.

Despite such minor flaws, the program went forward, the hawking of nostalgia and yore often being carried to extremes, while spokesmen for the region repeatedly swore that the Old West hadn't been tamed, as rumored. This in face of the fact that there was a disturbing decline in gunfights on saloon-lined dusty streets and hitching racks were getting hard to find. Even the dusty streets were gone, and apologies had to be made for the pavement, a necessary nuisance which progress-minded city fathers were said to have foisted upon unsuspecting residents. Then there was the matter of the dude ranchers, who had spent a good deal of effort and no little advertising money to show how safe the place was. They took a dim view of perpetuating the image of wildness.

But the tourist trappers had become used to the sound of the cash register; they had tasted blood, and nothing would stop them from continuing the charade. To keep the kettle boiling, they accelerated their advertising. Pinedale, Wyoming, let it be known that the town was 105 miles from a railroad, a fact that would have been buried six feet deep in an earlier day. The newspaper at Tombstone, Arizona, the famed *Epitaph,* labeled its obituary column "Hell's Bells," to suggest that the bad old days still were around, while Cheyenne rather pathetically reported a gun battle that any other place would have recorded as an ordinary shooting. Not to be left behind, a Colorado mining town repealed an ordinance that prohibited the gunning down of strangers on Sunday.

There is yet another twist to the tale of the tourists. By getting colorfully mean and by mimicking the orneriest old down-easter who ever snarled at those who were brave enough to venture near the coast of Maine, some of the westerners took up the pastime of lambasting the dudes. Charley Russell, the cowboy artist who never quite made it into the twentieth century in an emotional sense, heaped scorn on the tourists who frequented his summer neighborhood at Lake McDonald, Glacier National Park. Irvin S. Cobb, the humorist, visited there and gleefully wrote of the artist's bad disposition in this respect, saying that "Charley reserved the most sulphurous corner of his private Gehenna for tourists" because they cluttered up beauty spots with banana peels and empty pop bottles. Those who remember Cobb's visit recall with amusement the efforts to hoist the bulky writer aboard a docile trail pony so that he, too, could ride the West.

Coloradans who did not make a living milking the tourist trade had their objections to these strangers, or so they said. When World War II intervened and shut off some of the seasonal influx of visitors, the Denver poet Thomas Hornsby Ferril wrote that the prospect of slim pickings really ought to "delight all civilized people." It was, he said, a compensation for the tire shortage, and he allowed as how tourists "always should have been rationed anyhow." Why? Because, he judged, "There aren't more than a hundred choice spirits east of the Mississippi who deserve to come to Colorado in any year."

Exactly, said the tourists. This was the kind of talk they liked to hear from the aristocratic West. It showed discrimination. No peasants allowed. In this wonderful democratic land, one had to rise to royalty by his own efforts, to become one of the chosen through loyalty and good works. Far from being upset by such gruff talk from the denizens of never-never land, the tourists loved it. Steve Frazee, the novelist from Salida, Colorado, understood this when he wrote his prickly, humorous *More Damn Tourists*.

Despite the cuffs and curses, real or pretended, the tourists kept on coming West, by rail, automobile, and air. In this relatively new wrinkle in the story of colonialism, outsiders again demanded that the West play a role to their liking, this time providing not only food and fuel but also the chance to get away. Westerners learned to play the game to their advantage, taking the money and then, always in character, grousing about those meddling dudes who cluttered the summer landscape. By the 1950s, a new colonial tradition that traded on dreams rather than resources was firmly established. Frontier Airlines proudly advertised itself as ''The Dude Ranch Airline.'' Union Pacific Railroad advertising talked about ''lazy days on a Western dude ranch,'' a place where every day was carefree yet invigorating. Prospective dudes could obtain a thirty-two-page booklet, ''Dude Ranches out West,'' merely by writing. Hotels, motels, Chambers of Commerce, and endless others who were interested in the tourist trade advertised, and the faithful responded. By 1970 *U.S. News & World Report* found it necessary to advise travelers: ''Don't let those reports of bumper-to-bumper traffic in the national parks scare you away from a trip to the American West. This is still a big country.''

The legend of the Big Sky country still lived.

CHAPTER 8

THE FICTIONAL WEST

The West is dead my friend,
But writers hold the seed
And what they sow will live and grow
Again to those who read.
—Charles M. Russell

The booming tourist industry has fed upon those dudes who have had the time and the credit cards to go in search of what they have known in their hearts was waiting "out there." For millions of other Americans, however, the national game of westering remained a spectator sport, one in which, by necessity or by choice, they did their adventuring vicariously. The West of their dreams was a mixture of mental pictures, drawn from their reading and enhanced by brush strokes of their imaginations, fantasized embellishments that shaped for them an American utopia, occupied by an idealized people.

The emotional appetites of these stay behinds were fed by accounts of various kinds. These ranged from the descriptions by travelers, both foreign and domestic, to government reports filled with fascinating statistics—a constant flow of written reassurances that the western Eden indeed existed and that it lay waiting for a chosen people. Those who could not participate in the grand adventure did not feel short-changed; rather, they took comfort in the fact that something out there was being held in trust for them, a kind of early version of Social Security.

It is a truism that the more exciting and colorful the story, the wider the audience. So, writers, from as far back as colonial times, had larded their accounts of life in that untamed country to the west with all the picturesque language at their command. When frontiersmen crossed the Missouri and played out the final acts of the American pageant under that fabled big sky, contemporary scribes lit up the literary atmosphere with a pyrotechnic display of puffery that dazzled even the dull.

With a flourish of literary legerdemain the recently designated *160* "desert" was transformed into the Wild West, a place of action,

color, excitement, and drama. If the dime-novel authors were guilty
of exaggeration, and unfailingly they were, they had some help from
the land itself, for that rugged country was almost a geographical
overstatement. Its mountain heights, its endless horizons, its extremes of heat and cold—all provided fodder for authors and a field
day for future folklorists.

When writers thus improved upon the materials at hand, history
itself was drawn in terms that were broad enough to embarrass any
self-respecting Texan. All subsequent efforts to correct the proportions have been unavailing. This pleasant blur, depicting a land
where, as the saying goes, men were men and women were glad of it,
became a permanent part of the American legend, and any attempt
to dull its surface luster is warmly resisted even today.

While the various geographical Wests always have been touched
with wildness and while the last of them was liberally sprinkled with
it, Americans of the stripling twentieth century wanted even more on
their literary plates than their forebears had demanded. Violent
action and unrestrained excitement were not enough; they wanted to
watch the reenactment of the story through misty eyes. They
preferred a morality play with sentimental overtones, a soul-stirring
performance that depicted the final stages in the building of a nation.
They yearned for roots, for tradition, for more bricks to build the
monument of national pride.

The problem with the twentieth century was that it appeared to
demand maturity, and it promised the mundane rather than the
unusual. In other words, the game of westering appeared to be nearly
over. True, the Spanish-American War, that brief flurry described by
Secretary of State John Hay as a "splendid little war," had accelerated American pulses momentarily, but its aftermath suggested
responsibility in the family of nations and possible future international involvement. Confrontation with new and untested obligations
tends to make mortals want to break and run for the hills. Or at least
to fort up emotionally and look at the future with cautious concern.

In this situation a good many Americans were inclined to look
back, not ahead, and to relish what they had gained, before reaching
out for more and bigger things in an international sense. Curiously,
this search for an emotional anchor did not take them to the annals of
the Republic's earliest days; rather, it took them to later pages, which
told of the conquest of the last and most challenging of the successive
Wests. That most-recent frontier had scarcely disappeared before it
was being held up as an example of the individuality, the ingenuity,
and the healthy aggressiveness of a democratic people who were
building a new nation.

There would be a time of great metropolitan areas, with their skyscrapers, their wonders of rapid transit, and their marvels of mechanization, but that lay just ahead. For the moment the show-piece of national growth was best exemplified in the spectacular successes of western mining, railroad building, land speculation, town building, and cattle raising. It represented a boom economy at its best and most flamboyant. America loved it, for it seemed to epitomize the credo "can do," already regarded as something typically American.

It may have been the emergence of modern America, with its urbanization and industrialization, that sparked an additional inter-est among its people for a past that was more direct, more simple, more easily understood. The nation had, some held, grown too fast, had lost something in that process; and now there was a yearning to return to that fast-disappearing life on the soil. There now became evident a nervous feeling that the West either would go unrecognized in literature or that it would not develop a literature of its own. Sentimentalists wanted an American story, one of triumph, of surmounting odds, of hope. But, as Wallace Stegner has noted, there was a shift from hope to bitterness in our literature about the time when the frontier gave way to urban and industrial America. Perhaps the western, so frequently excluded from the category of literature, may have provided alternative reading, whether polemic or pep talk, that spoke to the masses, the less sophisticated, the boosters, the optimists.

As it had been in so many other instances, westerners were of two minds when it came to the telling of their story. They loved the heroics that eastern writers portrayed; they purred over the portraits drawn of these sundown supermen; and they reveled in their collective role as the Sagebrush Siegfried. Nevertheless, in the back of their minds there lurked a suspicion that perhaps there was irony in these praise-laden pulps, that writers might even engage in kidding the West a little, as was later said about Alfred Henry Lewis in his *Wolfville* stories. Westerners wanted to have a lot of nice things written about them, even exaggerated things, but still they wanted to be taken seriously. As early as 1902 a Denver writer tried to claim that no western man would show any interest in the "action" type of story about his region, because the West had matured. He was sure that the West had outgrown its dialects and that its pants no longer were tucked into boots. He wondered why the real West was not portrayed in fiction, why some "keen-eyed genius" had not yet discovered the actualities of the new country.

There were some difficulties with writing about the "real West" as
the Denverite saw it. To him it was a busy manufacturing, producing
community where golf links beckoned to tired businessmen and their
wives had a craze for grand opera. This might have been his West in
1902, but it wasn't one that was going to sell very readily to eastern
publishers. Rather, someone was going to have to come up with a
story that rose above the dime novel but still talked seriously about
men and horses. What was needed was a James Fenimore Cooper in
literary chaps. Fortunately, one appeared on the scene. His name was
Owen Wister.

Part of Wister's success was due to timing; he had a product that
filled a vacuum then being lamented by some important literary
figures. In 1902, the very year in which Wister's now-famous book
The Virginian was making its bid for fame, author Frank Norris fretted
that already the cowboy hero had ridden into the literary sunset. "No
literature has sprung up around him . . . and the American epic . . .
will never be written," Norris wrote gloomily. His contemporary
Emerson Hough also pondered the problem, worrying that such
literature as existed was superficial and transient, a variety of writing
that was still depicting the West as a crude and undeveloped place
without a solid future.

Even as Hough was complaining, the romantic writing continued,
its appeal undiminished. Those who read his comments could find, in
the same magazine, Frederic Remington's illustrated piece "A
Desert Romance," a story of bloodthirsty Indians, of dashing
cavalrymen, of rescue and romance in Arizona. A year earlier,
Hamlin Garland's "Her Mountain Lover" had run serially.

Wister, however, appeared to have hit the bull's-eye by offering
American readers something that transcended the common literary
fare of adventure laced with romance. His central figure, the cowboy,
had been around for some time, but usually in a supporting role and
certainly one that lacked heroic proportions. By putting the cowboy
on the center of the stage, Wister contributed heavily to the rise of the
western's popularity. Still, a lot of writers could have executed this
simple repositioning. Wister's rising reputation was given a boost by
easterners, both critics and readers, who saw him as a writer who
could portray men as men, without regard to place of residence, one
who might be "expected to deal with the concerns of polite life as
successfully as with the beefy West." As one reviewer of the day put
it, "Mr. Wister has . . . blazed the way to that quite possible
impossibility, the American novel," a contention that was supported
by the *New York Times*.

*Frederic Remington's "Colonel Simms" added
dash and color to "A Desert Romance,"
published in* Century Magazine *in 1902.
(Courtesy, Denver Public Library, Western
History Department)*

Time was to alter that judgment. While *The Virginian* made an enormous impact—it stayed at the top of the best-seller list for six months in 1902 and within three years had sold three hundred thousand copies—the acclaim that its author received was not sustained. As the years passed, he was increasingly judged to have been overly sentimental and too frequently obvious. "Wister was not a first-rate writer; his writings do not belong on a list of America's best fiction," commented a scholar of the 1970s. Why? One answer was that he became a willing prisoner of popular demand, that he yielded to the blandishments of money in exchange for serving the emotional needs of his readers, thus denying himself the freedom that he needed in order to treat his subject more thoughtfully. He has been charged also with laziness, of submitting carelessly executed and obviously padded work when craftsmanship was called for.

Given all this, Wister not only had written the first successful novel of the cowboy West, but in *The Virginian* he also had established the mold for what was to become the conventional western. Future generations of aspiring authors slavishly followed the literary recipe that the master chef had furnished to them, and despite some singularly bad writing on their part, it never let them down.

Scholars and critics have had a field day explaining the deeper meaning of *The Virginian* and the flood of westerns that it helped to spawn. Much of the comment hinges upon the novel as an example of the American dilemma at the turn of the century: the pull between changes implied by progressivism, on the one hand, and the comforting warmth of the nostalgic past on the other. Especially to a middle-class reading public, most of them Protestants of the old stock who had grown up in the countryside and small towns, the Virginian was an appealing and soothing figure. He was impeccably Anglo-Saxon at a time when immigrants from southern and eastern Europe were flooding into the country. More than that, as social changes of the industrialized Northeast were disturbing many readers, Wister's hero personified some of the best traditions associated with those parts of America—the South and the West—where industry and the industrial style of life had barely begun to make their mark. He blended the southern gentleman's chivalry and leisurely style with the virile individualism of the pioneer, and at the same time he managed to avoid the sedition associated with Dixie and the boorishness that some thought was typically western. In short, in the minds of many readers, the Virginian stood for the best of what America had been. To make it all go down even more smoothly, Wister made it clear that his cowboy could survive quite well, thank you, in the modern world of business and prosperity. Wister had discovered that the western hero could be the ideal spokesman for those who found that much was going wrong in the modern world. From then until today, in fact, the popular western has remained a vehicle for profoundly conservative, things-are-going-to-hell points of view.

Consistent with his earlier writings, Wister's final tribute to the frontier, a collection of stories published in 1928 as *When West Was West,* looked back fondly at simpler days. It was his last farewell to a yesteryear that seemed to be devoid of the problems of modern civilization. American developments during the years that paralleled Wister's writing career seemed to document the validity of the anxieties that were facing the nation when *The Virginian* made its appearance. In many ways the book seemed to epitomize the uncertain passage that was being negotiated into the twentieth century. His last book simply said "Amen."

Because Owen Wister has been written about so much, it may appear to some that he had invented literary prospecting, when, in fact, he merely was one among many—a very lucky one—who frequented those diggings. By the early twentieth century, quite a lot of writing about the recently departed Old West was available to readers. The magazine *Out West,* published at Los Angeles and edited by Charles F. Lummis, offered fiction, nonfiction, and poetry by such distinguished writers as David Starr Jordan, Joaquin Miller, Mary Hallock Foote, and Mary Hunter Austin. In the spring of 1902 the *Garden of the Gods Magazine,* sponsored by the Chautauqua Movement, appeared at Colorado Springs. Recognizing the magnetism of a name, the editors quickly changed its title to the *Frontier Monthly.* History repeated itself in 1920, when a university professor at Missoula founded a literary magazine called the *Montanan,* only to opt for a new title, the *Frontier,* in the second issue.

In the summer of 1906 a national magazine made reference to the renewed interest in what it called "this newer country." No longer did the public want books of foreign travel, nor did publishers and magazine editors desire this type of material, wrote one of its contributors. Rather, Americans were beginning to regard their own country as a rediscovered source of interest, and that view was said to reflect the drift of popular taste. Significantly, the article looked far beyond the cowboy horizon and anticipated an environmental theme when it observed that "the desert, the mountains, the forest, the inspiring note that rings in the big free life of the western country and its people, arouse more interest year by year."

Frederick Jackson Turner's move to Harvard in 1910 signaled that the study of westward expansion now was a respectable endeavor within the school's ivy-covered walls. Many teachers and historians were going to be surprised to learn, said the *Nation* in April 1912, that Harvard intended to make itself a leader in collecting western historical materials. It might have added that Yale also had such an intent, and one day it would be a leader in this field. The magazine explained that New England had a special interest in the West, because so many of its people had settled the frontier, and that there was a need to show the achievements of easterners in developing the newer part of America. Then there was the additional reason that Harvard could do it better because "so many state historical societies gather worthless material and improperly edit reams of narratives." The Kansas Historical Society was singled out as a particular offender. Kansas, a place that literally was "invented" by New Englanders and owed much of its early settlement to them, simply was not doing right by the West. It was bungling the care of a national treasure—sacred records of the American legacy.

Academic interest in the West certainly was well rooted, and it was real. In the years to come, colleges and universities from coast to coast would offer courses in the history of the American frontier, scholarly interest in the subject would remain strong, and a major historical association, aimed solely at developing that subject, would emerge and thrive. But all this lay in the future.

During the stripling years of the new century the main thrust of the West in print was to be found in fiction and popular presentation. And it was here that Americans gained much of their impression of the West, not from more formal writing or in the classrooms. True, there were increasing efforts to set the record of the West straight— the title "Fact or Myth?" appeared in a number of instances; but those who sought to realign their historical sights made little impression upon the public.

There were some reasons for this. During most of the nineteenth century, those who used or misused western history for background material saw it through a starry-eyed haze that warped and falsified the account. Despite later efforts at realism, fictional accounts were shaped with only a light historical covering. The only genuine westerns usually were portrayals of the land itself. So far as the characters were concerned, those who fought the land for an existence or who fought each other for the land, were described with a good deal of literary license. This is not because writers wanted to lie about the West; it was because readers wanted them to. Nineteenth-century audiences had come to believe that this never-never land beyond America's civilized neighborhoods was a place where it was high noon all day in every dusty little cow town and that heroic things were occurring in such places around the clock. To have given them anything less would have been a disloyalty to the western legend.

Thus, the American reading public was ready for Wister, and it was to make demands even upon him. He responded to them on the ground that the customer always is right. So did other writers who saw what was required and lost no time in following the Philadelphian's very successful lead.

The list of "hands" that signed on to ride with Wister is long and largely forgotten today, but a few who wrote for the popular taste stood out, if only by reason of the impressive volume of their efforts. A later generation, which regarded Zane Grey as passé, was devoted to Louis L'Amour, who, by the 1980s, has written more than eighty "horse operas," as De Voto called them. Neither is regarded as a creator of great literature, but both have won the admiration of Americans who set great store by productivity and occupational longevity. These authors were successful because readers wanted to buy their work; both wrote at a time when men were telling each other that the Old West was dead; the nostalgic theme has remained popular.

During the days of World War I and shorty thereafter, Zane Grey answered the emotional needs of Americans who wanted to look back, if only a few years, to the "old days" when life was simpler. Between 1917 and 1924 he never was out of the top ten of the best sellers. A half-century later, his books, some fifty of them, had sold around twenty million copies. While the old cow hand Andy Adams complained that Wister's *Virginian* was a cowboy novel without cows—a complaint that later would be lodged against A. B. ("Bud") Guthrie, Jr.'s *These Thousand Hills*—Zane Grey's cowboys actually herded cattle. They also sweated, grew saddlesore and bone weary aboard uncomfortable range ponies, occasionally got drunk in town, and even offered readers a mild cuss word now and then. True, they were almost dormant sexually, but even Grey could not anticipate the sexual revolution that lay in the future. When a later generation of western-fiction writers tried to remedy this situation, they were surprised at the negative reaction registered by veteran pulp readers. Apparently, sexual freedom in a more modern day did not mean the emancipation of the cowboy—at least the cowboy of fiction.

As Grey struggled for realism, his view of cowboys depicted the manner in which he thought the horsemen conducted themselves;

and through their eyes, it represented the West as he imagined it had existed, or at least what he had seen of it. By his own admission he would have drawn back from associating with these knights of the plains. While on a cruise to Hawaii in the autumn of 1932, he and Hamlin Garland had long talks about their own views, during the course of which Grey admitted that to please his mother he had taken the pledge and never had tasted whiskey. "I don't smoke and I don't tell smutty stories," he added, confiding that "I hate all this pornography of Hollywood, as you do." Garland decided that both men were just puritans, but what he called the former Ohio dentist's "peculiarities" both increased his respect for the writer and explained why Grey's stories did not offend readers.

Leslie Fiedler once remarked that in archetypal form the western was a fiction that involved the reactions of a transplanted WASP to wilderness conditions. In many ways, Zane Grey's protagonists fit this description in that the standard plot depicted the eastern "pilgrim" who countered the rigors of western life by adapting to the environment and thereby experienced a cultural and physical metamorphosis in the untamed part of America. In this Darwinian laboratory, Grey's heroes survived weaker men, while at the same time they offered moral, social, and even political lessons to less-fortunate brothers in the East. Perhaps unconsciously, he was offering the reading masses Turner's thesis on a fictional platter. He made some other inferences. Through the eyes of his WASP characters, Grey took an occasional swipe at early-day Mormonism and even anticipated, perhaps unconsciously, some of the ultra-Americanism that lashed out at minorities generally during the early 1920s.

While makers of the cowboy myth carefully fashioned their heroes to stand for everything that was strong, upright, and 110 percent American, there also was emphasis on the wholesomeness of the virgin land that served as a backdrop. Rex Ellingwood Beach, Harold Bell Wright, Gene Stratton Porter (an Indiana druggist's wife), and James Oliver Curwood reassured readers that Americans still were engaged in that courageous contest with nature, a combat against a respected opponent, in which only the best of men were successful. In these stories they were bridging a gap between accounts of primitive woodsmen and the modern nature lovers, who sought to recapture the arcadian grandeur of yesteryear that ordinary men of the early twentieth century were being denied by virtue of their urban imprisonment.

Harold Bell Wright, who once viewed life from the pulpit, now preached clean living, the purity of the wilderness, and the moral values to be mined in this new treasure trove. When he portrayed a wealthy easterner who abandoned the artificiality of a decaying society to seek a wholesome life somewhere out beyond, as he did in *When a Man's a Man* (1916), he touched upon an increasingly popular theme. As a contemporary critic pointed out, a great many Americans secretly were old-fashioned in their beliefs, people who looked upon the big cities as modern Sodoms and Gomorrahs; and as such, they found Wright's denunciations of the sins of society to be soul satisfying in the manner of the Puritans on their fire-and-brimstone Sundays. He called Wright's style Salvation Army tambourine-and-drum prose, but admittedly it was a form of revivalism that ruthlessly separated the sheep from the goats.

The popularity of the back-to-nature theme was a throwback to the day of earlier philosophical writings, of Rousseau's ideal (minus the "beautiful savages"), of purity drawn from the untouched landscape. The acceptance of the "outdoor" writers emerged as an offshoot of the cowboy scenario, with emphasis on the restorative influences of the life that this horseman, as well as others, experienced from contact with nature. Looking over the cowboy's shoulder at the azure and as-yet-unpolluted horizon, Americans were reminded in yet another way that this diminishing scene was, in part, the result of rapid urbanization and perhaps the consequent corruption of which Zane Grey and Harold Bell Wright had spoken. It was not difficult to project the notion that America gradually was slipping into a pattern that differed little from Old World decadence.

Anyone who grazes through novels like these will soon be aware of another related theme. Western fiction was and is overwhelmingly macho. Men are in charge, while women are important mainly as commentators and motivators. On the remote chance that we are not aware of the message, the heroine lets us know what it is, and beyond that, she gives the hero reasons to do his wondrous work, usually by demonstrating, at a crucial point, her inability to cope. In a crisis, she tends to swoon. This has been the case from the first westerns of the early nineteenth century. The women of Cooper's saga, one wag noted, were like his landscapes—flat as the prairie and sappy as maples. By the turn of the century this tendency was becoming, if anything, more deeply entrenched, because of the growing assertiveness of American women. The more mothers and daughters went after greater political power and social freedom and the more they organized to get it, the more westerns seemed to preach that the frontier had been a man's world.

The connection seems obvious enough. The "new woman" was just another example of how America was sliding toward decadence. Many who bought these westerns were paying off for comforting stories that assured them that our forefathers and foremothers knew that a woman's place was in the soddie and in the sidesaddle. The truth, of course, was something else. Pioneer women were always at least as tough and resilient as their men, and the record shows that they got along quite well when left to their own devices. But that message was not one that many men wanted to hear in America of the twenties. The modern western became more and more part of the hairy-chested school of literature that produced Ernest Hemingway and Norman Mailer as well as Zane Grey.

The turn of the century coincided with a last fling at frontier flamboyance and life in a raw environment as prospectors fought the wilds of Alaska for hidden gold deposits. For the "outdoor" writer these diggin's were rich, as Jack London and others discovered. As it was with earlier miners, these literary prospectors sometimes cashed in too early and failed to reap the full benefit of their finds. London, for example, sold his rights to *The Call of the Wild* to a publisher for $2,000, only to find later that this best seller would be produced in millions of copies. James Oliver Curwood turned out twenty-six wilderness novels in less than two decades, while Stewart Edward White, in such works as *The Blazed Trail* and *The Silent Places,* capitalized on the attractions of nature.

Continuing national curiosity about the West prompted westerners to look within and to think more about the significance of their own region. In the early 1920s, New Yorker Will Irwin made note of this interest, remarking that, if nothing else, it represented a "healthy provincialism."

Perhaps paternalism such as this generated some of the writing that came out of the West in this era. It has been said that Eugene Manlove Rhodes was moved to write out of indignation, from a resentment that the East was taking seriously some of the burlesques that were being handed out as western history and literature. Contending that his little patch of New Mexico ground might be agriculturally poor but that it sprouted strong men and leadership, he began to put some of his thoughts on paper. His desire for fidelity in writing the western story was the thing that brought him lasting fame.

There were others who felt the same urge. Montana housewife Bertha Sinclair (pseud., B. M. Bower) had only to look about her in that northern Montana dry-land farming country to come up with the title *Lonesome Land* (1912). While Wister had regarded the East as the norm, both Rhodes and Bower saw the West as that measuring stick. To them, easterners either adapted to it or they went back home as failures; it was as simple as that.

William MacLeod Raine was another writer who was regarded as a westerner, even though he had been born in London, the son of a merchant. As one of many who came to Denver to die of tuberculosis, young Raine settled down to a long and fruitful life in the mile-high climate. Before the turn of the century he had sold his first story to *Munsey's*. His long life in the West, as well as a brief experience as an Arizona ranger, provided his credentials as a "native" writer. His first novel, published in 1907, was entitled *Wyoming*.

During the 1920s, serious critics began to pay some attention to western authors and to the role of the region in American literature. Looking back a half-century later, a literary historian commented that these early postwar years marked a major divide in the quantity and quality of western writing and the crafting of stories about the West.

The role of such literature had been a matter of general interest for some years. Back in 1908, at a time when it still was building momentum, *Scribner's Magazine* targeted the problem, pointing out that easterners applauded "border dramas," not for their literary virtue, but because they believed that these stories accurately portrayed western life. Sooner or later, warned the magazine, writers would be unable to lean on the props of western scenery for support and would have to turn out work that was good literature, not just western literature. The failure to do so was what generated the run-of-the-mill western and made life difficult for those who wanted to write about the West without having their efforts damned by that term.

As serious writers shouldered their crosses, there were periodic reports that this budding genre had died an early death. In 1920, at a time when Zane Grey was riding tall in the saddle, a cynic announced that the "dark horseman of the Golden West" was nearing the end of his trail and that the "Stetson school of fiction" was finished. For years, skeptics of this kind—low-down and ornery dry-gulchers—would lurk in the shadows, gun in hand, ready to ambush the greasewood Galahad. But now the English author Clemence Dane (pseudonym of Winifred Ashton) was buying none of this doomsday talk. For her the saga of the American cowboy would find its place in the ultimate American epic, just as the romance of King Arthur was "the final version of a thousand legends based on long-forgotten

"On his mouthharp he cheerfully played 'I met my love in the Alamo!'"
The hero of A Texas Ranger *(1910), by the popular William MacLeod*
Raine, was a direct descendant of Wister's Virginian. (Courtesy, Colorado
Historical Society)

fact" in her own country. It was easy enough to sneer at "Wild
West" writers, she admitted; but she added: "I am not sure that their
stuff isn't in some sense literature already."

Westerners do not like to be reminded that theirs is a young
country, because this implies a lack of development, of polish, of

tradition. But they will use this excuse, as have generations before them, when accounting for poor marks in regional cultural achievement. "We are, like our forefathers, not a literary people," wrote one apologist in 1925. The West had been settled too rapidly, he explained, so fast that literature could not keep pace with the flow of the frontier; and much of its early history had vanished before it could be viewed by those who were able to tell the story.

There were a few exceptions. Some of the early authors of the mountain West came from Mormon settlements, because these people represented a group movement of migrants who had come west not only with deep attachments to their roots but also possessed of a solid cultural core that withstood the corrosive influences of frontier life.

If ordinary frontiersmen were too busy hacking away at a stubborn land to write the chronicles of their battle with nature, there were others who would do it for them. Early on, some of the New England writers saw what they regarded as an epic in the making "out beyond," and they incorporated the notion in their literary efforts. As Wilson Clough once remarked, these "earlier manipulators of the frontier symbol"—the Hawthornes, the Whitmans, and others— were not frontiersmen trying to tell their story; instead, they were "booklovers and library writers" who were trying to evaluate this new chapter of the national experience and to incorporate it into what they hoped would become a native literature.

When the descendants of the frontiersmen, who had more leisure time, tried to pick up the threads of that story, the temptation to mimic currently successful authors was too attractive to ignore. So when young Philadelphians and retired dentists hit pay dirt, manipulating the same symbol, the sons of the pioneers stole the blueprints and tried to cash in on a good thing. Thus far in the twentieth century, these home-grown purveyors of what South Dakota's John R. Milton terms the "subliterary form designed to exploit the myths of the Old West" not only have failed to declare a literary independence; they have so polluted the atmosphere and vilified the name that such writers as Wallace Stegner, Scott Momaday, David Lavender, Paul Horgan, Bud Guthrie, Jack Schaefer, Vardis Fisher, Frank Waters, Frederick Manfred, Walter Van Tilburg Clark, and John Williams have had to rise above their literary origins, so to speak, to avoid having the scarlet letter "western" branded upon their prose. The burden that these and other serious authors carry is how to write about the West and still earn the rating "literature" in the doing.

Yet, the writers of popular western fiction are no more guilty of seeking the quick buck than were the hordes of amateur miners who rushed westward in an earlier day to gather up nuggets reported to be lying around just waiting for the harvesters. The dime novel of the nineteenth century had established the pattern; the public had shown its demand for the product. All that happened later was the upgrading of the cowboy to hero status and the selecting of a literary cookie cutter of a slightly different design. As a critic commented a few years ago, the westerner who enters the traffic of myth peddling certainly looks for indigenous subjects, "but he sees western history only through the formulae of popular art," and he searches, not so much for new insight, as for the discovery of a fresh angle to an old approach.

In a sense the old-time "pulpers" and their literary descendants were participating in yet-another aspect of colonialism, because their view of the West was copied from a well-worn pattern, one that was not even western in its origins. They were the hired hands of eastern-based publishers, who, even today, have their own concept, not necessarily of what the West is all about, but of what they imagine the readers to view as the real McCoy. Any deviation from the norm, on the part of the author, brings a knuckle rap from the editor and a chance for the author to stand in the corner for a few minutes to reflect upon the ways of the publishing world. I once had a brief encounter with the never-never land of western fiction, in which a New York editorial mogul demanded and got the blood and guts that he imagined to be the authentic (or marketable) thing when recounting western history to the masses. An obedient colonial took the proferred money and bowed to the East.

But as it is in other parts of western life, there are signs here and there of an emerging independence, even from publishing houses, some of which have taken up the westward trek, but especially of a freedom from being considered a hack writer, a reputation so long associated with products from west of the Mississippi. Critics are increasingly inclined to respect those writers who live in the West or who have lived there long enough to get a feel for the land and for the mood of the people. That these authors are making their presence felt is evident in their collective harvest of prestigious literary prizes, giving strength to Professor John Milton's contention that there are novels about the American West that rank with the best about any other region in the country. Times have changed since De Voto argued that Thomas Hornsby Ferril was the only first-rate poet in the West. In the mid forties that comment brought no real disagreement, but during the intervening years both the prose and the poetry that have been generated in the "new country" have improved markedly in quality.

Since much of the subject matter basically is historically oriented, these writers—and this includes the "volume" writers, too—are being more and more discriminating when they use such material; for the Wild West aspects of the region's past are now being used less generously as high seasoning. Louis L'Amour, who is proud of his factual authenticity, has been accused, however, of perpetuating the Zane Grey theme that the West was a free and unfettered place in which men were offered fresh chances and new lives in an expanding economy. But this misses a point. L'Amour, who overmodestly sees himself as a storyteller rather than as an author, has remarked, "I'm the traveler who by word-of-mouth carries on the traditions of the people." Frederick D. Glidden (pseud., Luke Short) called himself an entertainer. Which says that the story of the West has its folk overtones and consequently is an important part of American culture, myth and all.

The myth is an essential part of the western past. The problem that has confounded writers is that of how to use the myth, how to separate it from fact, perhaps how to employ it as a subtle scent to create an ambience. It belongs in the historical mix and is what makes the story of the West genuinely western. Tom Ferril touched upon the need in a poem called "Something Starting Over," which appeared in his book *Westering* (1934).

> Will something old come back again tonight?
> Send something back to tell me what I want.
>
> I do not know how long forever is,
> But today is going to be long long ago.
>
> . . . .
>
> So I ask myself if I can still remember
> How a myth began this morning and how the people
> Seemed hardly to know that something was starting over.

And yet the myth, the indispensable myth, has become a roadblock to some writers, a signal for a detour. So they reject it. They have become so determinedly antimythological that they may be riding the pendulum too far in the opposite direction. Perhaps they are, as Wallace Stegner has suggested, reacting against those who have exploited the myth or have relied upon it too heavily and too long, trying to "substitute scenery for a society." Even writers of serious literature have yielded to the temptation and have made westerners stand for what De Voto called "innumerable magnificences" that these writers know full well never existed. What were in fact seedy, dull little communities, for instance, are portrayed as bustling, upcoming places, peopled by strong, fearless residents, who accepted the temporary presences of evil in their midst on the ground that good would triumph as the rough civic edges were sandpapered by time and clean living. This is sold as history, and the authors have assumed that because theirs was a message of lofty proportions, some tinkering with historical accuracy was not only justifiable but even helpful.

A California English professor has written: "Too few writers have been willing to tell the story of the West in its own terms." As a result, many people have identified the myth entirely with these superficialities and with shallow, ultimately unbelievable virtues. Quite naturally a lot of authors and readers have grown tired of this, but one may ask if such impatience implies an abandonment of the myth itself on the grounds that this faithful old support is worn out and is of no further use. There is another possibility. Perhaps the myth is multifaceted, and we have simply exhausted the usefulness of the plane that exaggerates the West's ever-pristine landscapes and the unreal heroics of its people. The Western myth is more than that, however. It has endured in part because it describes a deep current in our collective experience, and it speaks of what Americans believe has set them apart from others. In that sense, its job is far from finished.

Without delving into the virtues of recycled myths, there is, at least, the argument that every people needs its heroes, some of which are legendary, even mythical, and that Americans have made the most of their opportunities in this sphere. The cowboy, of course, was the favorite symbol for the American legend, not only because he represented the traditional "man on horseback," who was so popular in the nineteenth century both here and abroad, but also because he epitomized the virtues of individualism, masculinity, righteousness, and a personal triumph over hardship, the elements, and even the dreaded unknown. He was a hero for all seasons. And as John Milton tells us, it is hoped that the western, in print or on the screen, tells us something about ourselves, regionally and nationally, and perhaps helps to illuminate our dreams.

The cowboy was just one of the players on the stage, even though he was up front and had feature roles; there were also trappers, stagecoach drivers, scouts, hunters, troopers, and others. As the frontier closed, traveling Wild West shows helped to perpetuate the story of these heroes and to "give form and meaning to the profound mythology of the West," to quote a student of popular culture. Visually the movies and television picked it up there.

Another word that is used to describe the great western American experience is *epic*. It has been called upon many times and has been worked hard. *Webster's New Collegiate Dictionary* gives, as a third definition of the word: "a series of events or body of legend or tradition thought to form the proper subject of an epic (the winning of the American West was a great American epic)." The selection that was chosen for illustrative purposes is interesting for its implications.

Some have argued that the westering experience does not quite fill that bill. John Williams, a Denver novelist, is one. He contended that it was essentially a nationalistic movement, one in which the frontiersman pushed himself into the unknown, but without the sponsorship of a national force; and therefore it was adventure but was not essentially epical. Yet he judged Guthrie's *Big Sky* to have the quality of an epic because it displayed the "epical virtues of physical strength, courage and endurance in its chief characters."

It has even been suggested that since the underlying theme of a western saga is primarily one of success, triumph, and ultimate victory, it could not qualify as a traditional epic because it was deficient in the tragic ingredient. Many a pioneer who battled through a life of adversity in the barren new country would argue that indeed it had more than its share of tragedy. It might have comforted a burned-out, bankrupt eastern-Montana farmer of the dirty thirties to know that if his tragedy was not of epical proportions, at least it was historic and monumental.

Whether the story of the frontier West was epic or merely a part of American folklore, it lived and spread its influence, especially with the emergence of that additional dimension—the movies and, later, television. In this final refinement, neither literacy nor even comprehension was essential, because now, merely by staring at the screen, the passive viewer could experience emotion and a vague, warm contentment that may arise from the absence of thought. It was escapism at its best. As actor Jimmy Stewart has so aptly put it, there is a visual appeal on film that portrays scenery without explanation, not to mention the fact that "nobody talks very much in a western—thereby eliminating the language barrier."

A good deal has been written, and written well, about the role of the movie westerns, so there is not a lot to add here, except to make some generalizations that apply to the theme at hand. Although the

THE SCREEN'S SINGIN', FIST-SWINGIN' COWBOY

By the 1930s, such realistic early film stars as William S. Hart had given way to glamorized "singin' fist-swingin'" cowboys, like this one in Panamint's Bad Man. *(Courtesy, Denver Public Library, Western History Department)*

Edison Company produced *Cripple Creek Barroom* in 1898, *The Great Train Robbery* (1903) is most frequently mentioned as the first narrative western film; at least it is regarded as the cornerstone for one aspect of the emerging film industry.

Although the man-and-horse combination was always there, in one role or another, many of the better-known westerns, especially those of the 1920s, featured various kinds of heroism in what was hailed as the winning of the West. Some of the titles are indicative: *The Frontiersman, The Covered Wagon, The Iron Horse, Warpaint,* and *Winners of the Wilderness.* These were the gigantic production or "epic" type of movie, presumably several cuts above the horse opera that provided run-of-the-mill fare for the kids at Saturday matinees.

In the 1930s, when the nation was gripped in a major depression and movie houses were filled with unhappy people in search of escape, tastes changed. By early 1933 the market for film westerns was sharply declining, one explanation being that viewers were uncomfortable with the idea of watching the triumphal westward march of American civilization on the screen while it was falling apart just outside the door. It was not an escape for the impoverished to be reminded of yesterday's flush times. Perhaps more attractive was the notion of revolt against society, as depicted by gangsters and bank robbers, who offered all the violence and gunplay the viewer could want. In many ways these films simply bridged a gap by presenting modern "bad men," whose predecessors had shot up the frontier without any apparent disapprobation by the reading and viewing public. The "good guy" cowboy was replaced by the private-eye detective, who also could be violent and who had a gun but no horse.

Whatever the rationale, law and order made itself felt on the screen during the late thirties, just as it had during the maturing days of the fabled Old West. Like the cowboys, who earlier had done their share to make the little western town a fit place in which to raise kids and to live in by shooting it out with the itinerant gunmen, now the G-men contributed their part by going after the gangsters. Andrew Bergman put it well when he wrote: "The law was again granted dynamism and the grace of its old associations, and could be seen as a benevolent national force."

Although World War II was disruptive to family life, the films of those years offered numerous avenues of escape, and tried-and-true sagas of Stetson heroes were part of the visual fare. But as the 1940s faded, so did the traditional celluloid westerns. The adolescent audience in itself was no longer able to sustain Zane Grey in the theaters. The postwar generation of film makers either had to abandon an old stand-by or give it a thorough overhaul. The result was the "new" or psychological film, sometimes called the adult western.

Possibly there were other motivations. It has been suggested that the pressures that the House Un-American Activities Committee put on Hollywood during the 1940s prompted the film industry to look for less-controversial subjects; and the western was one of the most harmless choices. Another explanation is that the burgeoning television industry had gobbled up so many of the old westerns that producers had to come up with something new, even if it was no more than wide-screen scenery or some comparable innovation. That westerns comprised almost 25 percent of the motion pictures released in 1950 is evidence that there still was gold in the old mine; it just required a little deeper digging. In 1958 alone, fifty-four western feature films were produced.

So there was a shift in perspective; but in general, the old mythological qualities had not been destroyed or even damaged. There now appeared a story in which there was no hero or villain, in the conventional sense; instead, a film like *High Noon* or *The Gunfighter*

Roll 'em! Those who put the myth onto celluloid occasionally left the back lots of Hollywood to find a minimum of authenticity. Here a crew films Dodge City *in 1938. (Courtesy, Boot Hill Museum, Dodge City, Kansas)*

presented the audience with a normal man whose temptations were understandably human and who simply represented the personal struggle of daily life in his increasingly complex world. When Gary Cooper played such roles, *Time* referred to him as a sort of Lincoln in Levis.

Beyond this, there may have been some subtleties. Perhaps as a defiant gesture to congressional Red hunters, some producers laced their offerings with messages of social and political protest and even made a little fun of the traditional hero; but in the main the thrust of the stories now was communal, as opposed to individualistic.

Gary Cooper commented upon that trend: "In most of the TV shows and western movies I've done, the hero is a kind of father figure who fights alone for justice against the entire community. Humanity and decent human nature are always on the short end. This may be dramatically 'valid' but it gives the wrong impression of the way things get done." He promised that the only western he would ever do again was "one that has something to do with historical value."

The updated hero represented a group or an ideal; and meaningful social relationships recognized the need for stability, for restraint, as opposed to unfettered freedom. Now the climax portrayed hearth and home for the principal characters, but the protagonist frequently did not share these rewards; rather, he moved on, presumably to face fresh challenges.

This sort of exit provided an important safety valve for his vicarious companions in the audience. It helped to preserve the old belief that the wilderness was still offering a superior way of life, long believed to exist in a distant promised land peopled by noble, primitive, happy savages, an idyllic place of fresh air and freedom.

This seductive, solitary refuge offered sanctuary to the hagridden, to those who felt smothered by family responsibilities and who hungered for a chance to pursue the treasured western credo that silence is strength. There was a similar appeal to others who felt that they were being carried down a swift stream of modern life where technology was getting out of control and was beginning to command their lives.

The television viewer might well share the dewy eyes of families who watched the lonely hero mount up and prepare to leave, but at the critical moment, the armchair westerner made his decision and swung into the saddle, alongside his pardner, who was looking west. With them rode the nagging doubts shared by a group of stationary Americans who wondered if their country's course toward a powerful, capitalistic industrial giant had not taken something away from the national dream—or, at least, the dream as they saw it.

Film historians agree that in the 1950s, some of the finest westerns ever produced made their appearance. *The Wagonmaster, The Gunfighter, Broken Arrow, Shane, High Noon,* and *Invitation to a Gunfighter* are a few on which a consensus would be relatively easy to achieve. Aside from the trend toward films that tended to advocate Christian values, nonviolence, and stability and to emphasize the virtues of an older order, which appeared to be fading, there was a surprising softening of racial views. A West that actually had been highly racist now fictionally opened its arms to all, and the brothers—black, brown, and red—now rode together.

During the fifties the black cowboy was being written about, and shortly he and his fellow blacks would become more prominent in western films. By the 1970s the Negro audience for westerns would have increased so much that producers would be talking about the "black market" and trying to answer its demands. Meanwhile, Mexican-Americans also were to benefit from the fresh attitudes toward minorities that began to find their way toward silver-screen stories about the frontier. But first, the Indian.

Broken Arrow, in 1950, led the way in providing viewers with a more sympathetic portrayal of the American Indians. It received high praise, not only for its revisionism, but also for managing "the rare movie trick of making a social comment without overloading the scales." Although the film was decidedly pro-Indian, it did not immediately reverse a long trend of what a British critic called "pernicious lies" about the natives or of Hollywood's traditional devotion to the demonic stereotype of the red plainsman. Even in 1950 a white hero could not actually marry the Indian girl and settle down on the ranch; at least one of them had to meet with an unfortunate premature end. But a start had been made. By 1964 and John Ford's *Cheyenne Autumn,* some of the historical realities of Indian life were becoming more apparent. If nothing else, film makers were beginning to distinguish between native horsemen, in constant chase scenes, and Indian culture itself.

In the early seventies, New Mexican Indian tribes began to finance western movies; but rather than engaging in special pleading, they chose more conventional subject matter. In fact, old-time western movie buffs must have been somewhat taken aback when, in 1971, Lamont Johnson's *A Gunfight,* backed by money from the Jicarilla Apaches, turned out to be a western without Indians.

During the fifties, at a time when westerns were selling at an annual rate of thirty-five million copies in paperback, the popularity of the filmed versions found a great outlet through the television tube. With the appearance in 1955 of "Gunsmoke," "Cheyenne," and "Wyatt Earp," the TV western had arrived. Before the decade was over, the stampede was rampant, despite annual predictions that the bubble had burst. In the spring of 1959, eight of the top ten TV shows were oaters, with "Gunsmoke" firmly in the lead. At that moment, thirty of the prime-time programs were westerns. *Time* magazine puzzled over such wide acclaim by viewers and asked if an opiate of quick-and-easy escape was the answer. Or—and this was a perennial question—was it sex, that is, the gun as a sexual symbol. The magazine concluded that the reason was deeper, that westerns were an antidote for the complications of daily life that would offer simple solutions and a return to the restful absolutes of the past. It was an explanation that was common and had been heard frequently in the past.

Contrary to the gloomy forecast that the bloom was off the rose, there were a sustained interest in western films and only a slight decline in the number of such books during the 1960s. Films tended to emphasize a trend that had been in evidence since the end of World

War II: that of setting the scene near the very end of the frontier period. This seemed to sharpen the contrast between older virtues and the corruption of modern commercialized society. *Monte Walsh* (1970), in which an old cowpoke is shown as a victim of the depersonalized eastern corporate world, has been set forth as an extreme example of this theme.

Surrounded by strikes, social turmoil, a hopeless war in Southeast Asia, increasingly onerous taxes, dangerous new chemicals, and polluted cities, Americans of the sixties felt more strongly than ever the need to escape, even if only momentarily, to a mental Shangri-La, where the air was clear, where the horizons were uncluttered with billboards, and where a man was the master of his own movements. To many of those who lived in a hectic modern society, the frontier marshal, to pick one television character, represented above all a man who was relaxed, who had time to play cards or enjoy a social drink, who was cool enough during occasional times of tension, and who lived an orderly, regularized existence under the approving eyes of his fellow townsmen. Not burdened by any obvious property and invariably unmarried, this character appeared to represent the ideal of the unencumbered man, who, beyond all that, appeared to live an unhurried existence. Male viewers, especially, saw something here that appeared enviable, even if only in theory.

There was more to this, however, than simple escapism in a time of troubles. There always had been a fuzziness in the western fictional formula. On the one hand, the stories celebrated the coming of civilization in the form of towns, schoolmarms, laws, and the family; but on the other, the hero was the hero mainly because of his individualistic, free-roaming ways. In a situation like that, a nagging question was lurking between the lines: What would happen when the villains were all gunned down and the sheriffs and bankers were firmly in command? The hero would have little room to be and do what readers expected of him. Alan Ladd said as much in the classic Western movie of 1953, *Shane,* when he rode back into the mountains after taking care of Jack Wilson and the Riker brothers.

In the sixties—a time of hostility and cynicism toward authority and modern life, of countercultures and "dropping out"—movies and novels made heroes out of likeable misfits and anachronisms who were trying to survive on the cusp of the change between the older and newer America. Often they were amiable outlaws, such as Butch Cassidy and the Sundance Kid. These characters usually ended up dead, shot down by authorities, like Butch and the Kid, or otherwise crushed by impersonal forces. Jack Burns, the drifter-hero of *Lonely*

Are the Brave, a cult classic made from Edward Abbey's novel *The Brave Cowboy,* is run down by an enormous truckload of toilets. The lesson of the day was obvious, even heavy-handed. In modern America, many in the sixties thought, individualism was a fatal disease.

By the seventies the celluloid cowboy was still around, but barely. Such actors as Henry Fonda and William Holden occasionally took these golden roles; but John Wayne was about the last of the traditional movie saddle heroes. In this role his popularity was perennial and indestructible. Ben Johnson, who had appeared in a number of movies with him, thought that viewers wanted the kind of films Wayne made "because they make people feel good about this country and the way it was settled." When Wayne died in 1979, one editorial writer called him the true son of America, a man who epitomized justice in the Old West, where there were no gray areas between right and wrong and where fine points of the law did not rescue malefactors. Congress agreed; it struck off a medal for "the Duke," as he was called, the inscription stating simply "John Wayne, American." The legislators might well have said "American hero," for that was his role, on the screen and, in the eyes of many, off it.

For more than half a century the fictional cowboy, as the central figure in the conventional western, has trotted off the stage only to return for a curtain call. As early as 1914, readers of the *Moving Picture World* had been told that William S. Hart's day was over when that magazine deplored his first feature film, *The Bargain,* as being "an attempt to revive a style of motion picture which we had hoped was a thing of the past." True to the frontier legend, Hart stoutly responded: "The Western drama will never die."

The drama lived on, in spite of periodic reports that it was in poor health and perhaps had a terminal ailment. During the 1970s it was pronounced dead but was brought back to life with regularity. Sometimes this cycle was remarkably short. For example, in May 1976, Grace Lichtenstein wrote in the *New York Times* about the rebirth of the prairie morality play, but by March of the next year, Gene Siskel of the *Chicago Tribune* had written a new obituary. But wait. In February 1978, Jerry Buck of the Associated Press heralded the return of the western, only to have an AP television writer again watch it ride into the sunset in 1982. The cancellation of *Maverick* in June was offered as proof of the western's final passing. It was then believed that such programs were for people who craved nostalgia, who yearned to go back in time; but now it seemed that at last a modern generation was ready to reject the past in favor of the future or at least something more current.

If, indeed, Americans appeared to have grown weary of recounting this oft-told tale of conquest and glory in a wild country beyond the wide Missouri, there were others who might still be counted among the faithful. For years, foreigners have regarded our westering experience as the American odyssey. But rather than detachment, they feel a proprietary interest in this mythic West, which has vague boundaries of time and geography. This came out one time in a conversation that I had with an Englishman. When a remark was dropped about "our frontier," he countered with a quick and firm interjection: "But it isn't just *your* frontier. The frontier belongs to *everybody!*"

There have been many non-Americans who have been inclined to adopt the Old West. Most of them were readers, fans who not infrequently made a hobby of their interest, while others were travelers whose accounts sometimes were published. On occasion, novelists saw possibilities in the golden West and tried to strike it rich. Beyond doubt the European who achieved the greatest fame in this sphere was the German author Karl May. When he was a young man, his undisciplined imagination got him into all kinds of difficulty, including two prison terms, the latter experience perhaps compelling him to rechannel his fantasies, this time to the less-dangerous pursuit of writing about the American hinterland. During the latter years of the nineteenth century he cranked out dozens of potboilers about a western Canaan that he was never to see. The closest he ever came to an on-site visit was a brief tour of the eastern United States in 1908, four years before his death. However, the absence of original research proved to be no handicap. His ability to weave tales that satisfied his readers' appetite for romance and nostalgia resulted in a continuous sale that had totaled about twenty-six million copies by the 1960s. The magazine *Der Spiegel* asserted that his influence was greater than that of any other German writer between Goethe and Mann.

Among May's avid readers was young Adolf Hitler, who seems never to have lost his admiration for Germany's imitator of James Fenimore Cooper. As Europe's most dreaded warlord, Hitler maintained an unshakeable faith in the qualities of May's hero, Old Shatterhand. During those lonely nights when the war was going badly for the Third Reich, Hitler would, according to Albert Speer, "still reach for those stories that gave him courage, like works of philosophy for others or the Bible for elderly people." The somewhat incredulous Speer, who called the novelist the greatest dilettante of them all, added: "Hitler would lean upon Karl May as proof for everything imaginable, in particular for the idea that it was not necessary to know the desert in order to direct troops in the African theater of war." Just ask Old Shatterhand. In short, the message that May sent to Hitler was that one did not have to travel in order to know the world, a notion that the dictator found convenient and comforting.

Some of Hitler's troops believed in May's infallibility. During World War II, some German prisoners of war escaped from their Arizona internment camp and tried to cross the desert Southwest and get to Mexico. One of them later confessed, "Jurgen and I tried every trick we knew. . . . We walked backward in the sand, the way Karl May says the Indians did." They ended up back behind the wire.

The postwar years saw no diminution of May's popularity or that of the frontier image. When, in 1962, German movie makers struck gold with a film that featured Old Shatterhand and his faithful friend Winnetou (played by an American and a Frenchman), others joined the rush. Between 1963 and 1965, Italians turned out about 130 so-called spaghetti westerns. The French long since had shown their interest and had staked an early claim upon the West. Back in 1904 a French artist, who had spent six months on a Montana ranch, wrote *On the Trails of the Far West;* he later acted in some early French-made western films, one of which was called *Cowboy.*

The prairie fire of popularity was not confined to western Europe. In postwar years, "easterns" also appeared, produced by both Russians and Japanese, horse operas that sometimes were called parawesterns in that they might deal with the Foreign Legion or armored knights, but that appeared to portray thinly disguised cowboys. When a Czech director of puppet films sought to satirize American films, it was significant that he chose the western as his subject.

After European film makers appeared to have momentarily diluted the Stetson-and-chaps market, the western turned up in the form of rodeos, one of which was Larry Mahan's Ramblin' Rodeo Review, which opened in Belgium in 1979, a show that featured the cowboy as "the only true folk hero of America."

Even as Europeans and others were paying homage to the seemingly never-ending pageant of the Old West, in film, at local cowboy Disneylands, and then at rodeos, the legend continued to surface fictionally, even in nonwestern books. Here are a few samples. In Louis Bromfield's *Colorado* (1947), written when the sagebrush saga was booming, it was not surprising to learn that the principal characters "were all bound for the Promised Land to get rich. They were going west toward the setting sun with a little small change in their pockets. They were fleeing the crowded East . . . and the filthy overcrowded cities." But three decades later, the enduring myth had not lost any of its potency. The "beneficial West" again was seen, this time in Oakley Hall's *The Bad Lands* (1978), when one of the principals avowed that his true place was out there where every man has an equal chance and philosophized, "Perhaps we must always go to the frontier to find the fellowship that the nation's Founders intended."

At the same time the "negative West" lived on. In John Updike's *A Month of Sundays* (1975), a clergyman was "banished to one of those western states (what worse?) which is recognizably large and square and holds one refugee asthmatic and three drunken Indians in a Ford pickup per square mile." MacDonald Harris, in *Herma* (1981), dispatched an impulsive, disgraced heir of a well-to-do family off to a western exile, condemned "like so many other failures, dreamers, idealists, embezzlers, uncaught horse thieves . . . disinherited sons, and other victims of the American Dream." Perhaps the most effective blows against the legend came in the form of the fabulously successful comic western movies *Cat Ballou* (1965) and *Blazing Saddles* (1974), films that poked fun at the most hallowed traditions of the genre. The critic Pauline Kael compared the former to a buffoon at a party, ingratiating himself to his public by sacrificing his dignity.

In an odd way, however, these assaults were tributes to the western mystique. They worked precisely because the public had loved, so long and so well, the clichés and images that these books and movies were now ridiculing. The frontier West has produced America's most deeply rooted folk tale, the "hardiest weed that ever grew on the literary landscape," a myth that has survived abuse, ridicule, burlesquing, satire, and disdain. Despite the ongoing vilification of the western, Hollywood was not blind to that vehicle's monetary potential. It saw in that one general geographic location and in a saddlebag full of undeviating clichés a chance to capitalize and recapitalize on an apparently ever-renewable resource. No purveyor ever had a more constant or safer market. It existed because the public unfailingly showed its willingness to see the same thing again and again, a phenomenon that has been explained as "a ritualistic passivity similar to that which one finds in a [church] congregation," blended with the "same bewitching strength as an incantation: the magic of repetition."

This western story, chanted over and over like a mantra by the American public, began with the tales of James Fenimore Cooper and flourished in thousands of variations during the dime-novel era after the Civil War. In our century it has been sustained first by films and later by television, the glowing altar before which American families gather each night to pledge their cultural allegiances. The recent decline in the popularity of horse operas on the silver screen and on the picture tube has led some to announce the demise of the western. There is no need, however, for requiems for an old friend, rumored to have departed lately. For one thing, the literary tradition that stretches back to Leatherstocking shows no sign of flagging. Louis L'Amour has established himself as one of the best-selling authors in history. Customers are buying about half a million copies of his novels each month, or nearly seventeen thousand a day. Besides, the galleries are fickle, and tastes are cyclical. If western movies are not "in" this season, they probably will be discovered next time around by young people who think they have come up with something new. This has happened often enough before. The western, as a window to frontier America, will be as exciting to future generations as it has been to those in the past.

Because they need it.

CHAPTER 9

THE WILDERNESS EVANGELISTS

As Americans turned the corner from the nineteenth century into the twentieth, some of them believed they were watching the Old West begin to slip away. True, it was surviving on paper, but those who went looking for the place—tourists, scientists, writers, and even prospective settlers—were having trouble finding it. And that made them uneasy.

Part of their concern grew from doubts about the economic future of the region. The West always had seemed a limitless land of never-ending resources, but observers now were wondering whether it might indeed be finite. Its rich bounty was being devoured in enormous mouthfuls, and some questioned whether much would be left for their grandchildren. But behind these doubts was a vaguer anxiety over the great western wilderness, those immense sprawling spaces in the American outback. It, too, seemed suddenly to be in danger, and voices now were heard calling for its protection.

Both of these ideas, of course, ran counter to the traditional beliefs of the pioneers. The typical frontiersman thought the resources that unrolled toward the Pacific Ocean were endless, so there was no need to conserve them; such an attitude, in fact, was part of the general American tendency to equate progress with growth and development. As for the wilderness, the pioneer gazed upon it with a respect born of fear, hostility, and frustration. For generations, his ancestors had defined their success or failure through the assault on the forest. Telling such a westerner to be kind to trees was like urging a southerner to save the mosquitoes. Most who had come from that tradition still clung to the notion that the wild places were meant to be conquered and that the land of plenty would always be the land of plenty. They rationalized that while wastefulness was bad, in the beginning it was necessary to the process of digging in, getting started, setting roots. Aldo Leopold, who is so well known for his environmentalist writings, understood this and put it well: ''To the laborer in the sweat of his labor, the raw stuff on his anvil is an adversary to be conquered. So was the wilderness an adversary to the pioneer.''

190

Nonetheless, as the frontier days drew to a close, Americans in various walks of life began to have second thoughts about the "conquest" of the West. They were slowly discovering that the very condition which the pioneers had set themselves against—the fact that the wilderness was beyond human control—was part of the source of their excitement and affection for the West. This feeling grew stronger as the years passed, until it became an important force in political and social affairs. It evolved into something like a religion. Rooted in a stubbornly held faith, it attracted both wise men of vision and hot-eyed fanatics. Its bitter schisms produced a few martyrs and many shrewd princes of the church schooled in political games. There was even an occasional Moses, though unlike the original, this sort promised to keep the faithful wandering in the wilderness forever.

As the century opened, concern about the fate of the undeveloped West was still unfocused, but the government's land policy had already begun to reflect this uneasiness. Since the birth of the republic the question had been how to sell the land or give it away and to whom. Speculators, railroads, mining and timber companies, ranchers, squatters, and homesteaders took huge bites out of the pie, while a good part of the rest—eventually about 73 million acres in the West—went to the states to help pay for schools, canals, and roads. Now a new phase began. The government became the landlord; the people became the tenants. In 1891, Congress for the first time authorized the president to create forest reserves from the public domain, land that would be protected from development for the time being; and by 1901, 33 million acres had been set aside. Then Theodore Roosevelt moved into the White House. With characteristic enthusiasm, the president who had enjoyed playing cowboy started roping off great pieces of public land. By the time Congress applied the brakes in 1907, more than 150 million acres in 159 national forests had been put beyond the reach of westerners who were yearning to get at them. It had to be done, said the president. "If it had not been for the creation of the present system of forest reserves, practically every acre of timberland in the West . . . would be controlled or be on the point of being controlled by one huge timber trust."

The purpose was, not to leave the land untouched forever, but to divide the loot more fairly and sparingly, with an eye to the future. In 1897, Congress had spelled out the goal. The government was "securing favorable conditions of water flows, and [furnishing] a continuous supply of timber for the use and necessities of the United States." This fit well into the ideas of Roosevelt and his chief forester,

Gifford Pinchot. With wise, careful planning, plenty of the feast would be left for future generations to carve up. Their approach was democratic, utilitarian, efficient—and squarely within the traditional American mission to subdue the land and make it over. Forests, rivers, grasslands, and minerals—we should "take every part of the land and its resources," Pinchot wrote, "and put it to that use in which it will serve the most people."

Though the term would not be coined until 1939, this was the start of the government's policy of "multiple use." There is room for debate about how the Forest Service has applied this concept over the years; some observers argue that officials have always been ready to sacrifice watersheds and anything else to make sure that the nation has plenty of lumber. But at this point, early in the century, one point was clear. There was no mention of saving part of the national forests for recreation and scenic beauty. In time, utilitarians would do battle with those who wanted to allow such things under the multiple-use umbrella, but that lay in the future.

For now, the battle concerned, instead, how much land should be kept under supervision and how much the landlord should charge for its use. From the West came cries from cattlemen, sheepmen, lumbermen, hydroelectric interests, and those who were interested in coal and other minerals. They all claimed to be inheritors of the frontier tradition, sons of the pioneers, trying to eke an honest living from the lands that they always had used rather freely in their pursuit of happiness and prosperity. But now, they said, Washington was meddling in this most American of enterprises. An exasperated Arizonan told a meeting of his fellows: "Looks like every time one of the government scouts finds a tree in the West he wires Pinchot and Pinchot gallops into Teddy's office and says: 'Oh, Teddy, we've found a tree in the What-the-Hell Mountains; let's create a new forest.' "

It was not that westerners were unaware that their country had been torn up in many places as a result of ruthless exploitation. Many of them recognized the land's limitations. The humorist Bill Nye wrote that the West had more rivers with less water and more cows with less milk than anywhere else in the universe; and in the summer of 1908, Will C. Barnes wrote an article in *Out West,* praising the Forest Service and admitting that overgrazing had left too much western land vulnerable to erosion. A few influential officials spoke favorably of the government's actions; among them were Governor Joseph Dixon of Montana, Congressman William Kent of California, and Judge Ben B. Lindsey of Denver.

But a long list of other officials lined up against the president's conservation program, particularly a powerful group of western senators, Key Pittman of Nevada, James D. Phelan of California, Charles Thomas of Colorado, Reed Smoot of Utah, and Albert B. Fall of New Mexico. These men did not disagree with the lofty principles the president preached. Most westerners, in fact, would not have objected when Roosevelt told a Denver audience in 1910 that conservation meant "the utilization of . . . resources, under such regulation and control that will prevent waste, extravagance and monopoly." They did argue, however, that Roosevelt was taking out of immediate use great portions of the West, explaining that it all would be used at some distant future time. The president seemed to be putting most of the land far beyond the reach of most westerners during their own lifetimes. Beyond that, he appeared to be interfering with the hallowed dynamics of "progress."

The fight over western coal deposits illustrates the point. In 1906, Roosevelt withdrew some 50 million acres of coal-bearing lands. This, of course, increased the value of coal lands elsewhere in the country. Westerners quickly shouted discrimination and economic ruin. In Colorado, where 10 million tons of coal, worth $13 million, had been produced that year, coal lands naturally were a great attraction to outside investors. Now this new program was threatening to drive them away. A Yampa, Colorado, editor complained: "The coal land of Routt County is a treasure of which the people have always been proud, and we now have a chunk of it grabbed right while we were in the middle of a conversation with investors and homesteaders, trying to induce them to come, invest and help build up the country. Well, it doesn't look good, and the country don't feel good about it either." From another community came the lament that "actual settlers who are interested in developing her resources" were needed more than ever by the state. Roosevelt's latest move was merely one of "many notable wrongs the government had committed in its attempts to handle the lands and manage our affairs."

The last phrase revealed a lot. The particular issues at hand may have been new, but the squabbling over rentals and reservations also exacerbated an old dilemma. Westerners always had solicited federal aid, from land grants to army protection, but they could never control the agencies that administered these programs; and worse, the agencies themselves often collided with one another, causing local turmoil that inevitably ended in a general condemnation of the federal government. It became a habit. Westerners raged about the very intervention they had courted, even as they fought each other over the spoils. The result was a divided West, tenaciously held together by its common enmity toward Washington.

The complaints about conservation simply wrote a new chapter in this familiar story. It was the old and persistent resentment of paternalism at the hands of outlanders. The new restrictions on coal lands "established a system as obnoxious and repressive as English landlordism in Ireland," declared a Del Norte, Colorado, editor, who went on to call Uncle Sam a penny-pinching landlord, "preying on a class of pioneer citizens . . . trying to develop the wilderness."

With all the brickbats thrown in these disputes, it is easy to forget that the antagonists agreed on a crucial point: all of the West, sooner or later, should be developed. Another group, however, had radically different ideas. To the "preservationists," the American wilderness that this Colorado editor wanted to see developed had value in and of itself, not in how it might be made over. To develop the wilderness would be to destroy its worth. Its potential would be realized precisely by leaving it alone.

This was certainly a minority viewpoint at the time, but the idea was not new. It had roots going back at least to the Leatherstocking saga of James Fenimore Cooper, who believed that by some strange alchemy the American forests and prairies had transformed fresh arrivals into a new and distinctive breed. Even as Americans were fighting the wilderness, he wrote, it had become part of them. During these same years, Ralph Waldo Emerson, Henry David Thoreau, and the transcendentalists of the "Concord school" were preaching that the simplest creations of nature reflected profound truths. It followed that some of God's handiwork had to be saved so that man could reflect upon it and learn. The transcendentalists' universal message had a special power in their own country, because Europeans always had thought of this land as what the entire world must have been like before modern man had begun to make it over. "In the beginning," as John Locke had put it, "all the world was America." Now, however, more and more of God's garden seemed to be going the way of the Old World. For those who were looking for what was left, the directions were simple. "We go eastward to realize history and study the works of art and literature," Thoreau wrote; "the West is but another name for Wild." By 1900 there was a dawning awareness that time and land were starting to run out, but westward some of each remained—past the hundredth meridian, up in the hills, beyond the towns—Out There. It had to be saved.

As early as 1832, in fact, the painter and ethnographer George Catlin, after observing the vast herds of bison high on the Missouri,

The West's scenic extravaganzas proved to be some of its most marketable resources. In the selling of beauty, the Grand Canyon of the Yellowstone has been among the most popular products. (Courtesy, Colorado Historical Society)

suggested that "some great protecting policy of government" might make of the Great Plains "a *nation's Park*," where "rudenesses and wilds in Nature's works" would be kept untouched for future visitors. Predictably, Thoreau proposed the same: "Why should not we . . . have our national preserves . . . in which the bear and panther, and even some of the hunter race, may still exist, and not be 'civilized off the face of the earth?' "

Why not, indeed? As the nineteenth century ticked away, this cluster of ideas, all of which agreed that somehow the meaning of the American spirit and experience depended on the survival of part of the wilderness, began to attract more attention. The focus, for a while, was upon a few places of spectacular beauty. The most obvious candidate was the Yellowstone country of northwestern Wyoming, with its geysers, grizzly bears, and waterfalls. Congress made it the first national park in 1872. The movement, Wallace Stegner wrote later, turned into a backfire, "burning back upwind against the current of claim and grab and raid." By 1900 there were Sequoia, Mount Rainier, and Yosemite, which Washington had first given to California as a park back in 1864. Soon Crater Lake, Mesa Verde, Glacier, Lassen, and others were added to the list. In 1916 Congress created the National Park Service, under the Department of the

Interior, to oversee eighteen islands of protected scenery and wildlife, all of them in the West.

In these early years, the leading apostle of preservation was John Muir, a former Indiana farm boy who had given up a career as an inventor in favor of the wilderness cause. His lineage went straight back to the transcendentalists. He had a gift for translating their philosophy in a way that has held up well; in the 1970s his aphorisms on the unity of life ("We all travel the Milky Way together, trees and men") and nature's wisdom ("The clearest way into the Universe is through the forest wilderness") would find their way onto glossy posters of aspen groves and mountain peaks. Throughout this urban, industrial century, Americans have been fascinated by the primitive. By 1900 they were already looking for wild men, and Muir played the part beautifully. Thoreau had withdrawn to Walden Pond, within earshot of Concord; Muir tramped for weeks through the most rugged reaches of the Sierra Nevada, talking to bears and sitting atop pine trees during raging thunderstorms. Stories like these quickly became part of the Muir mystique.

They miss the main point, however. Muir was much more than an American Tarzan. He understood clearly that a good part of the public was stirring restlessly as it watched the "real West" begin to disappear, and more than anyone else of his generation he began to transform that vague uneasiness into a political force. He was convinced of the need for government help. God had always protected trees from drought and avalanches, he said, but "He cannot save them from fools—only Uncle Sam can do that." Between retreats to Yosemite, he would rush to Washington to testify and to bend the ears of politicians. He wrote a shelf load of books to move Americans to his ideas. In 1892, with two dozen other people, he founded the Sierra Club, and he served as its first and only president until his death in 1914, shaping what might have been only a hiking club into a powerful preservationist lobby, the nation's first. Later, after World War II, it would be so again.

Muir was a symbol and a pattern for much that would follow, the taproot of the modern wilderness crusade. He was everything that would inspire some and infuriate others—part mystic, part hardball lobbyist, an unlikely blend of Henry Thoreau and Ralph Nader.

Muir's blind spots also tell a lot about the early preservation movement. He often seemed to have nothing particular against the coming of big business to the West, and the admiration for progress and technological wizardry never quite died in him. Among his closest friends he counted such captains of industry as E. H.

Patron saint of the preservationists and founder of the Sierra Club, John Muir (left) rides through Yosemite Valley with President Roosevelt in 1903. (Courtesy, California Historical Society, San Francisco)

Harriman. When Harriman died, Muir called the railroad czar a great and benevolent glacier who made crooked ways straight and brought Americans ever closer together. Preservationists during those years concentrated on saving a few magnificent jewels in the vast expanse of the West. Men like Harriman appreciated such places. They could afford to. To them, a Yellowstone or a Yosemite was a restful haven of recreation and contemplation. Riding in Harriman's private railroad car through those great yawning spaces east of the Sierra, it would have been difficult for Muir to grasp the revolution that capital and technology eventually would bring. The real enemies, he thought, were the utilitarians such as Pinchot and the western go-getters, descended from the restless squatters who had first bulled their way into Kentucky, those who found no value in wilderness whatsoever and who saw nothing wrong with flooding Hetch Hetchy Valley in Yosemite and in grazing sheep in Yellowstone. These were the true infidels, the violators of holy places.

The hostility, of course, was mutual. Pinchot called Muir a fuzzy-thinking sentimentalist and elitist. Native westerners had spent their lives thinking of the wilderness as an antagonist to be overcome. To them, the preservationists, who saw it as a sacred temple, were almost beyond comprehension. Especially irritating was the prominent role being played by academics, intellectuals, and artists—soft-handed esthetes, they seemed, who had no appreciation of western realities. The governor of Wyoming fumed that government policy was being shaped by "college professors and landscape gardeners." Coloradans reacted similarly when Hamlin Garland and some eastern colleagues proposed setting aside, for good, part of the White River preserve. "Along comes a poet and suggests a national park in an area that ought to teem with inhabitants," an editor raged. "Away with him!" The natives were starting to worry that the dudes were taking over.

Stephen T. Mather, another demigod of the preservationist cause, showed another contradiction among the wilderness evangelists. A wealthy California borax manufacturer with a genuine passion for the West's beauty, Mather came to Washington in 1915 to administer the national parks. By the twenties he recognized that developers would soon be sniffing around his territory. When the government could seriously consider damming Lake Yellowstone, as it did in 1921, nothing was safe. So he and Horace Albright, his assistant and successor, set out to educate the public on just what a treasure was waiting for them. Mather hired publicists, turned out books and pamphlets and maps, and courted politicians and businessmen with his considerable charm and his slide shows of sequoias, geysers, and limpid lakes. It became a crusade. He "preached parks, pictured parks, planned parks, played parks on the clangorous cymbal and cooing lute until one is afraid not to go see parks," a journalist wrote. "One dreads a parkless death." With this publicity blitz came a campaign for roads to make the parks more accessible. In 1929, the year when Mather retired, Congress appropriated $51 million to the project.

The results of all this were spectacular. About 750,000 visitors entered national parks in 1919. By 1931 that number had multiplied four times over. During the same years the number of automobiles that rolled annually through the gates grew from 97,721 to 897,038. Never again would Yellowstone, Glacier, or Crater Lake face the danger of being ignored to death.

Victories like these brought other problems, however. According to the law that created the park system, its fundamental purpose was to provide for public enjoyment of the scenery, historical objects, and wildlife, while keeping it all "unimpaired for . . . future generations." In other words, bring people to the wilderness without changing it in any way. Here was the "unimpaired doctrine" that supposedly has guided the park system until today. It is a contradictory goal, as Mather's crusade already was making clear. Mather was full of assurances that roads and public promotions would not threaten the purity of the parks, but some were not so sure. After fighting the crowds in Yosemite (where Mather once sponsored jazz concerts), a visitor observed in 1931 that there was only one difference between this national park and a Los Angeles intersection: "They had trees and no traffic cop in Yosemite Valley, while at Seventh and Broadway they had no trees and a traffic cop." It was a refrain that would be heard repeatedly in the years to come.

Muir and Mather recognized that the crusaders of their day needed above all to alert the public to the wonders of the West and to focus the energy among those who were already dedicated to the cause. But they did not anticipate the full range of threats to the wilderness or the subsequent problems that their own actions would bring. How could they? Though the preservationist idea was sunk deep into the American experience, as a political movement it was still in its infancy. Muir and Mather were master publicists and organizers, but they and their friends were just starting to define what they wanted and how to go about getting it. Besides, in 1900, or even in 1930, it was hard to foresee what development and tourism would bring. The West was a big place. Part of its mystique lay in the fact that contradictory dreams and ideas could live and grow there without

"Summer Bedouins," such as these visitors to the San Isabel National Forest in Colorado, contributed millions of dollars to western coffers. (Courtesy, Colorado Historical Society)

bumping into one another. Only a good while later would the inheritors of the preservationist cause begin to learn the meaning of human glaciers such as Harriman and the slick promotions and packaging of the wilderness idea. When the West finally began to fill up, the implications became clear enough.

Meanwhile, as advocates of different ideas about the future of the West maneuvered within the government, changes in its official land policy continued. Without much fanfare, most of those who were concerned with the disposition of the public lands were moving toward the assumption that what was left of the national domain would remain in the government's hands, probably forever. The best farmland had long since passed into private holdings. Mining companies had every reason to continue leasing from the government on terms that amounted to a cheap ticket to a feast. At this point, at least, the timber interests still were relying almost totally on private forest lands.

There remained the question of grazing. Much of the land that was still in the public domain was suitable for raising cattle and sheep. Though it was unlikely that anyone would ever file claim on the millions of arid and semiarid acres, ranchers and sheepmen ran their animals on it, and overgrazing was taking a terrible toll. Cattlemen often had called for Washington to give the land to the states, but the states showed little interest in taking on such an enormous administrative burden, especially during the depression years. The veteran Colorado congressman Edward T. Taylor, by now a dedicated proponent of the multiple-use philosophy, eventually devised a solution to this stand-off. Taylor proposed that most of the remaining federal ranch land—a good part of the domain—be withdrawn from entry under homestead and be given over to a new Grazing Service, under the Department of the Interior. Ranchers would pay to use this land, and the fees would finance conservation projects. To soothe local interests, part of the rentals would go to the states, and cattlemen and sheepmen would play a role in making decisions for their grazing districts.

The Taylor Grazing Act of 1934 was a giant step in the process begun half a century earlier. By the end of the year, President Franklin Delano Roosevelt had closed most of the public domain to homesteading. This land, eventually more than 170 million acres, remained under the control of the Grazing Service until this office was merged in 1946 with the old General Land Office to form the Bureau of Land Management (BLM), but even this was considered a temporary expedient. Only in 1976, after years of study and deliberation and the usual gas and buncombe, was the BLM rescued from purgatory and made permanent. It was more of less official: as a realtor, Uncle Sam was saying, he had gotten out of sales and promotional giveaways and was getting into rentals and public stewardship.

Meanwhile, friends of the wilderness naturally were chafing. The Taylor Act was more of the same, they said, an accommodation over how the country should be sliced up and exploited. It was true that

Aldo Leopold combined scientific expertise with gentle but powerful prose to chide the public for its wrong-headedness and its abuse of the wilderness. (Courtesy, Sierra Club)

Pinchot's ideas still ruled the Forest Service, but by the twenties there were some who were beginning to fidget and raise questions. In fact, two of the most influential wilderness advocates of the interwar years worked within the government to temper the policies that had ruled the government's forest preserves from the start.

Aldo Leopold came to the Forest Service in 1909 as a believer in Pinchotism, but his early years in New Mexico and Arizona turned him away. He found that the government's conservation policies, like the pioneer's view of the land, rested on the false and dangerous belief that the world is man's personal possession. "We abuse the land because we regard it as a commodity belonging to us," he wrote later. "When we see the land as a community to which we belong, we may begin to use it with love and respect." Before and after he broke with the Forest Service in the late twenties, Leopold argued the need for a "land ethic," a sense of responsibility toward the world and everything in it. Given our growing numbers and our precocity at changing the environment, he warned, we are flirting with disaster unless we change our ways. He had a knack for mixing moral lessons with just enough scientific dissection to give his statements a hard-nosed credibility, and his *Sand County Almanac,* published shortly after his death in 1948, became a classic in the preservationist library. To Leopold, the West, with its huge but shrinking islands of surviving wildernesss, provided a classroom, a laboratory, wherein modern man could be schooled in these lessons. What better place to go, in his words, to learn to "think like a mountain"?

And there was Robert ("Bob") Marshall, the son of a prominent New York jurist. Marshall was a hiker extraordinaire and a plant pathologist who had graduate degrees from Harvard and Johns Hopkins. During the thirties, first as director of forestry in the Office of Indian Affairs and later as head of the Forest Service's Division of Recreation and Lands, Bob Marshall preached an idea that would gain popularity in the years to come. The West, he said, was essential for our psychological survival. Everyone needed the emotional and spiritual balm that only time in the wilds could bring. The leafy and needled solitudes would be a kind of national sanitarium. Psychology being all the rage in those years, this had a nice ring to it, but just as effective were Marshall's skills at administrative infighting. A master of the memorandum, he worked well within the New Deal power structure. The preservation of the wilderness was a "productive" use of the land, he argued, just as much as farming and ranching and timbering. It kept us sane, recharged our souls, reminded us of beauty beyond man's making.

The West could always teach us these lessons, so we needed to keep it as wild as we could, Leopold and Marshall were arguing. Like coal and oil, the wilderness was a nonrenewable resource, but there was a lot less of it, and unlike other resources, there was no substitute for it. It could never be increased, only diminished, and the shrinkage ought to stop. Shrewdly, Leopold and Marshall played on the jealousy of Forest Service officials over the growing popularity of the national parks. They called on their bosses to put aside large pieces of

Founder of the Wilderness Society and brilliant lobbyist for the preservation movement, Bob Marshall stands ready for a hike of thirty miles or so through the Alaskan back country. (Courtesy, The Bancroft Library)

the wildest deserts and mountains, and then to leave them alone—no roads, no rustic lodges, nothing. Let people come on the land's own terms. In 1924, under Leopold's goading (and with the support of sportsmen's groups), Congress made the Gila National Forest the first designated wilderness recreation area. By the time of Marshall's death in 1939, sixteen wilderness areas had been set aside in Indian reservations, and 14 million acres in national forests had been withdrawn from development by administrative fiat under what were called the "U" regulations. Gradually, the wilderness ideal was easing its way into the government's concept of multiple use.

During the decades between the two world wars, advocates of private development, conservation, and wilderness preservation continued to regard one another uneasily. The various sides were sharpening their ideas and arguments and were jockeying for position within the government. Looking back, it is easy enough to see a coming confrontation, but at the time there still was an unfocused quality to it all. The implications of what was happening were not so obvious.

World War II, however, would remedy that. During the four years of that conflict, forces were set in motion that would leave very little in the West unchanged. The debate over the land and its meaning was no exception. The war triggered a new western boom far more spectacular than anything the region had ever known. This, in turn, forced those with strongly held ideas about the country and its uses to dig in and defend their positions. This postwar boom also brought these advocates face-to-face with uncomfortable contradictions within their own beliefs and with clashing viewpoints among their own ranks.

The biggest story since World War II has been a phenomenal surge in the West's population, which has left statisticians scrambling to keep up. In 1947, about one out of every nine Americans lived in the seventeen westernmost states. By 1980, about one in five did. Colorado, Utah, and New Mexico grew most rapidly at first, but during the sixties, Idaho, Montana, and Wyoming took off too. After 1960, the population of the mountain and southwestern states has grown usually twice as fast as that of the Northeast and the Midwest. In fact, of the twelve fastest-growing states during the seventies, eleven were beyond the hundredth meridian. And the trend seems to be continuing. The results of a recent poll that asked Americans where they would like to live showed the Rockies and the Southwest well ahead, followed by the Pacific Coast and the South. Puffing and wheezing, the Northeast and the Ohio Valley brought up the rear.

Starting in World War II, the federal government has showered the West with billions of dollars to establish scientific research centers. One of the first and most famous was at Los Alamos, New Mexico, a facility that helped give birth to the atomic age. (Courtesy, Los Alamos National Library)

The greatest stimulus to this stampede has been federal spending. During World War II the western heartland got much more than its equal share—steelworks and supply depots in Utah, chemical-weapons arsenals and even shipyards in Colorado, and the instant city of Los Alamos, New Mexico—to name a few obvious examples. On the plains, the rain finally returned. Farmers and cattlemen found a hungry market in armies (wholly funded by the government) and steak-hunting workers, flush with pay checks from Uncle Sam. A bushel of wheat again was bringing a dollar by 1941, then two dollars by the end of the war, and it kept going up. Once more the land seemed to be smiling.

Since the war, Washington has continued to spend billions for testing grounds, aircraft and missile bases, scientific complexes, and "think tanks." More than ever, the West has been what historian Joe B. Frantz has called a "child of subsidy," and a spoiled child at that. In 1976 the government spent $32.00 per person on defense-industry salaries in New York but $275.00 in Colorado. Massachusetts got $58.00, while Utah took in $306.00. This has had a siphon effect. Public money has drawn in private investment for subsidiary businesses, particularly of the clean, "high tech" type, which are so dear to town fathers looking for industries with low profiles and little pollution, industry that has its hair combed and its shoelaces tied. Businesses easily moved and reestablished—"footloose industries," one writer has called them; and they looked with increasing affection to the new West, with its young, affluent newcomers. It was not all so neat and tidy, however. During the government's push in the seventies for energy development, coined "Operation Independence" under Nixon, strip mines were opened or expanded on the northern plains, and oil boom towns, with their prostitution rings and thousands of mobile homes stretching to the horizons, blossomed around the Four Corners area—where Colorado, Utah, New Mexico, and Arizona come together—and in wind-swept Wyoming.

Another spin-off of the postwar boom was the remarkable growth of tourism and the service industries that feed upon it. In the affluent society after 1945, families had money to chase all sorts of fantasies, and the West contained the stuff of dreams—exotic natives, magnificent backdrops, a John Ford movie that anyone could star in. Helping them along was a revolution in transportation. Once again, federal money played the largest role. In 1956, Washington provided $15 billion in grants to states for highway construction. The result was a spreading web of new lines across the map. Part runaway roads and part umbilical cords, they made it far easier for outsiders to come and look for the elephant, then, after two weeks, to run home to the office and junior-high carpools. Along the highways in the West an average of a thousand new motels appeared each year between 1945 and 1960, and with them, countless restaurants, service stations, and false-fronted gift shops selling rubber tomahawks, leather vests, hats of great gallonage, and other "authentic" frontier gimcracks.

Simultaneously the government was contributing to the growth of air transportation. Airports, financed for the most part by federal funds, sprang up in what had been the most out-of-the-way parts of the western outback. Friendly tax laws encouraged the great carriers, as well as a host of new, smaller companies, to expand their routes and schedules. All of a sudden, getting Out There was not much of a problem. The isolation of such places as Moab, Utah, and Darby, Montana, was over, probably for good.

With this spectacular new growth and prosperity, the older image of the West as a place of glittering possibilities, which had been so badly battered during the depression, was reborn, shinier than ever. The pendulum was swinging back by the end of the fifties, when a business executive, heading with his company across the Big River, spoke of "a new surge of life in the West much like the frontier spirit . . . an excitement . . . an alertness." A founder of Boulder's High Altitude Observatory said: "It's the people, the open spirit, the informality. . . . There is a chance for the fresh start, the something better."

The vision of a vibrant, forward-looking West revived with a vengeance, and with it the picture of an abundant land, a bulging storehouse that would satisfy all the needs of the hungry Republic. Did baby-boom families with money in the bank yearn for more and larger houses? If so, the western forests could give them what they wanted. In the fifties, for the first time, the lumber industry began to bite deeply into the national forests. By the seventies, nearly a quarter of all commercially cut timber was coming from national-forest land—11.5 billion board feet in 1971, up from just 1.5 billion twenty years earlier; and in 1981 a government official talked of 40 billion board feet per year by the end of the century. Some critics have charged that the production of timber has been the Forest Service's top priority virtually from the start. A national forest may be "the land of many uses," they say, but one of those purposes has shoved the others aside whenever it has pleased. Whatever had been true in the past, however, it was clear that the public forests were now being seen mainly as a source of lumber for a national orgy of construction. Environmentalists put it more bluntly: the Forest Service, they said, was fast becoming the lackey of Weyerhaeuser and Boise-Cascade.

The pattern was similar for underground resources. Since 1948 the United States had been importing more oil than it sold abroad, but it took the oil embargo, twenty-five years later, to really dramatize the problem. But the response was one of optimism; the West would bail us out. Suddenly the public heard about huge oil and gas reserves in Wyoming, Utah, Idaho, and Montana, as well as shale oil to be squeezed from marl beds in Colorado and Utah. And in addition, half the country's recoverable coal lay in the Rocky Mountain states, experts reported. With just part of this energy tapped, corporate and government analysts said, America would become self-sufficient and safe from international blackmail. True, there were some words of caution. Many of the methods of extraction were untested and expensive, and the new facilities would gulp enormous amounts of the region's most precious resource—water. But the prevailing mood was hearty and confident, and the boosters were quick to remind us that more than coal and oil waited underground. Seventy percent of the nation's gold and silver also came from the western heartland. Arizona alone provided more than half the American output of

Exxon's Colony Shale Oil Project near Parachute, Colorado, in 1981.
Americans were looking to the West to rescue them from oil shortages and
foreign economic pressures. The myth of abundance endures. (Courtesy,
Exxon Company, U.S.A.)

copper; and Idaho produced most of its lead and zinc. The postwar
generation learned new names, like uranium and molybdenum,
which are essential for producing lightweight alloys and for building
nuclear weapons and nuclear power plants. They also heard that
these exotic minerals were to be dug from western deserts and
mountains.

The land of plenty. Ever since the pioneer flood spilled over the
Appalachians at the time of the Revolution, the moving West had
been portrayed as the key to economic expansion and genuine
independence. As the wilderness gave up its riches, this bounty would
keep us growing, would sever for good the bonds that tied us to the
corrupt Old World. So it was in the new western boom after 1945.
The cast of characters changed, of course. In the nineteenth century,
Americans heard that western riches would pay to cut the apron
strings to England and to keep us from the clutches of Continental
despots. In the 1950s the villains were the Soviet Union and the
"Red menace," and a little later, the oil-rich sheiks of OPEC. But
the point was the same. The West, with its trees, its bombstuff, and

Colorado photographer Robert Adams's images capture the look of recent
western growth. Shown here are newly completed tract houses near Colorado
Springs, Colorado. (Courtesy, Robert Adams, The New West: Landscapes along the Colorado Front Range; *used by permission of the*
photographer)

the raw fuel for a nation of energy junkies, would keep America
secure and comfortable and on the move.

The better life, the land of individual renewal and national
redemption—these familiar images were strutting around in the
fifties as cockily as they ever had a hundred years before. But there
were also some undeniable differences. Numbers, for instance. The
sheer weight and rush of the postwar population far outstripped
anything that had been experienced previously. That, plus the
prodigious gobbling of resources, generated unprecedented pressures
on the land and on what lay within it and lived upon it. The look and
feel of the country seemed to be changing in a short lifetime, as
anyone driving around the West could see.

It was just as clear that this growth and change was taking place in
a new context. After World War II, doubts that had been building
since the turn of the century—questions about the West's limits and

the value of its untouched lands—took even deeper root in the
public's mind. Even as Americans took heart from the region's
development, some were listening attentively to those who warned
that we were looting the nation's birthright and fouling our own
nest—an unstable situation, to say the least, full of possibilities for a
scrap. It was not long in coming.

In 1953 the Eisenhower administration inherited and quickly
endorsed the Colorado River Storage Project, a massive reclamation
program that called, among other things, for damming the Green
River near the Colorado-Utah border. As the reservoir filled, it would
have left the Echo Park country of Dinosaur National Monument,
some of the most spectacular canyons of the desert West, deep under
water. The parallel to Hetch Hetchy was too obvious. Preservationists jumped to the defense.

The fight lasted for four years. Politicians and boosters of the basin
states and their neighbors said the reservoir would make the desert
blossom like the rose, and they predicted ruin if the project were
scuttled. The *Denver Post* warned that publicity against the dam would
be "disastrous to the economic welfare and growth of the Rocky
Mountain West." Some charged that the "Sahara Club" was in
league with Californians and eastern fat cats—the twin ghouls of the
western heartland—to keep the locals in bondage to Wall Street and
to keep the water flowing downstream toward Los Angeles. Residents
of the area formed groups of "agualantes" and sold sheriff's badges
for a dollar apiece to help finance the cause. The standard attacks on
"armchair" preservationists and "wilderness aristocrats" were
heard again.

This time, however, fifty-seven environmental groups organized
into several lobbies against the dam. Congressmen heard testimony
that the water would evaporate from the reservoir almost as fast as
farmers could take it out, and by one estimate the cost to taxpayers
would come to sixteen times the assessed valuation of all farmland
and farm buildings in the basin states. Why, asked such eastern
politicians as Senator John F. Kennedy, should so many pay so much
to help so few? Opponents of the dam were effectively knocking the
props out from under the utilitarian arguments. Then, taking the
high ground, preservationists argued the need to save retreats such as
Echo Park so that Americans could go there and "renew their souls
and gain a fresh perspective on life." Alfred A. Knopf, a staunch ally,
published *This Is Dinosaur,* with glossy illustrations and a text by
Wallace Stegner. Bernard De Voto attacked the project in the *Saturday
Evening Post,* and *Collier's* and *Life* ran similar articles, accompanied

by lush photographs. Wilderness lobbies organized campaigns that sent a blizzard of ten thousand letters of protest to Congress.

It worked. When Congress finally approved the larger water-storage project in 1956, it promised that no dam would be constructed within any national park or monument. It had been quite a coming-out party. Preservationists gained valuable experience in the pull and tug of politics, and they learned which arguments worked best with the public and its officeholders. Preservationists got a heady taste of using the media to shape popular attitudes. The simple fact of victory over powerful opponents and a popular president gave the preservationist lobby what it needed most—confidence—and left the disciplines of growth decidedly off balance.

During the ensuing years, the older division between the utilitarians and the preservationists blurred considerably. The preservationist ideal enjoyed a great surge of support, and as it did, the conservationists, descendants of Pinchot, recognized, sometimes grudgingly, that the wilderness held a place in their ideas of efficiency and multiple use. Preservationists, in turn, added many conservationist arguments to their own arsenal. Differences still remained, and the two sides still could disagree among themselves about just what should be protected and how, but both understood that the explosive growth in the new West threatened what each was fighting for. It made sense to cooperate in the common goal of shielding the public lands from the rush of population and development.

The twenty years after Echo Park showed dramatically how preservationist values were finding their way into public-land legislation. At least as official policy, the government was committing itself to saving some of the dwindling wilderness for the next century. In 1960 the Multiple Use–Sustained Yield Act officially recognized the multiple-use doctrine and then expanded it to include the "judicious use of the lands" for outdoor recreation, wildlife, and fish, as well as the old standards of soil, timber, and watersheds. Five years later the Land and Water Conservation Act set aside money (initially from a tax on motorboat fuel) to expand national parks and to purchase private lands within them. In 1976 the Federal Land Policy and Management Act (FLPMA, or "Flipma," to its familiars) finally gave the BLM a permanent charter and stewardship over nearly 300 million acres. FLPMA left the bureau with some sobering responsibilities—management according to the ideal of multiple use, for instance, as well as a fair return to the Treasury for the private use of the land, and long-range planning for its huge domain. Included on the list were the prevention of the "undue degradation of the land," the preservation of natural scenery, and an inventory to decide what should be set aside forever as untouched wilderness.

The jewel in the preservationists' crown was the Wilderness Act of 1964. The product of eight years of lobbying, rewriting, and compromise, this law carved out fifty-four areas from the national forests—9.1 million acres, all of it in the West—and decreed that they would be kept safe and secure from all development whatsoever. It further set up an inventory and review procedure by which this newborn National Wilderness Preservation System could be expanded. By 1980, 15 million acres had been added from the national forests and parks and from the BLM, and in that year an astonishing 56 million acres more were set aside in Alaska.

This was the culmination of a long administrative and legal process. The system of national parks had long been protecting certain glittering spots, though it did allow the accommodations needed for the ever-growing numbers of tourists. A few parts of the national forests had been protected as wilderness through their organic acts, and the "L-20" and "U" regulations had given Forest Service bureaucrats the power to set aside "primitive areas"—and also, of course, the right to change their minds.

In another sense, however, this new law went well beyond all this to create an expanding system that forbade the asphalt and lodges of Yellowstone and also shielded the wilderness lands from the shifting whims of administrators. More than that, the government had bound itself, apparently for good, to an idea: there was a point at which the slightest tinkering with the land, even if done with maximum efficiency and for the greatest good for the greatest number, hurt us more than it helped us. If part of the national domain could be held apart, just as close as possible to its virginal state, America would be the better for it. It would be difficult to conceive of a notion that would clash more glaringly with the laws and popular philosophy that had directed the treatment of the western lands from Jamestown to the opening of the twentieth century.

Clearly, something was afoot. Part of the explanation is found in the powerful postwar preservationist lobby, which first felt its oats in the Echo Park controversy. Scores of local and state groups have appeared since then and have generally flourished. Nationally a few prominent figures took the lead. In the Wilderness Society, founded in 1935 by Bob Marshall, were the naturalist Olaus Murie and the editor Howard Zahniser, of *Living Wilderness,* who drafted the Wilderness Act. There were Rosalie Edge of the Audubon Society, the attorney Richard Leonard and the photographer Ansel Adams of

David Brower, the charismatic, persuasive "archdruid" who, as director of the Sierra Club and founder of Friends of the Earth, became one of the most influential and controversial preservationists of recent years. (Courtesy, Friends of the Earth)

the Sierra Club, and others in the National Wildlife Federation and the Izaak Walton League—all of them talented political amateurs who had set out to do battle on their opponents' own turf, in Washington and in the public forum.

Most controversial and characteristic was the man that journalist John McPhee called the movement's "archdruid," David Brower,

who took over as executive director of the Sierra Club in 1952. Since
Muir's death, the club had turned mainly to publishing coffee-table
books and organizing outings for its seven thousand members, most
of whom lived in California—a "posey-picking hiking society," one
disgusted activist called it. Brower made it once again the best known
and most effective preservationist pressure group in the country. The
New York Times called it the "gangbusters of the conservation
movement." He led the fight over Echo Park during its early stages.
He courted politicians and opinion shapers and took out full-page
advertisements in the *Times,* at $20,000 a shot. He could snap off
aphorisms as glib as those of the prophets of growth: "We don't flood
the Sistine Chapel so tourists can see the ceiling." By 1969, when he
was pushed out of his job, the club's debt had swollen enormously,
but its membership had grown to seventy thousand. Brower admired
Muir for his "ability to transcend his powers as an observer and to
become in addition a keen advocate." The same might have been
said about Brower himself and about the rest of the new wilderness
evangelists.

Brower and company, however, probably would have made little
headway in an earlier day. The times, as much as their talents,
explain their success. The climate was right, and the public was ready
to listen to what they had to say. Most responsible were the changes
triggered by the world war, developments that brought into sharper
focus the contradictions that friends of the wilderness had found it
possible to ignore in the past.

Take, for instance, the case of tourism. Vacationers were nothing
new, of course, but the postwar boom brought some important
changes, among them a new multimillion-dollar outfitting industry.
A proliferation of new products became part of the landscape: simple
camper shells, great lumbering Winnebagoes, trail bikes, snow-
mobiles, Land Rovers, fiberglass kayaks, lightweight dome tents and
backpacks of aluminum and nylon, jackets and leggings of Gortex
and Cyclone Cloth, sleeping bags stuffed with Hollofil and Quallofil,
fifteen-ounce camp stoves, and other bits of gadgetry. In great cities
and small towns, thousands of "outdoor stores" appeared, super-
markets of the new technology of escape.

Buying such wares and taking to the new highways and airline
routes, Americans set their eyes westward. A few statistics suggest the
dimensions of what was happening. In 1950, national parks reported
33 million visitations—that is, warm bodies passing through the
gates. In 1983 there were 327 million, a number roughly equal to one
and a half times the population of the entire country. Park tourism

was increasing at a rate sixteen times that of the national population. In 1955, about 70 intrepid souls floated the Colorado River through the Grand Canyon; in 1972, 16,428 persons made the trip. And so on, and on, and on.

Seasoned tourist watchers noted, above all, a change in the nature of the beast. Earlier travelers had found charm and excitement in the country's isolation, its unpredictability, and its contrariness. By contrast, the new breed demanded two things above all else: the wonders of the West must be accessible, and the action must unfold on schedule. They knew what they wanted, and if it was not forthcoming, they would speak to the management. Planners of national parks built ever-more roads and facilities for the Bermuda-shorts crowd, who arrived asking the three most pressing questions of the postwar tourist: Where's the john? Where's the Coke machine? How long does it take to see this place? A western tour was becoming less and less an adventure and more and more an entertainment. And a big, big business. Edward Abbey coined the best term for it— "industrial tourism"—mass produced, streamlined, and with a high yield of pollutants.

It was a delicious irony. Muir and Mather and others like them had set out to save the western wilderness from the philistines by promoting its romantic image and by begging Americans to come and see just what a treasure they might lose. But what if everyone accepted the invitation? The contradiction had always been there, but it took the westward rush to bring it fully into the open. By the seventies the movement that had been set in motion at the turn of the century was bearing down on the wilderness with all the subtlety of a road grader.

Much of the same story could be told, with variations, in a dozen other ways. The West, or rather that part of it that made it unique in the eyes of outsiders and many of its own children, was in desperate danger of dying from too much affection. The publicity about the westward migration and its effects was beginning to alter the public's perception of what always had been the golden land. Even the early preservationists had been somewhat mesmerized by the march of development, the magic of technology, and the prospect of "progress," but it was hard now to miss some of the uglier and most disturbing results. Westerners themselves blinked hard at the "Gillette syndrome," new boom towns, like the Wyoming oil center, that were spreading over the landscape like scabs, fouling the watercourses and the air itself.

The sprawling growth of this Wyoming boom town in the late 1970s and early 1980s created problems and tensions that sociologists have called the "Gillette syndrome." (Courtesy, Gillette News-Record *photo by Kevin Doll)*

In fact, by the sixties, Americans were feeling more and more at home with a series of new clichés that would have flabbergasted their great-grandparents. More and more they heard about the fragile West, a land of delicate environments and endangered species, of erosion that was chewing at pasturelands after overgrazing had destroyed the natural grasses, of aquifers that had been sucked almost dry, and of great rivers like the Colorado, which had been reduced to pitiful dribbles—all because, to quote the California geographer Carl O. Sauer, Americans with the older pioneer mentality had "not yet learned the difference between yield and loot." The face of the West was changing. The image of an occasionally bullying adversary was giving way to something quite different—a virtually helpless maiden, facing a villain with a gleam in his eye.

All this led, naturally enough, to much talk about the "rape of the West." The phrase was the centerpiece of a thousand news stories and magazine articles that sold particularly well in the East. It inspired scores of task forces and "fact-finding" committees, congressional investigations, and law suits filed by environmental groups. One New York journalist, sent to Denver to cover the country's violent loss of virginity, heard of little else in the public forum. "If this was rape," she wrote later, "it was taking place in broad daylight with a crowd watching."

Critics of public-land policies sensed these currents and rode with them. They contributed to the deepening sense of limits and also took good advantage of it. They were shrewd enough to keep their arguments varied, to push all possible buttons, but always they returned to a central theme. They might argue that government leasing amounted to a series of rip offs, that cattlemen were paying only a fraction of the average rate charged on public lands, that hard-rock mining corporations were handing over only a nominal filing fee rather than a percentage of their profits, and that the "stumpage rate" that was being charged to the lumber companies took into consideration none of the costs of reforestation, administration, or construction of logging roads. They might, in other words, play like sharp-eyed clerks watching over the public coffers, but the heart of their appeal was elsewhere. With the disappearance of the wild lands, they said, would come a withering of the American soul. The pursuit of the old, enduring western vision of a land of abundance and the main chance was leading to a national calamity that was as much spiritual as environmental.

Drawing on the lessons of Echo Park, they called upon the shapers of public opinion to back them up. The somber, authoritative Eric Sevareid, once described as "God in a suit," wrote in *Reader's Digest* that development in the Rockies was closing in on "our last frontier of serenity and space, the ultimate Holy Grail, the spirit of the West." Those who were shaped by the land's openness and challenges shared a largeness of soul and "an electric feeling about the future" that were distinctively American. Unless the assault on this spiritual heartland were controlled—the reader could almost see Sevareid shaking his great gray head—"we will become a different people, a diminished people."

The responses from those who held friendlier views toward western development were especially interesting. To be sure, most of the older charges and complaints were repeated. Ranchers cried "meddling" and "interference" about the new laws, just as they had about the old ones. The natives railed against "elitist" outlanders, who were trying to keep too much of the West as a playground for themselves at the expense of healthy growth and an income that at long last would make the West truly independent. Besides, growth was in the national interest. Everyone needed what the West had plenty of. The coal under Montana belonged to all the country's citizens, a BLM official told a writer for *National Geographic*. "Are the people in Chicago going to shut down their refrigerators so people in Montana can have uninterrupted vistas?"

Not much new here: noises like these had been floating eastward for generations. But there was something new in the air. The wilderness rhetoric was now creeping in among the words of the most ardent disciples of development, for instance. With the growing sensitivity elsewhere to the blights of pollution and overcrowding, western boosters realized that the image of sweeping vistas and an unspoiled land was one of their strongest drawing cards. The annual army of tourists expected to drive directly into a Sierra Club calendar. Migrating executives were looking for much the same, and promoters were quick to tell them what they wanted to hear. "The magnificence of our mountains has been matched by a per capita tax burden below the national average," boasted the president of the Colorado Association of Commerce and Industry, and the head of the Rocky Mountain Energy Company agreed. "Open, clean, uncluttered space is the siren's song," as he saw it, with abundant jobs in the West matched only by its residents' zest for living. In the booster business, snow-dusted peaks and silent forests suddenly were full partners with optimism, friendliness, vast resources, and low taxes.

For their part, native westerners were becoming infected by the spreading sense of limits and loss. They always had thought of the opposite of growth as death, but now some of them were seeing full development of their country itself as a kind of dying. They found themselves pulled between a besieged way of life and all the possibilities offered by the swirl of changes after the war. A joke that made the rounds in the sixties summed it up. No rancher wanted to be the first to sell out to the coal companies, but there were quite a few who wouldn't mind being a close second. It was a situation that many found uncomfortable, but most were quick to assure all comers that they were as dedicated to their land's natural beauty as anyone else was. Some could even quantify their divided feelings. "I guess I'm about two-thirds environmentalist," one cowboy said to a reporter from the *Wall Street Journal.* Western politicians, even as they courted coal companies and petro dollars, assured their voters and potential immigrants that their states would not become "the boiler room of the nation." The West still should be made to give up its treasure. Now, however, there was broad agreement on the need to keep its finest scenery unmolested and to keep part of its great spaces wide and wild.

So the very sorts who traditionally had pushed most vigorously for development, who had rolled their eyes at talk of the blessings of forest solitudes, were thinking in terms of the limits of growth and the value of keeping some things unchanged. They still might cuss and stomp about government meddling, but when Congress passed the new laws putting millions of acres beyond the reach of development, it was responding to a spreading concern that was no longer limited to the Sierra Club. If Washington, as usual, was everybody's scapegoat, it was because, as usual, it was expressing the contradictory, muddled concerns of the public, both East and West.

Specifically, events seemed to be forcing all sides to confront the same dilemma. Purity and growth: the first promoted the second, and the second destroyed the first. It was an irreconcilable conflict, and out of it came a deepening worry about what was being lost. Things had surely changed since the days of Theodore Roosevelt. Before, the wilderness had been, by broad consensus, a barrier to civilization, a worthy opponent to be conquered—tough, enduring, seemingly without limits. Now it was a priceless resource—irreplaceable, shrinking, vulnerable.

This dilemma was really part of the larger paradox at the heart of the western mystique. To Americans and to the rest of the world, the West has always been the land. Space. Room. As late as the seventies, a New Yorker, who was visiting the West for the first time, defined it as "a few white folks in a great big place. It was this simple concept that threw me for a loss the moment I got past the hundredth meridian, and it throws me still." This openness has always seemed to offer one thing above all others: opportunity. But to do what, to be what? The traditional answer was simple enough. People fought the land, they filled and transformed the space, in order to make money and to make their lives better. Overlanders of the 1840s shouted to each other that in Oregon a man could "plant a nail and it'll come up a spike!" All those who headed West have promised themselves the same thing, in one way or another; and often enough to keep the dream alive, the land has given them something of what they wanted.

This faith, however, has been periodically shaken during this century. With a mounting sense of the limits of the land has come a predictable, and generally sensible, effort to save what is left of western resources for efficient use in the future. But something else, something more surprising, has happened as well. Another kind of faith has taken root and has spread as the pressures on the West have grown. Evangelists of this new ecological gospel say that the land has always offered other sorts of opportunities—the chance to learn what only the wilderness can teach, a feeding of the spirit as well as the belly, the hard-earned qualities of self-assurance and independence— to name just a few. According to this dogma, the contact with the new land has given us both a better life and a distinctive national character. Looking for the first opportunity, we found the other too. Whether Americans realized it or not, it was part of the deal they had made.

More and more converts have flocked to this new gospel, particularly since the Second World War. According to its catechism, the surviving wild lands have come to stand for the special nature of American history and the special promise of its future. It follows that the disappearance of the wilderness will threaten much more than the chance to turn a profit. The most rabid go-getters, the most dedicated arm-waving developers of the modern West, admit as much, crowing about the untouched scenic marvels of the country and the ways in which living and doing business in the last of the "real West" will gird up the spirit and cleanse the soul.

This has not meant the end of the conflict between preservationists and their foes, of course. In fact, the old fight over the control and use of the land flared with a special ferocity during the seventies. Roused in particular by the flurry of lawsuits brought by environmentalist groups, developers and cattlemen called once again for Washington to hand over the control of the land to the western states. Newspapers and periodicals ran scores of articles on the "Sagebrush Rebellion," and in September 1979, *Newsweek* featured a rifle-toting rancher on its cover, to introduce a story on "The Angry West." The controversy was at its hottest during the first administration of Ronald Reagan and the tumultuous tenure of his secretary of the Interior, James Watt.

Amidst all the loud words and red faces, however, it was easy to miss a significant point. What is striking today is the extent to which at least the assumptions of the wilderness gospel have carried the day. Though the combatants in these debates might disagree totally on the specific ways in which policies are carried out, they are likely to agree that Out There has been the source of Americans' greatness and originality. Keeping some of it around would remind us of that, at least, and keep alive our confidence and sense of uniqueness. "The wilderness is an anchor to windward," as Senator Clinton Anderson of New Mexico has put it. "Knowing it is there, we can also know that we are still a rich nation, tending to our resources as we should— not a people in despair searching every last nook and cranny of our land for a board of lumber, a barrel of oil, a blade of grass, or a tank of water."

That has been both the gift and the burden of the wilderness: an optimism, an expansiveness of mind, a damn-your-eyes attitude toward the rest of the world, and with it, the nagging knowledge that when it's all gone, when we've beaten back and paved over what pioneers have fought and cussed for three centuries, something basic in the American grain will have gone with it.

From the beginning, everyone who has been drawn to the West has been acting out this American dilemma. "We were in subtle ways subdued by what we conquered," Wallace Stegner has written. Beyond its resources and even its value for recreation, he went on, "we simply need that wild country available to us, even if we never do more than drive to its edge and look in." Like every long and stormy marriage, our coupling with the new land has left us bound to it in ways that are ultimately beyond reason and articulation. The mountains and deserts and great spaces, and the threat and challenge of it all, somehow have become part of our belief in who we are and where we have been, and so it feeds our faith in what we might still be. "The geography of hope," Stegner called it.

Whether or not such hope is justified is beside the point. Where the land's promises have been concerned, the fulfillment has always been less important than the anticipation, the dream. In the face of the transformations of this century, the flourishing of this faith testifies to the hold that the elusive, ephemeral West continues to have on the American imagination.

CHAPTER 10

THE MAN,
THE LAND,
THE LEGEND

By the formative years of the twentieth century, Americans had accumulated about a hundred years of experience with the plains and the mountain West. They could look back to the heyday of the fur traders and relive the ensuing decades, which saw explorers, goldminers, cavalrymen, wagon masters, railroad builders, cattlemen, and farmers cope with the American vastness that challenged the hardy, the resolute.

In its extremes of distance, altitude, aridity, temperature, and overall topography, the region presented barriers to man that were unexampled in the history of this people. As this last frontier was "conquered," it was generally believed, both here and abroad, that the surmounting of its demanding conditions had cast a new mold and produced a unique subculture, one that represented the best of a new people. Personifying this group was an idealized American type called a westerner. In both history and literature the term is one of male gender, as women entered all too infrequently into descriptions of this new American. Working with that limitation, one approaches the questions as to who this westerner was, or was believed to be, and was he the result of special western conditions that had not previously been encountered by the westering pioneers.

Certainly "pioneer," or primitive, conditions long had influenced the character and the life style of Americans on their trek from the Atlantic as far as the Mississippi River, but beyond that tremendous waterway the West changed, conditions grew dramatically different, and the price of admission to the next frontier went up. The accumulated craftsmanship of log-cabin pioneering, refined by repeated settle-then-sell experiences that had covered about two hundred years, simply did not fit these new and unfamiliar conditions of barren space, desolation, and other strictures of nature. Worse, there was no fixed set of rules, no standard or formula for meeting these special frontier conditions, because the terrain and climate, while having certain general similarities, varied widely from section to section.

What was once the West now became a collective title that represented several Wests: the desert Southwest, the plains West, the mountain West, and the Great Basin West—all regions in which elements and dimensions were vastly exaggerated. Out of this topographical and climatic mix, human variations emerged which are now lumped together in the public mind as products of what is mistakenly called the Old West, when, in fact, it is the newest of the Wests in terms of the American experience.

One characteristic that strikes all newcomers to the West is that of space and mass, and invariably it has some effect upon them. Walt Whitman felt it. Standing atop the grandly named but modestly scaled Mount Oread in Lawrence, Kansas, the poet gazed westward toward the plains and sensed "that vast Something, stretching out on its own unbounded scale." Millions of those who have visited the West for the first time would know what he meant. The earlier Wests had had distance, if you were high enough up the mountain, but this one has distances that fade into infinity. That is because of its exceptionally clear air, the lack of intervening objects to obstruct the view, and the absence of anything so familiar to the original pioneers as forests, shrubs, or, in some instances, any greenery. This, of course, speaks of the high plains or of the Southwest's deserts.

The West also has great vertical space—towering massive upthrusts that soar skyward and cause Coloradans to boast of how many of the state's peaks exceed fourteen thousand feet. From these heights, far above the timber line, you can see forever, as the song expresses it. But to have those mountain peaks, you have to accept valleys. Traditionally, valleys have been sought by miners, and later by settlers, because they had streams.

To many westerners, mountains offer, not a barrier, but shelter and sanctuary. Yet, some strangers feel trapped, boxed in. A young easterner, honeymooning in Glacier Park, complained of being enveloped, smothered by the mountains. "We thought Glacier Park would be the ideal place for a honeymoon," he wrote. "When we got there I found it was a different story—mountains, mountains, mountains, nothing but mountains, nothing to do all day but sit and stare at the mountains. After three days it really began to get on my nerves." Someone should have mentioned to him that Glacier has a reputation for providing great fishing.

Obviously, the exaggerated topography and the climate affect people in different ways. Mary Hunter Austin, reaching for words to somehow capture the meaning of the desert Southwest, finally chose

*Strangers sometimes feel smothered and trapped in the western high country.
"Mountains, mountains, mountains," complained a young eastern visitor to
Glacier National Park in Montana; "nothing to do all day but sit and stare
at the mountains." (Courtesy, Denver Public Library, Western History
Department)*

four: God, death, beauty, madness. Author J. B. Priestley was drawn
by that region's "terrifying spell of absolute silence." A German
prisoner of war, interned in Arizona, appreciated the vastness of the
desert because it reminded him of the sea, while nature writer Joseph
Wood Krutch saw the country as a desirable place for those who
wanted seclusion but still felt the need of having other people within
reach when loneliness touched them.

The desire for privacy without loneliness is common in the West.
As mentioned earlier, some of the first homesteaders put down
temporarily on adjacent corners of their quarter sections and lived in
the kind of proximity that was experienced by European peasants,
but before long they tended to move to the other side of the holding
because, as one of them said, "their chickens got mixed together."
Some of these settlers had come from Europe, but a great many of
them were Americans who were supposed to possess a crusty
individuality inherited from a generation or so of isolated living. Yet
ultimately, they sought, as Krutch later inferred, a privacy that did
not necessarily involve solitude.

So whether one is surrounded by towering mountains or situated in the midst of elongated distances where the skyline seems unreachable, the bigness of it all takes some getting used to. Thomas Wolfe called the apparently limitless West itself "America's horizon."

The desire of eastern asthmatics, retirees, and those who simply wanted to get away from crowded areas to seek out less populated areas in the West is not a modern phenomenon. Aside from the pioneers, who desired independence, Americans have thought about this for some time. In the twenties and thirties, at a time when the Old West was about to disappear, at least in the eyes of its eastern admirers, a good deal appeared in national magazines about a place to the westward where streams ran clear, forests beckoned hikers, and outdoors men could find an unspoiled paradise. They spoke of skies of Maxfield Parrish blue, of a land where "mile upon mile the world rolls on without a fence." And that image persisted. In the 1980s a western governor fondly recalled the "good old days," a mere three decades earlier, when he had been able to ride a horse for miles in a fenceless land. As a transplant from the Midwest, he reveled in the fact that "you could escape the regimentation of the civilized world. You could be free."

The spread of this sentiment accelerated an incipient movement to the mountains and to the Sun Belt, one that was highly publicized, especially in the East; and much was written about an increased desire on the part of those living in densely packed areas to migrate to the "wide open spaces of the West," as one magazine put it.

Westerners are not ones to miss opportunities, and so it was that space, once regarded as emptiness that must be filled, again became a commodity, one that, this time, western realtors were to hawk to emotionally cramped dudes. Prospective buyers were told that if they came out west, they would discover several thousand dollars worth of scenery and climate in any job they took. Some of the disillusioned young college professors and teachers who bit on this one were later to grumble that "you can't eat scenery."

But that didn't stop the promotional program. As Mary Hunter Austin had written of this country, there is more sky there than in any place else in the world. Later, Montanan A. B. ("Bud") Guthrie, Jr., used the term "big sky" as the title to his best-selling novel, and the Chamber of Commerce in his state later adopted it as a slogan.

The natives take this "open top" of the West as one of their freedoms, a necessary one. During the twenties a waitress in Las Vegas, New Mexico, advised a California-bound tourist about the limitations that he would face upon reaching the Coast. "No elbow room, no open range, no cattle. . . . Nothin' goin' on," she warned him. Perhaps a Nevadan put it best of all. When asked to characterize his state, he paused and then remarked, "Well, it's all out-of-doors!" This need for space was significant, wrote North Dakota–born Eric Sevareid; and it was more than regional—it had national implications to him. He defined the West as space and contended that if that quality should ever be missing, "we will become, I swear, a different people, a diminished people."

Western expanses create different mental horizons. In those endless stretches, distances often are not measured by miles but by time. Natives will tell you that your destination is a day's drive, or perhaps it will be given in hours. This may be a carry-over from the days when Indians measured distance by time. Another view suggests that in the West it is always mentally a long way from here to there, but it is invariably just a little way from here to a wilderness such as a desert or the mountains.

These expanses do other things for the mind and for attitudes. As Charley Russell put it, "Speakin' of liars, the Old West could put in its claim for more of 'em than any other land under the sun." He meant that the dimensions of the mountains and the plains provide a whole new set of mental yardsticks. "A man in the States," continued Charley, "might have been a liar in a small way, but when he comes west he soon takes lessons from the prairies, where ranges a hundred miles away seem within touchin' distance, streams run uphill and Nature appears to lie some herself."

This was being said long before Charley. The pioneers who made their way west by wagon train invariably wrote about the exaggerations of this land. To them the trees were the tallest, the winds the strongest, the rains the heaviest, the thunder the loudest, the grasshoppers the biggest, the temperature changes the greatest. The land certainly encourages boasts like these. The northern plains, for instance, claim several world records in temperature variations. In one spot in North Dakota, during a single year, the mercury ranged over one hundred and eighty degrees Fahrenheit—from a low of sixty degrees below zero to a blistering high of one hundred and twenty. In eastern Montana the temperature once dropped a hundred degrees in a day, and in Spearfish, South Dakota, in 1943, it rose an astonishing forty-nine degrees in two minutes. No wonder such a land seemed to inspire larger-than-life experiences among those who were seeing it for the first time. One of the overlanders remarked in his diary that even sex was better out West. As he put it, "love is hotter here than anywhere that I have seen when they love here they love with all thare mite & sometimes a little harder."

Technology, of course, reduced space in the West and sharply diminished the number of "moons" that the Indians once had to travel between points. The railroad made the first major cut in time; the automobile and the airplane finished it. Farmers, ranchers, and residents of small towns eliminated barriers of distance with their automobiles while at the same time they greatly lengthened the range of their social and business contacts. And in so doing, they not only revolutionized their own life styles; they also changed the face of the urban West by eliminating little "whistle-stop" towns and by contributing to the growth and economic welfare of larger cities within their reach. This greater mobility accounted for the creation of a number of agricultural ghost towns, little places whose booster occupants once had hoped to see crowned as queen cities.

In addition to changing the daily habits of westerners, space and the gradual conquest of it, or at least the modification of it, is believed to have molded character and to have contributed heavily to the creation of this new being, the westerner. Emerson noticed the influence that the land had upon Americans back in the 1840s, when he commented: "The vast majority of the people of this country live by the land, and carry its quality in their manners and opinions. . . . I think we must regard the *land* as a commanding and increasing power on the citizen."

It has been widely argued that this particular West, or set of Wests, magnified Emerson's contention and bred a special kind of people who were almost more American than the Americans they had left behind. Bud Guthrie wrote of this, saying that space breeds its own kind of man. He did not think the westerner was necessarily better or worse than the person who grew up in a heavily populated area, but he felt that the result was a freer, more open, friendlier type. Guthrie's westerner did not tend to be suspicious; he was democratic and had a sense of humor; and he philosophically accepted the climatic extremes that were doled out to him as an aid or a detriment to the immediate task at hand.

The legend that western men were men, and all that this implied, does not always make clear whether they had the makings before they arrived or whether the magic additives of bracing climate, rugged conditions, and fresh opportunities worked wonders even on scrawny newcomers. The extent to which life in the West could build men—or perhaps merely recycle stress-ridden, tattered personalities—has been the subject of much discussion.

Some students of the West have argued that the demanding country beyond the Big River acted more as a screen, selecting the strong and filtering out the unfit in true Darwinian fashion, that it held out little hope for the frail who were seeking some new source of strength. Colorado's Hal Borland opted for this explanation in one of his poems, part of which argued that

> The High Plains are tough, tough as rawhide,
>   uncompromising;
> And they choose their people.
> Drought drives out the weaklings, back to a gentler land.
> Flood sweeps them away, grasshoppers starve them out.
> Dust blows them away, drives them scurrying like
>   tumbleweeds.
> But the tough ones send down roots like the sagebrush,
>   and become Plainsmen.

A few years later, J. B. Priestley argued for this approach, if in somewhat harsher terms, when he wrote that the vast distances of the desert West "and huge nights of stars and silence frighten away the riff-raff."

A more romantic view is that the West actually made Men out of men, as the army top sergeant profanely promises his recruits he will do for them. But this comes largely from fiction that dates back to the dime novels of the nineteenth century and later was emphasized by writers of westerns, in which effete easterners were transformed into muscular beings from whose chests hair sprouted as profusely as range grass in a particularly rainy spring.

The promoters, especially those who tried to create humming commercial centers out of crumbling, sleepy little western towns or those fast-talkers who hawked land that buyers consistently had ignored, did their share to show the tonic effects of the climate. It was here that exaggeration of the purified atmosphere's marvelous restorative powers, already badly overblown, grew to proportions that gave it an honored place in western folklore. Roger L. Welsch's *Shingling the Fog and Other Plains Lies* deals at length with the projection of weather and climate to mythical proportions. It became a part of western humor.

Almost from the time when Americans first encountered the mountain West, the crisp, bracing air has been a subject of comment among those who were experiencing it for the first time. The efforts of enthusiasts to outdo one another in describing it has led, in part, to exaggerations of the powers of clean atmosphere. Long before the twentieth century, Colorado, in particular, had been regarded as a

These tuberculosis patients at the Cragmor Sanitarium in Colorado Springs were part of the "one-lung army" drawn westward by the clear, dry air as well as the spectacular vistas. (Courtesy, Colorado Historical Society)

health spa, especially for those suffering from pulmonary difficulties. In commenting upon Denver's air and altitude, one visitor said: "It keeps everyone keyed up to the trembling point, inciting the population to tireless, incessant effort." This, about 1900. He thought the resultant "mental exaltation" of the residents indeed would alter the community's course of history. But as time passed and as Denver grew into a large city with a reputation for a high incidence of smog, the influences of this promised mental exaltation never had a chance to surface; rather, people now are advised to stay inside on high-pollution days, especially if they have health problems. Those who are seeking the fabled "champagne" air head for the higher mountains, to the resorts, where salesmen still sell blue skies and pure air as one of the state's choice products.

The dry climate of the high altitude, which has been so widely advertised, yields humidity readings that are often so low that newcomers find the figures hard to believe. But that characteristic in itself has had an effect on work habits, the types of clothing worn, recreational customs, and, to no small degree, the dispositions of western people. It also has posed some problems. Furniture tends to dry out and come apart at the joints to a degree that calls for special glue to hold it together. Humidifiers pump moist air through hot-air furnace systems to achieve more efficient heating and to increase comfort.

The clear, dry climate also thrills tourists because of the miles of unobstructed views that it provides. Photographers have written that their exposure meters tell them surprising things, that western images affect film about three times as rapidly as in, say, New York, because there is so little blurring due to moisture or pollutants in the air. For years the aridity has struck newcomers, has impressed them, especially an old engineer who once, upon visiting Nevada, was asked what he thought of the place. "Less mud than any other state in the Union," he chortled.

These were physical matters, reactions that might affect the body or a person's daily living habits, but for years there have been references to the influence that open spaces have upon man's outlook and his character. A Colorado governor contended, in 1898, that great sweeps of western land had their influence. "The world of the stockman upon the prairie had a broad horizon; it made him a broad man. There is a mental tonic in the atmosphere of the unfenced plain." Shortly thereafter, the president of a western university said much the same thing to a gathering of stockmen, that there was something in the physical extent of the West "that makes men broadminded."

Coupled with this was the belief that the great open land had an emotional influence. Early in the century the *North American Review* reported that immigrants to the West, both of foreign and of domestic origin, reflected the influences of their new surroundings "in their energy, freedom, enthusiasm of the West." That quality seemed to endure, for a quarter of a century later, a popular eastern monthly reassured readers that the ability of the West to transform its adopted people still was significantly evident and that, as in earlier years, they tended to put their origins behind them and become "natives" in a very short time.

All these were positives, characteristics that westerners boasted about and that prospective settlers showed an eager interest in; but behind all this lay more subtle and often dangerous qualities in this enigmatic land. "History is a social expression of geography and western geography is violent," wrote De Voto. The earlier farmer-frontiersmen were used to certain climatic outbursts, but that is not why they shied away from this sparse country to the west. They did so for the very sensible reason that there appeared to be little reward in trying to subdue such a harsh and unpromising piece of geography. It was a long time before anyone went out to the plains and the Rockies with the intention of living there.

Penetration was an exploitative proposition from the start, one in which risks were traded for possible gains. It was, as the saying goes, "git and git out." Early explorers, trappers, and miners saw this, and they built in the risks when they calculated their chances. Theirs was a game, a gamble for profit, an adventure that did not imply putting down roots. All that the arid West did in this last great frontier poker game was to raise the stakes, make the play more challenging—sometimes fatal. As De Voto said of the West, it must be loved as you love a woman you know you cannot trust.

Those who decided to stay and to pit their lives against climatic extremes gradually came to understand the odds. Hal Borland spoke of the deadliness of plains winters, commenting, "You lived with winter and let it make the rules." His experience in eastern Colorado left a deep impression on him, and one of his novels, called *The Seventh Winter,* dramatized the hazards of life on the plains.

This defensive posture suggests Joseph Wood Krutch's impression of the desert, when he said that the heroism it encouraged was not one of conquest, but rather was one of endurance, of accommodation. Those who did not flaunt and fight the desert found the snowy season fascinatingly attractive. One person who spent a winter in Taos wrote that "the West in snow is unutterably beautiful" and concluded that one is never the same again after a winter in the West. Many an embittered old Dakota homesteader or beleaguered Montana stockman must have said the same thing, but in grim humor, for the West is actively, not passively, violent toward living things.

Right from the start, climatic and geographical extremes, as well as the availability of fuel, the water supply, and the problems of daily living, impressed Americans who came to the high plains and the Rockies. We get some strong hints of this by looking at the names that were selected for little mining camps and later for agricultural communities. For years, town builders had favored the names of their hometowns back east or in Europe, and while they did not abandon this practice, the western environment had a strong influence on them when they encountered new and sometimes dramatic conditions in their deeper penetration of the West.

The miners came first, in terms of town building, and the names that they chose delight today's tourists, who gaze admiringly at these mineral ghost towns. The choices frequently reflected the flamboyance of that frontier. Local conditions often were new and challenging, and they tell us much about the hopes and aspirations of those who suggested the names. Some random examples, taken from Colorado only, are representative of the names that appeared all across the mining regions of the West.

That gold was the dominant mineral in the early camps is apparent. Gold Lake, Gold City, Gold Hill, Gold Park, Goldfield, Quartzville, Oro City, and Ophir are typical; they are found throughout the mining west. The next favorite metal was silver, and we have Silver Creek, Silver Park, Silver City, Silver Cliff, Galena, La Plata, and even Silver Heels, named after a late-lamented prostitute. Leadville, dominated by its argentiferous lead ores, became the greatest silver producer of them all.

Some of the names were influenced by geographical or even social conditions. Whiskey Spring, Chance, Royal Flush, and Poverty Bar made a suggestive sequence. Others included Bugtown, Horseshoe, Mosquito, Tin Cup, Bachelor, Wagon Wheel Gap, Summitville, Spook City, and Music City. Mining terms were used, as in the towns of Apex, Nugget, Tungsten, Placerville, and Arrastra Gulch. Ethnic characteristics brought forth such names as Swede's Gulch and Nigger Gulch.

Those who ventured forth to make homes on the homesteaders' frontier and who planted their forlorn little farming settlements in this discriminating land of arid plains, acknowledged the odds when the time came for naming their towns. They took two points of view: either they used boosters' exaggerations and lures, or they were grimly realistic as to their chances. Some of the descriptive choices that suggested local conditions were Slick Rock, Hard Rocks, Rocky Point, Chalk Buttes, Mud Butte, Deadwood, Bitter Creek, Alkaline Lake, Cactus Flat, Lone Tree, Lost Cabin, and Paradox. Some others were Dull Center, Loco Hills, Skull Valley, Hell's Canyon, Wolf Hole, Horsethief Basin, and Tombstone. More promising, but sometimes less realistic, were Richland, Goodland, Wheatland, Fruitland, Garden City, Fairacres, Evergreen, Sunshine Valley, Pretty Prairie, Pleasant View, Grassy Butte, and Friendly Corners. These suggested rich soil, farming opportunities, and a bucolic life.

Water was vital to the West. It is featured in unnumerable town names, some of which are Clearwater, Sweetwater, Bluewater, Whitewater, Running Water, Red River, Green River, Warm River, and Big Springs.

On a grander scale were such all-encompassing appellations as Ideal, Superior, Grand View, Oasis, Carefree, and Inspiration. Topping them all in terms of promise were Eden and Paradise, the popularity of which can be seen by glancing at a western highway map. Then, there was the ultimate stumper, when the baffled fathers of a southern-Arizona town simply gave up and called it Why.

What sets this town naming apart from practices that pioneers followed on earlier frontiers is not so much a response to geography or local conditions, for this was nothing really new; rather, it was the newcomers' reaction to the exaggerations of this vast and different West. It also revealed an enthusiasm on the part of the settlers that was mixed with a grimly humorous determination by those who were resolved to make this, the great adventure of their lives, a success. Be it bravado or courage, it was their way of telling the world about their intentions, and through this medium, they revealed much about themselves to others.

Granted, this is but one small facet of the western character. The obvious and larger questions ask Who was the new westerner? Was he any different from his forefathers? and If so, why? These are difficult to answer, not only because they call for vulnerable generalizations but also because much of the writing on the subject reflects more what others thought of these people than what they themselves have told us. Tricky, also, is the problem of handling the changes that have taken place in the West since the turn of the century, changes that have wiped away much of what even westerners thought of as the Old West and its occupants.

There are some characteristics, however, that can be looked at and perhaps measured. The yardstick has to be that of what earlier frontiersmen were believed to be, as well as an understanding of the mainstream of an American society that watched the young branches of settlement sprout and grow. If the new communities did in fact breed a different sort of people, it is important to know why.

The academic father of frontier historians, Frederick Jackson Turner, saw traits that he thought were representative of frontier life, among them democracy, individualism, freedom, coarseness, strength, acuteness, ingeniousness, materialism, exuberance, and optimism. Westerners, he said, also were innovators in material things, were impatient of restraint, and were highly nationalistic. These were log-cabin types, small farmers who nibbled their way westward across the map, repeatedly settling and selling, eking out an existence at subsistence farming, living in isolation, and of necessity developing a way of life that was shaped for them by their environment and their daily experiences.

Their descendants, who lived in the twentieth-century trans-Missouri West, were thought to have retained some of the same traits. At least, eastern fans of the Old West wanted to think so.

Conditions of equality, freedom, and even individualism historically were equated with frontier democracy. This belief arose largely
because of the easy availability of land. Dating back to the earliest
America, the franchise was usually tied to property qualifications.
Even when this no longer was true, land ownership continued to
mean a measure of freedom and independence; this concept was
invariably associated with farming.

In the successive Wests, man's ability to solve his own problems,
with or without a gun and with relative freedom from governmental
control, was one of his trademarks. This projected easily into the final
West, and for a time it served as part of a treasured possession
brought west by the pioneers. As late as 1912 a sociologist told
readers of *Century Magazine* that the sterling frontier quality of
independence was still flourishing in the West. "Today in the recesses
of the Rocky Mountains you come upon steady-eyed, eagle-faced
men with tawny mustaches, whose masterful, unswerving will and
fierce impatience of restraint remind you of their spiritual kinsmen,
the heroes of the Icelandic sagas," was his assessment. He had no
way of knowing it, but he had just painted a word portrait of the
Marlboro Man, later to be created and made famous by the Philip
Morris Tobacco Company.

This belief about western independence persisted, especially
among foreign observers. Nevertheless, although the modern world
had been overtaking the West for some time, even westerners were
still trying to kid themselves into thinking that times had not
changed. They had. And gradually it dawned upon this developing
people that except for a brief moment, they never had been independent, at least in a collective sense, and each passing year showed them
the increasing unlikelihood that they could free themselves from their
political colonial status or from their dependence upon marketing
vagaries associated with single-crop or subordinate industry endeav-
ors. Belatedly they were aroused, and cries were heard that these key
components of their heritage had been lost, or perhaps stolen.

Not that westerners hadn't been warned. Quite early in the
century there had been rumblings along the Atlantic seaboard to the
effect that equality born of independence already was becoming one
of the West's endangered species. Bear with the westerners' assumptions of individualism, of egalitarianism, one writer urged, because if
this delicate organism were crushed, the result would be a servility
that already was surfacing in the East. True, he admitted, in the East,
social conventions were working to preserve the form, but beneath
the surface the substance tended to atrophy. "Our westerner is the
substance, the real thing," he concluded.

During the ensuing years, eastern sentiment on this score did not tend to weaken. Katharine Gerould argued that the tacit assumption of equality among citizens was the first social principle of democracy but that when the assumption became vocal, the principle degenerated. She took hope from the belief that in the real West the assumption was both tacit and sincere. To her, America was growing unrecognizable as America, and she recommended that concerned people look back upon the development of a section of the nation in which, at least for a time, democracy had blossomed as a workable theory that neither glorified Mammon nor canonized mediocrity.

The Great Depression struck a paralyzing blow at the concept of the free and independent westerners, especially those who lived on farms or ranches and had prided themselves upon having achieved liberation through land ownership. A dust-bowl farm wife, whose family lay marooned as if on a desert island, took a rueful look at this legend in 1935. She decided that the deeply rooted American myth about rural people's living off wild game, fish, fruit, "and in general on the free bounty of heaven" not only was wrong but was one that had entrapped many a prospective westering young family. Most people had no idea, she wrote, about the expense of operating a farm. It was impossible to try to combine modern methods with the income of earlier pioneers, who used to cover a year's expense with $200.

The idea of the independent yeoman was thoroughly enmeshed in the American agrarian myth. Long after the bitter dust-bowl years, Eric Sevareid recalled and defended the pioneer spirit of his and other North Dakota families and their fight to save their homesteads. These stubborn, tough people accomplished this, he remembered, "with damn little help from anybody but their neighbors." This is probably true, despite the fact that these and thousands like them were trapped and were largely defenseless; the federal government's aid spelled the difference in their survival. I saw much the same thing in Montana, where I grew up at that time of dust and tumbleweeds among a people who were forlornly waiting for help. The sons of the pioneers survived because they had no place to go and because relief agencies helped a great many of them through the crisis.

Still, the back-to-the-land ideal persists. A generation after the West's big dry up, President David McKay of the Mormon Church decried the drift of his young people into such employment as the missile industry on the ground that it led to dependence upon the government. Urging them to work the land whenever possible, he advised that "people should keep cows and chickens, have small farms and stay independent." This feeling went far beyond the confines of the church; it was a feeling that many a westerner subscribed to, but now only in a theoretical manner. Life on the farm or ranch was a diminishing characteristic; it was being priced out of the market. The sentiment was one more of nostalgia than of expectation, a longing look back over the shoulder, really an attempt to have it both ways.

In addition to being thought of as independent and democratically inclined, westerners were also said to be friendly, optimistic, and outgoing. Residents of the "last West" have inherited this reputation, one that newly arrived easterners expect to see at once. Sometimes they are disappointed.

Part of the reputation for easy, open, forthright relationships derives from an ancient frontier heritage of periodically cooperating with neighbors that other settlers might not have associated with for some time. It reaches back to the days of sewing bees, communal barn raisings, and other cooperative activities that were social as well as practical. While this spirit of cooperation and social intercourse was not lost upon modern westerners, the need for association was somewhat mitigated by mechanical and manufacturing advances that offered to the individual farmer or rancher assistance that had once been available from a neighbor. On the big western ranches and farms, even the near neighbor now was less common than earlier, because the average western farm had become larger, not smaller, in recent times. Still, at harvest time, farmers often shared machinery, and even labor, to gather in the crops.

So-called western hospitality is partly inherent friendliness, which sometimes derives from loneliness, and partly the pleasure that a rancher often got from hearing all the news from a passing stranger. Hospitality wasn't all give; the host received a good deal in return. The day of the radio, the telephone, and, later, television satisfied the need for communication. The passer-by still would be helped if he were in need, but he was less apt to be dragged into the house and shoved before a hot meal.

Foreigners often were surprised by this outgoing attitude. A pair of Russians, touring the West in 1935, encountered this attitude in New Mexico after their car had slid off the road. So delighted were the visitors with the immediate offers of assistance that they were almost pleased by this small accident, which opened another window on the American character to them. They were equally impressed by the offhand way in which their tendered thanks were received; a laconic nod, a wave of the hand, an inference that help along the road out here was not regarded as being any special virtue.

This squared with the impressions that easterners had of proffered courtesies to visitors. One magazine writer explained that "there's a bluff welcome about the country which enfolds one." The bluff welcome was as old as the frontier, something that many of the earlier travelers had commented upon, and apparently it was of a lasting quality, for it is one that is not unusual in less-settled parts of the West today. An offer of help, of course, is not necessarily an offer of friendship, but even the latter comes naturally. Ready acceptance of people is given as a matter of course and without reservations, only to be withdrawn upon cause.

Beyond the warmth of their welcome, visitors to the West long have felt that the natives were more courteous than the man on the street in the East. Perhaps this is because the pace of life is slower or because people have more time to respond to the needs of others, or conceivably it is a developed or innate quality. Katharine Gerould swore that you could tell you were out West simply by the infinitely better manners of the people, that their consideration for others was noticeable to visitors. That this reaction has persisted was evidenced in the early 1980s when a newswoman, fresh from the East, was charmed by the custom of merchants in a western town who went out of their way to refer her to a competitor if they did not carry the wanted item. She wondered if it was a case of "an easterner running into a Western phenomenon." In any event she labeled the action an example of western courtesy.

Along with the quality of politeness there is a candor, an openness, that often surprises strangers. The westerner easily tends to speak his mind and to expect an equally frank response. Sometimes this is taken for naïveté, giving rise to the suspicion that perhaps one has come across a rustic or even a rube. Now and then, dudes have made serious errors on this assumption.

If, on the other hand, the word naïve is used to explain a lack of artificiality or even an absence of sophistication, as opposed to meaning childlike or a foolish lack of worldly wisdom, it helps to explain westerners. De Voto hastened to make it clear that this was the correct interpretation when he suggested that there were no hicks west of the Missouri River.

Part of this is a spillover from frontier days, a quality projected into the present by certain cigarette advertisements. In lustier days, when—if we are to believe the novelists—daily life revolved around a hero, two basic characteristics stood out: action and simplicity. Out in those open spaces, where man was to be tested as an individual man, whether against the elements or against a human adversary, his course of action usually was direct and uncomplicated. "It was simplicity itself," wrote Wilson Clough, "like the fraternity of those who knew the trenches of World War I, whose members needed no mumbo jumbo or secret grip but only experiences shared. The common knowledge in both cases was masculine, physical, immediate, a mostly wordless knowledge, spoken sparingly."

An old-time newsman saw the trait of simplicity as being characteristic of a new country. The westerner, he said, is a relatively uncomplicated person, one who "enjoys the naivete of a youthful people." Youth, in a collective sense, then, is a quality, not only of the American people at large, but especially of those in the most recently settled parts of the country. It has not been very many years since the native son was something of a rarity among westerners. As late as the mid twenties, an eastern commentator noted that it still was "rather a distinction to be a native son in one of these states" and that among western senators, one of the most vigorous critics of the federal government was a native of Maine. It was not until 1932, when Pat McCarran became a United States senator, that Nevada could claim a native-born solon.

Outsiders have used the relative newness of the Old West to show its close linkage with the recent past, a time when those sterling American virtues that are so admired by conservative easterners were presumed to be alive and well out in that favored country. At the same time it has been employed by westerners themselves as an excuse for the lack of cultural development, the argument being, as it was all along the advancing frontier, that the tasks at hand prohibited such refinements but that beyond all doubt these improvements lay just ahead.

As late as the years of World War II, writers were still arguing that the West was too new to have produced political and cultural leaders of noteworthy stature. It was suggested that the crisis of 1929 may have been a turning point, but it does not follow that the place started to produce men to match its mountains overnight. During the postwar years, in many respects a transitional period for the West, the area still could not boast a list of great names in statesmanship, economics, social science, or education. However, it is not hard to prove that in the next generation this situation altered considerably. Even so, the region remains thinly populated, rapid as its growth has been, and despite demonstrable advances, it is not yet impressively strong nationally in these areas.

There are, however, some hopeful things to say about the youthful qualities of the West. While this characteristic, one that Walt

Whitman once saw as making it the most American of all the regions, certainly is fading with the passage of time, there is room for argument that the attribute already has shaped the way of the people who live there. While it is true that the West dragged its heels over the matter of entering the twentieth century, once that transition was effected, the residents often demonstrated their legendary adaptability by readily accepting innovations of the modern world. It has been suggested that in so doing, the West made the passage much more easily than did the South, and as one writer put it, the region never has been seduced in the manner of the East "by every fancy breeze that blew from Europe." Although it has been somewhat preoccupied with its own innocence, the West has accepted the fact that change was part of the westering process, and even with its youthful ways, it has taken a few halting steps in the direction of sophistication.

As Eric Sevareid once remarked, "You grew up in the West with a sense of change, of growth and improvement that even a kid could see and feel. . . . The future seemed as wide as the horizon." Having little or no past, the new communities had only their future to consider. Many of the newcomers resolved that come hell or high water, they were going to dig in, stay with it, and succeed. Townsmen bragged about their new municipalities, "boosted" them to a point that the practice became an art; and they did so unashamedly, fully believing their own rhetoric.

These accolades had a resilient quality about them; they never seemed to wear out. During the twenties, despite a deteriorating western agricultural situation, the economic picture superficially appeared bright. Tourism boomed, and visitors still glowed at what they viewed as the pristine West, its beauties, its invigorating climate, and its continued promise. They never seemed to grow tired of reading the colorful literature that praised this romantic, exciting land, the outpouring of which never seemed to diminish. An easterner, who noted the flow of western propaganda and was aware that it was sheer hucksterism, nevertheless admitted that he was so impressed by the West that he wanted to accept what he read and heard. "What it says is all true," he maintained. "The publicity manager tries to sin, but he cannot. Even the railroad folders are true." He thought there was so much to believe that the problem became one of how to decide.

This generation, then, both of the East and of the West, remained stubbornly convinced that the land of promise had shown only part of its treasures and that somehow it would never fail them. Standing on the brink of economic disaster, they looked beyond reality and savored a rosy future. Ray Lyman Wilbur, Hoover's secretary of the Interior, assured his listeners that the West was on the very threshold of its ultimate progress and that it intrigued the imagination to consider the years that lay ahead. He had these thoughts in 1929.

The western boom-and-bust notion that it takes three bankruptcies to make a farm died hard. There was always tomorrow, and somehow nature was due to deal out a better hand. In the 1960s the president of the University of Nevada marveled at the indefinable spirit of optimism that seemed to permeate the western air. There is something about the country, he said, that holds you, that gives you a feeling of great things just about to happen, "that mighty forces are converging and focusing." This is part of an old mirage, one that allowed the optimist to look at a lonely grain elevator alongside a railroad track or perhaps only at an unpainted wooden water tank and to visualize a growing metropolis all around that seedling.

There was an implicit faith in the idea of growth and development, one that certainly was American; but in the West it seemed to have a sense of the preordained about it. As late as the twenties, an eighty-year-old woman who had come west by covered wagon told a passerby in Colorado's Gunnison country that the thrill of life was to get out into new and untouched country, "where you can help build it up from the bottom." Confidently she added: "That's what counts. There ain't anything better." This "original settler" and a legion of those like her not only wanted to build; they were firm in their convictions that what they were doing would succeed. Theirs was the land of tomorrow. As the saying goes, these folks faced the future with the calm confidence of a Christian holding four aces.

Travelers and journalists who visited the West at various intervals after 1900 and who commented upon its characteristics frequently touched upon the question as to whether this developing country, in all its youthful and sometimes blindly optimistic ways, was cosmopolitan or painfully provincial. In the early years of the century, admirers of the region rather apologetically admitted that in such a large country, with such great distances between settlements, the resultant lack of contact produced what one of them called a "certain amount of provincialism."

Another argument held that the place really was cosmopolitan. This was said to be true of all recently settled parts of the country simply because these people had come from somewhere else and had, as a consequence, two points of view and a generally broader outlook. They had not yet had a chance to become narrow or rustic. This definition of cosmopolitanism, however, hung on the notion that the term equated with tolerance in social habits and customs, that in the free and easy society there were few suffocating social disciplines as compared to those in older America. In practice, the argument had some weaknesses.

The fence riders on this question contended that while the West was just as liable to be provincial as were parts of the East, still, on the whole, westerners knew the East better than easterners knew the West. Westerners were surprisingly well informed, said one historian, when writing about the people of Idaho. These folks knew a good deal about what was going on in the rest of the country, but that was about as far as it went; they really didn't care about problems elsewhere. Lorena Hickok, in writing to Harry Hopkins about Nevada's problems during the depression, was quite irritated by the narrow outlook of the people. "Dammit, they've got the 'gimmies' that's all. . . . They think only in terms of their own county. They aren't even state-minded, some of them, let alone national-minded."

Native sons sometimes turned on their region and called it provincial. Young De Voto showed that when he defected to the East and wrote devastatingly bitter things about the West that he had forsaken. Later, after becoming fascinated with the region's history, he changed his mind, deciding that there were fewer clodhoppers out there than he had first thought and that a healthy provincialism was something to be cultivated, because the West was for westerners and it should shrink back from any comparisons with Grand Rapids. Now he wanted the region to get rid of "alien ideals and alien ideas" and to develop a native civilization.

In 1937, Thurman Arnold, formerly of Laramie but now famous and successful in the East, said that no lawyer or professor who had any sense would settle in Wyoming, where money, intellectual contacts, and everything else were in short supply. Much the same was heard from Carey McWilliams, who contended that there was almost no intellectual communication between Denver, Salt Lake City, Boise, and the West Coast cities and that despite all the drum beating by westerners, the area remained "a rather dismal and uncivilized region."

One characteristic that might suggest provincialism, but that simply is true of all new areas, was the westerners' emphasis on the present and on the concerns of their own neighborhoods. The newcomers had a sense of the past, but it was a past that geographically was far away and one that many of them wanted to forget. In their new homes there was only today and the future; preoccupied with digging in, getting a firm root, they had little time for history.

When westerners finally did look into this matter, they tended to think of ancestor worship as history, or they glorified the Old West notion that had been handed on to them by eastern enthusiasts. Often they simply commercialized what they thought was western history, setting up roadside tourist traps that supposedly depicted former days of glory and conquest. Western highways are littered with the façades of fake forts, flying Old Glory and admonishing travelers to bring in the kids for an instant course in frontier history. History, in this sense, merely has been prostituted to pluck a quick dollar from the unwary dudes, and it speaks more of materialism than even of an ersatz culture. However, if one looks more closely, there are some very fine museums and historical societies in the West, but you have to look beyond Stuckey's roadside rest stops to find them.

Unfortunately, westerners have been sold the Old West of John Wayne for so long and so thoroughly that their view of what they believe to be their past is extremely limited. In short, to many of these people it is the record of WASP participation in empire building, the remaining portions of the cast being little more than offscourings, shavings on the floor of the workshop that really "built the West." The Chinese have suffered in the mining camps and larger towns. The blacks have been more or less ignored, often not being numerous enough or noticeable enough even to attract prejudice. The Mexican-Americans, the principal minority of the Southwest, historically have been denigrated and dismissed as being suitable primarily as sugar-beet workers. The Indians, of course, simply were savages, to be corralled, fed, and defanged.

An example of the attitudes that have been handed down to the present generation was capsulized in a conversation that journalist Bill Moyers had with his seat mate on an airplane as they flew over the plains one day in 1971. The man told Bill that he had sent his son to Kansas State University at Manhattan, as opposed to the University of Kansas at Lawrence, because there was "too large a foreign element at KU." He explained that by this he meant "kids from the East and colored fellows brought in to play football and a bunch of hippies."

There has been much change in the West, as in the turbulent sixties, but things evolve slowly in this conservative, cautious region, which the myth always said was so liberal and far-reaching in regard to advanced ideas. Minorities have made solid advances, but not without considerable gear grinding on the part of the western establishment, which is very slow in catching up with the rest of America in matters social and cultural.

Politically this is a hangover from earlier days, when larger interests, ranging from stockmen's associations to large corporations—Anaconda, for example—ruled the legislators. As De Voto remarked, westerners have "never been on the side of change nor have we ever granted the right of a minority to exist." This region is not only politically conservative; it is one in which eccentricity in dress, behavior, or belief is shunned, if not openly boycotted—college campuses, of course, being excepted.

These characteristics go back quite a long way in the West, back to the changing of the guard, when the cattlemen gave up the throne and surrendered to the nesters. Charley Russell was merely one of those who fought the coming of the "stink-wagon," as he referred to his automobile, the plowing up of the sod, and the resentment toward the "pilgrims," who were moving in and fencing off the ranges. A little later, dude-ranch hands showed some of this fixed-in-time attitude in their resentment of eastern women visitors who affected malelike costumes and refused to look female in the eyes of the beholders.

The western press reveals this conservatism. De Voto once called it "astonishingly reactionary" and averred that the western radical, who occasionally frightens the East, more often than not is advocating nothing more revolutionary than proposals that were set forth when Mark Hanna was a pup. De Voto thought that the average western Republican editor was more in tune with the social and economic assumptions of immediate post–Civil War capitalism than with anything of a more recent origin. But, he said, this was neither Democratic nor Republican; it was just western.

And "just western" more or less describes today's voter who enters the polling station to give his preference. He is so little Republican or Democratic that he drives both parties to distraction. Maverickism is the word of the day, a form of independence that has candidates of all stripes at their wits' end trying to find out what the constituents want. Colorado is a particularly good example of a state in which the politically disciplined are hard to find, with the exception of certain traditional party enclaves. All that Colorado voters seem to want is a man of the world, sophistication being only hinted at, who wears cowboy boots. And so cowboy boots are part of the uniform of the day. Visitors at the university's commencement exercises take no notice of boots that stick out from under academic robes as they view the governor or other visiting bigwigs on the platform.

The roots of this political maverickism possibly lie less in an old western tradition that insisted upon freedom of choice at all levels

than they do in the high mobility of a naturally peripatetic people.
This practice of picking up and leaving was an old one, but it has
persisted. In the early 1980s the Census Bureau said that westerners
were the most likely of all Americans to move; each year, 26 percent
of them changed residences. As a result they were little tied to any
one location, they were not as involved with their neighbors as
elsewhere, they had a lower rate of church affiliation, and as a
consequence of these characteristics, they were slower to develop any
sense of community responsibility. In the 1960s, Neil Morgan wrote
that all this had created loosely drawn community patterns which
frustrated the aims of western towns. "Many of the problems of city
planning in the West are attributable to mobility," he wrote. Looking
at it from a slightly different angle, Wallace Stegner commented that
this constant movement broke up forming regional patterns that, if
left alone, would have taken shape in rural isolation. Consequently
there has been little opportunity for "a native character to form and
to find its voice."

The habits and attitudes of westerners are not always quickly
apparent to outsiders. What visitors often expect to find upon
arriving in the "big sky" country are natives who look and sound like
the characters they have watched in Hollywood "oaters" on television. In 1977 a woman reporter, assigned to Denver out of New York,
said that as she got to know them, the people whom she met were not
what she had anticipated; most of them looked and acted just like
ordinary Americans. She discovered, however, a satisfying supply of
colorful characters "who looked as if they had just stepped out of the
back lot at Universal," and this was comfortably supportive of the
preconception that she had brought with her.

These replica cowboys and "western types" are not hard to find,
even in the larger cities, where a number of affectations of costume
and conduct are to be found. Beyond that, westerners have an uneasy
feeling, perhaps a subconscious guilt complex, which tells them that
they ought to look the part. So, not infrequently, the natives try to
accommodate this demand upon them, partly because many of them
have been kidded into the idea that these range-land outfits somehow
set them apart from lesser beings, especially the dudes, and partly
because it just makes them *feel* more western by following the
prescription that clothes make the man. Boys in small towns like to
affect ranch working garb, even if it is sometimes not entirely
appropriate, because it seems to ooze manliness and virility beyond
hinting at the notion of mounted horsemen. They can go around
their hometowns in these getups without causing any comment,

because the rural backdrop seems to accommodate the idea. This idea is so infectious that newcomers invariably head for the nearest bootery and limp around in restrictive footwear and wear awkwardly large headgear because they want to be accepted. Nobody laughs at them; westerners can be tolerant, even flattered, by mimicry. After all, it's part of the big act that has been going on for some time in the West.

On the other hand, when a western boy goes east, he is sometimes ill at ease, and sartorially he feels more like Montgomery Ward than like Hart, Schaffner & Marx. When Thurman Arnold left Wyoming for Princeton early in the century, he felt uncomfortable in his new surroundings. "My western clothes, mannerisms, and speech did not fit," he recalled a half-century later. "I was immediately classed as a queer character. I was not admitted to any club; indeed I was never admitted to anything at Princeton." Later, having worked at shedding some of his westernisms, he fared better at Harvard.

There is, of course, what is accepted as a western language or patois, one of the characteristics of which is its limited boundaries. Any account of open-range days will, at some point, tell the reader that the cowboys were stingy with words. Tall, silent types, who spoke through their actions, abound in western fiction. Gary Cooper easily made it across an entire movie career with a single word: yup. And John Wayne amassed a fortune simply by repeating "Aw, shut up" to his leading ladies. He once admitted to an interviewer that if you could make a living that easily, you would be a fool to pass it up. Beyond the saddle heroes, other westerners tended toward taciturnity—such as trappers, lone prospectors, and dog-tired homesteaders who tried to wrest a living from a lonely, defiant countryside. It was a quiet land.

Beyond *yup* and *nope,* there are words that are western because they had to be invented to describe a new and different land, or certainly new conditions in that vast expanse. Eastern terms often just didn't fit the West. Turner said that the pioneers brought their cultural baggage with them, and they did. In some cases, however, old paradigms broke down under the impact of western circumstances, and a regional language evolved.

The Spanish influence upon geographical designations is strong, as a cursory look at the western map will reveal. The cowboy legend, so dominant in the region, left a whole new vocabulary of terms, many of which also are of Spanish origin. Ramon F. Adams gathered them together in his volume *Western Words.* These expressions have lingered and are not uncommon in the daily conversations of westerners today. Newcomers often notice them, but as a rule the natives are not employing them consciously or for effect.

Somewhere in the background, behind the societal veneer of folks running around in Levis, boots, and Stetsons, howdying each other, there is a West today that is invisible, gossamer, spiritual, indefinable. It is the unseen and unheard West. It tells us that the West is something more than just a place of dwelling, that it creates a pride that blossoms early in the transplants who arrive daily, and the acceptance that is accorded to them turns them into "natives" very quickly. As was once said, a person doesn't reside in the West; he lives there. The process seems to take place naturally with recent arrivals.

This has been recognized for a long time. Very early in the century an eastern magazine writer commented that nothing in the western atmosphere was more surprising than the degree to which it brought outsiders under its sway. "So compelling is the western tone, as regards the making of Americans, that frequently one generation completes the process seemingly as well as ten generations; in every way the westerner upsets calculations." Vachel Lindsay made much the same remark on a trip across the Dakotas during the early twenties, where he thought the Russian, Swedish, and German immigrant children, "swallowed up . . . by distances and the primitive," would soon gain from this a western consciousness.

Westerners generally are outdoors people. Those who come here, especially from the East, desire that opportunity, and they become the most avid outdoors men of all. They are born-again wilderness children. The native, on the other hand, accepts the outdoors as part of his way of life, and while he is not apt to be much of a picnicker, he often spends a lot of leisure time along the flashing mountain trout streams. Or he just wants to be "out beyond" in a camper for the solitude of the thing and for a chance to be, as Stegner said, "where both illimitable freedom and perfect sanctuary may be found." There is something comforting in the feeling that in these untouched sections there remains an Old West that never can be completely conquered, and outdoors men find solace in that challenge.

Whatever the reason for penetrating the high country or any of the remote western spots, there is an implied search for the conditions of another time, a day when man stood against the wilderness and was bigger because of it. Somehow that solitude shouts out that this is the genuine article.

One day during the twenties, at a ranch in Taos, D. H. Lawrence and Joseph Foster were talking about the previous century, when

Westerners, both natives and newcomers, seem to feel obliged to spend much time outdoors. This dapper group has found the perfect picnic spot in Colorado's Big Thompson Canyon. (Courtesy, Denver Public Library, Western History Department)

things were less complex, and Lawrence quickly interjected: "Yes, . . . the frontier. The crisis in your history. Everyone was *real* then."

That is what the lone back packer is looking for today—something real—because he knows that populated western areas have lost that quality and that only in more remote areas is the elusive atmosphere he is seeking apt to be found.

Somewhere, deep in those woods, lies the mythic West.

EPILOGUE

THE GENESIS OF
THE MYTHIC WEST

From the outset the emergence of the mythic West
was a sure thing.

Along the way it has been nurtured by many things—economic
frustrations and dreams, an awakening sense of history, a feeling of
kinship with the land, and suspicions about the modern world, to
mention only a few. But at the start and forever afterwards one of the
basic ingredients has been ignorance. As the seaboard colonists clung
to the coastal region, trying to establish a permanent beachhead,
their notion about what lay westward, in an apparently unlimited
expanse, was so vague as to be unreal. With their information level
hovering near zero, it was not difficult for them to accept oral reports,
largely imaginary, of a legendary land Out There, where bubbling
fountains, succulent plant life, virgin forests, and an abundance of
wild game beckoned to those with the gumption to pick up and move.

While English colonials thought about this western pastoral paradise, the Spanish were as easily taken in. Stories that the Indians told
about the unimaginable mineral riches north of Mexico, of whole
cities built of silver, whetted their appetites. So Coronado spent man-
killing days herding his forces northward in search of the fabled and
fictitious Seven Cities of Cibola, and for years afterward the Spanish
stubbornly pursued the myth. The locals had "hustled" the first
tourists in the American Southwest.

Meanwhile, as those who were soon to be known as Americans
penetrated the passes of the Allegheny front and as little settlements
began to emerge beyond the mountains, a mythology with sartorial
trappings sprang up. Now and then in the streets of Richmond,
Virginia, people would appear in outfits topped by tailed coonskin
caps, clad in moccasins, and from whose jackets wicked looking dirks
might peep.

The "boys in buckskin" came to town, perhaps for some small
trading or for powder and ball, and during their visits they often
related to the wide-eyed townsmen some tales of western life that
excited imaginations. They told of outdoor life, of hunting experi-

ences, of picking off marauding Indians who were bent upon mischief, and they repeated oft-told tales of a free and uninhibited life where nature simply forced its plenitude upon the settler.

Or sometimes the visitors had land to sell, and endowed with great imaginations and an abundant supply of superlatives, they described the possibilities for those who might want to come out and settle down. These clear-eyed men had charm; they had stories that were colorful and exciting; some merely were accomplished liars. Thus, the modern land promoter or subdivision developer was born.

Through accounts that were brought back by those who had visited these remote settlements, the "civilized" communities of the East began to get a picture of westerners, one that set this breed apart from other Americans. In one of the early outlying subcolonies, newcomers were attracted by privileges that exempted them from taxes for the first year and outlawed all debts that had been contracted elsewhere. Into the new areas poured the impoverished, the fugitives from a stratified society, and the traditional honest plowmen, who sought upward social and economic mobility.

Since all was new, life was crude. Justice was dispensed over taproom tables; written records were few; and legal needs were attended to under exceedingly primitive conditions. Many of the settlers were Scots-Irish—aggressive, independent, and often contentious folks. One of William Penn's agents called them "bold and indigent strangers" and remarked that when questions arose over land titles, as they did almost daily, these hardies stood by their claims, arguing that it was against the laws of God and Nature that Christians who were willing to work should be denied the use of the land.

They were Christians when it came to invoking their presumed right to fructifying the earth, but frequently that sentiment did not extend to the Lord's day. The absence of religious facilities meant that Sunday often was just another day of the week, and the West began to get a name for being Godless. This reputation stuck, and for decades it would be applied to later frontiers as a characteristic of newer regions. It was just another facet of the Wild West myth.

Despite the later erroneous labeling of the plains and the Rockies as the Old West, this early tramontane frontier was the real and original Old West. It furnished manpower and experience for later westward thrusts. It sent forth men who harbored their own notions about individual enterprise, land ownerhsip, and social, religious, and political independence—qualities that their sons and grandsons

inherited and passed along to the successive frontiers that rolled
westward across the continent.

Once the pressure along the eastern slopes of the Alleghenies had
built up sufficiently, the geographical dam broke, and what had been
a trickle of leather-clad adventurers, mixed with a handful of hunter-
husbandmen, now became a flood of practiced farmers in search of
fresh, cheap lands. Westering families poured through the Cumberland Gap, exploded across Kentucky and Tennessee, and pressed
forward into the unknown in hopes of improving their lot. From that
time on, the West, a continent-wide expanse, was discovered over
and over again.

But always, ahead of the agrarian army was the advance guard,
outriders who sought quick money, at first in deer hides, then in
beaver pelts. Another group looked for precious minerals but settled
for the lead mines of Missouri or Illinois. While this process was
going on, the far-western fur brigades had advanced deep into the
unknown and daily were bringing back pelts and fresh geographical
knowledge. As they rendezvoused at such places as Jackson Hole,
Wyoming, and as they probed the Rockies ever more deeply, another
breed of entrepreneurs, traders this time, opened the Santa Fe Trail
and thrust their heavily laden wagons into what would be the
American Southwest.

Inspired by the success of prairie schooners that sailed deeply into
uncharted seas of grass, the Oregon migration of the 1840s set in, and
thus another gathering of adventurous Americans felt its way westward. Then came California gold and a literal traffic jam on the
plains, one that in itself triggered even more rushes that fingered their
way into virgin mountain recesses.

This traffic across the prairies, in turn, produced a new frontier.
When it was discovered that oxen which had been written off by
wagoners as being worn out and therefore had been abandoned would
often turn up the following spring fat and sleek, having survived the
winter by pawing into the snow in search of dried but highly
nutritious gramma grass, the range cattle industry sprang into
existence. About this time came still another breed of exploiters: the
hide hunters, who were determined to capitalize on the buffalo trade.
These elements of the advance guard, as always, were followed by the
farmers who, after a long reluctance, finally ventured out into the
Great American Desert, determined to gamble with the others.

The farmers came because the railroads had preceded them,
making possible the pursuit of a cash-crop economy, which had not

existed before. And with the coming of the railroads the day of the nomadic Indian ended, as these steel bands fenced them off and sliced up their hunting grounds. The rails were branches and subbranches of a huge framework, from which were suspended thousands of new farms, agricultural towns, and fenced sections of land that turned a once-open range into a monotony of squares of grain where gramma grass once grew and buffalo grazed. In many ways the railroads that spawned the farmer frontier brought an end to most of the earlier frontiers, although this was not to be evident for a while.

Meanwhile, the first flush of mineral extraction began to wane, and placer mining gave way to more traditional methods of mining. The process of digging deeper for gold, silver, and, later, copper turned temporary mining camps into towns that hoped to, and sometimes did, become permanent settlements. Then, as those industries declined, mountain towns turned to the building of resorts, and some advertised themselves as health spas. What might be called the tourist frontier blossomed and did so to such an extent that today in Colorado, this business is referred to as an "industry," one that ranks second only to agriculture in annual income.

The successive waves of Americans who rushed westward in leapfrogging frontiers were not mythical; they were real. But in many cases they developed because of highly inflated stories of continuing success in this new land, overblown advertising, much of which was not even true. Also, in later stages of the great invasion—the occupation of the trans-Missouri West—the color of cowboys, cavalrymen, stagecoach drivers, wild Indians, spectacularly rich miners, and many other sets of "characters," discussed earlier, themselves added to the legend. They contributed their share to the creation of a mythical land, a sort of sagebrush Shangri-La where everyone was prosperous, happy, and young.

Myths and legends are not made out of pure cloth, and the West was able to produce enough "miracles" to give substance to stories coming out of this fabulous land. Just when eastern confidence began to weaken, an enormous nugget would be discovered in some remote mining area, or the longest, fullest head of wheat yet seen would go on display. Periodically, millionaires—yesterday's welfare candidates—would turn up in the East and spend their new-found wealth prodigally. These things would draw reporters out to learn of the latest western wonders, and when they had finished embellishing their accounts, eastern readers experienced a renewed faith, a reassurance that the modern Eden had not let them down.

*No one packaged and sold the myth better than William F. ("Buffalo Bill")
Cody, here surrounded by stylized Indians from his troupe. His flamboyant
Wild West Shows had one message for his audiences: "You Should've Been
There!" (Courtesy, Colorado Historical Society)*

In addition to news stories about specific "finds," a great deal of
published nonfiction and fiction—discussed in an earlier chapter—
went on the market. Bored Americans, living quiet, uneventful lives
in eastern villages, got away from the monotony of their security by
escaping momentarily into a vicarious West, set before them in print.
Demand generates production, and the more this mythic West sold,
the more of it there was on the market. It was self-generating.
Publishers had found their own Golden West.

There were some westerners who did not yield to the blandishments of writers eager to retail their exploits in the eastern market.
The reviewer of a new biography about frontiersman Joseph Walker
(*Time,* 4 July 1983, p. 70) said that he stubbornly refused "to
embroider achievements for legend-hungry Eastern journalists," and
therefore his outstanding successes as a guide and explorer had gone
relatively unnoticed. The reviewer went on to say that "the True
West is not always the most appealing of places" and suggested that
"those in search of myth should try Louis L'Amour or Zane Grey."

Even so, as is the case today, journalists of Walker's day knew what
sold and what did not sell, and they wisely opted for the myth when

submitting their efforts to management. Such reading material titillated the minds of nineteenth-century Americans and enhanced their national pride as they watched the great westward crusade unfold. There were also added elements of excitement as that expansionistic century drew to a close. The Spanish-American War had satisfied superficial needs for diversion and patriotic fervor, but it was only a brief encounter, and its ability to curtain off some of the problems of rising conflicts in industrial America was limited. Coincidental to the ending of that brief international adventure was the apparent closing of the frontier. Overnight a great quiet fell across the nation.

Now came the American dilemma. Those enthusiastic liberals who endorsed Wilson's New Freedom and Teddy Roosevelt's progressivism were seeking to retain the rewards earned from benefits bestowed by the recent industrial advance, but at the same time they were seeking somehow to retain the individual freedom so thoroughly woven into the country's traditions. To them, as to the ordinary man on the street, the West was the repository of freedom and individualism, perhaps the last stronghold of those qualities. Somehow the frontier ambience had to be preserved "as a sacred bulwark against profane industrialism." That the new industrialism posed its own threats was noticed by Owen Wister, when, in 1911, he wrote the preface to a new edition of *The Virginian*. He explained that his novel was an expression of the American faith that currently was being attacked by "enemies both in Wall Street and in the Labor Unions."

America, having burst out onto the world scene as a result of the Spanish-American War, was standing on the threshold of an even larger international conflict in which airplanes, machine guns, tanks, and gas warfare would display, on the battlefields of France, the results of industrial production; this would, in part, announce the arrival of the modern world. Less dramatic but still in evidence were the emergence of crowded cities, tenement living, and the reduction of the everyday American to a nameless, faceless nonentity who was at the mercy of forces over which he had little control and who was possessed of few choices.

But the stories that these entrapped people were reading suggested that the traditional West was still out there and was, even at this late date, a place of opportunity, a big land that bred large men, a sanctuary possessed of an atmosphere that breathed American ideals and hinted a fulfillment of the old dream that had been around so long. Of course, the man on the street was shackled in many ways, unable to try for the main chance that his ancestors might have contemplated, but perhaps he would not have pulled up stakes if given the opportunity. However, that did not prevent him from taking the dream to bed with him or from finding it in the reading available to him. If, as has been suggested, the West really provided no safety valve in a physical sense, still it could be argued that one existed in the mind, the imagination, in the hidden hopes of those "huddled masses" in the East, about which we have read so much. The West of the mind did indeed exist.

It was not only the working man who savored a western dream; far from it. Americans of all classes—especially authors, journalists, the literati in general, and the dreamers—not only subscribed to the legend; indeed, they helped it to develop.

Over the years, as settlement had edged westward, the frontier simply had been a place where the majority of Americans did not live; to them it was a great vacant parcel of land awaiting ultimate settlement. While it lay there, raw and undeveloped, it was the original "open space," a place where nature ruled and where valuable lessons were to be learned. Henry David Thoreau, one of the first environmentalists, published his *Walden; or, Life in the Woods* in 1854, and he became a much-quoted literary figure on the subject of the wilderness. In many ways he personified the developing myth. "Eastward I go only by force; but westward I go free" was one of his oft-quoted remarks which suggested an unfettered existence in a less-crowded countryside. He and those like him envisioned it as nature beyond control, a sea of grass which Whitman later talked about. They saw a resemblance to the wild and stormy oceans that both fascinated and challenged seafarers.

Earlier Americans had found comfort and hope in the western myth; those who lived in the late nineteenth and the early twentieth centuries continued to see it as a need, a necessary support, a crutch. The latter group, faced by the technology and impersonality of a modern world, grasped out for roots, for tradition, for a past whose values one could lean upon or at least look to for guidelines. Older nations had their legends, and for Americans the great westward sweep, with all its implications, had been the national epic.

"The story of the West is our Trojan War, our Volsunga Saga, our Arthurian Cycle, our Song of Roland," wrote a California professor of English some years back. He thought that our own saga, one which he regarded as a symbol and a myth based upon an enlargement of the facts, was important to the American people and that it "exerts a strange power over us." Denis W. Brogan, the Englishman who understood America so well, said much the same thing in his

At the peak of his climb, Judge E. C. Winchell, here christening
California's Mount Winchell in 1888, symbolized man in the West—
standing alone, vigilant, heroic, robust, a true American (literally wrapped in
the flag), and with a threat of violence. (Courtesy, the Bancroft Library)

confession that "I would be the last one to forget . . . that the United States is the only country since the Middle Ages that has created a legend to set beside the story of Achilles, Robin Hood, Roland and Arthur." The film director George Stevens wanted to enlarge the western legend in the belief that the pioneers who were presented in films filled "the same role for Americans as King Arthur and his knights hold in English mythology." Even the Germanist Herbert Frenzel was quoted as having placed the American frontier epoch alongside the European age of knighthood. In an effort to create legends and somehow to catch up with the rest of the world, we have made heroes of individuals who really were not of the heroic mold, and we have popularized and idolized military and naval figures simply to answer popular demand generated during wartime. After the shooting was over, we broadcast bronze statues of these overnight heroes across the land to satisfy a desire of the burghers to have a local warrior, preferably in an equestrian form, ensconced in the town square. The outbreak of such commemorations was particularly virulent after the Civil War, and it must have kept sculptors and foundries busy trying to answer the demand. Nor was it just generals and admirals that were so honored. While lower ranks could not expect to find themselves cast in bronze, democratic America chose also from the ranks and produced the Sergeant Yorks and the Audie Murphys for the reading public and, later, for the movie audiences.

We have even made heroes of western "bad men," ordinary bank robbers and psychopathic killers such as Billy the Kid. Mounted gangsters, Jesse James being one, were figuratively outfitted in Robin Hood garb and passed off as individuals who had revolted against society to help the poor and the unfortunate.

Our heroes—both military and civilian—have been associated with horses. While we could not match Russia's colorful Cossacks or Europe's traditional man-on-horseback figure, we did invent the cowboy, a man who was armed, who was a horseman, and who did violent but presumably good things even though he was largely a nameless, faceless figure who simply herded cows on the open range for a living. In our short history we have probably created more "heroes" by means of publicity and manufactured myth than have any of our older sister nations during their long histories.

All of which means that in our brief tenure as a nation, possessed of relatively few traditions, we have needed heroes and legends, as well as roots. When I once lectured for a year in Great Britain, giving courses in American history to students who displayed a mild interest in such folklore, colleagues teasingly asked: "*American* history? I didn't think there was such a thing!'' Historically we were still confined to playing with Lincoln Logs. These were people whose past stretched back to infinity, and to them we were relative newcomers on the scene, whose past lay in the future. Americans have been self-conscious about this, even defensive.

That the need for roots exists comes back to us in many ways. As Wallace Stegner has remarked, ''Fearing the loss of what little tradition we have, we cling to it hard; we are hooked on history.'' Or what we think is history. When Archibald MacLeish made his comment that the West is a country of the mind and is therefore eternal, he was referring both to the factually historical article as well as the inherited ''romantic'' version of our past, made so popular in the nineteenth century. The latter, perpetuated in novels and movies, is so well established in the American mind as to be real in itself.

Just because the historian uncovers the truth, which does not coincide with the myth, does not mean that the myth is not useful or that it is not important. The Australian author Thomas Keneally put it very well: ''For the thing about a myth is not whether it is true or not, nor whether it *should* be true, but that it is somehow truer than truth itself.'' So, when some writers have jiggered the facts a bit, and have upset historians, we must remember that the mythical West has been a great comfort to a lot of people who really didn't give a snap about the mint item, historically speaking.

The mythic West has left some deep and lasting impressions on the European mind. Given the proper setting, the emotional impact can even get out of hand.

During the 1930s a small group of Russian immigrants, traveling in two parties, started west, bound for California. Somewhere in the Southwest they found themselves on an off-trail, meandering road, and before long, one of the vehicles, an old broken-down truck, became stuck in the mud. Some Navajo Indians who were passing that way saw the difficulty and approached the beleaguered travelers, hoping to be of assistance.

''It's Indians,'' the leader of the Russians announced. Where-upon, he later related, ''Anna Feodorovna went on her knees, crossed herself and started to pray out loud. His Excellency [Anna's father] jumped off the unpacked sofa where he was resting and started throwing fire tongs and walking canes and pokers around like a crazy man. 'Where's my sword? My sword! My sword!' Ermak turned the kitchen table over, piled chairs up, crouched down behind it. 'Don't be afraid' he said to Madame Greskin, 'before I die I try to shoot you and Luba, too, but if God wills otherwise. . . .' He opened a drawer in his barricade and pulled out a butcher knife, 'use this, but don't ever let them take you alive.' ' "

The confused Navajoes, trying to ignore the uproar, freed the truck. Somewhat calmed down and glad to be alive, the Russians bought a sheep from the Indians, killed it, and prepared a fire. In turn, the Indians contributed another sheep for the spit, and a combined barbeque party resulted. There were no casualties.

Less dramatic, but no less emotionally involved, were hundreds of Europeans who have shown great interest in the Wild West throughout the twentieth century and whose fascination is still evident today.

Parisians who are addicted to the West buy the appropriate garb at a store called the Western House, not far from the Arc de Triomphe, and some of them spend weekends in an outlying "western" village, lifted from the nineteenth-century American high-plains scene. Here they lose themselves briefly, transported to another world, and with their faces painted or covered by a bandanna, they brandish tomahawks or six-guns as they reenact that internationally favorite saga known as the Conquest of the West.

On the outskirts of Cologne, post–World War II Germans constructed a replica of a log blockhouse, which served as a clubhouse for the Prairiefreunde, or Friends of the Prairie, where weekend warriors, both Indians and cavalrymen, could rub elbows with momentary cowboys and plainsmen. It was one of dozens of such clubs in Germany. The existence of at least two chain stores specializing in western garb that catered to the needs of the well-dressed German frontiersman further suggested the widespread interest in this fantasizing over the buckskin days of yore. Admirers of the cowboy also bought a deodorant called Lasso and Rodeo aftershave. The *real* buffs refused to watch TV westerns unless they were dressed for the occasion in frontier outfits.

In the 1980s the Old West was still flourishing in England. The Double H Western Club of Coventry, as described by one of its members, is made up of a group of men and women, ranging in age from seventeen to eighty-five, "who dress up as cowboys, mountain men, American Indians, etc. We also sometimes put on country and western dances to raise money for charities." I am the proud possessor of the Double H badge, which stands for "his and hers," and am a member in good standing in the foreign branch of the organization; the other two stateside members reside in North Dakota. The Double H group will find enjoyment in this recreation if they don't carry things too far; westernizing can be dangerous to your health. For example, a Glasgow health officer has complained that

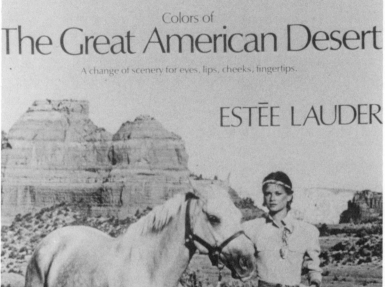

There is a place of golden canyons, apricot sands, terracotta mountains and mauve shadows.
There is a place where colors are quite unlike the way they are anywhere else.
Only Estée Lauder could take you there with such style.

Colors of

The Great American Desert

A change of scenery for eyes, lips, cheeks, fingertips.

ESTĒE LAUDER

To sell products promising to enhance and preserve feminine beauty, manufacturers have called upon themes and images of a land that left its women sun-leathered and wind-chapped. (Courtesy, Estée Lauder, Inc.)

young Scots are getting round-shouldered and hollow-chested from
mimicking the slouchy walk of the western gunslingers.

The American publishing community is well aware of this market on the other side of the Atlantic. In 1972, Flora North, of Howell-North Books in Berkeley, California, said, "We sell more western Americana in Paris and Switzerland than we do in New York."

Europeans have been less critical of the American epic than have some Americans. During the nineteenth century, at a time when the westward expansion was at full tide, eastern communities that were watching the population drain sometimes were less than enthusiastic about the great national movement. A drop-off in census figures threatened a weakening of political clout in Washington, D.C., and the flight of young people forecast future economic stagnation in these older communities. For example, in the spring of 1879, when the great Leadville, Colorado, mining boom was at its height and when stories of fabled wealth were circulating freely in the East, there was a concerted "anti-Leadville" editorial campaign in Maine newspapers. They were filled with forebodings of "go broke in Leadville" and with sneering remarks to the effect that when the railroad came to that transient camp, those who were "busted" could get home faster. Avoid Texas, too, said the editors, for it was a place of bad crops, hog cholera, horse thieves, and cattle rustlers. Stay in Maine, they urged, where one's long-run chances were better.

Even westerners tried to cool off the effusive praise of the wonderland they had discovered. Stories about wide-open mining and about cattle towns that were populated by whores, gamblers, and gunslingers were driving off some of the prospective businessmen who wanted to settle in the West with their families, invest their money in these communities, and become the economic and political leaders of the new towns. To counter the myth of wildness, western publicists poured out articles that stressed the culture of the new country, the high types who were leading the West onward and upward educationally, socially, and culturally, and the peace and quiet that had descended upon a once-wild frontier country.

It was only the best blood of the East that peopled the plains and mountains, said Charles Moreau Harger, the Abilene, Kansas, editor, in 1900. While these folks might be poor in worldly goods, he went on, they came from families that traced their origins to hardy American stock. Out in the newly settled communities were the brothers and cousins of men whose names were nationally famous for their "eminence in church or law or State." These were said to be bright, progressive people whose morals were beyond reproach, good citizens who were products of that great selective process that the West provided, and they would be the builders of a bigger, better, and more American America.

By the twenties, in that period of "updating" the young businessman's West, which we discussed earlier, the campaign for reassessing the old Wild West myths continued. When Emerson Hough's *North of 36* appeared in 1923, Stuart Henry, who had been reared and educated in Kansas, attacked it on the ground that its exaggerations did an injustice to the true history of the region. He, in turn, was assailed by outraged old-timers who chose to remember it otherwise. Writers such as Andy Adams, Charles A. Siringo, and William MacLeod Raine, who were aficionados of the mythic West, came to Hough's defense.

Later in that decade, De Voto made his attack upon the "purity of the pioneers" legend, saying that, aside from mining rushes that tended to attract transients of a less-stable nature, the great migration was made up of three classes: restless, unadjusted people such as old soldiers, rivermen, and roustabouts; people who for one reason or another found it necessary to evade the law; and—this, the largest class—those who were driven out of the East, where the competition was too much for them, "which is to say, further, the unfit." De Voto thought that the agrarians who moved west weren't even good farmers; if they had been, they would have stayed home and made a success of it there. But in this he fell for the biggest myth of all: that the bulk of the settlers were displaced misfits, forced westward because they couldn't make it anywhere else. Looking at the entire sweep of land seekers who made the move, both from the East and from Europe, De Voto was shooting from the hip in this latter assertion. The evidence simply doesn't support his generalization, popular as that notion has been.

One aspect of the American legend is that, in general, these western settlers were highly individualistic people, given to personal solutions of problems, and that it was their ability to innovate that got them out of trouble where ordinary mortals failed. Over the years this notion was appropriated by the general public and was applied to Americans at large. One sees this myth running all through our military history, where the Yank, falling back upon his native inventive qualities, invariably confounds the enemy, who has to rely blindly on "book training" and cannot think for himself. This quality was believed to be an inheritance from the frontier experience, from "the most American part of America," part of the heritage that has been passed down by those who learned it while

Bold, Honest, Heroic.
A genuine fragrance of the American West.
Colorado Sage.

COLORADO SAGE COLOGNE BY JESS BELL 8 FL. OZS.

For stores, call toll free.
1-800-321-9985.
In Ohio, call collect.
216-221-9191.

© Jess Bell, Inc.

*The myth appeals to all senses. Did a sophisticated eastern reader of this
advertisement in the* New Yorker *believe that when he slapped on some
Colorado Sage, he would smell like a cowboy? (Courtesy, Bonne Bell, Inc.)*

hacking away at a wilderness to which they hoped to bring a new
civilization.

The lone settler, far removed from any kind of assistance—
medical, religious, commercial, or any other type—had no choice but
to solve his own problems. Sometimes he could call upon a neighbor,
who might live within several miles, but often even this was not
possible. So the successive generations of frontiersmen moved westward, pretty much on their own, and gained a reputation for being
great individualists.

But when the high plains were reached and farming had to be
carried on under an entirely different set of circumstances and rules,
the highly prized quality of making it on one's own faded in the glare
of realities. Walter P. Webb has written that life for the traditional
frontiersman was supported by a three-legged stool, these supports

being land, water, and timber; but when the high-plains country was reached, two of these legs were removed. Only land remained. And now the pioneer farmer had to rely upon importations to keep his operations going. Grand Rapids supplied the furniture; barbed wire and windmills were shipped in; coal had to be purchased; and if the farmer did not want to live in a soddy, he bought lumber that had made a long and expensive trip to reach his outpost. Turning from a subsistence type of living, he now engaged in a cash-crop economy— wheat, corn, or livestock—and immediately became the prisoner of the market price for his produce. The Populist Revolt was one of the responses to this new dilemma.

The old individualistic frontiersman, whose long rifle was a key to the meat market, whose forests were his fuel and housing supply, and whose irrigation system was sufficient rainfall, now joined the ranks of regimented eastern workers, because, in effect, the new westerner also was working for wages. And when times were tough, he was in no better position than was the eastern worker. For example, in the North Dakota of 1940, one sociologist discussed the emergence of a permanent relief population of "employable unemployed" farmers. The mining of the land in the form of bonanza farming had altered the status of the traditional honest yeoman, who had tilled his soil and had lived from the fruits of his labors.

While individuals who lived beyond the hundredth meridian, or in the land of little rain, had to maintain a certain degree of self-reliance, which they had inherited from their forebears, the odds against them were great enough to require a good deal of cooperative action. The Mormons, who were said to have made the desert bloom, are a good example not only of cooperative efforts but also of disciplined collective action dictated by the church.

Yet as Joe Frantz has pointed out, the West, which is so full of contradictions, furnished another example of maverickism among the presumably docile Latter-day Saints. Even in a strict theocracy, one that is based upon joint effort, the Mormons have given us some of the "most vocally rampant individualists that this nation has produced." Possibly they surfaced as a reaction to the restrictiveness of their society or because they believed the legend of western individualism. Their conduct might have been an effort to deny the existence of any yoke in a land that was supposed to be so free.

Despite the erosion in the role of the agrarian as the independent American, a development dictated by a new and unremitting climate west of the hundredth meridian, the old myth of the loner making his way in the world, unassisted and unhampered, died very slowly.

During the 1970s, writers were still talking about the mountain-states
region as a place where "the pioneer ethic of rugged individualism seems to be greatly cherished." One of them pondered the question as to whether this was because of regional ideology "or some more ordinary Darwinism," but he concluded that any attempts by the government to channel future population growth would "reduce the freedom that individuals have had and cherished in the past." He contended that the West still was the last refuge from the tentacles of organizational restrictiveness and also—quite incorrectly—that while corporate power was present in the West, it had not yet thoroughly fastened its grip, as was the case in the East.

Perhaps it was the notion of individualism that popularized the cowboy myth, rather than the colorful trappings he wore or the presumed acts of derring-do he carried out at his lonely prairie outpost. The boots, big hats, chaps, and holstered guns were just the means of identifying this particular westerner. In many ways, he may have been an accident. It has been argued that Rousseau's "natural man," who was romanticized in the eighteenth century as a symbol of the free and the unfettered, started his American trek in the backwoods of Kentucky as the buckskin-clad hunter and made his appearance on the Great Plains a century later under a Stetson hat.

In a collective sense the cowboy became a hero largely because fiction made him so, but one would be hard pressed to name a particular cowboy hero, any individual who became nationally known just for being a cowboy. Actually, he didn't even call himself a cowboy—the title was bestowed upon him; rather, he thought of himself as a ranch hand or a rider. The earlier version of this American "natural man" could show some individual heroes—Davy Crockett, Daniel Boone, and, later, Jim Bridger, Jedediah Smith, Hugh Glass, and quite a few more—but the cowboy normally remained anonymous, usually died broke, a physically "stove in" hired hand who may have ridden the range but didn't want to end up there, as the plaintive lines "bury me not on the lone praire-e-e-e" suggest.

As historian Lewis Atherton has pointed out, there is difficulty in explaining why the ordinary cow hand, who really lacked the traits from which heroes are cast, should have been elevated to that pedestal. How, also, could this employee of a conservatively inclined rancher become a symbol of individualism and freedom when he was a mere wage earner as surely as was any clerk working in a New England hardware store or as a midwestern farm hand. The only independence that the cow hand had was the right to quit at the drop of a hat. Possibly the notion that he was independent arose from the locale of his job: out on the open range, where people were few and far between and social restraints were loose.

The average cowpoke had little interest in saving his money; usually he was a floater; he was momentarily interested in women but not necessarily in marriage; and he frequently showed little desire to rise to the management level. Some sought upward mobility, an opportunity to have a little spread of their own, where independence could be more a reality and there would be a chance for family life. Those who made it beyond owning a small outfit and became successful, perhaps even achieving the title "cattle king," were not made into heroes. The owners who gained wealth and prominence often went into politics and became well known for their influence in that field, rather than as cowherds.

Possibly the relative few who made it to the top surrendered their chances to join the American heroes of the saddle, because now they represented capital and were people who herded around their own wage slaves. During the early twentieth century the progressive movement was strong, and there was a shift from the earlier worship of the wealthy to a suspicion of them as being exploiters. The cattle king was just another member of "big business," one who chased off squatters, crushed small cattlemen, brought in hired guns to stage such wars as the famed Johnson County shoot out in Wyoming. They "owned" western legislatures, whose members obediently carried out the conservative policies of their political masters.

In a sense, this left the cowboy as the oppressed worker, or at least one who apparently had little chance to rise to a higher level, something that ran counter to the American tradition. Futilely he tried to object, as did eastern workers, and there were efforts to organize and to strike. The Knights of Labor had a good many cowboys on its rolls. But management was in the saddle, so to speak, and the strikers had very little luck.

It is worth mentioning that perhaps this, in part, brought sympathy from a public whose attitudes were shifting, and it helped to make a hero of yet another little man who was trying to maintain his identity. The setting was right. He was a loner, out in that great, wide West, where he had to fight distance, isolation, the elements, and, now, big business. He was on a much better stage—sagebrush and sunsets—than was his fellow worker in a New England textile mill, for the public had a weakness for the Wild West, a place where, in its view, heroes sprang forth much more readily.

The cowboy himself wanted to preserve the legendary status that the mythmakers had accorded to him. Carey McWilliams said that his father, a pioneer cattleman in northwestern Colorado, had "no end of difficulty" in keeping the hired hands from playing cowboy. He recalled that these employees spent long hours in the bunkhouse on dull days, "devouring cheap romances" of the West, and they insisted upon wearing the proper garb and acting in the manner of their favorite fictional characters. McWilliams was sure that many of their activities and pranks had a literary origin.

This had been going on for some time. As early as the 1880s, wrote John C. Van Dyke, ranch hands were taking their role rather seriously. "They even accepted the popular estimate of themselves that they were a distinct genus of their own, and a bold bad lot into the bargain." He argued that most of these young men never belonged to the vaquero class, the members of which usually were raised with cattle, had ridden since boyhood, and were herdsmen who frequently remained on the hacienda for all of their lives; rather, these were "wandering Willies," who worked around from ranch to ranch. Van Dyke said the cowboys he knew had little or no education, had no great intelligence and very little sense of responsibility. They were men who generally recognized property rights and were not given to thievery but who had no reservations about shooting to kill under the proper circumstances and showed a disposition to get out of the country aboard a stolen horse if necessity demanded such an exit.

So may it have been. Nevertheless, the myth survived, undamaged and perhaps even a little enhanced. Teddy Roosevelt kept things going by organizing his famous Rough Riders, former cowboys, as support for what he hoped would be his personal exploits in the Spanish-American War. Things did not work out that way. The "charge" up San Juan Hill was carried out on foot, and much of the real fighting and dying was done by a regiment of black soldiers. The hill that Teddy climbed, in fact, was Kettle Hill; the more romantically named San Juan was next door. No matter. With the help of the press and a painting by his friend Frederic Remington, who knew something about making heroes of western-style figures doing battle with those southern Europeans whom he found so unsavory, Roosevelt realized the possibilities of gaining fame with his own version of cow-country Cossacks. He was very unhappy when Woodrow Wilson would not send him over the Atlantic to turn his Stetson cavalry loose on the Germans in World War I.

However, all was not lost. In the next round, known as World War II, the flamboyant George S. Patton, packing his ivory-handled pistols in the approved gunslinger manner, impressed even the Germans, not to mention other Europeans, who saw "Two Gun George" figuratively stalking Main Street at high noon, looking for someone upon whom he could freshen up his quick draw. He was a holstered Rommel, who did a lot of swaggering around, but at least he put his money where his mouth was and came out shooting, as compared to Douglas MacArthur, who merely sucked a corncob pipe, in the manner of a Missouri farmer, and promoted himself to fame through self-aggrandizing press conferences. Nor should we forget a milder character, Dwight D. Eisenhower, who neither savored a corncob nor packed a shooting iron on his hip, but all the same was unreservedly devoted to "westerns" and found refuge in them right up to the eve of D-day.

Theodore Roosevelt and Patton proved the power of the western mystique in boosting and hyping a career in public life. Many others have followed their lead. During the 1960s and 1970s, as the horse opera seemed to be fading first from television and then from the silver screen, the western theme was gathering strength in politics. John F. Kennedy, the only elected president between Franklin Roosevelt and Jimmy Carter from east of the Mississippi, called his program of reforms the New Frontier. Lyndon Johnson and Barry Goldwater made a habit of posing in cowboy garb, often on horseback, and affecting the unblinking, straight-from-the-shoulder style of the B-western hero.

In the 1970s the derring-do of the cowboy image was still going strong. German-born Henry A. Kissinger knew the international legend. He told the Italian journalist Oriana Fallaci—though he later denied it—that he liked to act alone, that Americans admired that quality enormously. He then used as an example the cowboy riding into a small town, sometimes even without a pistol, "because he doesn't go in for shooting. He acts, that's all: aiming at the right spot at the right time, a Wild West tale, if you like." Perhaps young Henry had read his Karl May and had absorbed the Teutonic version of the American legend. At least he found it not uncomfortable. Neither did his boss, Richard M. Nixon, who once urged Americans to leave Vietnam only "as a cowboy, with guns blazing, backing out of a saloon." By the end of the decade there was little indication that this theme was losing its appeal. In 1980, voters overwhelmingly elected a former star of several oaters and the former host of "Death Valley Days."

In any event, out of the story of the horseback herders came one of
our most enduring legends. Not only was it universally accepted; for
decades it has been presented over and over again to world readers
and viewers. Critics constantly swear that it is worn out and that it
has faded away forever; but then, that beautiful image surfaces again
in perhaps a slightly varied form, possibly because a new generation
has come along and finds it fascinating or even reassuring.

Meantime, Americans are just as prone to play at being western as
are some of their European counterparts. It just takes a little different
form. While they don't run around on weekends in Indian headdress
or holstered six-guns, the flavor of the West touches them in many
ways. As one writer remarked, "western lifestyle always has been
more fashionable than living in the West itself." Ranch-style houses
have been popular for decades. Ranch-wagon automobile body styles
are a common sight. And of course, "western-wear" clothing for
both men and women has had its appeal for some years.

Without doubt the best-known commercialization of the western
motif has been the Marlboro cigarette advertisements. By the
autumn of 1970, when the last television cigarette commercial ran,
the announcer stated that "today the West is everywhere." Indeed,
television commercials, as well as newspaper and magazine advertisements, had helped to make it so. But if one looks more closely at the
Marlboro Man, one will notice that in most of these advertisements
he is no mere cowpoke. He is a stockman, a mature American with
the proper wrinkles around his eyes to prove that he has been out of
doors, but his dress is that of an owner, not of an employee—a
businessman with roots, with property; and he is not a drifter. He is
solid and conservative; and beyond all doubt he votes the straight
Republican ticket.

Marlboro ran a large and expensive advertisement in *Time*, on 25
October 1982, announcing that once more the Marlboro Country
Store was open. Available to buyers were such items as hats,
sheepskin coats, boots, leather vests, concha belts, and red-flannel
shirts. Also for sale were bunkhouse lanterns, Hudson's Bay
blankets, snowshoes, Son-of-a-Gun stew sets, and a genuine chuck-
wagon supply box made of ponderosa pine, with metal bindings. For
the true followers of the western legend, branding irons were on sale
at only $32.00 each. These nostalgic items could be acquired, at a
hefty price, by placing an order with the Country Store, the address
of which was Westbury, New York.

Of course, to get suited up in such "duds," as the westerners call
them, could be the equivalent of wearing a three-piece suit to the

office. All right for the classes, but what about the masses? What if you wanted to look like the real article? According to one New York newspaper reporter who scanned the western sartorial scene in the seventies, the average construction worker or laborer, arriving in a Montana or Wyoming town and wanting to appear in proper garb, would head for the nearest western-wear store to get himself outfitted. A straw hat, cut stockman's style, Levis, cowboy boots, and a tooled leather belt would cover the basics. Then, if possible, the mount. This time it was apt to be a pickup truck sporting a gun rack and a rifle mounted below the cab's rear window. With a can of Coors beer firmly in his grasp and with the windows rolled down "to show he can get properly filthy," our modern hired hand comes riding into the West. If they met on the street, the Marlboro Man probably would give him a look of proper disdain, accorded the working class, and continue on his way to the local membership club that did not admit such riffraff.

By the early eighties the craze for cowboy getups had posed some problems for working ranchers. An outfitter in Livingston, Montana, complained that the dudes had made off with all the goods, and when local farmers and ranchers came in for boots or Levis, the shelves were pretty well stripped. Worse, the demand had driven prices sky-high, and old-timers had difficulty in coping with the idea that high-grade boots were going from around $150 and that the better hats were commanding $65. Retailers blamed the rush on the movie *Urban Cowboy,* a film that set off the nationwide craze.

It was more than a national desire to look like cattle-range folks. Anything western was "in." In the fall of 1982, western clothing that featured the "prairie look" offered pioneer-style dresses. Montgomery Ward advertised the Santa Fe look: "ruffles and denim." That autumn a New York mail-order house promoted what it termed "a celebration of the American style" and stressed that it was a tribute to those who were possessed of a highly individual, refreshing sense of fashion. "Sensual suedes" made one look like an Indian maiden. Also there were "prairie living" dresses, "frontier flannels," and a combination of calico and boots called "the new frontier" models. Black, lacy Victorian formal wear promised the lady buyer "unabashed glamor."

But alas, another western boom had gone bust—an old story in the promised land. By the spring of 1983, fashion experts had announced the demise of western wear and the advent of "active wear," for the new outdoor-activity craze. Once-empty store shelves now stood high with unsold western wear. There was a glut in the boot market.

Rodeo stars, both male and female, still bought shirts and other
articles of clothing, but the mass market was dead, and western retailers who once had outfitted urban cowboys were in despair, not a few of them closing up or turning to other items. But since nothing is more fickle than fashion, there were expectations that the Old West, sartorially speaking, was not yet dead and that perhaps some new movie or television series might set off yet another rush to the clothiers.

Not to worry. The tall hats, leather vests, and other bits of frontier foppery stand for only a small part of a much larger phenomenon. Western fashion is simply one of a hundred ways in which Americans celebrate a myth that has endured for two centuries.

This myth is firmly set in one part of the country, that ephemeral West found somewhere between the Missouri and the Sierra. But those who are trying to assess and explain its strength and longevity often underestimate the obvious—that this myth's appeal and implications are more national than regional. The South has a literature of its own and writers who deal with it as an entity; so has the East. But there is a difference. Americans admire Faulkner and love *Gone with the Wind,* but they do not spend millions to dress like Rhett Butler. Nor have they stood in line, generation after generation, to buy paperbacks and to watch B movies about cotton pickers and pellagra. There are westerns, but there are not southerns. The West alone seems to be a national possession. Its experience speaks for all Americans, not just for those who live there.

Why? Partly because the myth is rooted in the experience of the frontier, surely one of the most important chapters of the American story. The frontier moved slowly at first from the southern tidewater and Puritan villages into the piedmont and into New England forests. Then, from the day when the first curious, adventuresome frontiersmen breached the passes of the Appalachians and gingerly felt their way out into the openness of the continent, they marked out a continuous wilderness road that reached out for the Pacific Ocean. Some reached that body of water and stayed; others who got that far curled back, followed the mining frontier inland in an eastward movement, and ultimately met the main westward-moving body of settlers who had halted short of the Rockies. Together they put down stakes in that untapped hinterland and began to wind up the American pioneering experience. This plains-and-Rockies region was the last frontier, and as time passed, it was here that the fluidity of the westward surge ground to a halt. As De Voto put it, this "set the first full stop to the American dream."

That moving line of settlement has helped to shape every part of the land. New Jersey plumbers, computer programmers in Indiana, lawyers and fry cooks in Atlanta and Minneapolis—all of them, if they care to look, can find some part of that grand tale in their neighborhoods, and many feel that they have a personal stake in it. Their great-grandparents might have lived it, for one thing, and after adding a few embellishments, the old folks were sure to let the youngsters know about it. In that sense the stories set on the plains and in the high country stand for a historical experience that has touched each acre of this nation.

The myth's appeal goes far beyond that, however. After all, each year carries us farther from that frontier heritage, yet the myth survives. The western historian Ray Billington enumerated three main reasons for its persistence during these waning years of our century—a strong back-to-nature urge among a sizeable body of Americans, a growing irritation over the strictures of conventionalism, and a desire for greater opportunities for individual expression in a highly industrialized society that itself is being more and more circumscribed by governmental controls. Each of these feelings has inspired people who have nurtured their own images of the frontier, bits of folklore and legend that came to them from diverse sources. They have imagined the frontier in a certain way, and whether or not that time, place, or condition ever existed is less important than the fact that their beliefs give psychological support to those who have that vision.

The insight is helpful, but the national fascination with the West seems to run even deeper. Something more than modern frustrations is keeping the myth alive. Perhaps the answer is to be found in an even-more-basic urge—a search for identity. People seem to need to know who they are, individually and collectively. They need to believe they are set apart from the rest of the world by something peculiarly theirs. The bewildering diversity of our society has deepened this urge. We are a stew into which the world has thrown whatever scraps have been at hand, and with so little in common, our people have reached out for something—anything—to bind them together. In the Western myth, many have found exactly what they were looking for. Significantly, the images and the simple story of the western legend first caught on in the early nineteenth century, those years when the young Republic, like a proud and gawky adolescent, was trying to decide who and what it was. This myth has been around ever since, simply because it has always done its job.

The legend is rooted in a story with which just about anyone can identify. It tells what happened when ordinary people moved into an extraordinary land. Often enough they overcame the challenges that they met there, but the real point of the story is not what happened to the land, but what happened to the people. They were changed, the legend insists—transformed, reborn. And they were better for it. The ordeal in the wilderness created the American, we believe: free-thinking, open, tough, optimistic, self-reliant—the litany goes on and on. The western hero has embodied these virtues and this message. He is us, only a little bigger, tougher, braver. From James Fenimore Cooper to John Wayne, whenever anyone has told us this story and has done it well, we have clapped and made him rich.

This story has had many settings, but by this century it had found its final home in the plains and the deserts and the mountains between Iowa and Reno. This was partly because that part of the country was the last stop for the pioneers and because it produced figures, like the cowboy, who seemed to fit snugly into the hero's big boots and broad-shouldered suit. But much of the reason is the land itself, its exaggerated weather and topography, its yawning distances that seem to swallow sound and time, its lingering dangers, its feel of great forces that will not be tamed, its beauty that can clutch your stomach and make you want to cry. As the cars, factories, and condominiums have intruded more and more into this country, the public has awakened to the fact that in a way the land, as much as the steely eyed frontiersman, is the hero. In a strange and finally indefinable way, it, too, is us writ large.

The simplicity and apparently endless repetition of this myth have made it an easy mark for critics such as Dwight Macdonald, who has called the western "one of the most vapid and infantile forms of art ever conceived by the brain of a Hollywood movie producer." It certainly has spawned a lot of silliness, from mechanical bulls in barrooms to accountants who spend their evenings and weekends dressed like Clint Eastwood. From the start it has appealed to the ugly side of the national character, our fascination with violence, our fears, our biases and narrow insecurities about uppity women and swarthy foreigners. It has left us vulnerable to the manipulations of politicians and advertising executives, those two creatures who know so well which buttons to push to get us to throw votes and money at them. Overly romantic, shallow, playing fast and loose with the facts—the scoffers have said all that and a lot more about the legend, and they have been right.

Beyond a certain point, however, such sniping becomes irrelevant. Born of the closest thing we have to a collective experience, fed by our need to discover or invent who we are, the myth endures. C. L. Sonnichsen put it so well: "It comes closer than the fiction of any other region to providing an index to America." Within us the wilderness still lingers, another writer has argued, the legacy of the pioneers: "What they dreamed we live; what they lived, we dream. That is why our western story still holds us, however ineptly it is told."

And it has been told badly, yet the story of the westering experience has still drawn packed houses for a long time. Whether we think of it as the West of the mind or as something geographical, it has been an enormous stage, with its characters set in place, ready to create the illusion that the audience has expected. This audience has paid its admission fee expecting to be enchanted, and the fact that it understood that this was all an illusion does not mean it was not satisfied. Nor does it mean that the characters were not telling the truth in their own way. If believed ardently enough, long and strongly enough to shape the way in which we live our days, anything becomes true.

The mythic West, then, is more than an emotion or a state of mind, more than a fantasy floating around the American mentality on gossamer wings—ethereal, hard to define, impossible to corner. It is real. It is not only the westerner but also the American at large who, knowingly or not, lives in two worlds: the day-to-day scene and the make-believe or fantasized world that has, for a great many people, actual substance. And there is no real conflict between the two. We live with both quite comfortably—one world filled with the immediate problems at hand, the other serving as a spare tire, a numbered emotional bank account, a fall-back position that is reassuring, comforting. Agreed, the factual frontier is gone, but the possibilities, the promise that it held, are very much alive in the national mind. This quality may be fugitive, buried deep in one's conscience, but it is there, and this is the place where dreams are manufactured.

Thankfully, though the legend can bring out many of our weaknesses, it more often speaks to the best in us and reminds us that we can be better than we are. Americans continue to go West, whether by car or movie ticket or pulp paperback, in part because, as one writer put it, they see that land as "the setting for a large moral fulfillment." It is home to the loveliest and most enduring of our myths, the only one to be universally accepted, Bernard De Voto

said. "In that mythology," he added, "it has worn many faces. It has
meant escape, relief, freedom, sanctuary. It has meant opportunity, the new start, the saving chances . . . the birth and fulfillment of a race."

We created this dream as we were growing up as a people, though we realized it only dimly as it was happening, and in turn the dream has continued to give us back a sense of who we are. It has been a case of mutual midwifery, with Americans and the myth helping each other into the world. For a dozen generations, Americans fought their way into the wilderness and, like me, when I visited my grandfather's Montana ranch as a boy, they could not wait to put that life behind them. But as with that place along the Missouri breaks, we have found that leaving is exactly what we cannot do.

The western mystique will be with us for a while longer. With so much to keep it alive, within us and all around, how could we ever forget?

ESSAYS ON SOURCES

---

1. THE EPHEMERAL WEST

For more comments about the terms *West* and *frontier* being used synonymously see T. K. Whipple, *Study out the Land* (Berkeley: University of California Press, 1943). See especially his essay "The Myth of the Old West," pp. 59–69.

Wister's observations were taken from Ben Merchant Vorpahl's *My Dear Wister: The Frederic Remington–Owen Wister Letters,* with Foreword by Wallace Stegner (Palo Alto, Calif.: American West Publishing Co., 1972), pp. 12, 20, 34, 301–2. Some of Nye's writings have been reproduced in T. A. Larson's *Bill Nye's Western Humor* (Lincoln: University of Nebraska Press, 1968, see p. 182). The reprint of this piece also appeared in the Ouray *Solid Muldoon* for 4 July 1884. The Creede reference is from Duane A. Smith, *Song of the Hammer and Drill: The Colorado San Juans, 1860–1914* (Golden, Colo.: Colorado School of Mines Press, 1982), p. 107. The "western newspaper" quotation is from Anthony J. Hensen, "We Restless Americans," *Salt Lake Tribune,* 13 Aug. 1905. The Frank Norris material came from his "The Frontier Is Gone at Last," *World's Work* 3, no. 4 (Feb. 1902): 1728–31, and was republished in his *The Responsibilities of the Novelist and Other Literary Essays* (New York: Greenwood Press, 1968).

Teddy Roosevelt wrote his predictions for *Century Magazine* (see "Ranch Life in the Far West," Feb. 1888, p. 510). G. Edward White, in *The Eastern Establishment and the Western Experience* (New Haven, Conn.: Yale University Press, 1968), talks about Roosevelt's western-oriented "Americanism" (see p. 191). Woodrow Wilson mentioned the passing of the frontier in "The Making of a Nation," *Atlantic Monthly,* July 1897, pp. 1–14. As early as 1901 Emerson Hough spoke of the passing of the frontier in "The Settlement of the West: A Study in Transportation," *Century Illustrated Monthly Magazine,* Nov. 1901, pp. 91–107, and Dec. 1901, pp. 201–16. He commenced his book *The Passing of the Frontier* (New Haven, Conn.: Yale University Press, 1918) with a burst of nostalgia about the recent past (see pp. 1–3 and 172).

Modern writers who have quoted Catlin on this subject include Loren Baritz, "The Idea of the West," *American Historical Review* 66 (Apr. 1961): 618; and Edwin Fussell, *Frontier: American Literature and the American West* (Princeton, N.J.: Princeton University Press, 1965), p. 3. Turner's comments are found in "Contributions of the West to American Democracy," *Atlantic Monthly,* Jan. 1903, pp. 83–90, and "The West—1876 and 1926," *World's Work* 52, no. 3 (July 1926): 319–27. For more about America's foremost exponent of the frontier theory see Ray Allen Billington's prize-winning *Frederick Jackson Turner: Historian, Scholar, Teacher* (New York: Oxford University Press, 1973); see page 399 for remarks about the latter article and Turner's dissatisfaction with it.

"Where Is the West?" was discussed in *World Today* 8, no. 2 (Feb. 1905):
117. See also William R. Lighton, "Where Is the West?" in *Outlook,* 18 July
1903, p. 702. Morris Garnsey's penetrating volume *America's New Frontier:
The Mountain West* (New York: Alfred A. Knopf, 1950) contains an excellent
discussion about the location of the West. For boundaries of the fiction
writer's West see John R. Milton, *The Novel of the American West* (Lincoln:
University of Nebraska Press, 1980), pp. xii–xiii.

The "amoeba" reference is from Hector H. Lee, "Tales and Legends in
Western American Literature," *Western American Literature* 9, no. 4 (Winter
1975): 240. The searcher for "truest civilization" was Frank Waugh, who
wrote "Frontiering" for *Survey,* 1 June 1924, p. 291. Gerould's article, "The
Aristocratic West," appeared in *Harper's Magazine,* Sept. 1925 (see p. 467).
Much the same material may be found in her *The Aristocratic West* (New York:
Harper & Brothers, Publishers, 1925). For Stegner's reaction to the high-
plains country see his article "I Sing of America," in *Holiday,* Mar. 1976, p.
49. The Nebraska-panhandle story came from *Time,* Feb. 1982, p. 23.

The notion that the Pacific Coast really was not a part of the West was set
forth by Walter Lionel George in his article "On the Road to Canaan,"
Sunset Magazine, Nov. 1922, p. 9. The symbolic connotation of the word *West*
is dealt with in Carey McWilliams, "The Myths of the West," *North American
Review,* Nov. 1931, pp. 426–28. See also Garet Garrett, "How in the West?"
Saturday Evening Post, 22 Nov. 1924 (see p. 78). Albert W. Atwood agreed with
Garrett that the Pacific Coast states were not part of the West. See his article
"Why Go West?" *Saturday Evening Post,* 19 Feb. 1927, p. 19. Carey
McWilliams, in his "Myths" article, also makes this case, on p. 427.

Professor Earl Pomeroy, a widely known and highly respected western
historian, wrote about eastern traits as applied to these coastal states in his
book *The Pacific Slope* (New York: Alfred A. Knopf, 1965); see his Introduction. See also Stegner, in his "I Sing of America" article mentioned above.
Nicholas Murray Butler's views may be found in "Across the Busy Years,"
Scribner's Magazine, Aug. 1936, pp. 114–19. See also Garnsey, *New Frontier,*
pp. 41, 44. Bernard De Voto entertained the question as to the West's
delimitations in "Footnote on the West," *Harper's Magazine,* Nov. 1927, pp.
713–14, and in "The West: A Plundered Province," ibid., Aug. 1934, p.
356. As an illustration of the uncertainty as to the West's easternmost limits,
both De Voto and Carey McWilliams (in his "Myths" article) decided that
North Platte, Nebraska, was located in the Midwest. I would argue that, if
so, it is the West's "port of entry."

For remarks about the various cowboy Wests and the "Montgomery Ward
Buckaroos" see Struthers Burt, *The Diary of a Dude Wrangler* (New York:
Charles Scribner's Sons, 1925), pp. 309–10. Thomas Hornsby Ferril is the
well known Coloradan mentioned. He made his remark in *I Hate Thursday*
(New York: Harper & Brothers, 1946), a little book put together from
columns that he had written for *Harper's Monthly.*

Climatic characteristics are described by Bernard De Voto in "The West:
A Plundered Province," *Harper's Magazine,* Aug. 1934, p. 357, and by Ross
Calvin in *Sky Determines* (Albuquerque: University of New Mexico Press,
1948). A view from the inside may be read in Edward M. Miller, "A
Westerner Views the U.S.A.," *American Scholar* 12, no. 4 (Autumn 1943):

457. He was a native of Oregon who wrote features for the *Oregonian* (Portland).

The observations of Philip Ashton Rollins are found in his Foreword to Lawrence B. Smith, *Dude Ranches and Ponies* (New York: Coward-McCann, 1936), p. xvi, which he wrote in 1933. Peckinpah's West is described in Paul Seydor, *Peckinpah: The Western Films* (Urbana: University of Illinois Press, 1980), p. 287. John Fischer's quotation is from his book *From the High Plains* (New York: Harper & Row, 1978), p. 2. The conversation from John Steinbeck's *The Red Pony* came from pages 118–19 (New York: Viking Press, 1959; reprint of 1937, 1938 ed.).

2. How the Old West Was Lost

Edward Everett Dale's *Cow Country* (Norman: University of Oklahoma Press, 1942 and 1965) has a good discussion of the cattle industry's influence on high-plains states; see particularly part 6. More recent is Lewis Atherton, *The Cattle Kings* (Bloomington: Indiana University Press, 1961, and Lincoln: University of Nebraska Press, 1972). Joe Frantz is quoted in his "Cowboy Philosophy," in *The Frontier Re-examined*, ed. John Francis McDermott (Urbana: University of Illinois Press, 1967), p. 180. The suggestion that cattlemen represented a kind of cow-country nobility came from John L. Cowan, "Knights and Barons of Our Western Empire," *Overland Monthly*, Oct. 1906, p. 251.

The transition from cattle ranching to farming is described by Ike Blasingame in *Dakota Cowboy* (New York: G. P. Putnam's Sons, 1958), pp. 9, 15, and 32; Walker Wyman, *Nothing but Prairie and Sky* (Norman: University of Oklahoma Press, 1954), p. 202; W. M. Pearce, *The Matador Land and Cattle Company* (Norman: University of Oklahoma Press, 1964), chap. 3. The *Outing Magazine* reference is from Stuart L. Douglas, "Westward Ho!" Aug. 1906, p. 615. The "last West" historian was Agnes C. Laut, who wrote "The Last Trek to the Last Frontier," in *Century Magazine*, May 1909 (see pp. 102–3). The "modern youth and the gatepost" observation came from Arthur Chapman, "The New West and the Old Fiction," *Independent*, 9 Jan. 1902, p. 100. He was editor of the *Denver Republican*. More about the transition may be found in Randall R. Howard, "The Passing of the Cattle King," *Outlook*, 27 May 1911, pp. 196, 198, 204; and Henry Loomis Nelson, "The Spirit of the West," *Harper's Monthly Magazine*, July 1904, pp. 200, 202.

The "skirmish line" comments were made by Frederick R. Bechdolt in "The Field Agent of Settlement," *Collier's*, 18 Sept. 1909, p. 34. The Trail Driver's Association, founded by George Saunders, is mentioned in Atherton's *Cattle Kings* (p. 271). The Model-T-Ford and mail-contract incident comes from Hal Borland, *High, Wide and Lonesome* (Philadelphia: J. B. Lippincott & Co., 1956), p. 250. Emily Post's impressions are found in her book *By Motor to the Golden Gate* (New York: D. Appleton & Co., 1916), pp. 129–30. A good survey of the role of the cowboy is found in David Dary, *Cowboy Culture: A Saga of Five Centuries* (New York: Alfred A. Knopf, 1981). For a "counter-cowboy" view see John C. Van Dyke, *The Open Spaces* (New

York: Charles Scribner's Sons, 1922), chap. 4. In his view the cowboy was no
hero.

The account of the "wool-hat" people comes from Wyman's *Nothing but Prairie,* p. 199. Roosevelt's remarks may be found in his *Autobiography* (New York: Charles Scribner's Sons, 1913), p. 94. Statistics on the millions of acres occupied between 1870 and 1900 are from Gilbert C. Fite, *The Farmer's Frontier: 1865–1900* (New York: Holt, Rinehart & Winston, 1966), p. vi. The demand that the word *ranch* be abandoned in favor of *farm* was printed in several sources, the most conveniently found of which is David M. Emmons, *Garden in the Grasslands: Boomer Literature of the Central Great Plains* (Lincoln: University of Nebraska Press, 1971), p. 193. Remarks by Rawhide Rawlins may be found in Charles M. Russell, *Trails Plowed Under* (Garden City, N.Y.: Doubleday & Co., 1946); for this quotation see p. 159. The Idaho and Nevada population figures are from Earl Pomeroy, "What Remains of the West?" *Utah Historical Quarterly* 35, no. 1 (Winter 1967): 47. Sales of railroad land in Kansas and Colorado were referred to in an article by a Kansas promotional writer named Charles M. Harger; see his "Revival in Western Land Values," *Review of Reviews,* Jan. 1907, p. 65. Mary Wilma M. Hargreaves, in *Dry Farming the Northern Great Plains, 1900–1925* (Cambridge: Harvard University Press, 1957), pp. 73–74, discusses the prospect of food shortages and comments by experts as to the undesirability of western lands for wheat production. See her chapter 9 for details of Homestead Act modifications. Information about agricultural prices, 1900 to 1910, came from Howard Ottoson et al., *Land and People in the Northern Plains Transition Area* (Lincoln: University of Nebraska Press, 1966), pp. 48–50; see p. 59 for reference to Dakota lands being homesteaded. The estimate of 400,000 newcomers a year to the West is from Charles M. Harger, "To-day's Chance for the Western Settler," *Outlook,* 17 Dec. 1904, pp. 980–82. The nature of migration to the West, around the turn of the century, is discussed by William E. Smythe, "Real Utopias in the Arid West," *Atlantic Monthly,* May 1897, pp. 608–9. On occupation of part of the southern plains see Garry L. Nall, "The Farmer's Frontier in the Texas Panhandle," *Panhandle-Plains Historical Review* 45 (1972): 1–20.

Jim Hill's response to the new land boom is related on page 462 of Albro Martin's *James J. Hill and the Opening of the Northwest* (New York: Oxford University Press, 1976). The "well-known national magazine" referred to is the *Review of Reviews,* May 1892, pp. 394–95. The removal of Montana Indians in 1910 is well described by Verne Dusenberry in "The Rocky Boy Indians," *Montana: The Magazine of Western History* 4, no. 1 (Winter 1954): 1–15.

Ray Stannard Baker's assessment of the desert theory was set forth in his article "The Great Southwest," pt. 2, *Century Magazine,* June 1902, pp. 213–15 and 216. Enthusiasm for irrigation was voiced by Arthur W. Page, "The Great Conquest of the West," *World's Work* 15, no. 2 (Dec. 1907): 9691, and by C. J. Blanchard, of the U.S. Reclamation Service, in "The Spirit of the West," *National Geographic Magazine,* Apr. 1910, pp. 333–60. See also Walter V. Woehlke, "Modern Water Feuds in the West," *World To-Day* 14, no. 6 (June 1908): 663–67. W. F. G. Thacher, "St. Anthony, Idaho," *Sunset,* July 1911, pp. 108–9, is a good example of the new boosterism in "irrigation country." A little later in the century, and of a more general nature, is Albert W. Atwood's "Wealth in the Outdoor West," *Saturday Evening Post,* 8 Jan. 1927, pp. 35, 145, 149–50.

Waldo R. Smith, in "Is the Old West Passing?" *Overland Monthly,* Mar. 1916, p. 248, quoted the burned-out farmer. For a further reference to this period see Vance Johnson, *Heaven's Tableland: The Dust Bowl Story* (New York: Farrar, Straus & Co., 1947), especially p. 103.

World War I and the American agricultural problem is a subject well covered by Marion Clawson et al., *Land for the Future* (Baltimore, Md.: Johns Hopkins Press, 1960); see p. 212. See also Stuart Chase, "Disaster Rides the Plains," *American Magazine,* Sept. 1937, p. 66. Among those who urged greater wartime production was Albert Jay Nock, "The West Faces the Land Question," *Century Magazine,* Dec. 1917, pp. 296–98. The critic who urged the use of new equipment, commercial fertilizers, etc., was Edwin G. Nourse, "The Revolution in Farming," *Yale Review* 8, no. 1 (Oct. 1918): 90. See Howard Ottoson et al., *Land and People in the Northern Plains Transition Area* (Lincoln: University of Nebraska Press, 1966), p. 51, for comments about the prewar and wartime expansion of plains agriculture. A personal view of the wartime resurgence of plains agriculture is related in Hal Borland, *Country Editor's Boy* (Philadelphia: J. B. Lippincott & Co., 1970), p. 49. Gifford Pinchot made his remarks about land tenure in *The Fight for Conservation* (New York: Doubleday, Page & Co., 1910, and Seattle: University of Washington Press, 1967), pp. 12–13. Comments on the demand for land investment were made by O. L. Dickeson in "Evolution of the West," *World To-Day* 19, no. 4 (Oct. 1910): 1145–50. The item about work horses came from Carey McWilliams, *Ill Fares the Land* (Boston: Little Brown & Co., 1941), p. 103. William Allen White, in *The Changing West: An Economic Theory about Our Golden Age* (New York: Macmillan Co., 1939), mentions overexpansion during World War I on pp. 62–63.

The Kincaiders material came from Paul B. Sears, *Deserts on the March* (Norman: University of Oklahoma Press, 1935, 1947), pp. 54–55. Distress near Shelby, Montana, is described in *Not in Precious Metals Alone: A Manuscript History of Montana,* compiled by the staff, Historical Society of Montana (Helena: Montana Historical Society Press, 1976), p. 179. See also Chet Huntley, *The Generous Years* (New York: Random House, 1968), p. 96. The modern homesteading story is related by Courtney Ryley Cooper in "Present-Day Pioneers," *Saturday Evening Post,* 3 Apr. 1926; see pages 30 and 137. Charles M. Harger referred to the rise of tenant farming in "The West's New Vision," *Atlantic Monthly,* July 1917, p. 126. Labor turmoil on the plains is mentioned by McWilliams in *Ill Fares the Land* (p. 101). See also George Creel, "Harvesting the Harvest Hands," *Harper's Weekly,* 26 Sept. 1914, pp. 292–93; D. D. Lescohier, "With the I. W. W. in the Wheat Lands," *Harper's Monthly Magazine,* Aug. 1923, pp. 372–79.

Farm problems of the twenties are discussed by Charles M. Harger in "Why the West Will Not Revolt," *Outlook,* 13 June 1928, pp. 255–57. Secretary William M. Jardine expressed his opinions in "The Agricultural Problem," *Saturday Evening Post,* 16 Oct. 1926, pp. 3–5, 169, 173–74, 177, and in "The Farmer's Place under the Sun," *Century Magazine,* Mar. 1927, pp. 543–50. The remark about the absence of western representation on the

House Agriculture Committee came from Albert W. Atwood, "The Youngest Brother: The West and Its Share in the National Heritage," *Saturday
Evening Post,* 4 Dec. 1926, p. 19. For a show of concern over the farmer's
possible loss of individualism see "Shall We Have Factory Farms?" *New
Republic,* 31 Aug. 1927, p. 32. A very good brief treatment of the farm
problem of this era is Gilbert C. Fite's "The Farmers' Dilemma,
1919–1929," in *Change and Continuity in Twentieth Century America: The 1920s,*
ed. John Braeman, Robert H. Bremner, and David Brody (Columbus: Ohio
State University Press, 1968), pp. 67–103.

3. THE NERVOUS YEARS

The "nervous years" editor was Charles Moreau Harger, who in 1900 was
editor of the *Abilene Daily Reflector.* He wrote a number of articles about the
West in well-known American magazines, including this, "The West's New
Vision," *Atlantic Monthly,* July 1917, pp. 121–28.

Comments about bathtubs and indoor toilets on farms is from Harger's
"West's New Vision," p. 126. Plumbing in the new West also attracted the
notice of Allen Reed; see "The Empire of the Northern Prairies," *World Today* 14, no. 2 (Feb. 1908): 185.

The discussion about western characteristics came largely from the
following: Harger, "The New Westerner," *North American Review,* 2 Aug.
1907, pp. 755–57; Henry Loomis Nelson, "The Spirit of the West," *Harper's
Monthly Magazine,* July 1904, see especially pp. 198 and 203; Ray Stannard
Baker, "The Western Spirit of Restlessness," *Century Magazine,* July 1908, p.
468; Stuart L. Douglas, "Westward Ho!" *Outing Magazine,* Aug. 1906, p.
616; William R. Lighton, "Where Is the West?" *Outlook,* 18 July 1903, p.
703; Edward M. Miller, "A Westerner Views the U.S.A.," *American Scholar*
12, no. 4 (Autumn 1943): 458; Frank H. Spearman, "The Westerner,"
World To-day 8, no. 2 (Feb. 1905): 146. Edward Alsworth Ross, in "The
Middle West," *Century Magazine,* Feb. 1912, pp. 609–15, makes comparisons
between that area and the West. Harger, in his "New Era in the Middle
West," *Harper's New Monthly Magazine,* July 1898, pp. 276–82, does much the
same thing. For more about westerners' characteristics read Stephen M.
Dale, "The West through Eastern Eyes," *Independent,* 20 Oct. 1904, pp.
903–9. Richard Burton, in "Is the West Wild and Woolly?" *Bookman* 56, no.
2 (Oct. 1922): 147–51, also describes the typical westerner. Reference to a
slackening demand for physical types in the West was made by Robert Tudor
Hill, *The Public Domain and Democracy* (New York: Columbia University Press,
1910); see pp. 31–33. The comment by the Wyoming man about eastern
mercenary characteristics came from Edwin E. Slosson, "The East through
Western Eyes," *Independent,* 20 Oct. 1904, p. 910. For the searcher-of-culture
comment see Rollin Lynde Hartt, "Mid-westerners and That Sort of
People," *Century,* Dec. 1916, p. 178.

Comments about social conditions in the West, women's dress, etc., came
from Mrs. Reginald De Koven, "Western Society and Its Leaders,"
Everybody's Magazine, Feb. 1904, pp. 197–99. See also Shailer Mathews,
"Culture in the West," *World To-day* 8, no. 2 (Feb. 1905): 191–96. The New

York City magazine that called the West eastern was *World's Work;* see "Three Novelists of Sincerity and Charm," in vol. 5 (Nov. 1902), p. 2794. More about cosmopolitanism of the West is in David M. Steele, *Going Abroad Overland* (New York: G. P. Putnam's Sons, 1917), p. 196. He was a Philadelphia minister. Louis Howland, in "Provincial or National?" *Scribner's Magazine,* Apr. 1908, p. 455, expressed similar ideas.

The "well-known historian" who commented upon the West's future was Shailer Mathews, a history professor at Colby College and later the editor of *World To-day.* See his "Culture in the West," mentioned above, p. 196. The notion of industrial advance, in 1903, was put forward by William R. Lighton in his article in the *Outlook,* cited above, pp. 703–4. The contention that the "modern" western farmer knew exactly what crops to plant was held by Charles M. Harger, "The Revival in Western Land Values," *American Monthly Review of Reviews,* Jan. 1907, p. 64.

The absence of western slums was mentioned by Jacob Riis in "Heading Off the Slums in the West," *Charities and Commons,* 7 Mar. 1908, pp. 1704–6. References to westerners' theological narrowness are from Frederick M. Davenport, "On the Trail of Progress and Reaction in the West: The Persistence of the Pioneer Conscience," *Outlook,* 16 June 1915, p. 365. See this article also for the charge that Colorado was "economically brutal." The "specific gravity of kerosene" remark came from Harger's "West's New Vision," p. 123.

Owen Wister's ideas on southern European immigration were suggested by Richard Etulain, *Owen Wister* (Boise, Mont.: Boise State College, 1973), p. 35. For William Jackson Palmer's dreams of Colorado Springs see John Fisher, *A Builder of the West: The Life of William Jackson Palmer* (Caldwell, Idaho: Caxton Printers, 1939), pp. 202–3; and for Remington's opinion on "the rubbish of the earth" see G. Edward White, *The Eastern Establishment and the Western Experience* (New Haven, Conn.: Yale University Press, 1968), p. 109. The "hodge podge" observation is from Ross, "Middle West," p. 609. Ross was the University of Wisconsin sociologist quoted in the Nordic-strain discussion. Mention of the Italian, Hungarian, Russian, and Jewish farmers came from "West and New East," *Independent,* 8 Feb. 1912, p. 323. Governor Johnson's sentiments were published in "The Call of the West," *World's Work* 18, no. 6 (Oct. 1909): 12, 139–40. Emerson Hough talked about the dilution of the American bloodstream in *The Passing of the Frontier* (see p. 173).

The Idaho farm wife who commented on World War I was Annie Pike Greenwood, who wrote *We Sagebrush Folks* (New York: D. Appleton-Century Co., 1934), pp. 296, 298. Her comments on "pickled Americans" are on page 301. More about Angie Debo's experience appears in *Prairie City: The Story of an American Community* (New York: Alfred A. Knopf, 1944), pp. 154–57. See also Hal Borland, *Country Editor's Boy* (Philadephia: J. B. Lippincott Co., 1970), p. 227; and Norman Macleod's novel about wartime Montana, *The Bitter Roots* (New York: Smith & Durrell, 1941).

Frank Norris's statement is from his "The Frontier Is Gone at Last," *World's Work* 3, no. 4 (Feb. 1902): 1731. It was republished in his book *The Responsibilities of the Novelist and Other Literary Essays* (New York: Greenwood Press, 1968). Hough's *Passing* is cited above.

The prosperity of wartime western farms was discussed by Burges Johnson
in "That Elusive West," *Century Magazine,* Feb. 1923, p. 596, and by Charles
M. Harger in "The West's New Vision," *Atlantic Monthly,* July 1917, p. 127.
One of the apologies for western pacifism appeared in "The Great
Crusade," *Scribner's Magazine,* Mar. 1918, pp. 377–80. Tim McCoy's
quotation is from his book *Tim McCoy Remembers the West: An Autobiography*
(Garden City, N.Y.: Doubleday & Co., 1977), p. 120. Virginia Weisel
Johnson wrote about Montana's western tradition and the war in *The Long,
Long Trail* (Boston: Houghton Mifflin Co., 1966), p. 112. See Chet Huntley,
The Generous Years (New York: Random House, 1968), for comment on the
Montana census error. "Nauseating nonsense" is from "The Effeminate
West," *Independent,* 23 June 1917, p. 530.

Colorado's wartime "patriotism" is discussed briefly by Robert G.
Athearn in *The Coloradans* (Albuquerque: University of New Mexico Press,
1976), chap. 13. Joseph Hergesheimer mentions the lingering patriotism in
"The Magnetic West," *Saturday Evening Post,* 2 Sept. 1922, pp. 98, 141.

Garland's comments about something strong and free's passing from our
national life came from his article "The Passing of the Frontier," *Dial,* 4
Oct. 1919, p. 286. See also John Gould Fletcher on the passing, in his article
"The Passing of the West," *New Republic,* 23 June 1920, p. 124.

The author of the "perpetual West" term was Joseph Hergesheimer in
"The Magnetic West," *Saturday Evening Post,* 2 Sept. 1922; see p. 145.
Courtney Ryley Cooper, a very popular writer in the twenties, also
complained about Americans going soft: see his *High Country: The Rockies
Yesterday and Today* (Boston: Little, Brown & Co., 1926), p. 39.

4. EDEN IS JEOPARDIZED

The comments about a first generation without a frontier came from
Roderick Nash, *The Nervous Generation: American Thought, 1917–1930* (Chicago: Rand McNally & Co., 1970), p. 78. The Hal Borland reference is from
his *Country Editor's Boy* (Philadelphia: J. B. Lippincott Co., 1970), pp. 8 and
223. Frederick Simpich spoke of the speed cops cruising the countryside in
his "The Changing Southwest," *Century Magazine,* Feb. 1927, p. 494. For
Villard's impressions see his article "The West—Tamed and Combed," in
the *Nation,* 10 Dec. 1924, pp. 617–18. Gene Gressley's quotation is from his
book *Voltaire and the Cowboy: The Letters of Thurman Arnold* (Boulder: Colorado
Associated University Press, 1977), p. 14. Standardization of the West is also
the subject of Charles M. Harger in "The West Adopts Oratory," *Century
Magazine,* Jan. 1928, p. 304. The man who searched for the West that
delighted his youthful dreams was Richard Burton, in "Is the West Wild and
Woolly?" *Bookman* 56, no. 2 (Oct. 1922): 148.

Bernard De Voto's excoriation of boosterism is from his article "Footnote
on the West," *Harper's Monthly Magazine,* Nov. 1927, p. 717–19. The author
who said the western towns looked so much alike that they had to rely upon
boosterism and who said that the practice was taken seriously in the West was
Garet Garrett, in "How in the West?" *Saturday Evening Post,* 22 Nov. 1924, p.
10. The critic who sought to explain how western communities became ripe

for expression was Harger, in "The West Adopts Oratory," p. 305. It was he, also, who described the "brotherhood and singing" (p. 302) and quoted Will Rogers (p. 303). Joseph Hergesheimer said his goodbye to the Old West in "The Magnetic West," *Saturday Evening Post,* 2 Sept. 1922, pp. 141–46.

One of the scholars who assessed western change in the 1920s was Frederick Jackson Turner, in "The West—1876 and 1926," *World's Work* 52, no. 3 (July 1926): 327. Will Irwin watched the change, at Leadville, and spoke of it in "What Is the Western Spirit?" *Sunset Magazine,* June 1923, p. 24. The "replica of the life which built America" comment is from Courtney Ryley Cooper, "Present-day Pioneers," *Saturday Evening Post,* 3 Apr. 1926, p. 30.

An article entitled "Exit Frontier Morality," *New Republic,* 2 Jan. 1924, p. 138, spoke of the lingering pioneer conditions in the West. Only a few years later the western writer Struthers Burt talked about the West as the "real" America; see "The Dry West," *Scribner's Magazine,* Feb. 1928, p. 144. The account of the prairie schooner (1916) is from Hamilton Laing, "Bucking the Desert Trail," *Sunset,* Mar. 1916, pp. 76–88. The lady homesteader in Utah is described by Amy Armstrong in "Homesteading without a Chaperone," *Sunset,* June 1916, pp. 25–26 and 95–97.

The Englishman in Colorado in 1922 was Walter Lionel George, who wrote "On the Road to Canaan: An Englishman Discovers the Real West," *Sunset Magazine,* Nov. 1922, pp. 9 and 10. The Denver, Cheyenne, or Great Falls remark was made by Waldo R. Smith in "Is the Old West Passing?" *Overland Monthly,* Mar. 1916, pp. 243–44. The article in the popular weekly of 1927 that discussed westward-moving job seekers was Albert W. Atwood's "Why Go West?" *Saturday Evening Post,* 19 Feb. 1927, p. 42. Berkeley's lines are found in his *Works,* 1871 ed., vol. 3, p. 232.

The contention that the westerner really was aristocratic belongs to Katharine Fullerton Gerould (Mrs. Gordon Hall Gerould, wife of a Princeton professor), who wrote "The Aristocratic West," *Harper's Magazine,* Sept. 1925, pp. 466–77, taken from the manuscript of her book *The Aristocratic West* (New York: Harper & Brothers, 1925).

More about the agrarian myth and the garden of the world can be read in Richard Hofstadter's *The Age of Reform* (New York: Alfred A. Knopf, 1955), see chap. 1; and in Henry Nash Smith, *Virgin Land; The American West as Symbol and Myth* (Cambridge: Harvard University Press, 1950).

5. "The Dreaming Is Finished"

The Billington reference is from his *Land of Savagery, Land of Promise: The European Image of the American Frontier* (New York: W. W. Norton & Co., 1981).

Suitcase farming and bonanza farming are dealt with by Leslie Hewes in *The Suitcase Farming Frontier* (Lincoln: University of Nebraska Press, 1973) and by Gilbert C. Fite in "The Great Plains: Promises, Problems, and Prospects," in *The Great Plains: Environment and Culture,* ed. Brian W. Blouet and Frederick C. Leubke (Lincoln: University of Nebraska Press, 1979). A contemporary view of suitcase farming may be found in Walter Davenport,

"Land Where Our Children Die," *Collier's,* 18 Sept. 1937, pp. 12, 13, and 73–77. The Laramie County plow-up figures came from Avis Carlson, "Dust Blowing," *Harper's Magazine,* July 1935, pp. 148–58. She was the woman referred to in connection with the Colorado newlyweds.

The information about Hill County's decline was supplied by Toni Hagener, "Hill County Celebrates Its 70th Birthday," *Havre* (Mont.) *Daily News,* 22 Feb. 1982. The figures for out migration for Idaho and Montana came from F. Ross Peterson, *Idaho: A Bicentennial History* (New York: W. W. Norton & Co., 1976), pp. 140–44. The farm woman who talked about the gambler in us was Caroline Henderson, who wrote "Letters from the Dust Bowl," *Atlantic Monthly,* May 1936; see p. 550. See also Evelyn Harris and Caroline Henderson, "Letters of Two Women Farmers," *Atlantic Monthly,* Aug. 1933, pp. 236–45, and Sept. 1933, pp. 349–56.

The "not in our blood" remark is from Vance Johnson, *Heaven's Tableland: The Dust Bowl Story* (New York: Farrar, Straus & Co., 1947), p. 274. One of the best books ever to appear about dust-bowl days is Lawrence Svobida, *An Empire of Dust* (Caldwell, Idaho: Caxton Printers, Ltd., 1940), not only because it is well written but also because its author was one of those plains farmers who fought the losing fight, in his case for nine years. This is a highly recommended "inside" account; it has been reissued as *Farming the Dust Bowl: A First-Hand Account from Kansas,* with a new foreword by R. Douglas Hurt (Lawrence: University Press of Kansas, 1986). A very good and more recent work is Donald Worster's *Dust Bowl: The Southern Plains in the 1930s* (New York: Oxford University Press, 1979); see pp. 94–95 for his defense of the "regular" farmers and his quote on the "contriving hand of humanity." A brief account may be found in Robert G. Athearn, *High Country Empire* (New York: McGraw-Hill & Co., 1960), chap. 13. Walter Webb's remark is from his *Divided We Stand. The Crisis of a Frontierless Democracy* (New York: Farrar & Rinehart, Inc., 1937), pp. 19–37.

Comments about farmers' pointing the finger at foreigners who financed the cattlemen were made by Carlson in "Dust Blowing," p. 151. Reference to the 1931 Chicago meeting is from Worster, *Dust Bowl,* p. 184. He also furnished the figures as to the cost of the 1934 drought and the numbers on relief (p. 12). Carlson, in "Dust Blowing," mentioned farmers digging out their tractors in 1933 (see p. 156), and on p. 149 see her comment on Kansans making fools of themselves.

The account of extreme heat in 1936, of farmers confining their ducks, etc., came principally from "The West in Black Crisis of Drought," *Literary Digest,* 18 July 1936, pp. 3–5. The humorous stories are from Margaret Bourke-White, "Dust Changes America," *Nation,* 22 May 1935, pp. 597–98. See also Caroline Henderson, "Dust Bowl," pp. 542–43, and Walter Davenport, "Land Where Our Children Die," p. 13. The "ashes to ashes" remark is from Johnson's *Heaven's Tableland,* p. 194. Paul Bonnifield, in *The Dust Bowl: Men, Dirt and Depression* (Albuquerque: University of New Mexico Press, 1979), discussed dust pneumonia and other related diseases. Another contemporary account is Stuart Chase's "Disaster Rides the Plains," *American Magazine,* Sept. 1937, especially pp. 47 and 66. The rationalizations of the two women about staying on, etc., are in Carlson, p. 151, and in Henderson, pp. 540–41.

Margaret Bourke-White's remark about hopelessness' pervading the plains is on p. 597 of her above-cited article. Population shifts were discussed by Worster, *Dust Bowl*, p. 48; Elwyn B. Robinson, *History of North Dakota* (Lincoln: University of Nebraska Press, 1966), p. 401; Melvin E. Kazeck, *North Dakota: A Human and Economic Geography* (Fargo: North Dakota Institute for Regional Studies, 1956), pp. 235–38; and A. G. Mezerik, *The Revolt of the South and West* (New York: Duell, Sloan & Pearce, 1946), p. 50. "Big Ed" Johnson's "bum blockade" and Colorado's depression problems were taken from Robert G. Athearn, *The Coloradans* (Albuquerque: University of New Mexico Press, 1976), pp. 280–81. Richard Neuberger's statement of the "typical American frontiersman" is from his "Public Domain," *Survey Graphic,* Feb. 1941, p. 76.

Mumford's "spread and plunder" remark was quoted by Worster in *Dust Bowl,* p. 186. See also Lewis Mumford, *The Golden Day: A Study in American Experience and Culture* (New York: Boni & Liveright, 1926). Henry A. Wallace, in *New Frontiers* (New York: Reynal & Hitchcock, 1934), talked about the agrarian expansion being over, on p. 277. MacLeish's lines are from his *Land of the Free* (New York: Harcourt Brace, 1938), written in the summer of 1937. Worster quoted him also, on p. 48.

The "courage has returned" quotation came from Charles M. Harger, "Brighter Skies Out West," *Review of Reviews,* Oct. 1924, p. 423. Another "prosperity" comment may be found in "The Wealthy West," *Literary Digest,* 15 Apr. 1922, p. 23. More of the same was in Courtney Ryley Cooper's "This Is My America," *American Magazine,* Jan. 1933, p. 40, and in Albert W. Atwood, "Wealth in the Outdoor West," *Saturday Evening Post,* 8 Jan. 1924, p. 35. Mark Sullivan's statement is quoted by Michael P. Malone in *C. Ben Ross and the New Deal in Idaho* (Seattle: University of Washington Press, 1970), p. 36. The Idaho income figures for 1929–32 are from Peterson's *Idaho: A Bicentennial History,* p. 144.

The lady who was surprised at the ten-cent tip was Isobel Strother Walker, who wrote "We Do Our Part," in *New Republic,* 8 Nov. 1933, p. 359. Villard's "star of empire" remark is in Oswald Garrison Villard's "Western Melange," *Nation,* 11 Apr. 1934, p. 405. For more about the depression in western mining see Gerald D. Nash, *The American West in the Twentieth Century* (Englewood Cliffs, N.J.: Prentice-Hall, Inc., 1973), pp. 140–41 and 167; and Michael P. Malone & Richard B. Roeder, *Montana: A History of Two Centuries* (Seattle: University of Washington Press, 1976), p. 227. Petroleum difficulties in Montana are well outlined by Don Douma in "Second Bonanza: The History of Oil in Montana," a series of articles published in *Montana: The Magazine of Western History* in 1954; see, especially, pt. 2, in vol. 4, no. 1 (Winter 1954), p. 43.

The decline-in-tourism material came from Nash, *American West,* p. 141. The disheartened Montanan was Charles Vindex, who wrote "That Dwell in Dust," *Antioch Review* 11, no. 3 (Sept. 1951): 364; or see his "Survival on the High Plains: 1929–1934," in *Montana: The Magazine of Western History* 28, no. 4 (Oct. 1978): 2–11, much of which repeats the *Antioch* article. He was a wheat farmer who lived near Plentywood, Montana. The account of militants marching on the Colorado state Capitol are from Athearn, *The Coloradans,* pp. 278–79. The young people who headed for rural Nevada to "fort up" are described by Helen Borden Viets in "Wind in the Sage: Journal of an Amateur Pioneer in Nevada," *Saturday Evening Post,* 15 Feb. 1936. More general statements about "back to the land" are in Worster, *Dust Bowl,* especially pp. 47–48, a very good discussion.

The account of South Dakota bank failures came from Herbert S. Schell, *History of South Dakota* (Lincoln: University of Nebraska Press, 1961); see p. 285 of the 3d ed., rev. (1975). From the same book (p. 282) came the story of educational cuts. More on this subject may be found in Nash, *American West,* p. 142, and in Malone and Roeder, *Montana,* p. 278. How the West suffered from the depression, as compared to other parts of the country, is mentioned in Ernie Pyle, *Home Country* (New York: William Sloane Associates, Inc., 1947 ed.), p. 49. He thought South Dakota suffered the most. That help from Washington was relatively slow in getting to the plains is mentioned both by Worster in *Dust Bowl,* p. 38, and by Bonnifield in *The Dust Bowl,* p. 106. Lorena Hickok's rich letters about conditions in the Dakotas are found in Richard Lowitt and Maurine Beasley, eds., *One Third of a Nation: Lorena Hickok Reports on the Great Depression* (Urbana: University of Illinois Press, 1981); see especially pp. 61, 66, 83, 85, and 96.

Some references to the decline in cattle prices are available in Nash, *American West,* p. 145; T. A. Larson, *History of Wyoming* (Lincoln: University of Nebraska Press, 1965), p. 444; and Charles Morrow Wilson, *Roots of America* (New York: Funk & Wagnalls Co., 1936), p. 252.

A number of sources provide information as to the proportional amount of money that various western states received from the federal government during the depression. Some of these are: Morris E. Garnsey, *America's New Frontier: The Mountain West* (New York: Alfred A. Knopf, 1950), p. 133; T. J. Woofter, Jr., and Ellen Winston, *Seven Lean Years* (Chapel Hill: University of North Carolina Press, 1939), p. 142; Nash, *American West,* p. 172; Schell, *South Dakota,* p. 292; Robinson, *North Dakota,* p. 409; Malone and Roeder, *Montana,* pp. 229–31; James C. Olson, *History of Nebraska* (Lincoln: University of Nebraska Press, 1955), p. 311; and Donald A. Laird, "The Tail That Wags the Nation," *Review of Reviews,* Nov. 1935, p. 45. But the best of all, the most inclusive, is the writing of Leonard Arrington on this subject: see his "The New Deal in the West: A Preliminary Statistical Inquiry," *Pacific Historical Review* 38, no. 3 (Aug. 1960): 311–16, and his "The Sagebrush Resurrection: New Deal Expenditures in the Western States, 1933–1939," ibid., 52, no. 1 (Feb. 1983): 1–16.

The material about the Civilian Conservation Corps is from Peterson, *Idaho,* p. 150; Worster, *Dust Bowl,* p. 39; Malone and Roeder, *Montana,* p. 230; Schell, *South Dakota,* p. 293; Russell R. Elliott, *History of Nevada* (Lincoln: University of Nebraska Press, 1973), p. 297; and Robert Bruce Parham, "The Civilian Conservation Corps in Colorado, 1933–1942" (Master's thesis, University of Colorado, 1982).

Mention of the New Deal in Utah and Nevada came from Elliott, *Nevada,* p. 297, and from Frank Jonas, "Utah," in *Rocky Mountain Politics,* ed. Thomas C. Donnelly (Albuquerque: University of New Mexico Press, 1940), pp. 46–48. The reference to the "busted little town" is from my remembrance of the depression.

The notion that the plainsmen failed more as businessmen than as farmers was suggested by Richard Barry in *Theme Song: 1936: Give Us Back Our Independence* (Indianapolis, Ind.: Bobbs-Merrill, 1936), p. 41; and by Robert V. Hine, *Community on the American Frontier: Separate but Not Alone* (Norman: University of Oklahoma Press, 1980), p. 124. Western animosity toward the New Deal was discussed by Marshall Sprague in *Colorado: A Bicentennial History* (New York: W. W. Norton, 1976), p. 159; and by Nash in *American West,* p. 174.

The reference to money poured into Colorado during Roosevelt's first two terms is from Athearn, *The Coloradans,* p. 282. Colorado's resentment toward the New Deal is mentioned by A. G. Mezerik in "Journey in America," *New Republic,* 11 Dec. 1944, p. 795. See also Carl Abbott, *Colorado: A History of the Centennial State* (Boulder: Colorado Associated University Press, 1976), p. 231. Mention of this general resentment is made also by Robinson in *North Dakota,* p. 409. Another very good source on this topic is James T. Patterson, "The New Deal in the West," *Pacific Historical Review* 38, no. 3 (Aug. 1969): 317–27. In fuller form is James T. Patterson's *The New Deal and the States: Federalism in Transition* (Princeton, N.J.: Princeton University Press, 1969). The *Collier's* article about "puttering around" by the New Deal is from Davenport, "Land Where Our Children Die," p. 13.

The contention that New Deal efforts in the grasslands were partially the work of men who were inflicted with a missionary spirit is from Bonnifield, *Dust Bowl,* p. 184. The material from Great Plains committees came from Merrill Jensen, ed., *Regionalism in America* (Madison: University of Wisconsin Press, 1951), p. 348; and from Rupert N. Richardson, ed., "The 'Summary Foreword' of the Future of the Great Plains," *Mississippi Valley Historical Review* 30 (June 1943): 49–68.

A number of sources support the contention that with the New Deal's efforts to bail out the West during the depression and the Dust Bowl days there was "change of masters" and a shift in emphasis on colonialism. Arrington suggested it in his "Sagebrush Resurrection." So did Woofter and Winston, in *Seven Lean Years,* p. 499; Nash, *American West,* pp. 139, 173, 174, 191; Malone and Roeder, *Montana,* pp. 229–32; and Donnelly, *Rocky Mountain Politics,* p. 8.

The notion that the dream became an illusion is supported by Charles R. Hearn, *The American Dream in the Great Depression* (Westport, Conn.: Greenwood Press, 1977), p. 193.

6. COLONIALISM: THE ENDURING DILEMMA

A general statement about the West as a colonial hinterland may be found in Elwyn B. Robinson's "An Interpretation of the History of the Great Plains," *North Dakota History* 41, no. 2 (Spring 1974): 5–19. Bernard De Voto wrote a great deal about this in a series of articles in *Harper's Magazine:* see "The West: A Plundered Province," Aug. 1934, pp. 355–64; "The Anxious West," Dec. 1946, pp. 481–91; "The West against Itself," Jan. 1947, pp. 1–13; and in *Collier's,* "Our Great West—Boom or Bust?" 25 Dec. 1953, pp. 47–50 and 54–63.

The "sagebrush" articles are Bernhard Knollenberg's "Sagebrush
Rule," *Atlantic Monthly*, Mar. 1932, pp. 289–95, and A. Edward Newton's "Westward," ibid., May 1932, pp. 527–38. The Spokane lawyer was B. H. Kizer, whose rebuttal to these articles, "In Defense of the Sagebrush States," appeared in *Atlantic Monthly*, June 1932, pp. 746–52. General Sherman's ideas are set forth by Robert G. Athearn in *William Tecumseh Sherman and the Settlement of the West* (Norman: University of Oklahoma Press, 1956), p. 85. William E. Smythe expressed his views in "Real Utopias in the Arid West," *Atlantic Monthly*, May 1897, pp. 599–609; see p. 608.

The rate-differential bill, sponsored by Senator Gooding of Idaho, was referred to by Frederick Jackson Turner in "The West—1876 and 1926," *World's Work* 52, no. 3 (July 1926): 324. The reaction of Frederick Bonfils is discussed by Robert G. Athearn in *The Coloradans* (Albuquerque: University of New Mexico Press, 1976), p. 270. For the Moffat reference see Arthur Chapman, "Denver, a Typical American City," *World To-Day* 11, no. 3 (Sept. 1906): 983; and Steven Mehls, "David Moffat: Early Colorado Business Leader" (Ph.D. diss., University of Colorado, 1982). Albert W. Atwood made the comment about small-town groceries and big chains in his article "Why Go West?" *Saturday Evening Post,* 19 Feb. 1927, p. 40. Webb's reference to that subject is in his book *Divided We Stand: The Crisis of a Frontierless Democracy* (New York: Farrar & Rinehart, Inc., 1937), p. 87. The "offshoots of the nation" attitude was quoted by Eugene H. Berwanger in *The West and Reconstruction* (Champaign: University of Illinois Press, 1981), p. 214. Wyoming's farcical Jackson Hole is fully described in T. A. Larson, *Wyoming's War Years: 1941–1945* (Laramie: University of Wyoming, 1954), pp. 194–202. Robert W. Righter, in *Crucible for Conservation: The Creation of Grand Teton National Park* (Boulder: Colorado Associated University Press, 1982), p. 115, mentions it.

A discussion of population changes during World War II may be found in Morris E. Garnsey, "The Future of the Mountain States," *Harper's Magazine,* Oct. 1945, p. 335. The Thurman Arnold reference is from Thomas Hornsby Ferril, *I Hate Thursday* (New York: Harper & Brothers, Publishers, 1946), p. 183. More of Arnold is in *Voltaire and the Cowboy: The Letters of Thurman Arnold,* ed. Gene M. Gressley (Boulder: Colorado Associated University Press, 1977).

Shortly after World War II there was another outbreak of complaint about colonialism and especially the strictures of western rail rates: see Wendell Berge, *Economic Freedom for the West* (Lincoln: University of Nebraska Press, 1946), p. 24; Rufus Terral, *The Missouri Valley: Land of Drouth, Flood and Promise* (New Haven, Conn.: Yale University Press, 1947), pp. 155–56. Morris E. Garnsey, in *America's New Frontier* (New York: Alfred A. Knopf, 1950), enlarged upon these views of the West in the immediate postwar years, especially on pp. 139, 178, and 297; see also his *Harper's* article, quoted above, pp. 330–34. For this period read also A. G. Mezerik, *The Revolt of the South and West* (New York: Duell, Sloan & Pearce, 1946). Mezerik, a New York journalist, also wrote "Wasteland in the Making," *Nation,* 2 Apr. 1949, pp. 389–90, and "Report from the High Plains," *New Republic,* 5 June 1950, pp. 12–14. Mezerik made some general comments about the Mountain West in his "Journey in America," *New Republic,* 11 Dec. 1944, pp. 793–95. As viewed a generation later, some of Mezerik's ideas are subject to challenge.

Arrington's statistics were taken from his "The Changing Economic Structure of the Mountain West, 1850–1950," Monograph Series (Logan: Utah State University Press, 1963), p. 22. Another view of western prospects, as of 1940, is in Thomas C. Donnelly, ed., *Rocky Mountain Politics* (Albuquerque: University of New Mexico Press, 1940), p. 3. Elroy Nelson stated his conclusions in *Proceedings, Second Annual Western Area Development Conference,* 1955, p. 56; see also "What the West Must Do Next," *U.S. News & World Report,* 1 Apr. 1949, p. 30, for more on the increasing money supply. The material covering Colorado's search for "clean" industries came from Athearn, *Coloradans,* pp. 320–21.

Over the years the views on the extent of Anaconda's villainy underwent a change: see Joseph Kinsey Howard, "What Happened in Butte," *Harper's Magazine,* Aug. 1948, pp. 89–91, and compare it to Oswald Garrison Villard, "Montana and 'the Company,' " *Nation,* 9 July 1940, p. 39, and to Norman MacKenzie, "Mountain Empire," *New Statesman and Nation* (London), 4 Dec. 1948, pp. 479–80. More revisionism is evident in Michael P. Malone's "Montana as a Corporate Bailiwick: An Image in History," in *Montana, Past and Present,* William Andrews Clark Memorial Library Monograph (Los Angeles: University of California at Los Angeles, 1976), pp. 67 and 72.

Gilman Ostrander's book is *Nevada: The Great Rotten Borough, 1859–1964* (New York: Alfred A. Knopf, 1966); see pp. 203 and 214. The item about Nevadans' incomes by the 1960s is from Leonard J. Arrington and George Jensen, "Comparison of Income Changes in the Western States, 1939–1960," *Western Economic Journal* 1, no. 3 (Summer 1963): 208–9. For a recent report on the gambling income in that city of glitter see William R. Eadington, *The Economics of Gambling Behavior: A Qualitative Study of Nevada's Gambling Industry* (Reno: University of Nevada Bureau of Business and Economic Research, 1973).

The 1973 complaint about intellectual colonialism appears in Paul Jacobs's "Go East, Young Man," *Newsweek,* 12 Feb. 1973, p. 9. For Gerald Nash's comments see his volume *The American West in the Twentieth Century* (Englewood Cliffs, N.J.: Prentice-Hall, Inc., 1973), pp. 139, 173, and 195. Changes in residential land patterns are discussed by Daniel J. Elazar in "Land Space and Civil Society in America," *Western Historical Quarterly,* 5, no. 3 (July 1974): 276. For more about Romanzo Adams and land usage see his "Public Range Lands—A New Policy Needed," *American Journal of Sociology* 22, no. 3 (Nov. 1916): 234–51. Lorena Hickok's letter from Cheyenne may be found in Richard Lowitt and Maurine Beasley, eds., *One Third of a Nation: Lorena Hickok Reports on the Great Depression* (Urbana: University of Illinois Press, 1981), p. 334. The quotation by Wayne Aspinall is from "Where Money from Washington Is Being Turned Down," *U.S. News & World Report,* 16 Mar. 1964, p. 79. Connally's freedom declaration came from the *Boulder* (Colo.) *Daily Camera,* 5 Oct. 1979. The Montana federal-support figures came from Neal R. Peirce, *The Mountain States of America* (New York: W. W. Norton & Co., 1972), p. 109; and the amounts of 1981 federal aid were listed in *U.S. News & World Report,* 22 Feb. 1982, p. 8.

The case of Senator Wallace Bennett and the items about federal payrolls in Colorado, New Mexico, and Utah were noted by Paul R. Wieck, "In the West, Fear Is Uppermost," *New Republic,* 24 Aug. 1964, p. 11. Senator

McGee's experience is recounted in the same article. As an old personal friend of his, I have corresponded with him about the incident. The "West offers an industrial entity all its own" comment is from "Westward, Ho! The Shift across America," *U.S. News & World Report,* 24 Oct. 1958, p. 65. The 1978 "plundered province" story, by Richard Rhodes, is in *American Heritage,* Aug./Sept. 1978; see especially p. 6. Along with Rhodes read Wallace Stegner, *The Sound of Mountain Water* (Garden City, N.Y.: Doubleday & Co., Inc., 1969), especially p. 32. the well-known agricultural historian is Gilbert C. Fite; see his "The Great Plains: Promises, Problems and Prospects," in *The Great Plains: Environment and Culture,* ed. Brian W. Blouet and Frederick C. Luebke (Lincoln: University of Nebraska Press, 1979), pp. 197–200. For an excellent discussion of the government's aid to farmers read John T. Schlebecker, "The Federal Government and the Cattlemen on the Plains, 1900 to 1945," in *Probing the American West,* ed. K. Ross Toole et al. (Santa Fe: Museum of New Mexico Press, 1964), pp. 114–24.

7. THE DUDES' WEST

For more about the origin of the word *dude* see Peter Watts, *A Dictionary of the Old West, 1850–1900* (New York: Alfred A. Knopf, 1977), and Glenn R. Vernam, *Man on Horseback* (New York: Harper & Row, 1964), p. 394. The Canadian reference is from Patrick A. Dunae, *Gentlemen Emigrants: From the British Public Schools to the Canadian Frontier* (Vancouver and Toronto: Douglas & McIntyre, 1981), p. 127. Bill Nye's contribution is from T. A. Larson, *Bill Nye's Western Humor* (Lincoln: University of Nebraska Press, 1968), p. 182.

The changing tourist picture during the early twentieth century is discussed by Henry F. Cope in "A Nation's Playground," *World Today* 8, no. 6 (June 1905): 634 and 639; Stuart L. Douglas, "Westward Ho!" *Outing Magazine,* Aug. 1906, pp. 615–17; Agnes C. Laut, "Through Our National Forests," *Travel,* July 1911, p. 441; Clifton Johnson, *Highways and Byways of the Rocky Mountains* (New York: Macmillan Co., 1910), pp. 115 and 118–19; John T. Faris, *Roaming American Highways* (New York: Farrar & Rinehart, 1931), for a description of the "name" highways. The "freight doesn't complain" remark is from the author's experience, the railroad being the Denver and Rio Grande Western. Keith L. Bryant, Jr., in *History of the Atchison, Topeka and Santa Fe Railway* (New York: Macmillan Co., 1974), has a good discussion of the Harvey Houses; see chap. 4. Details about the Irma Hotel at Cody came from a quotation in Tim McCoy, with Ronald McCoy, *Tim McCoy Remembers the West* (Garden City, N.Y.: Doubleday & Co., 1977), p. 98. The New Mexico "arid and sun-burned" comment is from Johnson, *Highways and Byways,* p. 118. Cope (see above) made the "hordes of hoodlums" remark, p. 639.

On dude ranching the best source is Lawrence R. Borne, *Dude Ranching: A Complete History* (Albuquerque: University of New Mexico Press, 1983); see also his *Welcome to My West: I. H. Larom, Dude Rancher, Conservationist, Collector* (Cody, Wyo.: Buffalo Bill Historical Center, 1982). For Boorstin's thoughts on the differences between American tourists and continental varieties see his *The Image: A Guide to Pseudo-Events in America* (New York: Atheneum, 1971), chap. 3. Other viewpoints on dude ranching can be found in Vernam (see above) and in Struthers Burt, *The Diary of a Dude Wrangler* (New York: Charles Scribner's Sons, 1925). A Pennsylvanian like Wister, Burt came to Wyoming as a visitor and ended up running a dude ranch. Other dude ranchers or wranglers who are worth consulting are Floyd C. Bard, *Dude Wrangler, Hunter, Line Rider* (Denver: Sage Books, 1964), see pp. 12 and 25–26; and Dick Randall: see L. W. Randall, "The Man Who Put the Dude in Dude Ranching," *Montana: The Magazine of Western History* 10, no. 3 (Summer 1960): 29–41. Interesting from the dude's point of view is Mary Roberts Rinehart's *The Out Trail* (New York: George H. Doran Co., 1923). Earl Pomeroy's excellent *In Search of the Golden West* (New York: Alfred A. Knopf, 1957) has some good background material; the comment about Frontier Airlines' slogan came from his book, p. 169. Reference to the number of dude ranches in Wyoming, as of 1937, came from Henry J. Peterson, "Wyoming," in *Rocky Mountain Politics*, ed. Thomas C. Donnelly (Albuquerque: University of New Mexico Press, 1940), p. 122. For that period see also a description of ranch vacations in "On Peaks and Prairies," *Literary Digest*, 1 June 1935, p. 37. Garet Garrett, in "How in the West?" *Saturday Evening Post*, 22 Nov. 1924, p. 78, talks about the emerging dude-ranch business.

One of the best things available on auto tourism is Warren James Belasco's *Americans on the Road: From Autocamp to Motel, 1910–1945* (Cambridge: Mass.: MIT Press, 1981). Reference to the See America First conference and the praise for Spokane's restaurants came from Douglas, "Westward Ho!" p. 615. The material on the Colorado tourist traffic of 1906 is from Robert G. Athearn, *The Coloradans* (Albuquerque: University of New Mexico Press, 1976), p. 231. Earl Chapin May wrote about the 1909 Colorado women in "The Argonauts of the Automobile," *Saturday Evening Post*, 9 Aug. 1924, p. 89. Reference to the 1911 legislation to establish seven national highways is from *Harper's Weekly*, 6 Jan. 1912, p. 12. Statistics concerning roads, as of 1904, are in Oscar O. Winther, *The Transportation Frontier* (New York: Holt, Rinehart & Winston, 1964), p. 159.

The motor convoy to the West Coast in 1911 was described by John G. Monihan in "Across America by Auto," *Harper's Weekly*, 6 Jan. 1912, pp. 11–12. For an account of some of the "trails" being opened to autos see Frank E. Brimmer, "Autocamping—the Fastest Growing Sport," *Outlook*, 11 July 1924, p. 437. Milford R. McClelland talked of crossing the Dakota prairies in "Only Fifty-one Years Ago," *Montana: The Magazine of Western History* 12, no. 3 (Summer 1962): 34–42. The "last land on earth" comment is from Hamilton Laing's "Bucking the Desert Trail," *Sunset*, Mar. 1916, pp. 81–82. Emily Post's exploration of the high plains is recounted in her book *By Motor to the Golden Gate* (New York: D. Appleton & Co., 1916); see pp. 113, 243, 270–71, and 345.

References to the European situation of 1914 and 1915 came from "Go West," *Review of Reviews*, Feb. 1915, pp. 131–37, and from "Westward the Course of Tourism," *Independent*, 19 Oct. 1914, p. 82. The comments about Yellowstone Park are by Maurice O. Eldridge, "Touring Yellowstone Park on Government Highways," *World To-Day* 19, no. 5 (Nov. 1910): 1263–64. See also Johnson, *Highways & Byways*, p. 231. A good description of the

National Park Service's origins is given by Donald C. Swain in "The
Founding of the National Park Service," *American West* 6, no. 5 (Sept. 1969): 6–9; the entire issue is devoted to National Parks. The growth of the park system is mentioned in Marion Clawson et al., *Land for the Future* (Baltimore, Md.: Johns Hopkins University Press, 1960), pp. 144–45.

There are several good accounts of Denver's early efforts to attract campers. Quite detailed is Edgar C. McMechen's "A Home for the Migratory Motorist," *Outing,* June 1918, pp. 161–63. See also Garet Garrett, "How in the West?" pp. 77–78; May, "The Argonauts," p. 89; Brimmer, "Autocamping," pp. 437–39.

The figures for Yellowstone Park's entry rate in 1924 came from Garrett's "How in the West?" pp. 77–78; the "vagabonds" remark is from the same source, as is the statement about Boise. Figures for travel in Montana and Arizona for 1924 came from Albert W. Atwood's "Wealth in the Outdoor West," *Saturday Evening Post,* 8 Jan. 1927, p. 149. E. B. White's comments about North Dakota roads came from *Letters of E. B. White,* ed. Dorothy Lobrano Guth (New York: Harper & Row, Publishers, 1976), p. 51. Driscoll's opposition is described by Wayne E. Fuller in "Good Roads and Rural Free Delivery Mail," *Mississippi Valley Historical Review* 42 (June 1955); see p. 79.

B. H. Kizer, "In Defense of the Sagebrush States," *Atlantic Monthly,* June 1932, p. 748, provided figures on blacktop mileages. The information about pavement in Bozeman was from May, "The Argonauts," p. 25. Winifred Hawkridge Dixon, *Westward Hoboes: Ups and Downs of Frontier Motoring* (New York: Charles Scribner's Sons, 1926), p. 103, gave the reaction to Phoenix pavement and the "what they damn please" comment. The conservationist who worried about the Good Roads movement was Aldo Leopold; his article "Conserving the Covered Wagon," *Sunset,* Mar. 1925, was subtitled "Shall We Save Parts of the Far Western Wilderness from Soft 'Improvements'?"; see p. 21.

Western cuisine was evaluated by Bernard De Voto in "The Easy Chair," *Harper's Magazine,* Nov. 1946, p. 432. The complaint that dudes would not leave New Mexico's pavement was set forth by Jim Marshall in "Untaming the West," *Collier's,* 11 Apr. 1936, p. 64. It was Atwood, in "Wealth," who wrote that the roads were crawling with flivvers, p. 150. Figures on Arizona's tourism are from Waldo M. Waltz, "Arizona," in *Rocky Mountain Politics,* ed. Thomas C. Donnelly (Albuquerque: University of New Mexico Press, 1940); see p. 268. The author who made the observation about being "the right sort" was Arthur W. Little, Jr., in "The Tall Walls of the Rockies," *Scribner's Magazine,* June 1937, p. 88.

The "wilding up of the West" material came largely from Marshall, "Untaming the West"; see pages 52, 64, and 66. Atwood, in "Wealth," mentioned that tourists were in a receptive frame of mind for "wilding up" (see p. 150). Bernard De Voto, in "The Anxious West," *Harper's Magazine,* Dec. 1946, pp. 384–85, described "frontier day" celebrations. The "anti-tourist" material is from Irvin S. Cobb, *Exit Laughing* (Indianapolis, Ind.: Bobbs-Merrill Company, 1941), p. 415; and Thomas Hornsby Ferril, *I Hate Thursday* (New York: Harper & Brothers, Publishers, 1946), pp. 36–37.

The Union Pacific advertisement ran in *Harper's Weekly* in June 1948. The *U.S. News & World Report* article was entitled "Vacations Out West: 1970 Style"; it may be found in the issue for 22 June 1970, pp. 62–65.

8. THE FICTIONAL WEST

A note about the Russell poetry at the chapter's beginning: Charley was fond of children, and these lines were jotted down in 1912, at Great Falls, in a book the artist was autographing for a young boy. The episode was mentioned by Jessie Lincoln Mitchell in "C. M. Russell—The White Indian," *Montana: The Magazine of Western History* 10, no. 1 (Winter 1960): 5. The Denver writer who was concerned about fiction of the real West was the well-known Arthur Chapman, this time in an article "The New West and Old Fiction," *Independent,* 9 Jan. 1902, pp. 99 and 100.

Frank Norris's lament was quoted by Philip Durham in "The Cowboy and the Myth Makers," *Journal of Popular Culture* 1, no. 1 (Summer 1967): 59. Hough's comments appeared in his article "The Settlement of the West: A Study in Transportation," *Century Illustrated Monthly Magazine,* pt. 3, Jan. 1903, p. 369. Hamlin Garland's "Her Mountain Lover" ran serially in the same magazine during 1901. Remington's "A Desert Romance" appeared in the Feb. 1902 issue, pp. 522–30.

A good deal has been written about Owen Wister. The contemporary account that mentioned the "possible impossibility" appeared in "Three Novelists of Sincerity and Charm," *World's Work* 5 (Nov. 1902); see pp. 2790–94. See also E. S. Martin, "This Busy World," *Harper's Weekly,* 11 Aug. 1894, p. 754. The *Times* quotation about Wister was included in G. Edward White's *The Eastern Establishment and the Western Experience: The West of Frederic Remington, Theodore Roosevelt and Owen Wister* (New Haven, Conn.: Yale University Press, 1968), p. 196. Roy M. Meyer talked about Wister's sales records in "B. M. Bower: The Poor Man's Wister," *Journal of Popular Culture* 7, no. 3 (Winter 1973): 667.

Some background on Wister is to be found in Philip Durham's article, cited above, p. 59. The best evaluation of Wister as a writer is by Richard Etulain. There are some stimulating ideas in Etulain's book *The Popular Western: Essays toward a Definition* (Bowling Green, Ohio: Bowling Green University Popular Press, 1974); see also his "Origins of the Western," *Journal of Popular Culture* 5, no. 4 (Spring 1972): 799–805, and "The Historical Development of the Western," ibid., vol. 7, no. 3 (Winter 1973): 717–26. He had more to say about Wister in "Riding Point: The Western and Its Interpreters," ibid., pp. 647–51.

For thoughts on the Virginian and other western heroes as symbols of what many thought of as the best of an earlier America see David B. Davis, "Ten Gallon Hero," *American Quarterly* 6 (Summer 1954): 111–25. More on Wister can be found in Neal Lambert's "Owen Wister's Virginian: The Genesis of a Cultural Hero," *Western American Literature* 6, no. 2 (Summer 1971): 99–107, in which he compares Wister to James Fenimore Cooper, as does John Milton in *The Novel of the American West* (Lincoln: University of Nebraska Press, 1980), p. 5. Lambert, in "The Values of the Frontier: Owen

Wister's Final Assessment," *South Dakota Review* 9, no. 1 (Spring 1971):
76–87, discussed Wister's *When the West Was West.*

The "newer country" remark, of 1906, was made by Stuart L. Douglas in "Westward Ho!" *Outing Magazine,* Aug. 1906, p. 617. Harvard's earnest intentions toward western history were discussed in "Western History in the East," *Nation,* 18 Apr. 1912, p. 383. For more on the "falsification" of western history read Loy Otis Banks, "The Credible Literary West," *Colorado Quarterly* 8, no. 1 (Summer 1959), esp. p. 49.

The Zane Grey material came from Gary Topping, "Zane Grey's West," *Journal of Popular Culture* 7, no. 3 (Winter 1973): 681–89, and from Etulain's "Riding Point," p. 647. Topping also wrote "Zane Grey: A Literary Assessment," *Western American Literature* 13, no. 1 (May 1978): 51–64. The question that I raised about the literary cowboy's sex habits is enlarged upon by C. L. Sonnichsen in "Sex on the Lone Prairee," ibid., pp. 15–32. One of the best things in print on this subject is Clifford P. Westermeier's "The Cowboy and Sex," in *The Cowboy: Six-shooters, Songs, and Sex,* ed. Charles W. Harris and Buck Rainey (Norman: University of Oklahoma Press, 1976). Zane Grey and Turner are compared in John Cawelti, "God's Country, Las Vegas and the Gunfighter: Differing Versions of the West," *Western American Literature* 9, no. 4 (Winter 1975): 281. Roderick Nash, in *The Nervous Generation: American Thought, 1917 1930* (Chicago: Rand McNally & Co., 1970), pp. 1 and 140, made mention of sales records set by Grey and other popular writers of westerns. The conversation between Grey and Garland is found in Donald Pizer, ed., *Hamlin Garland's Diaries* (San Marino, Calif.: Huntington Library, 1968), p. 140. Leslie Fiedler's description of the western is from his book *The Return of the Vanishing American* (New York: Stein & Day, 1968), p. 24.

For a view of the back-to-nature writers consult Frederic Taber Cooper, "The Popularity of Harold Bell Wright," *Bookman* 40 (Jan. 1915): 498–500; and Peter Schmitt, "Wilderness Novels in the Progressive Era," *Journal of Popular Culture* 3, no. 1 (Summer 1960): 72–90. Nash, in *Nervous Generation,* assessed Bell and Curwood; see pp. 139 and 141. Andrew Sinclair's *Jack: A Biography of Jack London* (New York: Harper & Row, 1977) belongs with this group. For thoughts on turn-of-the-century feminism as an inspiration for the macho school of literature see Theodore Roszac, "The Hard and the Soft: The Force of Feminism in Modern Times," in *Masculine/Feminine: Readings in Sexual Mythology and the Liberation of Women,* ed. Betty Roszac and Theodore Roszac (New York: Harper & Row, 1969). Russel Nye, in *The Unembarrassed Muse: The Popular Arts in America* (New York: Dial Press, 1970), discusses some of the outdoor writers; see pp. 288–90.

Will Irwin's "healthy provincialism" remark was found in "What Is the Western Spirit?" *Sunset Magazine,* June 1923, p. 24. Provincialism was being discussed as far back as 1908; e.g., see Louis Howland, "Provincial or National?" *Scribner's Magazine,* Apr. 1908, p. 454.

A good example of the reaction of regional writers is seen in May Davison Rhodes's *The Hired Man on Horseback* (Eugene Manlove Rhodes) (Boston: Houghton Mifflin Co., 1938). For more about Bertha Sinclair see Roy Meyer, "B. M. Bower." William McLeod Raine is mentioned by Nye in *Unembarrassed Muse* (see p. 292) and by William J. Barker in "Wild Bill of the

Circle-WR," in *Rocky Mountain Empire,* ed. Elvon L. Howe (New York: Doubleday & Co., 1946), pp. 202–3. The "border drama" reference is from Howland's "Provincial or National?" (see p. 454). The literary historian who talked of the early postwar years as a major divide was C. L. Sonnichsen, in *From Hopalong to Hud: Thoughts on Western Fiction* (College Station: Texas A & M University Press, 1978), p. 7. The "dark horsemen of the Golden West" reference came from Philip Durham's "The Cowboy and the Myth Makers," p. 60, where he was referring to a remark made by Harold Waldo. Both Durham and Jay B. Hubbell, in "The Frontier in American Literature," *Southwest Review* 10, no. 2 (Jan. 1925): 86, are quoted in Clemence Dane. The apologist of 1925 who did not think westerners a literary people was Jay Hubbell in the above-cited article, p. 89.

Reference to Mormon settlements and early writers is from Ray B. West, Jr., *Rocky Mountain Reader* (New York: E. P. Dutton & Co., Inc., 1946), p. 14. For Wilson Clough's opinion see his *The Necessary Earth: Nature and Solitude in American Literature* (Austin: University of Texas Press, 1964), p. 144. John Milton's assessment of the "subliterary form" is from his *The Novel of the American West,* on p. xiv; see p. xv for his praise of indigenous novels. The critic who talked about the "fresh angle" to an old approach was Robert B. Heilman, in "The Western Theme: Exploiters and Explorers," *Partisan Review* 28, no. 2 (Mar.–Apr. 1961): 289.

More about authors who live or have lived in the West was dealt with by Max Westbrook in "The Authentic Western," *Western American Literature* 13, no. 3 (Fall 1978): 213–25, especially p. 216. De Voto's praise of Tom Ferril was published in a blurb opposite the table of contents for the Dec. 1946 issue of *Harper's Magazine.* The novelist's view of the western as being historical is touched upon by John Milton in *Three West: Conversations with Vardis Fisher, Max Evans, Michael Straight* (Vermillion, S.D.: Dakota Press, 1970), p. 101.

For further comments on romance versus history read Frederick Elkin, "The Psychological Appeal of the Hollywood Western," *Journal of Educational Sociology* 24, no. 2 (Oct. 1950): 74; and Michael T. Marsden, who said that as a romance, the western should not be expected to be historically accurate: see his article "The Popular Western Novel as a Cultural Artifact," *Arizona and the West* 20, no. 3 (Autumn 1978): 209. Jack Nachbar, ed., in *Focus on the Western* (Englewood Cliffs, N.J.: Prentice-Hall, Inc., 1974), briefly discussed the question of historical fidelity, pp. 4, 5; so did James K. Folsom, "Westerns as Social and Political Alternatives," in the same volume (see, e.g., p. 81). Philip French, in *Westerns: Aspects of a Movie Genre* (New York: Viking Press, 1974), p. 12, thought westerns reflected little genuine western history. The question of searching for the authentic West is covered also by Loy Otis Banks in "The Credible Literary West," pp. 28–50.

Louis L'Amour's assessment of himself was published in a syndicated column by Ronda Haskins under the title "Louis L'Amour Rides Again in 'Shadow Riders,' " *Boulder* (Colo.) *Daily Camera,* TV guide, 26 Sept. 1982, p. 9. Luke Short's "entertainer" description is in Robert L. Gale's *Luke Short* (Boston: Twayne Publishers, 1981), p. 152.

Stegner's judgment on myths is from Russell Martin, "Writers of the Purple Sage," *New York Times Magazine,* 27 Dec. 1981, p. 22. The California professor was T. K. Whipple, who wrote *Study Out the Land* (Berkeley:

University of California Press, 1943); see p. 64. De Voto's "unnumerable *297*
magnificences" remark was used in his article "Two Points of a Joke," *Essays*
Harper's Magazine, Oct. 1951, p. 76. The "seedy, dull little communities," *on*
unrealistically romanticized, were discussed by Ralph Willett in "The *Sources*
American Western Myth and Anti-Myth," *Journal of Popular Culture* 4, no. 2
(Fall 1970): 456.

Milton's comment about the West's telling us something about ourselves is
from his *Novel of the American West,* referred to above; see p. 1. The reference
to Wild West shows is from Joseph Schwartz, "The Wild West Show:
Everything Genuine," *Journal of Popular Culture* 3, no. 4 (Spring 1970): 664.

For John Williams's arguments on the term *epic* read his article "The
'Western': Definition of the Myth," *Nation,* 18 Nov. 1961, pp. 401-6. The
critic who pondered the "tragic" omission was Robert B. Heilman, in "The
Western Theme: Exploiters and Explorers," *Partisan Review* 28, no. 2
(Mar.-Apr. 1961): 291.

Jimmy Stewart's "language barrier" explanation was published in *U.S.
News & World Report,* 15 Nov. 1976, p. 86. Much the same thing was said
about the attractiveness of scenery and open space by John Cawelti in *Six-Gun
Mystique* (Bowling Green, Ohio: Bowling Green University Popular Press,
[1971]), p. 42. For some excellent background reading on early western films
see Elliott West, "An End to Dreaming: The American Vision in Recent
Westerns," *Red River Valley Historical Review* 5, no. 3 (Summer 1980): 22-39.
His article "Good Guys, Bad Guys: The Movie Western and the Popular
Mind," *Film and History* 5 (Dec. 1975): 105 and 112, also should be
consulted. References to early films are found in Jon Tuska, "The American
Western Cinema: 1903-Present," in *Focus on the Western,* ed. Jack Nachbar,
p. 27. One of the best general works on this subject is William K. Everson's *A
Pictorial History of the Western Film* (New York: Citadel Press, 1969). I have
much respect for the author's judgments because of his extensive experience
with films and their history. A Briton's view is Jenni Calder's in *There Must Be
a Lone Ranger: The American West in Film and in Reality* (New York: Taplinger
Publishing Co., 1975); see p. 4. Very good, also, is John G. Cawelti's *The
Six-Gun Mystique.*

The decline of filmed westerns in the 1930s is well covered by Andrew
Bergman in *We're in the Money: Depression America and Its Films* (New York:
New York University Press, 1971); see pp. 83 and 88. For a brief look at the
ups and downs of westerns, from the 1930s to the 1970s, see chap. 1 of
Robert L. Gale's *Luke Short.* The waning of the western during the 1940s is
mentioned by John G. Cawelti in "The Gunfighter and Society," *American
West* 5, no. 2 (Mar. 1968): 30-35, 76, and 77; see also his article "God's
Country, Las Vegas and the Gunfighter: Differing Visions of the West,"
Western American Literature 9, no. 4 (Winter 1975): 273-83.

Comparison of the cowboy to the 1930s gangster was made by Robert
Warshow in *The Immediate Experience* (New York: Doubleday & Co., Inc.,
1962), p. 137. The suggestion that producers saw westerns as "safe" subjects
came from Philip French, *Westerns: Aspects of a Movie Genre,* p. 13. Some
figures relating to the volume of westerns, in film and in print, may be found
in Durham's "Cowboy and the Mythmakers," p. 59; Frederick Elkin, "The
Psychological Appeal of the Hollywood Western," *Journal of Educational*

Sociology 24, no. 2, p. 72; Will Wright, *Six Guns and Society: A Structural Study of the Western* (Berkeley: University of California Press, 1975), p. 4; and Cawelti, *Six-Gun Mystique,* p. 2.

The best book on westerns since World War II is John Lenihan's *Showdown: Confronting Modern America in the Western Film* (Urbana: University of Illinois Press, 1980). See also Elliott West, "An End to Dreaming: The American Vision in Recent Westerns," *Red River Valley Historical Review* 5 (Summer 1980): 22–39. Much has been written about the advent of the "adult" or "psychological" western that emerged after World War II. For one of several explanations for the development read Martin Nussbaum, "Sociological Symbolism of the 'Adult' Western," *Social Forces* 39, no. 1 (Oct. 1960): 25–28. Also take a look at James K. Folsom, "*Shane* and *Hud:* Two Stories in Search of a Medium," *Western Humanities Review* 24, no. 4 (Autumn 1970): 359–72. Philip French, in *Westerns,* mentioned above, talked about postwar trends (see p. 86).

The "communal" type of film was discussed by Kathryn C. Esselman in "When the Cowboy Stopped Kissing his Horse," *Journal of Popular Culture* 6, no. 2 (Fall 1972): 337–49; and by Everson in *A Pictorial History,* p. 204. A good article called "Six Gun Galahad" treated this subject in the 30 Mar. 1959 issue of *Time,* pp. 52–60; I found the "Lincoln in Levi's" quotation in this piece. Gary Cooper offered his view in an article called "The West in Faction and Fiction," which appeared in *Senior Scholastic,* 22 Mar. 1961, p. 7. Jon Tuska dealt with the postwar generation of film makers in "The American Western Cinema: 1903 to Present," in *Focus on the Western,* ed. Jack Nachbar (see p. 27); see also Tuska's excellent book *The Filming of the West* (Garden City, N.Y.: Doubleday & Co., Inc., 1976).

Harry Schein, in "The Olympian Cowboy," *American Scholar,* 24, no. 3 (Summer 1955): 309–20, has some good points to make about postwar shifts in perspective. So does Michael T. Marsden in "The Popular Western Novel as a Cultural Artifact," pp. 203–14. The same goes for William W. Savage, Jr., *The Cowboy Hero: His Image in American History and Culture* (Norman: University of Oklahoma Press, 1979), pp. 3 and 42. The emergent popularity of Christian values of kindness and the loss of the hero's identity are discussed by Walker Percy in "The Decline of the Western," *Commonweal,* 16 May 1958, pp. 181–83. More on the changing role of the hero during the sixties may be read in Calder, *There Must Be a Lone Ranger,* pp. 214–15. A good discussion of public concerns and insecurities was set forth by Everson in *A Pictorial History,* pp. 12–13. The description of the frontier marshal as a man of leisure came from Warshow's *Immediate Experience,* p. 138. The "hag-ridden" notion is from "Six Gun Galahad," p. 53.

Reference to the growing number of minorities in western films was made by Everson in *A Pictorial History,* pp. 201 and 203. The "new" Indian was treated by George N. Fenin and William K. Everson in *The Western* (New York: Grossman Publishers, 1973), pp. 320, 366, and 371; and by Ralph Willett in "The American Western Myth and Anti-Myth," p. 456. See also Cawelti, "God's Country," p. 277; and French, *Westerns,* p. 84. My comment about the longevity of the western is based, in part, upon a passage in Everson, *A Pictorial History,* pp. 1 and 2; see page 3 for a statement about Wayne as the last of the traditional movie saddle heroes.

More about John Wayne, the movie hero, was discussed by Margaret Ronan in "Two Screen Cowboys Talk about the Reel West & the Real West," *Senior Scholastic,* 6 Dec. 1971, pp. 10 and 11. More of the same came from several articles in the *Boulder* (Colo.) *Daily Camera:* Vernon Scott, "John Wayne—The American Hero," a syndicated piece, 12 and 13 June 1979, plus a local editorial, "John Wayne: True Son of America," 13 June 1979. The 1914 comment by William S. Hart was quoted by John D. Weaver in "The Universal Appeal of the West," *Publishers Weekly,* 9 Oct. 1972, p. 60.

The periodic items that reported the western's death appeared in the press. E.g., the Siskel reference of 6 Mar. 1977 came from the *Boulder* (Colo.) *Daily Camera* for that date; the Buck item from the 12 Feb. 1978 and the Maverick reference, by Fred Rothenberg of the AP, from the 6 June 1982 issues of the same paper. Savage, in *Cowboy Hero,* wrote about the ups and downs of the 1970s (see p. 157). Banks, in "Credible Literary West," had pronounced the western dead in 1949: the obituary appears on p. 28.

Americans are almost as fascinated by the devotion of non-Americans to the frontier as they are to the western itself. Much has been written about it. Karl May, of course, is a pet among these foreign "Wild West" writers. A good place to start reading about him is in Richard H. Cracroft's "The American West of Karl May," *American Quarterly* 19, no. 2, pt. 1 (Summer 1967): 249–58. Very entertaining is Joseph Wechsberg's "Winnetou of der Wild West," *Saturday Review,* 20 Oct. 1962, pp. 52–53 and 60–61. John Toland mentioned Hitler's devotion in his *Adolf Hitler* (New York: Doubleday & Co., 1976), p. 13. Albert Speer talked about Hitler and Old Shatterhand in his *Spandau: The Secret Diaries* (New York: Macmillan, 1976), pp. 347–48. See also D. L. Ashliman, "The American West in Twentieth-Century Germany," *Journal of Popular Culture* 2, no. 1 (Summer 1968): 83. The escaping German prisoners were described by John Hammond Moore in *The Faustball Tunnel: German POWs in America and Their Great Escape* (New York: Random House, 1978), p. 194.

International interest, in general, has been touched upon by Everson, in *Pictorial History,* pp. 1 and 234, and by Fenin and Everson, in *The Western,* p. 343. The story of the French westerns has been told by my colleague Clifford P. Westermeier in "Sagebrush Galahads: The Cinema Cowboys," *Red River Valley Historical Review* 5, no. 4 (Fall 1980): 27–54. Philip French mentioned the "easterns" in his book *Westerns,* p. 21. The Czech puppet-film director was discussed by Schein in "Olympian Cowboy," p. 310.

The "hardiest weed" remark was made by Harry Sinclair Drago in the 1961 Introduction that he wrote for a reissue of Douglas Branch's *The Cowboy and His Interpreters,* p. v. Harry Schein, in "Olympian Cowboy," talked about the "magic of repetition" (p. 311). Repetition is discussed also by Peter Homans in "Puritanism Revisited," in *Focus,* ed. Nachbar, p. 87. For more on the western as national literature read Hubbell's article "The Frontier in American Literature," p. 85.

9. The Wilderness Evangelists

The recent interest in conservation and the preservation of the wilderness has inspired shelf loads of books and articles. For three that take a broad look at different aspects of the subjects the reader can turn to William K. Wyant,

Westward in Eden: The Public Lands and the Conservation Movement (Berkeley and Los Angeles: University of California Press, 1982); Frank E. Smith, *The Politics of Conservation* (New York: Pantheon Books, 1966); and Roderick Nash, *Wilderness and the American Mind,* rev. ed. (New Haven, Conn., and London: Yale University Press, 1973; 3d ed., 1982).

On the government and conservation before Theodore Roosevelt see Arthur H. Carhart, *The National Forests* (New York: Alfred A. Knopf, 1959); and Henry Clepper, ed., *Origins of American Conservation* (New York: Ronald Press Co., 1966), pp. 3–15. Robert Tudor Hill, in *The Public Domain and Democracy* (New York: Columbia University, 1910), has some interesting material on the conservation fights, written at the time, as does James Middleton, in "A New West," *World's Work* 31, no. 6 (Apr. 1916): 669–80. Gifford Pinchot speaks for himself in *The Fight for Conservation* (New York: Doubleday, Page & Co., 1910). On western opposition to government conservation programs see Samuel P. Hays, *Conservation and the Gospel of Efficiency: The Progressive Conservation Movement, 1890–1920* (Cambridge: Harvard University Press, 1959), chap. 12. Elmo Richardson's *The Politics of Conservation: Crusades and Controversies, 1897–1913* (Berkeley: University of California Press, 1962) provides an excellent overview of the period; see p. 28 for the "Oh, Teddy" quote. For Will Barnes's article see "The U.S. Forest Service," *Out West* 29, no. 2 (Aug. 1908): 89–109. G. Michael McCarthy has an excellent detailed treatment of the fight over Colorado coal lands in his *Hour of Trial: The Conservation Conflict in Colorado and the West, 1891–1907* (Norman: University of Oklahoma Press, 1977), chap. 8. The quotes from Colorado newspapers appear on pp. 171 and 188.

The best study of early champions of preservationism is Lee Clark Mitchell's *Witnesses to a Vanishing America* (Princeton, N.J.: Princeton University Press, 1981). For Catlin's thoughts on the need for a national park see Roderick Nash, *The American Environment: Readings in the History of Conservation* (Reading, Mass.: Addison-Wesley Publishing Co., 1968), p. 9. Thoreau's musing is quoted by Frederick Turner in "The Language of the Forest," *Wilderness* 47, no. 161 (Summer 1983): 7. Stegner's words are from his article "The Best Idea We Ever Had," *Wilderness* 46, no. 160 (Spring 1983): 5–6. In addition to John Muir's many writings the reader might wish to consult Nash's *Wilderness and the American Mind,* chap. 8, and Stephen Fox's *John Muir and His Legacy: The American Conservation Movement* (Boston: Little Brown & Co., 1981). For Muir's tribute to Harriman see George Kennan, *E. H. Harriman: A Biography* (Boston: Houghton Mifflin Co., 1922), vol. 2, pp. 382–84. The exasperated Colorado editor's comments are in McCarthy's *Hour of Trial,* p. 145. An interesting if somewhat controversial discussion of the origins of the national park system is to be found in Alfred Runte's *National Parks: The American Experience* (Lincoln: University of Nebraska Press, 1979).

Stephen Mather and his influence on the national park system are treated on pp. 126–38 of Donald C. Swain's *Federal Conservation Policy, 1921–1933* (Berkeley: University of California Press, 1963), a detailed look at conservation issues during those years. The quote about his "preaching parks" is on p. 129; that about cops and trees in Yosemite, on p. 131. On the transition period of conservation policy and one of the most important figures in it see

Steve Mehls and Carol Drake, "Edward T. Taylor and the Origins of a
'Multiple Use' Philosophy for the Public Domain," in *A Taste of the West: Essays in Honor of Robert G. Athearn,* ed. Duane A. Smith (Boulder, Colo.: Pruett Publishing Co., 1983), pp. 66–74. Aldo Leopold's masterpiece is *A Sand County Almanac* (New York: Oxford University Press, 1966); his statement on the land as a community appears on p. x. Nash, in *Wilderness and the American Mind,* chap. 11, discusses Leopold as a prophet of the movement; Nash also provides a succinct discussion of Marshall and his contributions on pp. 200–208.

Several books have considered the spectacular developments in the West since World War II. The best are Gerald Nash, *The American West Transformed: The Impact of the Second World War* (Bloomington: Indiana University Press, 1985); Neil Morgan, *Westward Tilt: The American West Today* (New York: Random House, 1963); and Peter Wiley and Wiley Gottlieb, *Empires in the Sun: The Rise of the New American West* (New York: G. P. Putnam's Sons, 1982). For the regional popularity poll see Bernard L. Weinstein and Robert E. Firestine, *Regional Growth and Decline in the United States* (New York: Praeger Publishers, 1978), pp. 28–30; and on defense salaries see Michael J. Greenwood, *Migration and Economic Growth in the United States: National, Regional and Metropolitan Perspectives* (New York: Academic Press, 1981), pp. 30–31. Daniel J. Elazar has some interesting thoughts on the movement of a "metropolitan-technological frontier" into the West after World War II in his "Land Space and Civil Society in America," *Western Historical Quarterly* 5, no. 3 (July 1974): 261–84.

The businessman and the scientist speak on the new frontier spirit in Morgan, *Westward Tilt,* pp. 32 and 275. Statistics on lumber production in national forests can be found in Dennis Hanson, "The Aspect of the Tally-Sheet," *Wilderness* 47, no. 161 (Summer 1983): 26. For a sampling of the scores of articles, both scholarly and popular, on the postwar western boom and some of its implications the reader can consult Robert Cahn, "The New Utah: Change Comes to Zion," *Saturday Evening Post,* 1 Apr. 1961, pp. 32–33 and 42–46; Frank McCulloch, "Will the West Take Over?" *Saturday Evening Post,* 8 July 1961, pp. 18 and 46–51; Albert Rosenfeld, "New Mexico Cashes In," *Harper's Magazine,* Jan. 1954, pp. 29–35; Earl Pomeroy, "What Remains of the West?" *Utah Historical Quarterly* 35, no. 1 (Winter 1967): 37–55.

The best survey of the politics of conservation during the immediate postwar years is Elmo Richardson's *Dams, Parks and Politics: Resources Development and Preservation in the Truman-Eisenhower Era* (Lexington: University of Kentucky Press, 1973). For the Echo Park fight see p. 129–52 in it and also Nash, *Wilderness and the American Mind,* pp. 209–19, and Owen Stratton and Phillip Sirotkin, *The Echo Park Controversy,* University of Alabama, Cases in Public Administration and Policy Formation no. 46. Smith, in *Politics of Conservation,* and Wyant, in *Westward in Eden,* have good summaries of some of the most important conservation and preservationist legislation during these years, as does Roderick Nash in "Path to Preservation," *Wilderness* 48, no. 165 (Summer 1984): 5–11. For a fine discussion of the preservationist lobby see Fox, *John Muir,* pp. 250–90; and on David Brower, consult Peter Wild, *Pioneer Conservationists of Western America* (Missoula, Mont.: Mountain

Press Publishing Co., 1979), pp. 151–59, and John McPhee, *Encounters with the Archdruid* (New York: Farrar, Straus & Giroux, 1971). For Edward Abbey's provocative and occasionally outrageous comments on industrial tourism see his *Desert Solitaire: A Season in the Wilderness* (New York: McGraw-Hill Book Co., 1968), pp. 45–67.

For some negative comments and dire predictions about new western growth see Richard H. Jackson, *Land Use in America* (New York: V. H. Winston & Sons, 1981), p. 139; James M. Rock, "Boomtowns in the Energy-Rich West," *Intellect,* Dec. 1976, pp. 155–58; and Doelzer, *Population and Development,* p. 227. Edward Abbey writes on "The Second Rape of the West" in chap. 16 of his *The Journey Home: Some Words in Defense of the American West* (New York: E. P. Dutton, 1977). Carl O. Sauer's oft-quoted words are from "Theme of Plant and Animal Destruction in Economic History," in *Land and Life: A Selection from the Writings of Carl Ortwin Sauer* (Berkeley: University of California Press, 1963), p. 154. The reporter who commented on the rape in broad daylight was Grace Lichtenstein: see her *Desperado* (New York: Dial Press, 1977), p. 123. Eric Sevareid warned: "They're Closing in on the Great Open Spaces," in *Reader's Digest,* Feb. 1963, pp. 196–98. On the debates about recent western growth in one state see Mike W. Edwards, "Should They Build a Fence Around Montana?" *National Geographic,* May 1976, pp. 614–57. The BLM official is quoted on p. 646. The sanguine remarks of the Colorado boosters on the state's scenic marvels come from Tom McCoy, "What Now, My Love?" *Colorado.* The "two-thirds environmentalist" cowboy spoke to a reporter in "Rebellious Mood in the West," *Wall Street Journal,* 16 Aug. 1979, p. 18.

Grace Lichtenstein, in *Desperado,* p. 5, is the source of the observation on the West as "a few white folks in a great big place." The *Newsweek* issue on "The Angry West" is that of 17 Sept. 1979. Sen. Clinton Anderson's remark can be found in Stewart L. Udall, *The Quiet Crisis* (New York: Holt, Rinehart & Winston, 1963), p. 181; and Wallace Stegner's observations on the "geography of hope" appear in his "Wilderness Letter," in *The Wilderness Reader,* ed. Frank Bergon (New York: New American Library, 1980), pp. 327–33.

10. THE MAN, THE LAND, THE LEGEND

New conditions that pioneers met in the trans-Missouri West are discussed by Bernard De Voto in "The West: A Plundered Province," *Harper's Magazine,* Aug. 1934, pp. 356–57; De Voto discussed distances in his article "The Anxious West," ibid., Dec. 1946, p. 487. For more about the West's climatic conditions see Thomas C. Donnelly, ed., *Rocky Mountain Politics* (Albuquerque: University of New Mexico Press, 1940), p. 2. The Glacier Park anecdote is from Meridan H. Bennett's "The Scenic West: Silent Mirage," *Colorado Quarterly* 8, no. 1 (Summer 1959): 15. Having spent my own honeymoon there early in a rainy June, I could not resist the urge to include this item. I didn't find the mountains oppressive!

Mary Austin's choice of words can be found in John R. Milton, *The Novel of the American West* (Lincoln: University of Nebraska Press, 1980), p. 61. The

German prisoner of war was Fritz Guggenberger, and his story is included in John Hammond Moore's *The Faustball Tunnel: German POWs in America and Their Great Escape* (New York: Random House, 1978), p. 66. Joseph Wood Krutch, in John D. Margolis, *Joseph Wood Krutch: A Writer's Life* (Knoxville: University of Tennessee Press, 1980), is quoted on the desirability of space, p. 184. The story of settlers' chickens getting mixed together is from Eugene V. Smalley, "The Isolation of Life on Prairie Farms," *Atlantic Monthly,* Sept. 1893, pp. 381–82. The comment about "Maxfield Parrish blue" skies and the descriptions of western open spaces may be found in Courtney Ryley Cooper, "This Is My America," *American Magazine,* Jan. 1933, p. 82. Wolfe's quotation about "America's horizon" is from Edward M. Miller's "A Westerner Views the U.S.A.," *American Scholar* 12, no. 4 (Autumn 1943): 464.

The western governor who said you could be free was Richard Lamm (D, Colo.): see his "Goodbye to My West," in *Rocky Mountain Magazine,* Mar. 1982, p. 49, or in his book *The Angry West: A Vulnerable Land and Its Future,* coauthored by Michael McCarthy (Boston: Houghton Mifflin Co., 1982), pp. 2 and 3. The book is more or less a polemic, but it serves as a good illustration of how the Old West syndrome can overpower a transplant to the region. For more on the idea of "escape to the West" see Miller, "A Westerner Views the U.S.A.," p. 462; "Americans 'Discover' the West Again," *U.S. News & World Report,* 21 June 1965, p. 80; Jon Wesley Sering, "Mary Austin's Land of Little Rain: The Country of Lost Borders," *Desert,* June 1981, p. 54; Bernard De Voto, "Our Great West—Boom or Bust?" *Collier's,* 25 Dec. 1953, p. 48.

The Las Vegas waitress was quoted by Dallas Lore Sharp in *The Better Country* (Boston: Houghton Mifflin Co., 1928), p. 137. He was an English professor who did some "outdoor" writing. Eric Sevareid, on space, can be read in his article "Why the Aspens Quake," *Saturday Review,* 20 Oct. 1962, p. 45. The suggestion that "it is always a long way from here to there," etc., came from Bernard De Voto, "The Wild West," *Holiday,* July 1954, p. 40. Charley Russell's remark appears in his book *Trails Plowed Under* (Garden City, N.Y.: Doubleday & Co., 1946), p. 191. The exaggerated land, as seen by pioneers, is described by John D. Unruh, Jr., in *The Plains Across* (Urbana: University of Illinois Press, 1979), p. 397.

Space, as a western commodity, was discussed by A. B. Guthrie, Jr., in "The West Is Our Great Adventure of the Spirit," *Life,* 13 Apr. 1959, p. 94. Emerson was quoted by Ernest Marchand, in "Emerson and the Frontier," *American Literature* 3, no. 2 (May 1931): 158. The idea that the West simply brought out the best in men was argued by David B. Davis in "Ten-Gallon Hero," *American Quarterly* 6, no. 2 (Summer 1954): 116. Borland's poem is found in his *America Is Americans* (New York: Harper & Brothers, 1941), p. 101. J. B. Priestley's opinions about the desert are treated by him in "The Wonder of the Desert," *American Magazine,* Feb. 1952, pp. 91–92.

Denver's one-time clear air was mentioned by Julian Ralph (and a few thousand others), but see his "Colorado and Its Capital," *Harper's New Monthly Magazine,* May 1893, p. 938. Dallas Lore Sharp, mentioned above, also was much struck by the clear sky; see p. 143 of *The Better Country.* Ross Calvin, in *Sky Determines* (Albuquerque: University of New Mexico Press,

1948), p. 29, talked about film exposures in the West. The remark about Nevada's aridity came from Albert W. Atwood, "Wealth in the Outdoor West," *Saturday Evening Post,* 8 Jan. 1927, p. 149.

The Colorado governor who said the land influenced man was Alva Adams; he is quoted by Don Walker in *Clio's Cowboys: Studies in the Historiography of the Cattle Trade* (Lincoln: University of Nebraska Press, 1981), p. 52. On the same page Walker quoted Dr. J. E. Stubbs, president of the University of Nevada, on the subject.

The manner in which the West brings outsiders under its sway was described by Frank H. Spearman in "The Westerner," *World Today* 8, no. 2 (Feb. 1905): 146. About this time, Charles M. Harger said much the same thing: see his article "The New Westerner," *North American Review,* 2 Aug. 1907, p. 756. A quarter-century later, Courtney Ryley Cooper thought the characteristic still persisted: read his "This Is My America," p. 41.

The violence of the land is often mentioned by De Voto: for some examples read his introduction to B. A. Botkin, ed., *A Treasury of Western Folklore* (New York: Crown Publishers, Inc., 1975), pp. vi–vii. His remark about loving a woman you can't trust is from his article "The Wild West," p. 72. Hal Borland talked about winter conditions in his book *Country Editor's Boy* (Philadelphia: J. B. Lippincott Co., 1970), p. 157. Krutch on the desert is from John D. Margolis's *Joseph Wood Krutch: A Writer's Life* (Knoxville: University of Tennessee Press, 1980), pp. 202–3. The comment about Taos winters was made by Joseph Foster in *D. H. Lawrence in Taos* (Albuquerque: University of New Mexico Press, 1972), p. 57.

Edward Alsworth Ross, in "The Middle West," *Century Magazine,* Feb. 1912, p. 611, was impressed by the "steady-eyed, eagle-faced" western man who lived in the "recesses of the Rocky Mountains." It was Frank Spearman, in "The Westerner," who thought we should bear with the westerners' assumptions of equality (see p. 146). Katharine Gerould's opinion on equality is expressed in her article "The Aristocratic West," *Harper's Magazine,* Sept. 1925, pp. 468 and 476. The farm wife of 1935 who commented on the desert's myths was Caroline A. Henderson, "Letters from the Dust Bowl," *Atlantic Monthly,* May 1936, p. 547. Eric Sevareid's remembrances of the dust-bowl days appear in his article "They're Closing in on the Great Open Spaces," *Reader's Digest* Feb. 1963, p. 197.

David McKay's desire to have his people on the land is related in Robert Cahn, "The New Utah: Change Comes to Zion," *Saturday Evening Post,* 1 Apr. 1961, p. 42. Reference to early cooperative efforts in rural communities is discussed by Robert V. Hine in his excellent *Community on the American Frontier: Separate but Not Alone* (Norman: University of Oklahoma Press, 1980), p. 104. The story of the Russians came from Ilya Ilf and Eugene Petrov's *Little Golden America: Two Famous Soviet Humourists Survey the United States* (London: George Routledge & Sons Ltd., 1944; first published in Russia in 1936), p. 134.

The friendliness of the westerner is often mentioned, but see Miller, "A Westerner Views the U.S.A.," p. 459. Katharine Gerould's comment is in her "Aristocratic West," pp. 467–68. Courtney Ryley Cooper, in "My America," also talked about the openness of the people. The lady editor who

thought she was an easterner running into a western "phenomenon" was
Janet Chusmir, in "Boulder Merchants Show Western Courtesy," *Boulder*
(Colo.) *Daily Camera,* 19 Dec. 1982.

The quality of simplicity is discussed by Frederick Elkin in his article "The
Psychological Appeal of the Hollywood Western," *Journal of Educational
Sociology* 24, no. 2 (Oct. 1950): 73. Wilson Clough's comment is in *The
Necessary Earth: Nature and Solitude in American Literature* (Austin: University of
Texas Press, 1964), p. 145. The old-time newsman who is quoted is Edward
Miller, "A Westerner Views the U.S.A.," p. 458.

Gilman M. Ostrander mentioned Pat McCarran's birthplace in *Nevada:
The Great Rotten Borough, 1859–1964* (New York: Alfred A. Knopf, 1966), p.
133. The scarcity of native sons in the West also was mentioned by Albert W.
Atwood in "The Youngest Brother: The West and Its Share in the National
Heritage," *Saturday Evening Post,* 4 Dec. 1926, p. 205. Edward Miller (see
above) discussed the West's youthfulness at some length (see esp. p. 465).
More of the same may be found in Ray B. West, ed., *A Country of the Mind*
(Sausalito, Calif.: Contact Editions, 1962), p. ix.

Eric Sevareid's comment about growing up with a sense of change is from
his article "They're Closing," p. 198. Garet Garrett talked about the
publicity manager's inability to sin in "How in the West?" *Saturday Evening
Post,* 22 Nov. 1924, p. 78. For Ray Lyman Wilbur's optimism see "Broaden-
ing Horizons," an interview reported by Frank J. Taylor in *Sunset Magazine,*
Apr. 1929, p. 19. De Voto made his "three bankruptcies to make a farm"
remark in "Two Points of a Joke," *Harper's Magazine,* Oct. 1951, p. 74. The
Nevada University president was Charles Armstrong, quoted by Frank
McCulloch in "Will the West Take Over?" *Saturday Evening Post,* 8 July
1961, p. 51. William T. Foster, in "The Spirit of the West," *Atlantic Monthly,*
July 1920, p. 90, talked about optimism as being a western characteristic. So
did Hal Borland, in *Country Editor's Boy,* p. 130. The line about the Christian
who held four aces was from McCulloch, "Will the West Take Over?" p. 51.
The pioneer lady who lived near Gunnison was quoted by Courtney Ryley
Cooper in "Present-day Pioneers," *Saturday Evening Post,* 3 Apr. 1926, p.
146.

The question of provincialism has generated no small amount of discussion, as well as some interesting rationalizations by westerners: for some
reading on this see Bernard De Voto, "Footnote on the West," *Harper's
Monthly Magazine,* Nov. 1927, p. 722, and his article "The Anxious West," p.
488. De Voto's own background, in this regard, is mentioned by Wallace
Stegner in *The Uneasy Chair: A Biography of Bernard De Voto* (New York:
Doubleday & Co., Inc., 1974), p. 15. The comment about the lonely
elevator's eventually becoming a town also is from De Voto; he mentioned it
in "The Wild West," p. 68. The admission that there might be a "certain
amount" of provincialism in the West was made by Hamilton W. Mabie in
"The Intellectual Movement in the West," *Atlantic Monthly,* Nov. 1898, p.
597. Katharine Gerould, in her "Aristocratic West" article, also talked
about this (p. 466). That new settlements are necessarily cosmopolitan was
argued by Thomas C. Donnelly, ed., in *Rocky Mountain Politics,* p. 5. Much
the same viewpoint was taken by the anonymous author of "The Spectator,"
published in the *Outlook,* 15 Aug. 1917, p. 581. Cosmopolitanism was argued

by the highly respected western historian John W. Caughey in "The American West: Frontier and Region," *Arizona and the West* 1, no. 1 (Spring 1959): 10–11. That Idahoans were well informed was argued by Lawrence H. Chamberlain, "Idaho," in Thomas Donnelly's *Rocky Mountain Politics,* pp. 164–65. Lorena Hickok's criticisms of Nevadans is from Richard Lowitt and Maurine Beasley, eds., *One Third of a Nation: Lorena Hickok Reports on the Great Depression* (Urbana: University of Illinois Press, 1981), p. 328.

Thurman Arnold's complaint was noted by Gene M. Gressley in "Colonialism: A Western Complaint," *Pacific Northwest Quarterly* 54, no. 1 (Jan. 1963): 3. Carey McWilliams talked about the lack of communication among western cities in "Myths of the West," *North American Review,* Nov. 1931, p. 429. The westerners' penchant for "tourist trap history" is discussed by De Voto in "The Anxious West," p. 485. See also Richard A. Bartlett, "The West Is Getting Lonely Again," *Reader's Digest,* Aug. 1969, p. 50. The Bill Moyers reference is from his book *Listening to America: A Traveler Rediscovers His Country* (New York: Harper's Magazine Press, 1971), p. 125.

De Voto's remark about the reactionary press is from his article "The West against Itself," *Harper's Magazine,* Jan. 1947, p. 7. For more on western conservatism see his "Footnote on the West," p. 718. Will Irwin talked about reactionary tendencies in western towns in "What Is the Western Spirit?" *Sunset Magazine,* June 1923, p. 24. An individual example of the western conservative can be seen in J. Frank Dobie, "The Conservatism of Charles M. Russell," *Montana: The Magazine of Western History* 2, no. 2 (Apr. 1952), reprinted almost verbatim in the same magazine, vol. 8, no. 4 (Autumn 1958); see pp. 58–59 of the latter version. Political maverickism is discussed by Daniel J. Elazar in *Cities of the Prairie: The Metropolitan Frontier and American Politics* (New York: Basic Books, Inc., 1979), p. 347.

Western mobility was mentioned by Miller in "A Westerner Views the U.S.A.," p. 459. I took some information also from a news item in the *Boulder* (Colo.) *Daily Camera* for 21 Aug. 1981, where Census Bureau figures were given. Neil Morgan discussed the subject in his article "The Great Westward Tilt," *Saturday Review,* 20 Oct. 1962, p. 64. Stegner's comment is from his *The Sound of Mountain Water* (Garden City, N.Y.: Doubleday & Co., Inc., 1969), p. 191. The comment about lower church affiliation came from Ladd Haystead, *If the Prospect Pleases: The West the Guidebooks Never Mention* (Norman: University of Oklahoma Press, 1947), p. 5. The New York reporter who didn't find westerners to be the people she anticipated was Grace Lichtenstein, who wrote *Desperado* (New York: Dial Press, 1977); see p. 5. Thurman Arnold's problems with his western clothes at Princeton is from Gene M. Gressley, ed., *Voltaire and the Cowboy: The Letters of Thurman Arnold* (Boulder: Colorado Associated University Press, 1977), p. 9.

The quality of taciturnity that has been attributed to westerners was mentioned by the movie actor William S. Hart (who once had been a cow hand) in *My Life East and West* (1929; reissued in 1968 by Benjamin Blom, Inc., Bronx, N.Y.), see p. 37. Western dress was mentioned by De Voto in "Plundered Province," p. 364, and in his article "Two Points of a Joke," p. 76. Vachel Lindsay was quoted by Stephen Graham in *Tramping with a Poet in the Rockies* (New York: D. Appleton & Co., 1922), p. 15. Stegner on illimitable freedom is from his article "I Sing of America," *Holiday,* Mar.

1976, p. 49. Joseph Foster recorded Lawrence's remark in *D. H. Lawrence in*
Taos (Albuquerque: University of New Mexico Press, 1972), p. 244.

11. EPILOGUE: THE GENESIS OF THE MYTHIC WEST

For material about the early frontiersmen and the myth, I have helped myself unashamedly to several large helpings of Carey McWilliams's "Myths of the West," *North American Review,* Nov. 1931, pp. 424–32. I have lifted some of the material from my own work: see Robert E. Riegel and Robert G. Athearn, *America Moves West,* 5th ed. (New York: Holt, Rinehart & Winston, 1971), chaps. 1 and 2.

Several sources talk about the conflict between the new industrialism and the desire to cling to individualism: see Gerald Nash, *The American West in the Twentieth Century* (Englewood Cliffs, N.J.: Prentice-Hall, Inc., 1973), p. 185; Russel Nye, *The Unembarrassed Muse: The Popular Arts in America* (New York: Dial Press, 1970), p. 290; Jenni Calder, *There Must Be a Lone Ranger: The American West in Film and in Reality* (New York: Taplinger Publishing Co., 1975; previously published in England), pp. 219–20; Richard Etulain, "Origins of the Western," *Journal of Popular Culture* 5, no. 4 (Spring 1972): 802. Ralph Willett, in "The American Western Myth and Anti Myth," *Journal of Popular Culture* 4, no. 2 (Fall 1970): 456, also had something to say about the troubled urban man.

That the frontier West simply was a place where most Americans did not live is taken up by James Oliver Robertson in *American Myth, American Reality* (New York: Hill & Wang, 1980), p. 115. He also mentioned Thoreau's interest in the West (p. 115), as did Loren Baritz, in "The Idea of the West," *American Historical Review* 66, no. 3 (Apr. 1961): 639. That the frontier experience was the American epic is discussed by T. K. Whipple in *Study Out the Land* (Berkeley: University of California Press, 1943), a set of essays: see "The Myth of the Old West," pp. 59–69. Whipple was a professor of English. W. H. Hutchinson, in "A Candle for the Sun," *American West* 3, no. 4 (Fall 1966): 64, quotes Denis Brogan. The connection between fact and myth is discussed by John R. Milton in *The Novel of the American West* (Lincoln: University of Nebraska Press, 1960); see especially pp. 42 and 300. Director George Stevens was quoted by Harry Schein, "The Olympian Cowboy," *American Scholar* 24, no. 3 (Summer 1955): 317. D. L. Ashliman, in "The American West in Twentieth Century Germany," *Journal of Popular Culture* 2, no. 1 (Summer 1968), quoted Herbert Frenzel (see p. 90). See also Bernard De Voto, "The West: A Plundered Province," *Harper's Magazine,* Aug. 1934, pp. 355–64, for more on the enduring myth.

Reference to Wister's Introduction in *The Virginian* was noted by Russel Nye in *The Unembarrassed Muse: The Popular Arts in America,* p. 290. Ralph Willett, in "The American Western Myth and Anti-Myth," *Journal of Popular Culture* 4, no. 2 (Fall 1970), talked about the problems of the urban man, the entrapped eastern workers, and their West (see p. 456). For more on the wage slave's dreams of the West see John D. Weaver, "The Universal Appeal of the West," *Publishers Weekly,* 9 Oct. 1972, p. 61.

Wallace Stegner's "hooked on history" remark is from his *The Sound of Mountain Water* (Garden City, N.Y.: Doubleday & Co., Inc., 1969), p. 192. Archibald MacLeish was quoted by John Milton in *The Novel of the American West* (Lincoln: University of Nebraska Press, 1980), p. 41. C. L. Sonnichsen, in his book *From Hopalong to Hud: Thoughts on Western Fiction* (College Station: Texas A & M University Press, 1978), mentions our need for roots and tradition (see p. 17). Hector H. Lee, in "Tales and Legends in Western American Literature," *Western American Literature* 9, no. 4 (Winter 1975), stresses the value of the myth (see p. 240). Thomas Keneally defined the myth in his excellent *Schindler's List* (New York: Simon & Schuster, 1982), p. 232.

The Russian immigrants' encounter with the "savages" is taken from George and Helen Papashvily, *Anything Can Happen* (New York: Harper & Brothers, 1940), p. 81. A great deal more about western village sets in France can be found in Clifford P. Westermeier's "Sagebrush Galahads: The Cinema Cowboys," *Red River Valley Historical Review* 5, no. 4 (Fall 1980): 27–54. Some of the German material was taken from "The World Image of the American Frontier," by Ray A. Billington. This was published in *The Congressional Record—Senate*, 9 Mar. 1976, upon the request of Barry Goldwater (see p. S 3008). See also D. L. Ashliman, "The American West in Twentieth Century Germany," p. 89. The Double H story is from correspondence that I have had with one of the club's members, Jim S. Hurst of Coventry. It was he who sent the Double H badge and membership.

Flora North's comment may be found in Kenneth Lamott, "Anatomy of a Specialized Publisher," *Publishers Weekly*, 9 Oct. 1972, p. 63. For an example of Maine's "anti-western" attitudes see the *Lewiston Evening Journal*, 24 May 1879. Efforts of writers to tone down the Wild West notion are exemplified in Charles Moreau Harger, "The West's Higher Life," *Independent* (New York), 12 July 1900, p. 1727; and in Carey McWilliams, "Myths of the West," p. 426. Stuart Henry's criticism of Hough was detailed by Lewis Atherton in "Cattleman and Cowboy: Fact and Fancy," *Montana: The Magazine of Western History* 11, no. 4 (Autumn 1961): 10–12 and 13. He said much the same thing in his volume *The Cattle Kings* (Bloomington: Indiana University Press, 1961), chap. 12. De Voto talked about the myth quite a lot: as an example see his article "Footnote on the West," *Harper's Mgazine*, Nov. 1927, p. 718.

The erosion that the individualism myth suffered under rigid high-plains conditions is discussed by Daniel J. Elazar in *Cities of the Prairie: The Metropolitan Frontier and American Politics* (New York: Basic Books, Inc., 1979), p. 150; and by Bernard De Voto in "The West: A Plundered Province," *Harper's Magazine*, Aug. 1934, pp. 357–58. The sociologist who talked about a dependent class emerging in North Dakota in 1940 was J. M. Gillette, in "Social-Economic Submergence in a Plains State," *Rural Sociology* 5, no. 1 (Mar. 1940): 62. Reference to the individualism of the Mormons is from Joe B. Frantz's "Western Impact on the Nation," *Western Historical Quarterly* 1, no. 3 (July 1970): 253. Robert Morris, in "East-West," *New Republic*, 17 Dec. 1977, made the "ordinary Darwinism" comment (see p. 13).

The remark about Rousseau's natural man is from Marshall W. Fishwick's "The Cowboy: America's Contribution to the World's Mythology,"

Western Folklore 11, no. 2 (Apr. 1952): 77. Discussions of the cowboy as being an illogical choice for the American hero is found in Bernard De Voto, "The Wild West," *Holiday,* July 1954, p. 39; Virginia Weisel Johnson, *The Long, Long Trail* (Boston: Houghton Mifflin Co., 1966); Lewis Atherton, "Cattleman and Cowboy," pp. 4 and 5, as well as his *Cattle Kings,* p. 247; and Don Walker, *Clio's Cowboys: Studies in the Historiography of the Cattle Trade* (Lincoln: University of Nebraska Press, 1981), p. 57. The Carey McWilliams quotation is from his "Myths," p. 428. John C. Van Dyke's *The Open Spaces* (New York: Charles Scribner's Sons, 1922) is an antihero reminiscence (see pp. 59–61, esp.). Comments from the Kissinger interview came from Oriana Fallaci, "Kissinger," *New Republic,* 16 Dec. 1972, p. 21; and Richard Nixon's thoughts about backing out of a saloon are noted by Clifford P. Westermeier in "Cowboy Sexuality: A Historical No-no?" *Red River Valley Historical Review* 2, no. 1 (Spring 1975): 105.

The "last television commercial" item came from William W. Savage, Jr., *The Cowboy Hero: His Image in American History and Culture* (Norman: University of Oklahoma Press, 1979), p. 118. Morris, in "East-West," said western life styles were more fashionable than living in the West (see p. 12). The New York reporter who commented on western wear was Grace Lichtenstein in *Desperado* (New York: Dial Press, 1977), p. 56. Complaints that high prices for cowboy gear annoyed old hands is from an Associated Press release by Warren Wintrode, published in the *Boulder (Colo.) Daily Camera,* 7 June 1981. The New York mail-order house that featured the "American Style," was FBS of New Rochelle, New York, a trademark owned by Molbe Shoes. I used their fall 1982 catalog. The "bust" in western wear was from a feature story by Linda Castone in the *Boulder* (Colo.) *Daily Camera,* 14 Apr. 1983.

Billington's statement is from his book *Land of Savagery, Land of Promise* (New York: W. W. Norton & Co., 1981), p. 313. C. L. Sonnichsen remarked on western fiction as the best index to America in his *From Hopalong to Hud: Thoughts on Western Fiction* (College Station: Texas A & M University Press, 1978), p. 4. The quotation "What they dreamed, we live," etc., came from T. K. Whipple, *Study Out the Land* (Berkeley: University of California Press, 1943), p. 65; while the thought on the West as a large moral fulfillment is from Don Walker's *Clio's Cowboys: Studies in the Historiography of the Cattle Trade* (Lincoln: University of Nebraska Press, 1981), p. 51. De Voto's assessment of the myth as our loveliest and most enduring is from his article "The West: A Plundered Province," *Harper's Magazine,* Aug. 1934, pp. 356 and 364.

INDEX